BLUE AND GOLD

DAN JURGENS
writer

**RYAN SOOK • CULLY HAMNER • KEVIN MAGUIRE
DAN JURGENS • PHIL HESTER • ERIC GAPSTUR
PAUL PELLETIER • NORM RAPMUND
WADE VON GRAWBADGER**
artists

**CHRIS SOTOMAYOR • RYAN SOOK
STEVE BUCCELLATO**
colorists

ROB LEIGH
letterer

RYAN SOOK
collection cover artist

Booster Gold created by
Dan Jurgens

BLUE AND GOLD

Brittany Holzherr — Editor - Original Series & Collected Edition
Jamie S. Rich — Editor - Original Series
Chris Rosa — Associate Editor - Original Series
Steve Cook — Design Director - Books & Publication Design
Ryane Lynn Hill — Production Editor

Marie Javins — Editor-in-Chief, DC Comics

Anne DePies — Senior VP - General Manager
Jim Lee — Publisher & Chief Creative Officer
Don Falletti — VP - Manufacturing Operations & Workflow Management
Lawrence Ganem — VP - Talent Services
Alison Gill — Senior VP - Manufacturing & Operations
Jeffrey Kaufman — VP - Editorial Strategy & Programming
Nick J. Napolitano — VP - Manufacturing Administration & Design
Nancy Spears — VP - Revenue

BLUE & GOLD

DC Comics, 100 S. California Street, Burbank, CA 91505
Printed by Solisco Printers, Scott, QC, Canada. 8/19/22. First Printing.
ISBN: 978-1-77951-678-7

Library of Congress Cataloging-in-Publication Data is available.

PEFC Certified

This product is from sustainably managed forests and controlled sources

PEFC/26-31-02 www.pefc.org

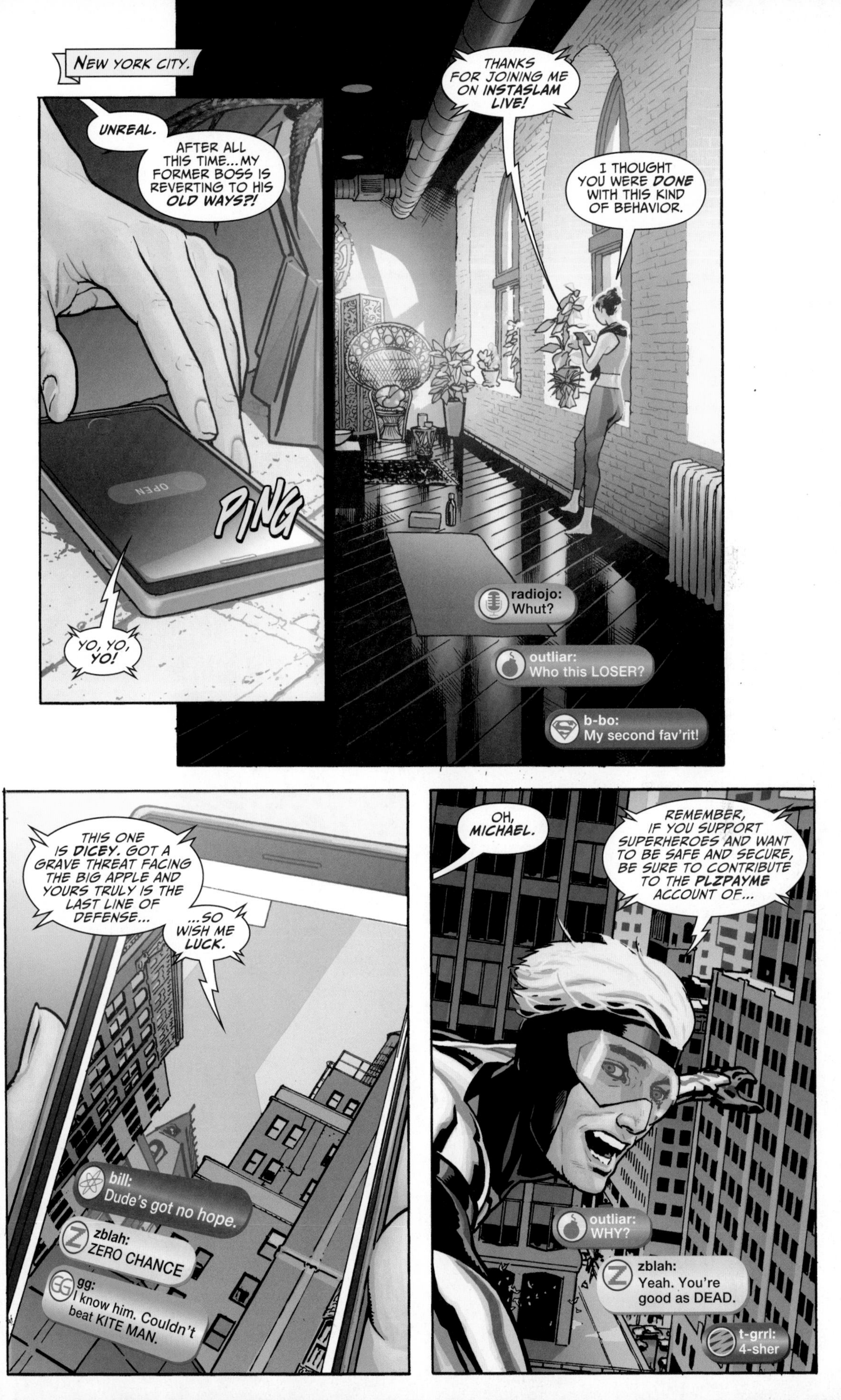
NEW YORK CITY.
UNREAL.
AFTER ALL THIS TIME... MY FORMER BOSS IS REVERTING TO HIS OLD WAYS?!
OPEN
PING
YO, YO, YO!
THANKS FOR JOINING ME ON INSTASLAM LIVE!
I THOUGHT YOU WERE DONE WITH THIS KIND OF BEHAVIOR.
radiojo: Whut?
outliar: Who this LOSER?
b-bo: My second fav'rit!
THIS ONE IS DICEY. GOT A GRAVE THREAT FACING THE BIG APPLE AND YOURS TRULY IS THE LAST LINE OF DEFENSE...
...SO WISH ME LUCK.
bill: Dude's got no hope.
zblah: ZERO CHANCE
gg: I know him. Couldn't beat KITE MAN.
OH, MICHAEL.
REMEMBER, IF YOU SUPPORT SUPERHEROES AND WANT TO BE SAFE AND SECURE, BE SURE TO CONTRIBUTE TO THE PLZPAYME ACCOUNT OF...
outliar: WHY?
zblah: Yeah. You're good as DEAD.
t-grrl: 4-sher

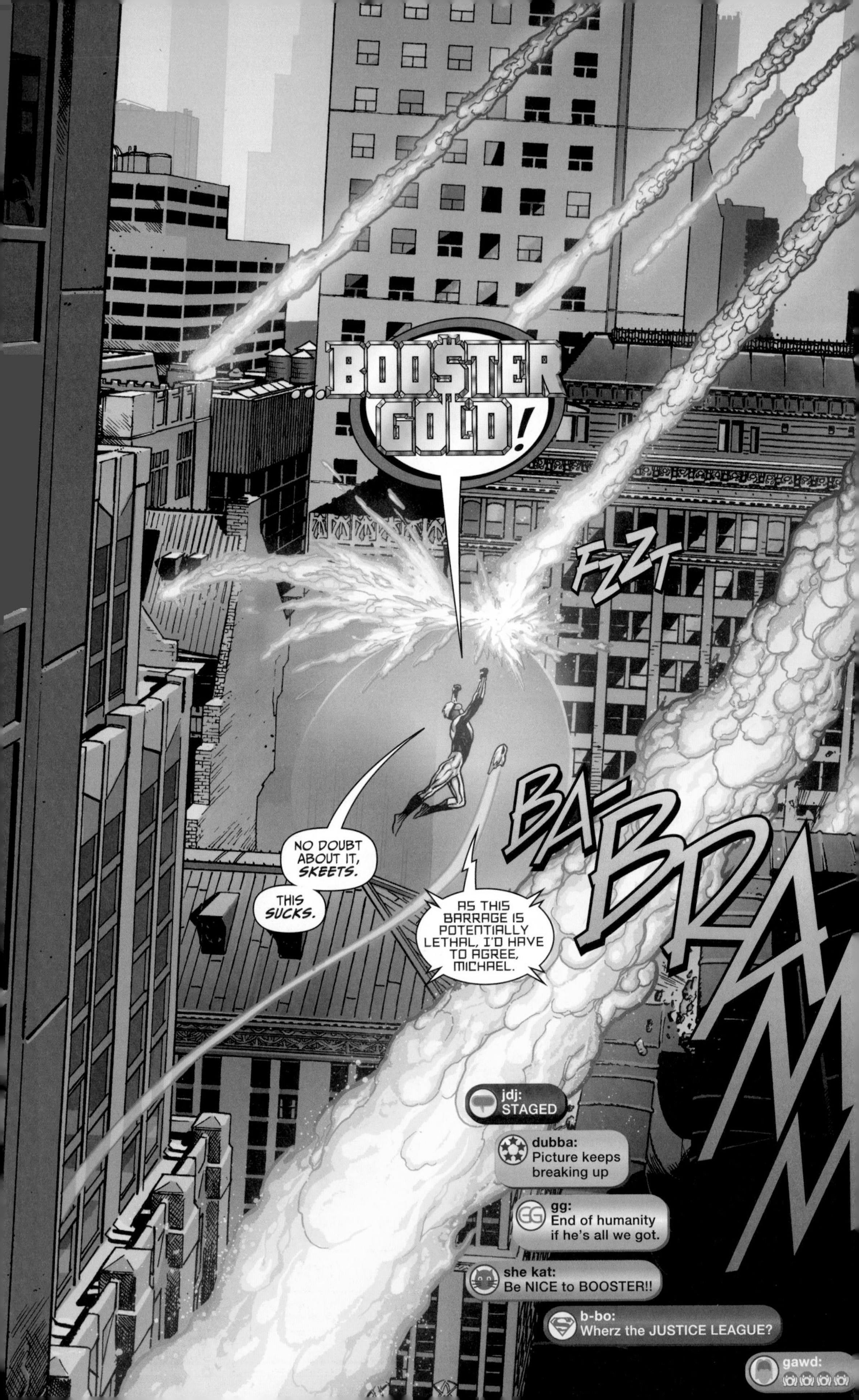
...BOOSTER GOLD!
FZZT
NO DOUBT ABOUT IT, SKEETS.
THIS SUCKS.
AS THIS BARRAGE IS POTENTIALLY LETHAL, I'D HAVE TO AGREE, MICHAEL.
BA-BRAM
jdj: STAGED
dubba: Picture keeps breaking up
gg: End of humanity if he's all we got.
she kat: Be NICE to BOOSTER!!
b-bo: Wherz the JUSTICE LEAGUE?
gawd:

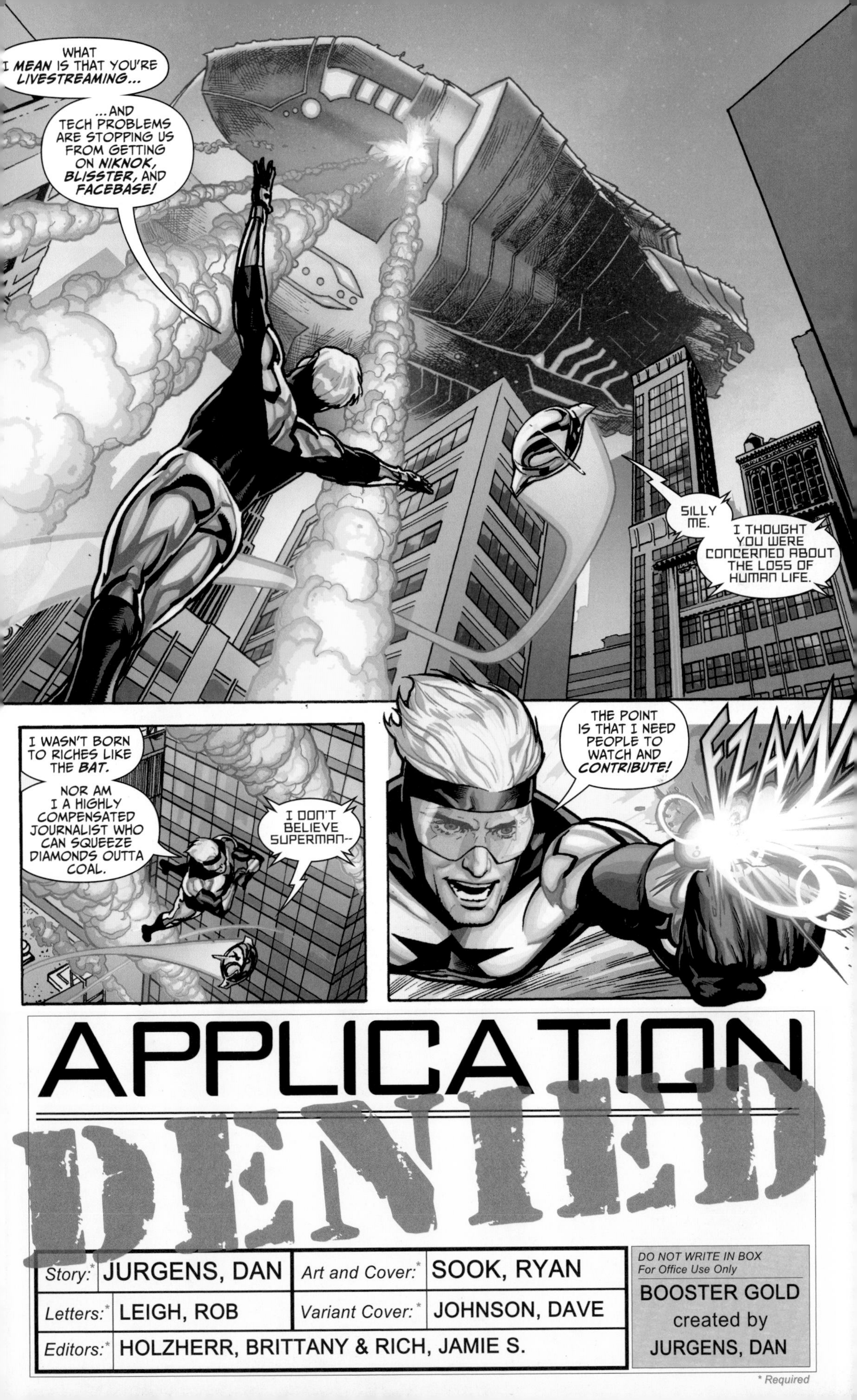
WHAT I *MEAN* IS THAT YOU'RE *LIVESTREAMING...*
...AND TECH PROBLEMS ARE STOPPING US FROM GETTING ON *NIKNOK, BLISSTER,* AND *FACEBASE!*
SILLY ME.
I THOUGHT YOU WERE CONCERNED ABOUT THE LOSS OF HUMAN LIFE.
I WASN'T BORN TO RICHES LIKE THE *BAT.*
NOR AM I A HIGHLY COMPENSATED JOURNALIST WHO CAN SQUEEZE DIAMONDS OUTTA COAL.
I DON'T BELIEVE SUPERMAN--
THE POINT IS THAT I NEED PEOPLE TO WATCH AND *CONTRIBUTE!*
FZAM!

APPLICATION DENIED

Story:*	JURGENS, DAN	Art and Cover:*	SOOK, RYAN
Letters:*	LEIGH, ROB	Variant Cover:*	JOHNSON, DAVE
Editors:*	HOLZHERR, BRITTANY & RICH, JAMIE S.		

DO NOT WRITE IN BOX
For Office Use Only

BOOSTER GOLD
created by
JURGENS, DAN

** Required*

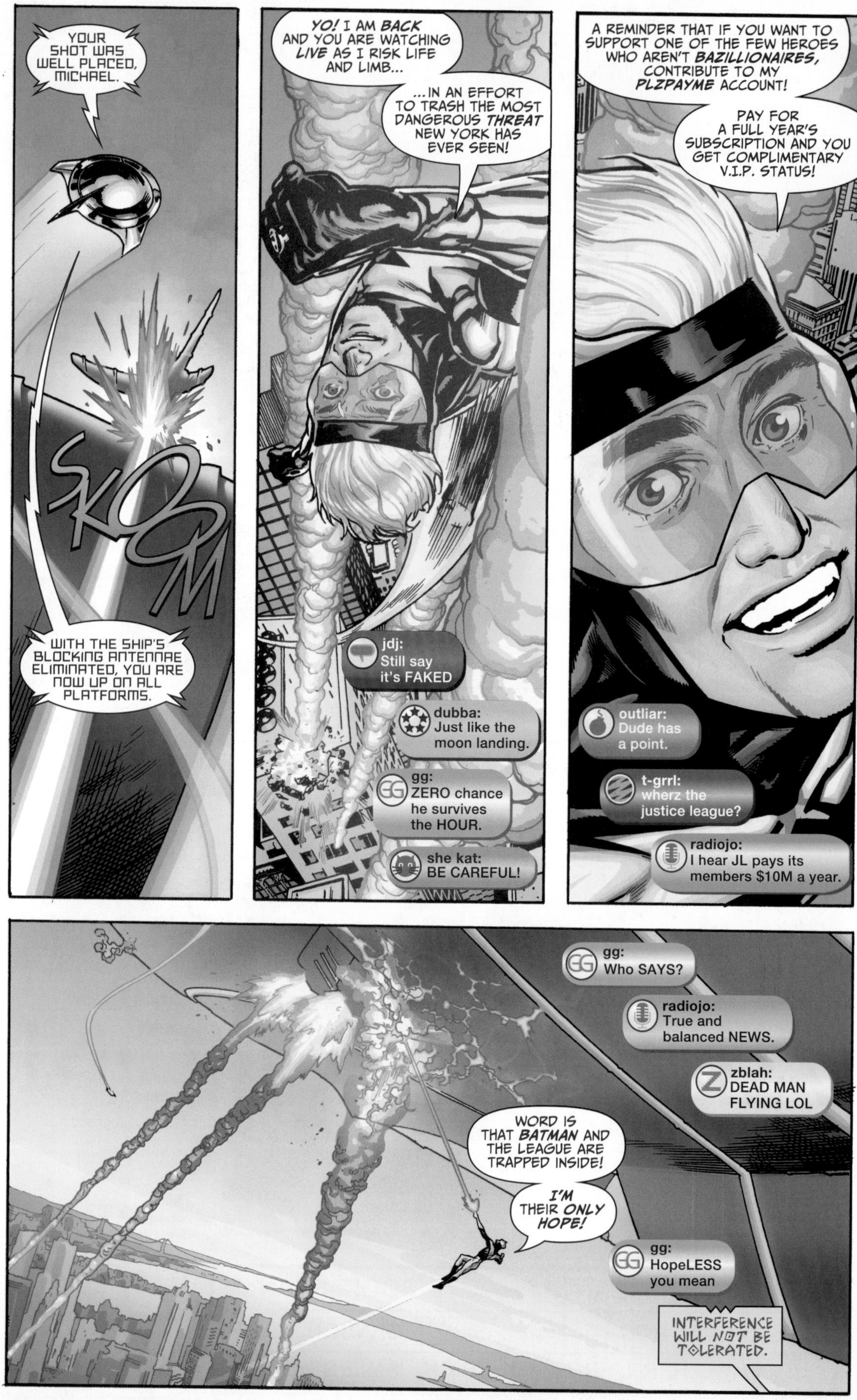
YOUR SHOT WAS WELL PLACED, MICHAEL.
SKOOM
WITH THE SHIP'S BLOCKING ANTENNAE ELIMINATED, YOU ARE NOW UP ON ALL PLATFORMS.
YO! I AM BACK AND YOU ARE WATCHING LIVE AS I RISK LIFE AND LIMB...
...IN AN EFFORT TO TRASH THE MOST DANGEROUS THREAT NEW YORK HAS EVER SEEN!
jdj: Still say it's FAKED
dubba: Just like the moon landing.
gg: ZERO chance he survives the HOUR.
she kat: BE CAREFUL!
A REMINDER THAT IF YOU WANT TO SUPPORT ONE OF THE FEW HEROES WHO AREN'T BAZILLIONAIRES, CONTRIBUTE TO MY PLZPAYME ACCOUNT!
PAY FOR A FULL YEAR'S SUBSCRIPTION AND YOU GET COMPLIMENTARY V.I.P. STATUS!
outliar: Dude has a point.
t-grrl: wherz the justice league?
radiojo: I hear JL pays its members $10M a year.
gg: Who SAYS?
radiojo: True and balanced NEWS.
zblah: DEAD MAN FLYING LOL
WORD IS THAT BATMAN AND THE LEAGUE ARE TRAPPED INSIDE!
I'M THEIR ONLY HOPE!
gg: HopeLESS you mean
INTERFERENCE WILL NOT BE TOLERATED.

TERMINATION REQUIRED.

TECHSTROSITY ALERT!

she kat: LOOK OUT!

b-bo: But you gotta save SOOPERMAN!

WHAT AM I DEALING WITH HERE, SKEETS?

ALLOYS I DO NOT RECOGNIZE. ALIEN TECHNOLOGY, NO DOUBT.

outliar: Kiss the JL goodbye

zblah: Dude fighting BACK

SHAKK

CRANKING IT TO MAX SO I CAN BLOW THIS SUCKER ALL THE WAY TO GOTHAM!

zblah: Has more juice than I thought

VRRRMMMMM

C'MON...

Uh-oh...

outliar: OR NOT

t-grrl: LMAO

gg: Reminds me of when DOOMSDAY crushed him

jdj: Staged. FAKE death

dubba: This is one hero that'll STAY DEAD!

radioz: TOASTER is running away!

gawd: LOL LOL LOL

WHOOOAM

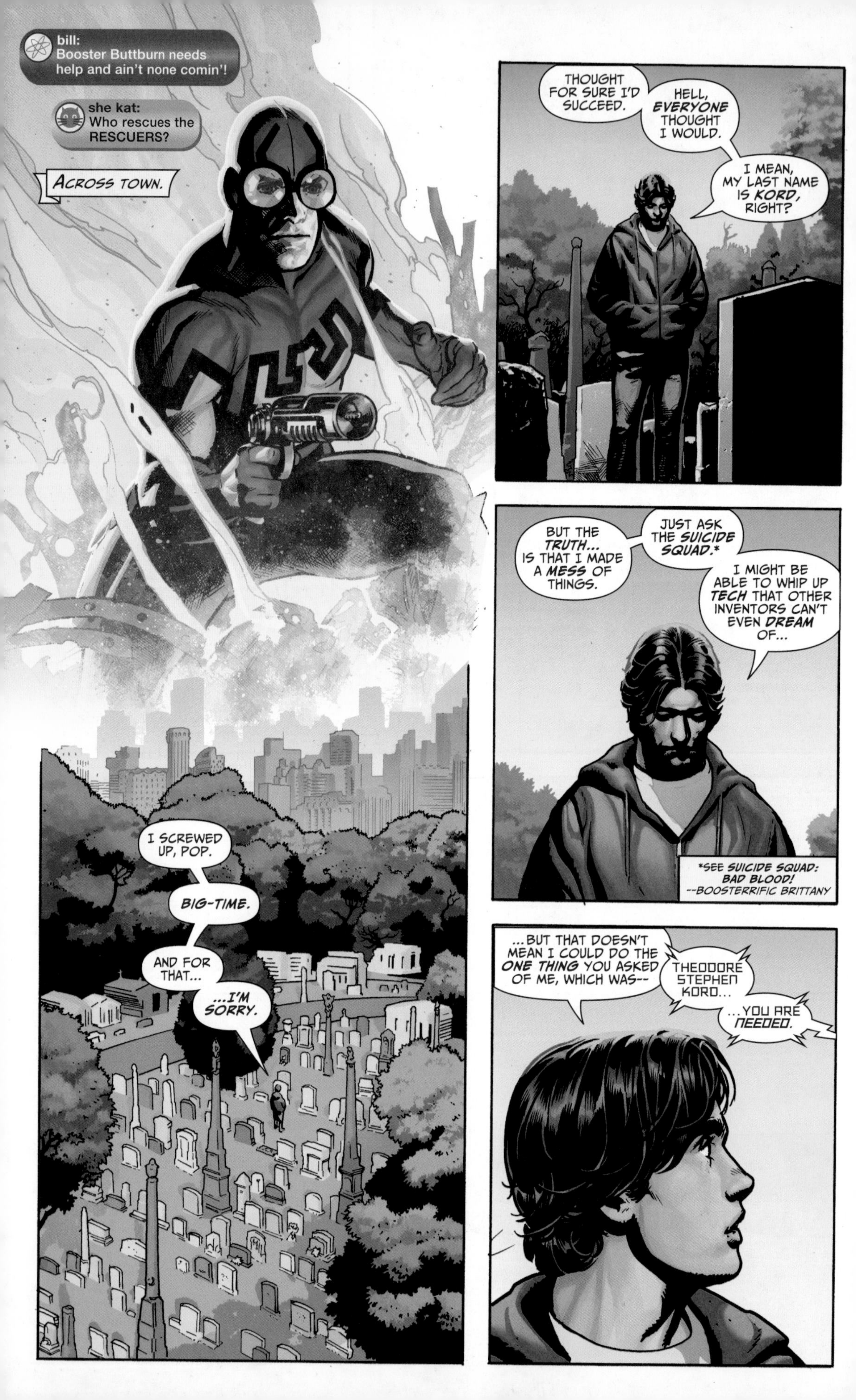
bill:
Booster Buttburn needs help and ain't none comin'!
she kat:
Who rescues the RESCUERS?
ACROSS TOWN.
THOUGHT FOR SURE I'D SUCCEED.
HELL, EVERYONE THOUGHT I WOULD.
I MEAN, MY LAST NAME IS KORD, RIGHT?
BUT THE TRUTH... IS THAT I MADE A MESS OF THINGS.
JUST ASK THE SUICIDE SQUAD.*
I MIGHT BE ABLE TO WHIP UP TECH THAT OTHER INVENTORS CAN'T EVEN DREAM OF...
*SEE SUICIDE SQUAD: BAD BLOOD! --BOOSTERRIFIC BRITTANY
I SCREWED UP, POP.
BIG-TIME.
AND FOR THAT...
...I'M SORRY.
...BUT THAT DOESN'T MEAN I COULD DO THE ONE THING YOU ASKED OF ME, WHICH WAS--
THEODORE STEPHEN KORD...
...YOU ARE NEEDED.

SKEETS?!

YES. BOOSTER GOLD'S SECURITY 'DROID.

NOT TO MENTION, LOGISTICS EXPERT, MORAL COMPASS, AND *LIFE COACH*.

I'VE COME BECAUSE MICHAEL NEEDS *HELP*.

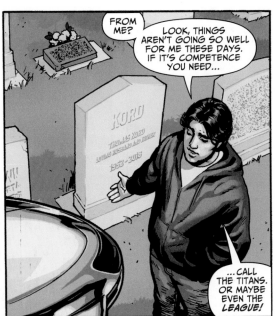

FROM ME?

LOOK, THINGS AREN'T GOING SO WELL FOR ME THESE DAYS. IF IT'S COMPETENCE YOU NEED...

KORD

THOMAS KORD
LOVING HUSBAND AND FATHER
1953 - 2019

...CALL THE TITANS. OR MAYBE EVEN THE *LEAGUE*!

THAT IS THE *PROBLEM*, MR. KORD.

BOOSTER IS BATTLING AN ALIEN CRAFT HOVERING OVER NEW YORK...

...WHICH IS ALREADY HOLDING THE *JUSTICE LEAGUE* AS *PRISONERS*.

I'D LIKE TO, BUT...

I HAVE SCANNED YOUR MEDICAL RECORDS AND BELIEVE YOUR HEART TROUBLES TO BE SETTLED.

WITHOUT HELP, BOOSTER WON'T SURVIVE THE *HOUR*.

WITH MY RECENT RECORD...

...I MAY END UP SHORTENING THAT.

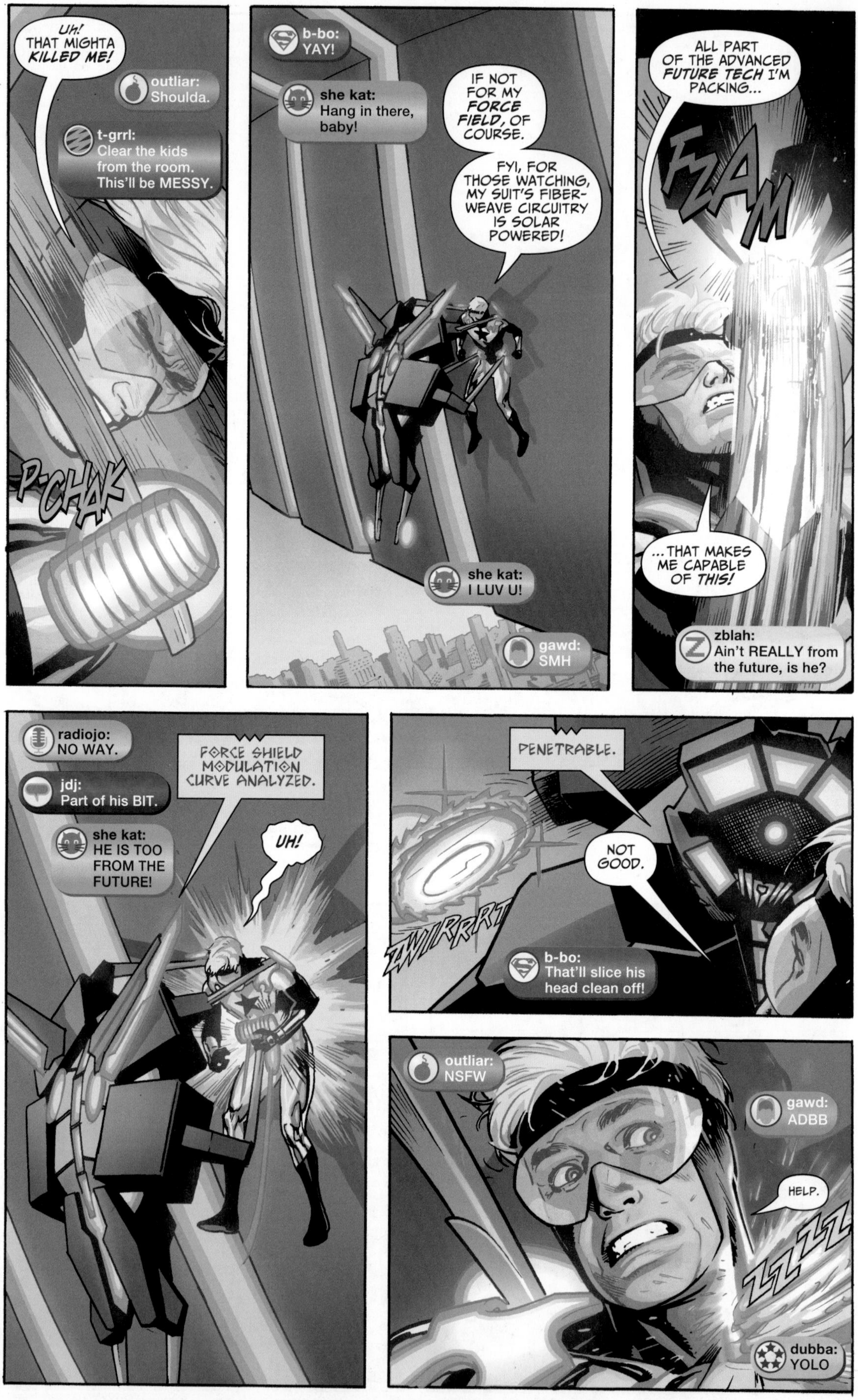
UH! THAT MIGHTA KILLED ME!
outliar: Shoulda.
t-grrl: Clear the kids from the room. This'll be MESSY.
P-CHAK
b-bo: YAY!
she kat: Hang in there, baby!
IF NOT FOR MY FORCE FIELD, OF COURSE.
FYI, FOR THOSE WATCHING, MY SUIT'S FIBER-WEAVE CIRCUITRY IS SOLAR POWERED!
she kat: I LUV U!
gawd: SMH
ALL PART OF THE ADVANCED FUTURE TECH I'M PACKING...
FZAM
...THAT MAKES ME CAPABLE OF THIS!
zblah: Ain't REALLY from the future, is he?
radiojo: NO WAY.
jdj: Part of his BIT.
she kat: HE IS TOO FROM THE FUTURE!
FORCE SHIELD MODULATION CURVE ANALYZED.
UH!
PENETRABLE.
NOT GOOD.
ZWIIRRRT
b-bo: That'll slice his head clean off!
outliar: NSFW
gawd: ADBB
HELP.
ZZZZZ
dubba: YOLO

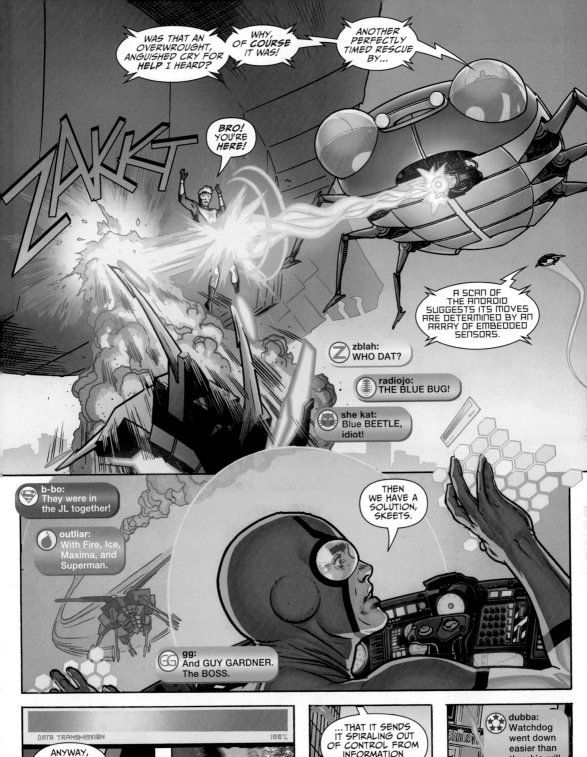

WAS THAT AN OVERWROUGHT, ANGUISHED CRY FOR **HELP** I HEARD?

WHY, OF **COURSE** IT WAS!

ANOTHER PERFECTLY TIMED RESCUE BY...

ZAKKT

BRO! YOU'RE HERE!

A SCAN OF THE ANDROID SUGGESTS ITS MOVES ARE DETERMINED BY AN ARRAY OF EMBEDDED SENSORS.

zblah: WHO DAT?

radiojo: THE BLUE BUG!

she kat: Blue BEETLE, idiot!

b-bo: They were in the JL together!

outliar: With Fire, Ice, Maxima, and Superman.

THEN WE HAVE A SOLUTION, SKEETS.

gg: And GUY GARDNER. The BOSS.

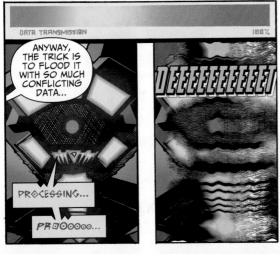

DATA TRANSMISSION   100%

ANYWAY, THE TRICK IS TO FLOOD IT WITH SO MUCH CONFLICTING DATA...

DEEEEEEEEEET

PROCESSING...

PR☐OOOOO...

...THAT IT SENDS IT SPIRALING OUT OF CONTROL FROM INFORMATION OVERLOAD!

jdj: Pressing a button is all it took?

dubba: Watchdog went down easier than the ship will.

BWOOOSH

t-grrl: KEWL.

she kat: I LUV them BOTH!

TED! YOUR TIMING COULD *NOT* HAVE BEEN BETTER!

WAIT. MY IDENTITY...

STREAM'S *OFF.* BREAK TIME FOR THE FANBOYS.

GOOD. THE WORLD DOESN'T KNOW TED KORD AND THE BLUE BEETLE ARE THE SAME GUY AND I'D LIKE TO KEEP IT THAT WAY.

SKEETS? YOUR FAITH IN MY ABILITY TO SURVIVE WAS SO MINIMAL THAT YOU THREW UP THE *BEETLE SIGNAL?*

NICE MERCHANDISING IDEA, COME TO THINK OF IT.

YOUR SITUATION WAS *DIRE,* MICHAEL. MR. KORD WAS YOUR *ONLY HOPE.*

WOULDN'T WANT TO MAKE BATMAN MAD...

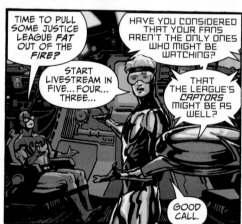

TIME TO PULL SOME JUSTICE LEAGUE *FAT* OUT OF THE *FIRE?*

START LIVESTREAM IN FIVE... FOUR... THREE...

HAVE YOU CONSIDERED THAT YOUR FANS AREN'T THE ONLY ONES WHO MIGHT BE WATCHING?

THAT THE LEAGUE'S *CAPTORS* MIGHT BE AS WELL?

GOOD CALL.

LET'S STICK WITH WHAT'S *REALLY* IMPORTANT. SUCH AS...

...THE WORLD'S GREATEST *SUPERHERO* TEAM *EVER* IS REUNITED!

BLUE AND GOLD

RIDE AGAIN!

THAT'S *GOLD AND BLUE,* TED.

DOESN'T SOUND RIGHT, BOOSTER.

MAYBE, BUT THE *BOSS'S* NAME *ALWAYS* COMES BEFORE THE *SIDEKICK'S.*

WAIT. I THOUGHT I WAS THE BOSS AND *YOU* WERE THE SIDEKICK.

I REALIZE YOU TWO FALL INTO COMPLETE ADOLESCENT MODE WHEN TOGETHER, BUT WE ARE BEING *TARGETED...*

WIRRRRP

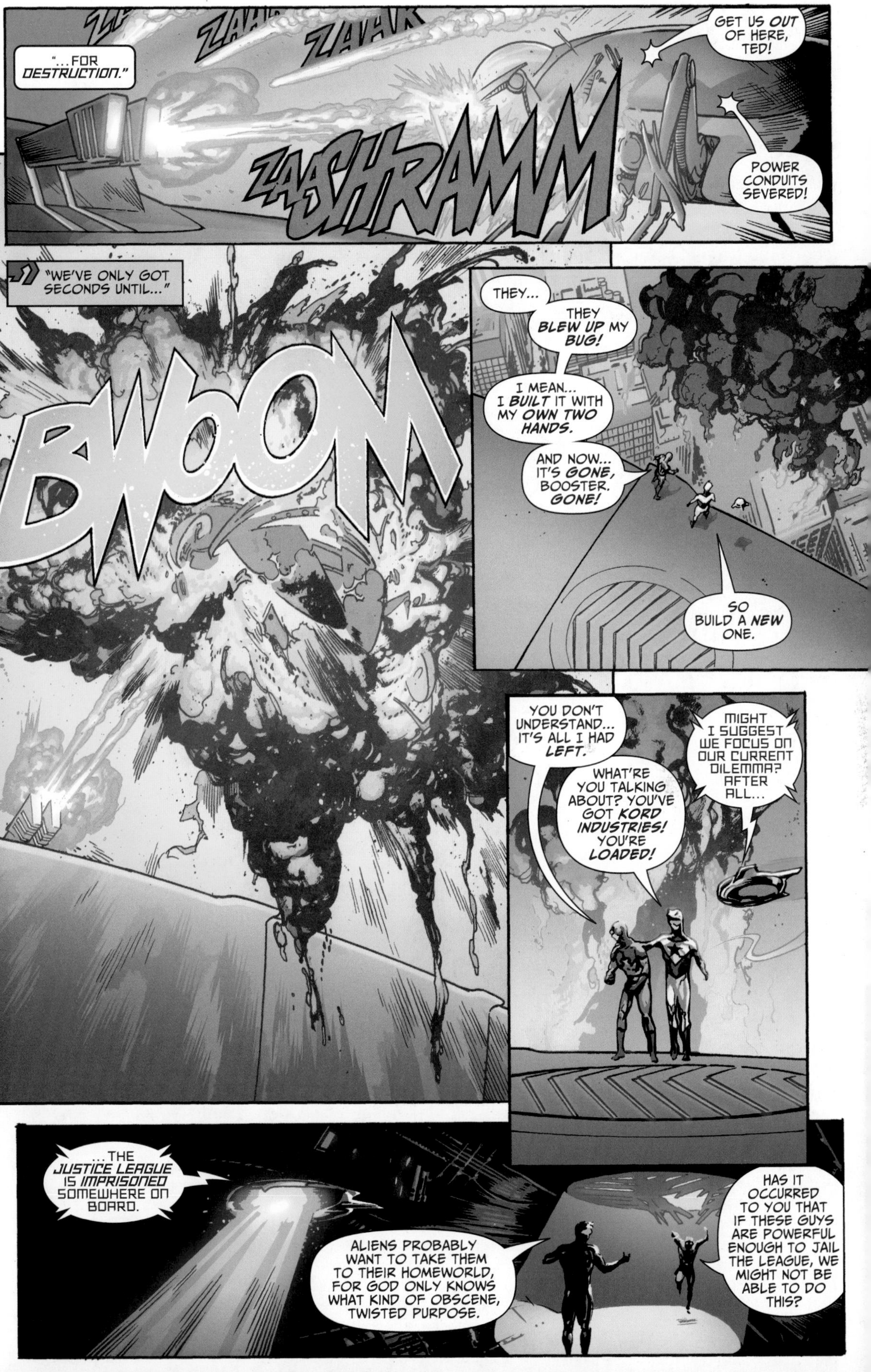
"...FOR DESTRUCTION."
ZAHR
ZAVAR
GET US OUT OF HERE, TED!
ZAASHRAMM
POWER CONDUITS SEVERED!
"WE'VE ONLY GOT SECONDS UNTIL..."
BWOOM
THEY...
THEY BLEW UP MY BUG!
I MEAN... I BUILT IT WITH MY OWN TWO HANDS.
AND NOW... IT'S GONE, BOOSTER. GONE!
SO BUILD A NEW ONE.
YOU DON'T UNDERSTAND... IT'S ALL I HAD LEFT.
WHAT'RE YOU TALKING ABOUT? YOU'VE GOT KORD INDUSTRIES! YOU'RE LOADED!
MIGHT I SUGGEST WE FOCUS ON OUR CURRENT DILEMMA? AFTER ALL...
...THE JUSTICE LEAGUE IS IMPRISONED SOMEWHERE ON BOARD.
ALIENS PROBABLY WANT TO TAKE THEM TO THEIR HOMEWORLD, FOR GOD ONLY KNOWS WHAT KIND OF OBSCENE, TWISTED PURPOSE.
HAS IT OCCURRED TO YOU THAT IF THESE GUYS ARE POWERFUL ENOUGH TO JAIL THE LEAGUE, WE MIGHT NOT BE ABLE TO DO THIS?

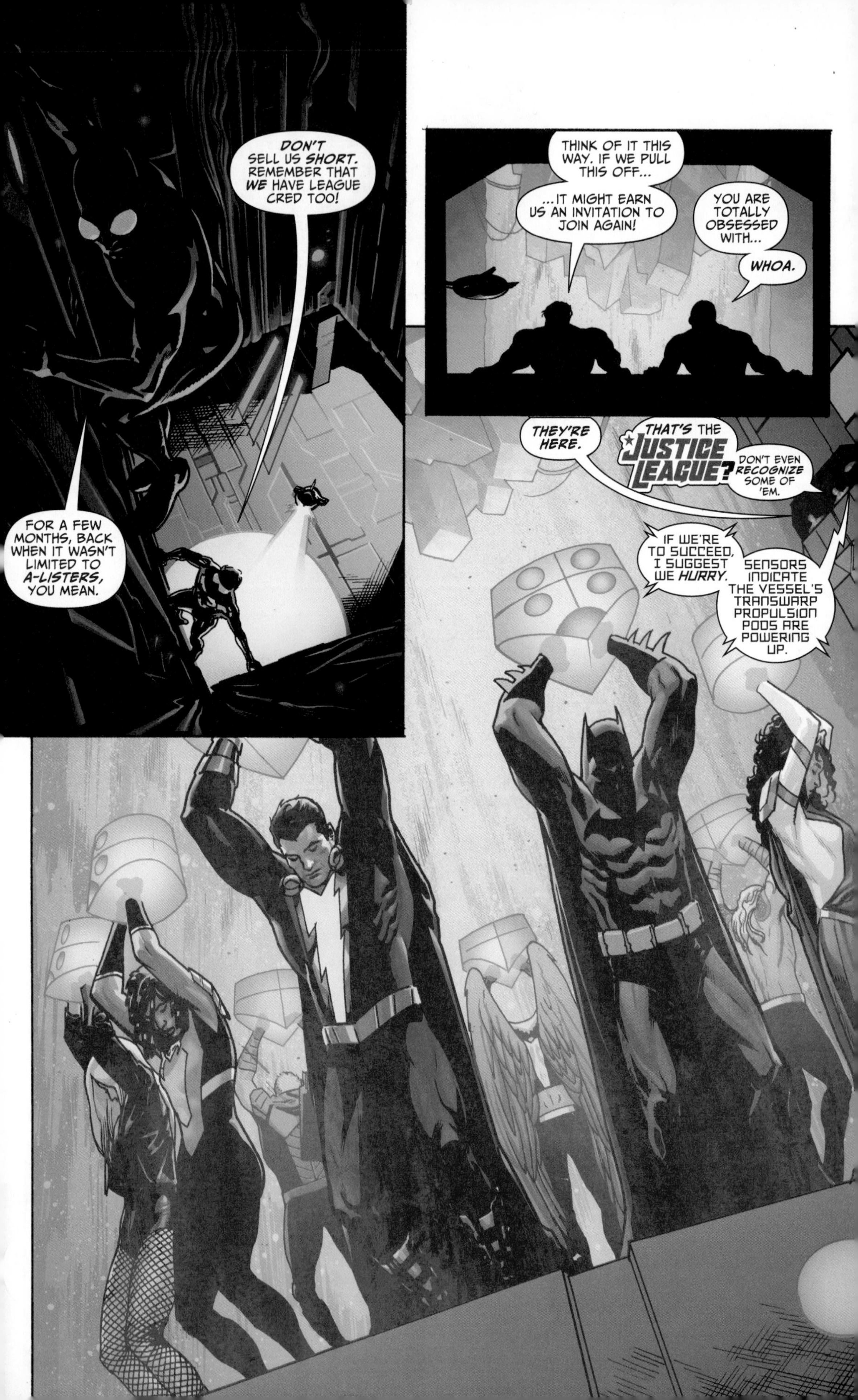
DON'T SELL US SHORT. REMEMBER THAT WE HAVE LEAGUE CRED TOO!
FOR A FEW MONTHS, BACK WHEN IT WASN'T LIMITED TO A-LISTERS, YOU MEAN.
THINK OF IT THIS WAY. IF WE PULL THIS OFF...
...IT MIGHT EARN US AN INVITATION TO JOIN AGAIN!
YOU ARE TOTALLY OBSESSED WITH...
WHOA.
THEY'RE HERE.
THAT'S THE JUSTICE LEAGUE?
DON'T EVEN RECOGNIZE SOME OF 'EM.
IF WE'RE TO SUCCEED, I SUGGEST WE HURRY.
SENSORS INDICATE THE VESSEL'S TRANSWARP PROPULSION PODS ARE POWERING UP.

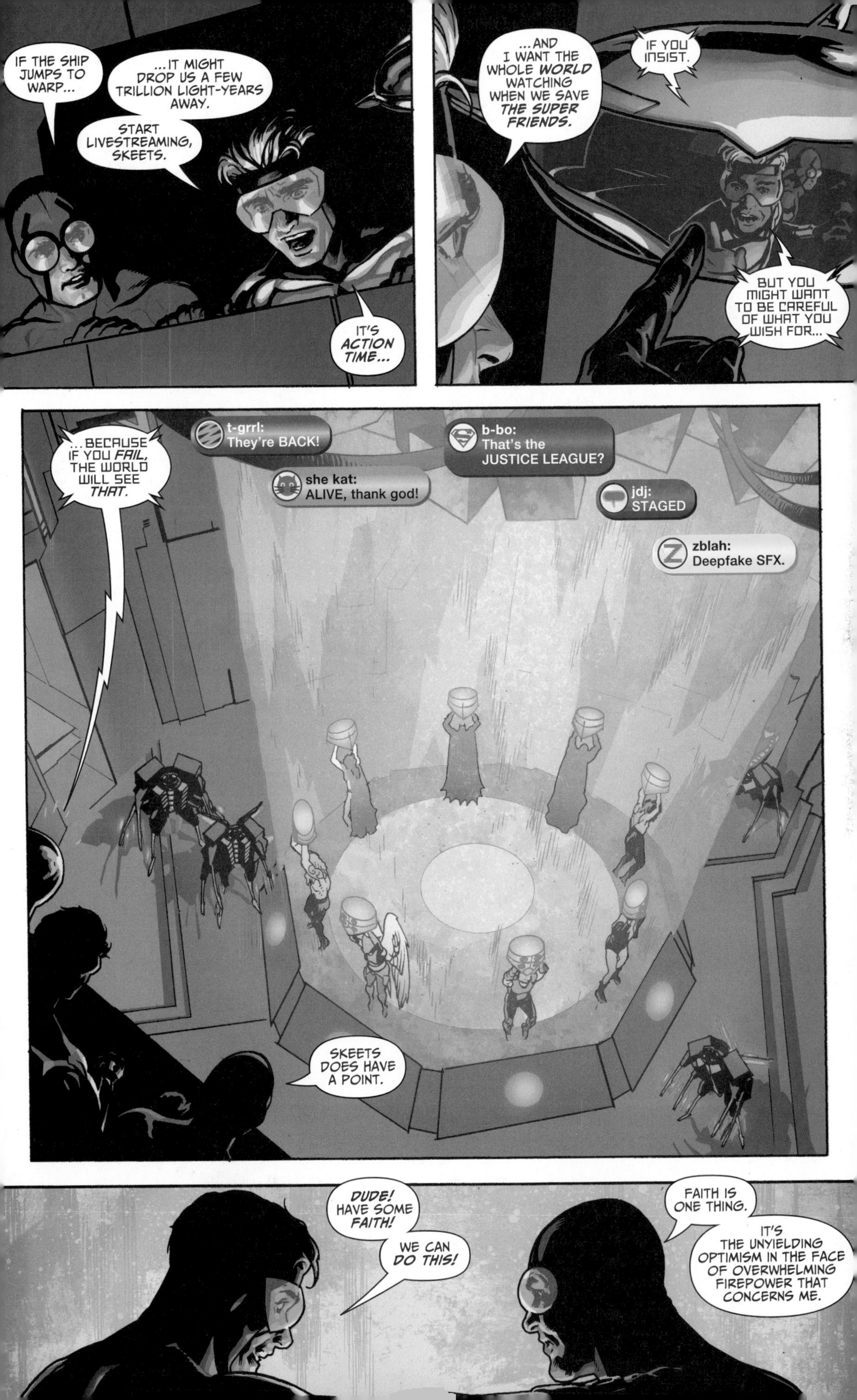
IF THE SHIP JUMPS TO WARP...
...IT MIGHT DROP US A FEW TRILLION LIGHT-YEARS AWAY.
START LIVESTREAMING, SKEETS.
IT'S ACTION TIME...
...AND I WANT THE WHOLE WORLD WATCHING WHEN WE SAVE THE SUPER FRIENDS.
IF YOU INSIST.
BUT YOU MIGHT WANT TO BE CAREFUL OF WHAT YOU WISH FOR...
...BECAUSE IF YOU FAIL, THE WORLD WILL SEE THAT.
t-grrl: They're BACK!
b-bo: That's the JUSTICE LEAGUE?
she kat: ALIVE, thank god!
jdj: STAGED
zblah: Deepfake SFX.
SKEETS DOES HAVE A POINT.
DUDE! HAVE SOME FAITH!
WE CAN DO THIS!
FAITH IS ONE THING.
IT'S THE UNYIELDING OPTIMISM IN THE FACE OF OVERWHELMING FIREPOWER THAT CONCERNS ME.

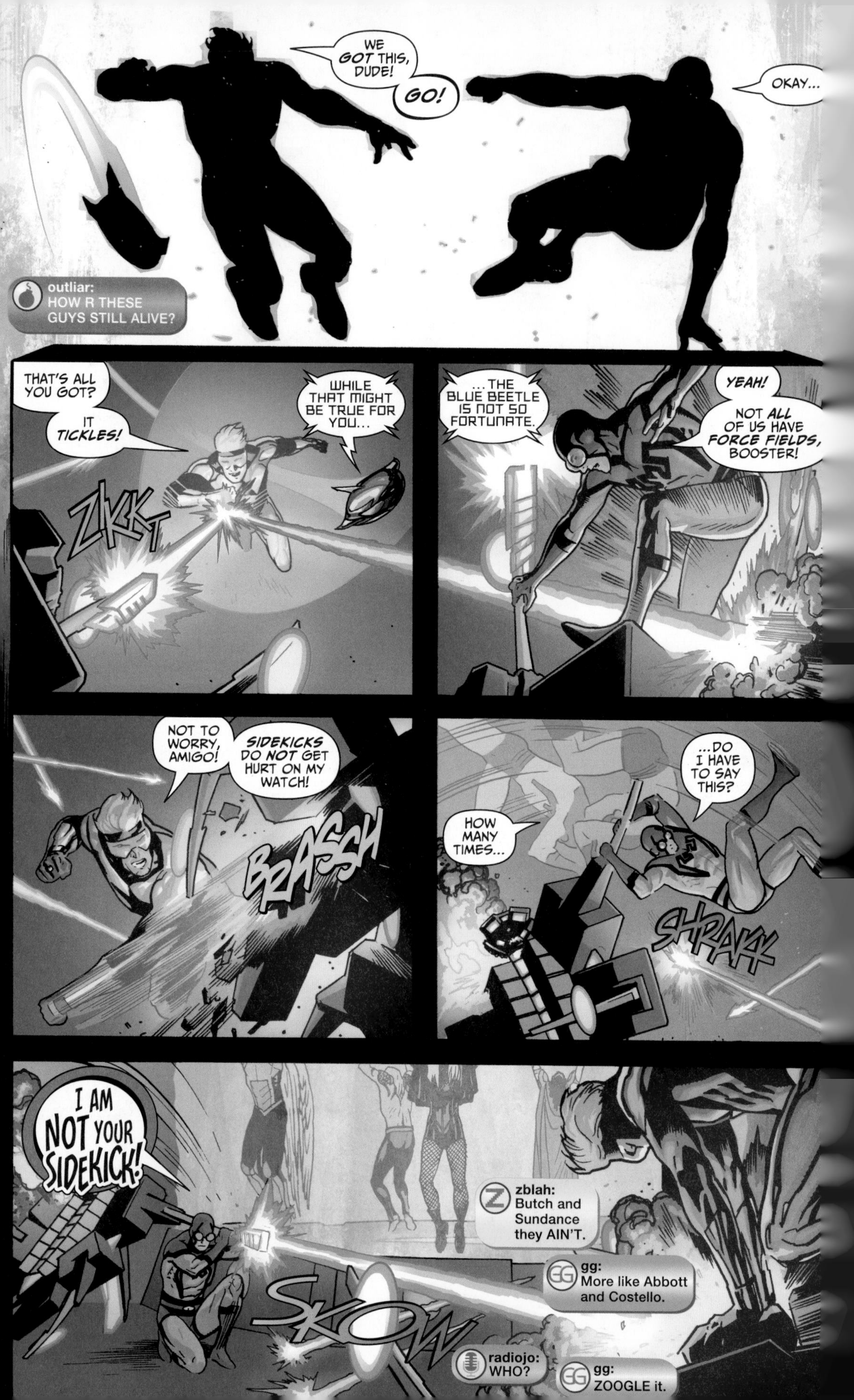
WE GOT THIS, DUDE!
GO!
OKAY...
outliar: HOW R THESE GUYS STILL ALIVE?
THAT'S ALL YOU GOT?
IT TICKLES!
WHILE THAT MIGHT BE TRUE FOR YOU...
ZIKKT
...THE BLUE BEETLE IS NOT SO FORTUNATE.
YEAH!
NOT ALL OF US HAVE FORCE FIELDS, BOOSTER!
NOT TO WORRY, AMIGO!
SIDEKICKS DO NOT GET HURT ON MY WATCH!
BRASSH
...DO I HAVE TO SAY THIS?
HOW MANY TIMES...
SHRAKK
I AM NOT YOUR SIDEKICK!
zblah: Butch and Sundance they AIN'T.
gg: More like Abbott and Costello.
SKOW
radiojo: WHO?
gg: ZOOGLE it.

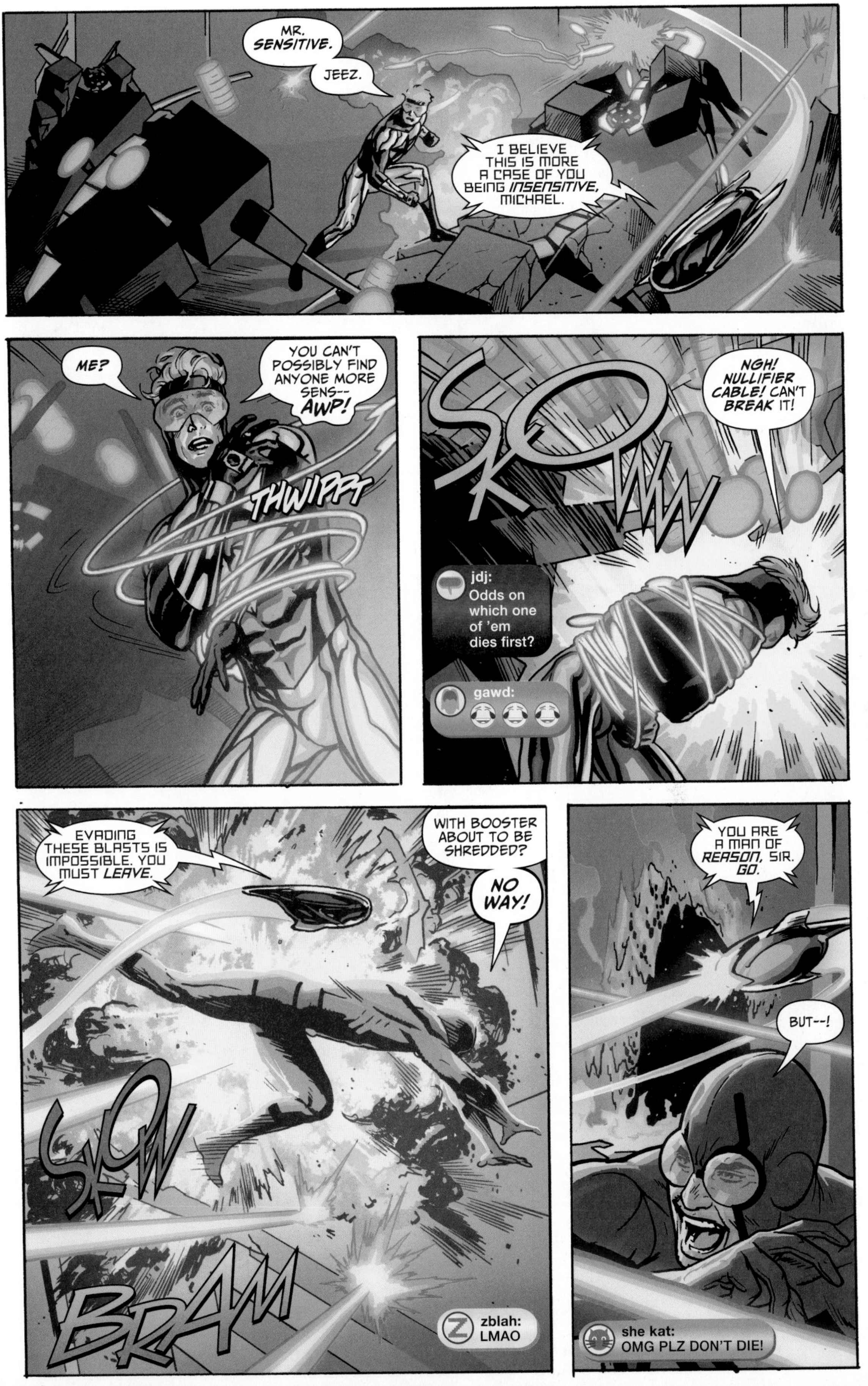
MR. SENSITIVE.
JEEZ.
I BELIEVE THIS IS MORE A CASE OF YOU BEING INSENSITIVE, MICHAEL.
ME?
YOU CAN'T POSSIBLY FIND ANYONE MORE SENS-- AWP!
THWIPPT
SKOWWW
NGH! NULLIFIER CABLE! CAN'T BREAK IT!
jdj:
Odds on which one of 'em dies first?
gawd:
EVADING THESE BLASTS IS IMPOSSIBLE. YOU MUST LEAVE.
WITH BOOSTER ABOUT TO BE SHREDDED?
NO WAY!
SKOW
BRAM
zblah:
LMAO
YOU ARE A MAN OF REASON, SIR. GO.
BUT--!
she kat:
OMG PLZ DON'T DIE!

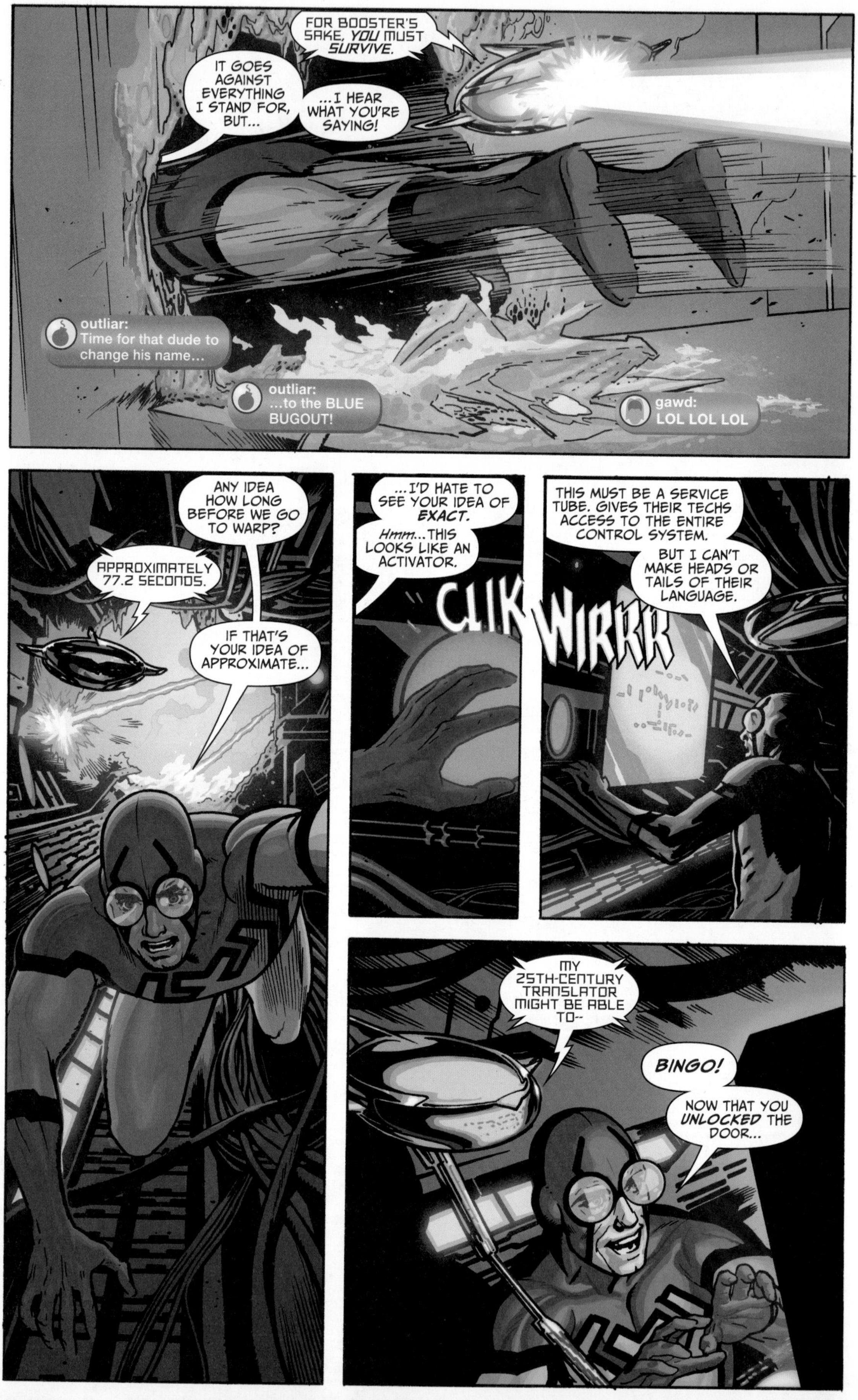
FOR BOOSTER'S SAKE, *YOU* MUST *SURVIVE.*
IT GOES AGAINST EVERYTHING I STAND FOR, BUT...
...I HEAR WHAT YOU'RE SAYING!
outliar: Time for that dude to change his name...
outliar: ...to the BLUE BUGOUT!
gawd: LOL LOL LOL
ANY IDEA HOW LONG BEFORE WE GO TO WARP?
APPROXIMATELY 77.2 SECONDS.
IF THAT'S YOUR IDEA OF APPROXIMATE...
...I'D HATE TO SEE YOUR IDEA OF *EXACT.*
Hmm...THIS LOOKS LIKE AN ACTIVATOR.
CLIK
WIRRR
THIS MUST BE A SERVICE TUBE. GIVES THEIR TECHS ACCESS TO THE ENTIRE CONTROL SYSTEM.
BUT I CAN'T MAKE HEADS OR TAILS OF THEIR LANGUAGE.
MY 25TH-CENTURY TRANSLATOR MIGHT BE ABLE TO--
BINGO!
NOW THAT YOU *UNLOCKED* THE DOOR...

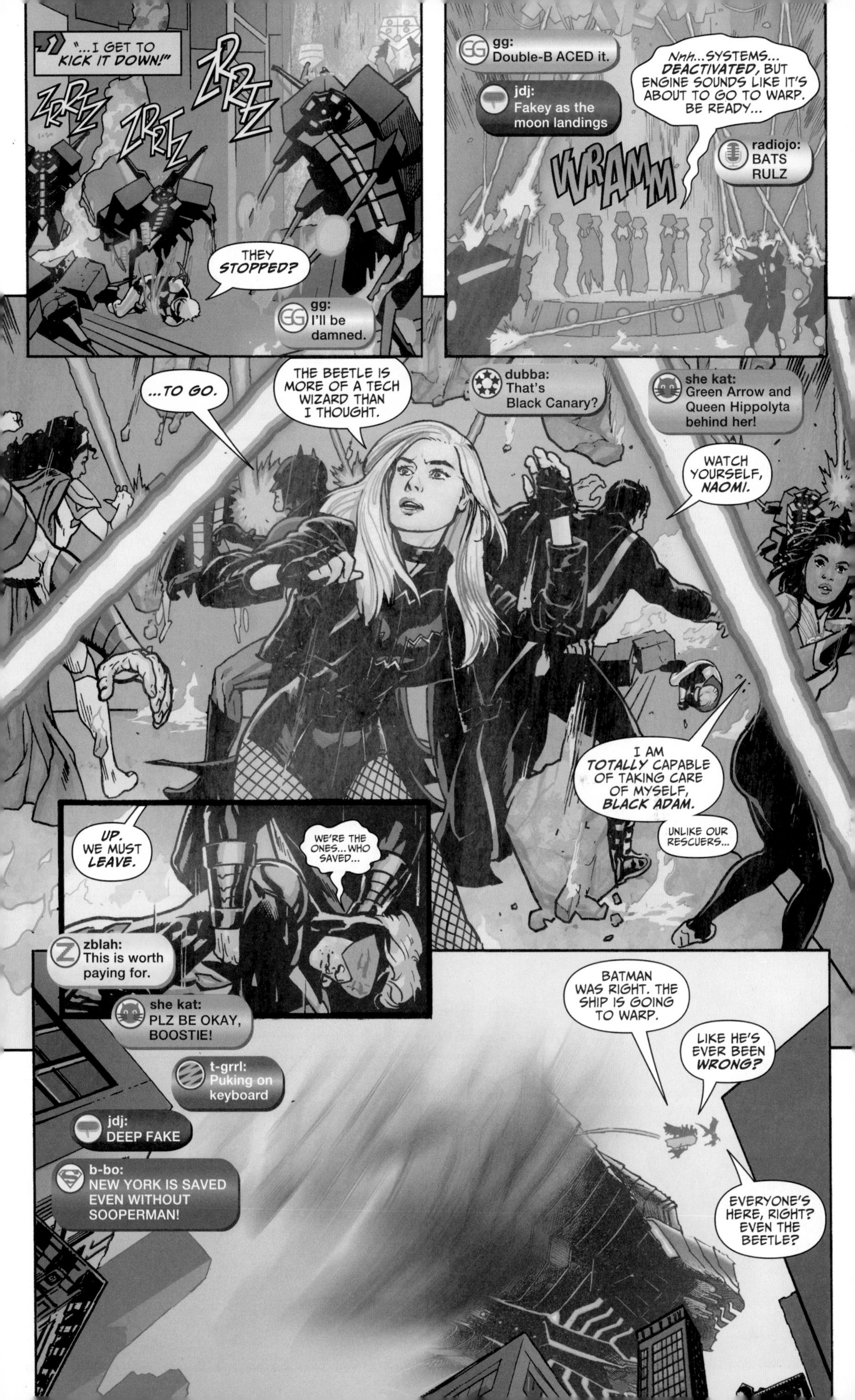
"...I GET TO KICK IT DOWN!"
ZRRZZ
ZRRZZ
ZRRZZ
THEY STOPPED?
gg: I'll be damned.
gg: Double-B ACED it.
jdj: Fakey as the moon landings
Nnh...SYSTEMS... DEACTIVATED, BUT ENGINE SOUNDS LIKE IT'S ABOUT TO GO TO WARP. BE READY...
VVRAMM
radiojo: BATS RULZ
...TO GO.
THE BEETLE IS MORE OF A TECH WIZARD THAN I THOUGHT.
dubba: That's Black Canary?
she kat: Green Arrow and Queen Hippolyta behind her!
WATCH YOURSELF, NAOMI.
I AM TOTALLY CAPABLE OF TAKING CARE OF MYSELF, BLACK ADAM.
UNLIKE OUR RESCUERS...
UP. WE MUST LEAVE.
WE'RE THE ONES...WHO SAVED...
zblah: This is worth paying for.
she kat: PLZ BE OKAY, BOOSTIE!
t-grrl: Puking on keyboard
jdj: DEEP FAKE
b-bo: NEW YORK IS SAVED EVEN WITHOUT SOOPERMAN!
BATMAN WAS RIGHT. THE SHIP IS GOING TO WARP.
LIKE HE'S EVER BEEN WRONG?
EVERYONE'S HERE, RIGHT? EVEN THE BEETLE?

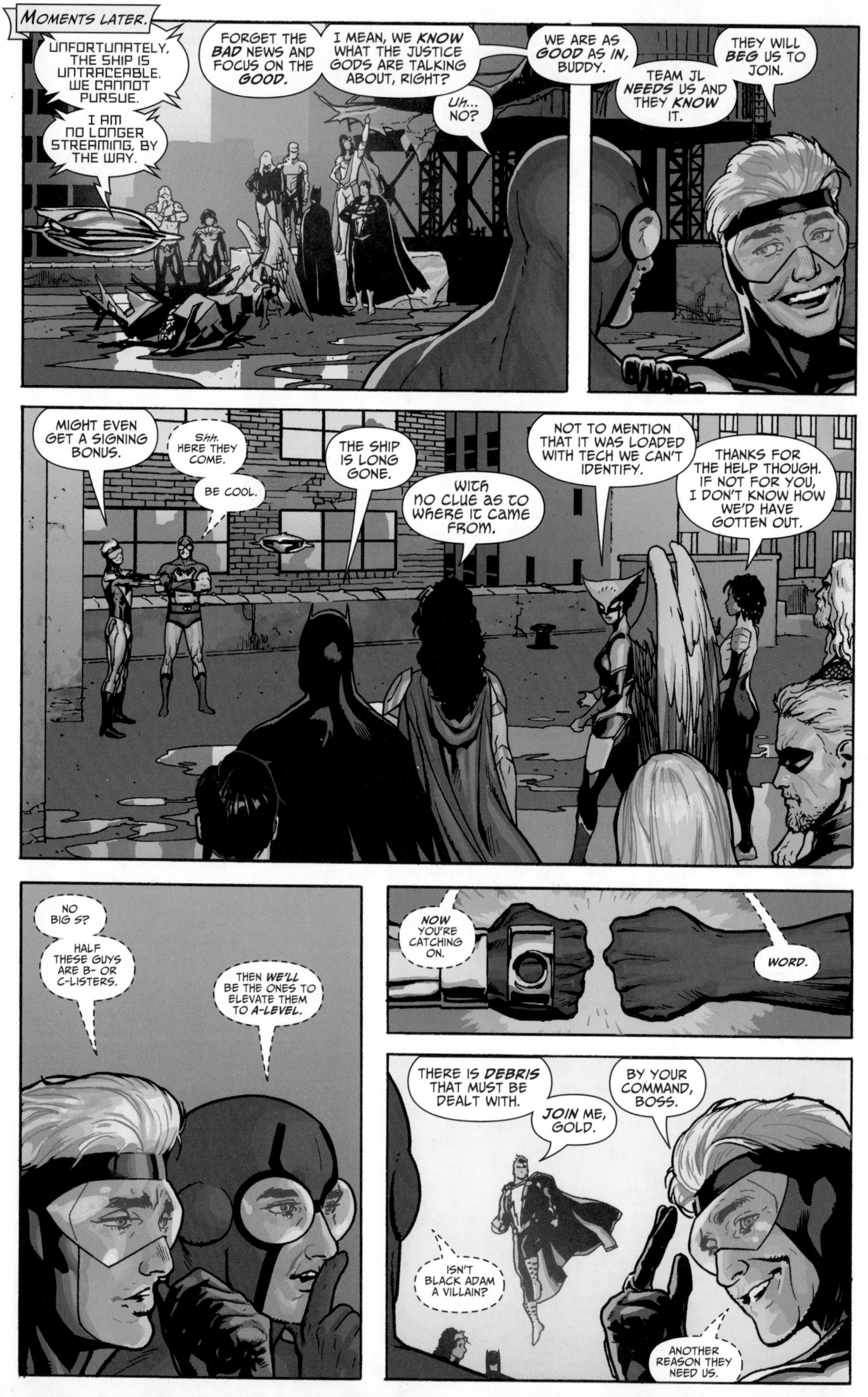
MOMENTS LATER.
UNFORTUNATELY, THE SHIP IS UNTRACEABLE. WE CANNOT PURSUE.
I AM NO LONGER STREAMING, BY THE WAY.
FORGET THE BAD NEWS AND FOCUS ON THE GOOD.
I MEAN, WE KNOW WHAT THE JUSTICE GODS ARE TALKING ABOUT, RIGHT?
Uh... NO?
WE ARE AS GOOD AS IN, BUDDY.
TEAM JL NEEDS US AND THEY KNOW IT.
THEY WILL BEG US TO JOIN.
MIGHT EVEN GET A SIGNING BONUS.
Shh. HERE THEY COME.
BE COOL.
THE SHIP IS LONG GONE.
WITH NO CLUE AS TO WHERE IT CAME FROM.
NOT TO MENTION THAT IT WAS LOADED WITH TECH WE CAN'T IDENTIFY.
THANKS FOR THE HELP THOUGH. IF NOT FOR YOU, I DON'T KNOW HOW WE'D HAVE GOTTEN OUT.
NO BIG S?
HALF THESE GUYS ARE B- OR C-LISTERS.
THEN WE'LL BE THE ONES TO ELEVATE THEM TO A-LEVEL.
NOW YOU'RE CATCHING ON.
WORD.
THERE IS DEBRIS THAT MUST BE DEALT WITH.
JOIN ME, GOLD.
BY YOUR COMMAND, BOSS.
ISN'T BLACK ADAM A VILLAIN?
ANOTHER REASON THEY NEED US.

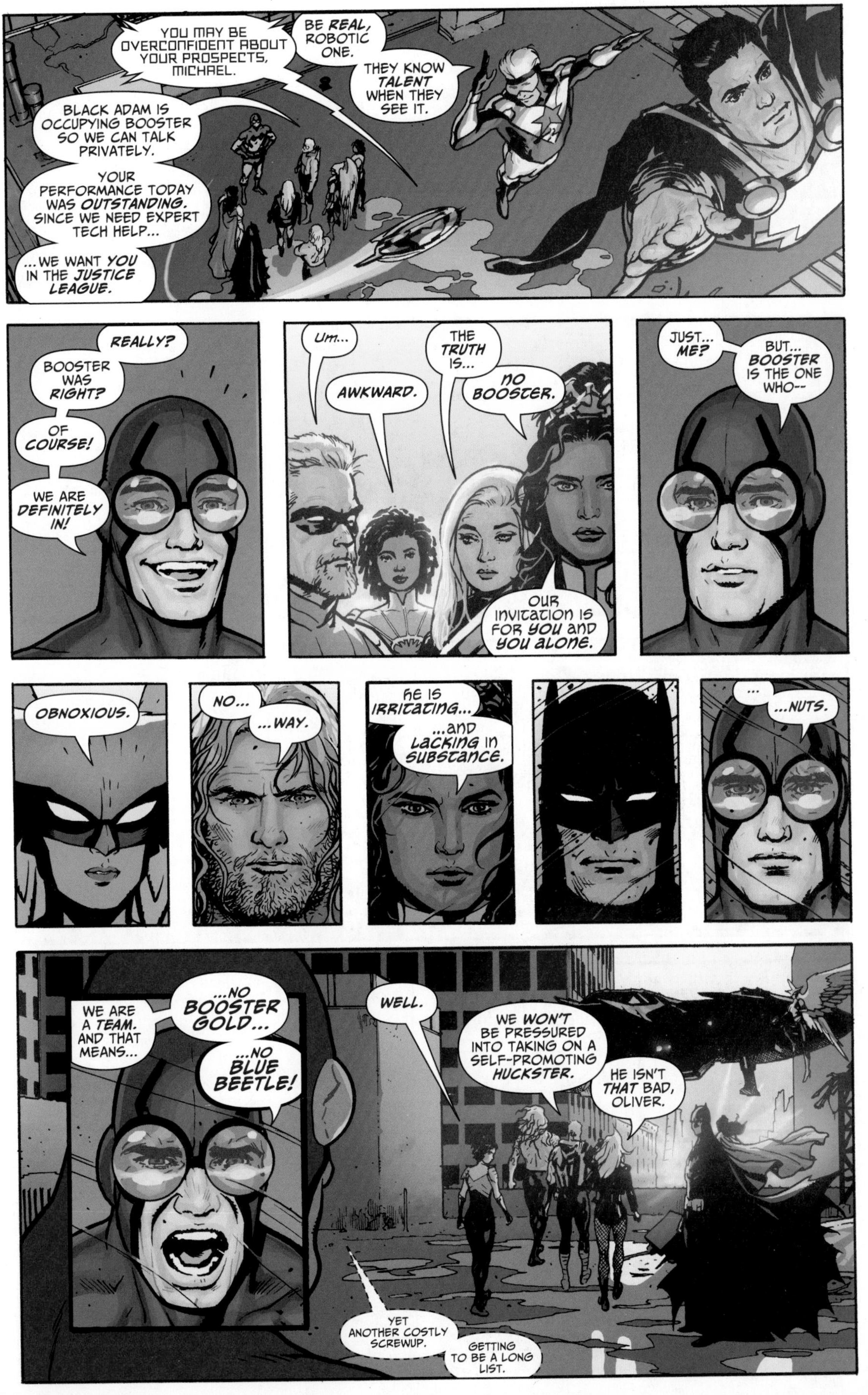

YOU MAY BE OVERCONFIDENT ABOUT YOUR PROSPECTS, MICHAEL.
BE REAL, ROBOTIC ONE.
THEY KNOW TALENT WHEN THEY SEE IT.
BLACK ADAM IS OCCUPYING BOOSTER SO WE CAN TALK PRIVATELY.
YOUR PERFORMANCE TODAY WAS OUTSTANDING. SINCE WE NEED EXPERT TECH HELP...
...WE WANT YOU IN THE JUSTICE LEAGUE.
REALLY?
BOOSTER WAS RIGHT?
OF COURSE!
WE ARE DEFINITELY IN!
Um...
AWKWARD.
THE TRUTH IS...
NO BOOSTER.
OUR INVITATION IS FOR YOU AND YOU ALONE.
JUST... ME?
BUT... BOOSTER IS THE ONE WHO--
OBNOXIOUS.
NO...
...WAY.
HE IS IRRITATING...
...AND LACKING IN SUBSTANCE.
...
...NUTS.
WE ARE A TEAM. AND THAT MEANS...
...NO BOOSTER GOLD...
...NO BLUE BEETLE!
WELL.
WE WON'T BE PRESSURED INTO TAKING ON A SELF-PROMOTING HUCKSTER.
HE ISN'T THAT BAD, OLIVER.
YET ANOTHER COSTLY SCREWUP.
GETTING TO BE A LONG LIST.

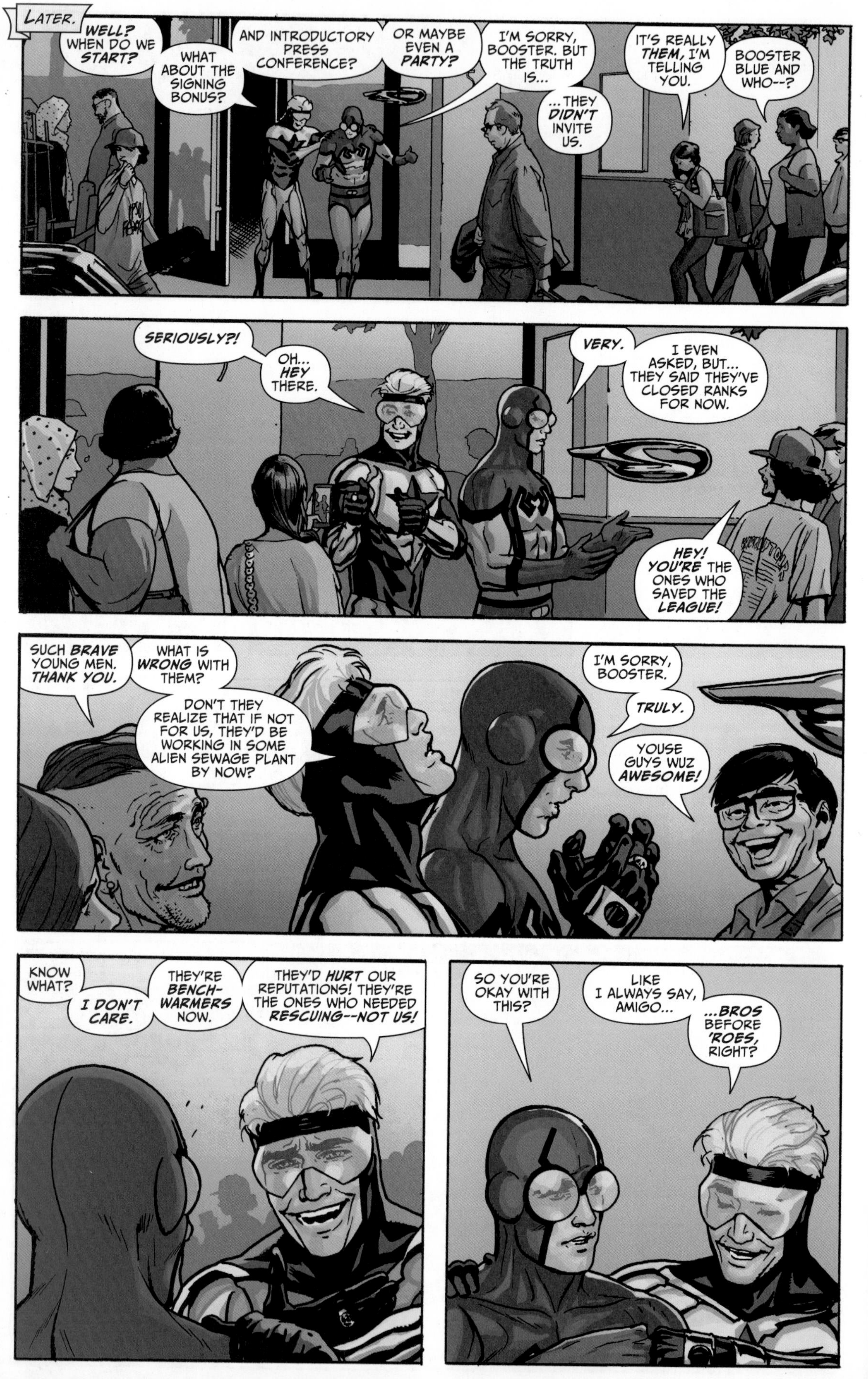
LATER.
WELL? WHEN DO WE START?
WHAT ABOUT THE SIGNING BONUS?
AND INTRODUCTORY PRESS CONFERENCE?
OR MAYBE EVEN A PARTY?
I'M SORRY, BOOSTER. BUT THE TRUTH IS...
...THEY DIDN'T INVITE US.
IT'S REALLY THEM, I'M TELLING YOU.
BOOSTER BLUE AND WHO--?
SERIOUSLY?!
OH... HEY THERE.
VERY.
I EVEN ASKED, BUT... THEY SAID THEY'VE CLOSED RANKS FOR NOW.
HEY! YOU'RE THE ONES WHO SAVED THE LEAGUE!
SUCH BRAVE YOUNG MEN. THANK YOU.
WHAT IS WRONG WITH THEM?
DON'T THEY REALIZE THAT IF NOT FOR US, THEY'D BE WORKING IN SOME ALIEN SEWAGE PLANT BY NOW?
I'M SORRY, BOOSTER.
TRULY.
YOUSE GUYS WUZ AWESOME!
KNOW WHAT?
I DON'T CARE.
THEY'RE BENCH-WARMERS NOW.
THEY'D HURT OUR REPUTATIONS! THEY'RE THE ONES WHO NEEDED RESCUING--NOT US!
SO YOU'RE OKAY WITH THIS?
LIKE I ALWAYS SAY, AMIGO...
...BROS BEFORE 'ROES, RIGHT?

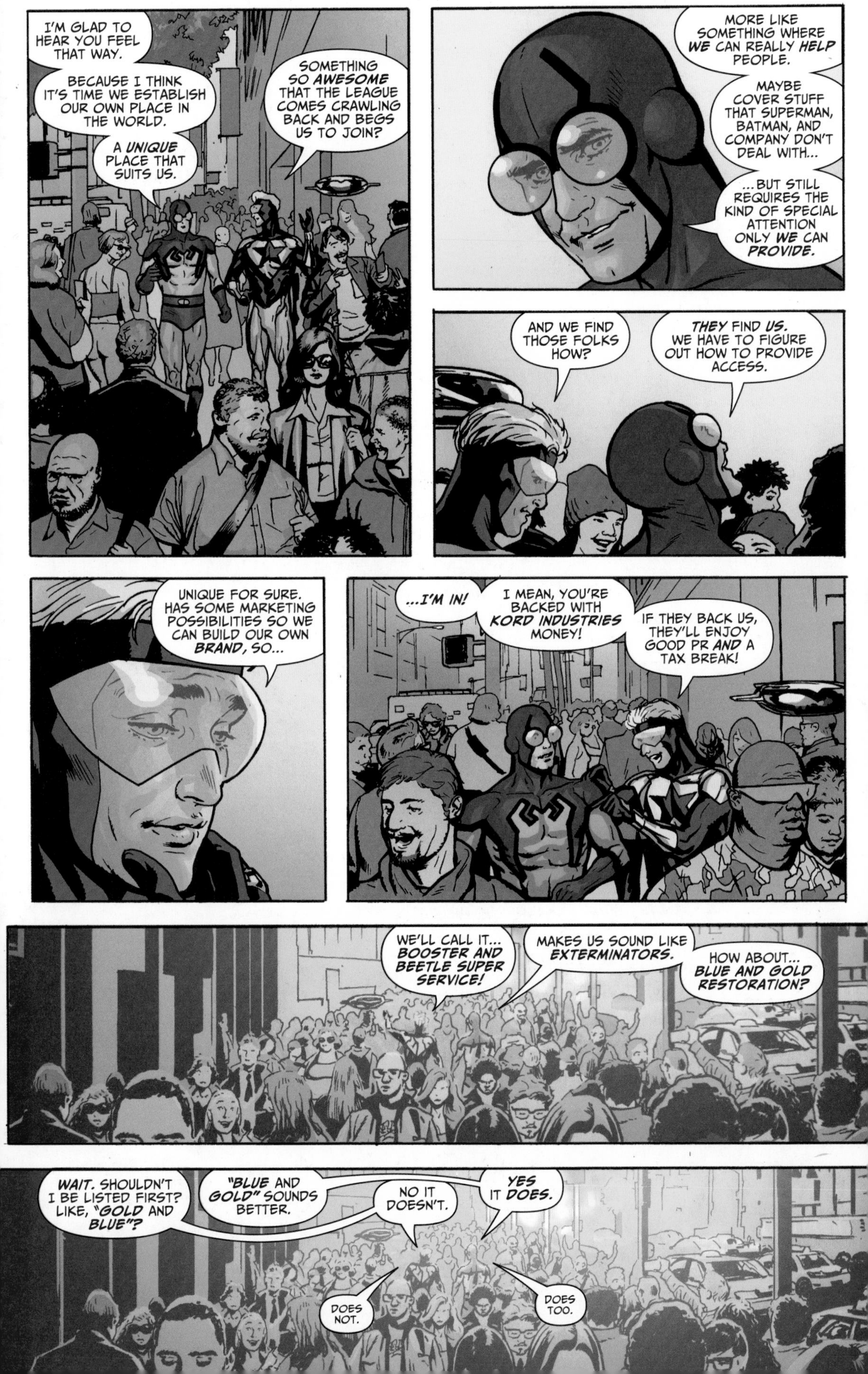
I'M GLAD TO HEAR YOU FEEL THAT WAY.
BECAUSE I THINK IT'S TIME WE ESTABLISH OUR OWN PLACE IN THE WORLD.
A *UNIQUE* PLACE THAT SUITS US.
SOMETHING SO *AWESOME* THAT THE LEAGUE COMES CRAWLING BACK AND BEGS US TO JOIN?
MORE LIKE SOMETHING WHERE *WE* CAN REALLY *HELP* PEOPLE.
MAYBE COVER STUFF THAT SUPERMAN, BATMAN, AND COMPANY DON'T DEAL WITH...
...BUT STILL REQUIRES THE KIND OF SPECIAL ATTENTION ONLY *WE* CAN *PROVIDE.*
AND WE FIND THOSE FOLKS HOW?
THEY FIND *US.* WE HAVE TO FIGURE OUT HOW TO PROVIDE ACCESS.
UNIQUE FOR SURE. HAS SOME MARKETING POSSIBILITIES SO WE CAN BUILD OUR OWN *BRAND,* SO...
...I'M IN!
I MEAN, YOU'RE BACKED WITH *KORD INDUSTRIES* MONEY!
IF THEY BACK US, THEY'LL ENJOY GOOD PR *AND* A TAX BREAK!
WE'LL CALL IT... *BOOSTER AND BEETLE SUPER SERVICE!*
MAKES US SOUND LIKE *EXTERMINATORS.*
HOW ABOUT... *BLUE AND GOLD RESTORATION?*
WAIT. SHOULDN'T I BE LISTED FIRST? LIKE, "*GOLD* AND *BLUE*"?
"BLUE AND *GOLD"* SOUNDS BETTER.
NO IT DOESN'T.
YES IT *DOES.*
DOES NOT.
DOES TOO.

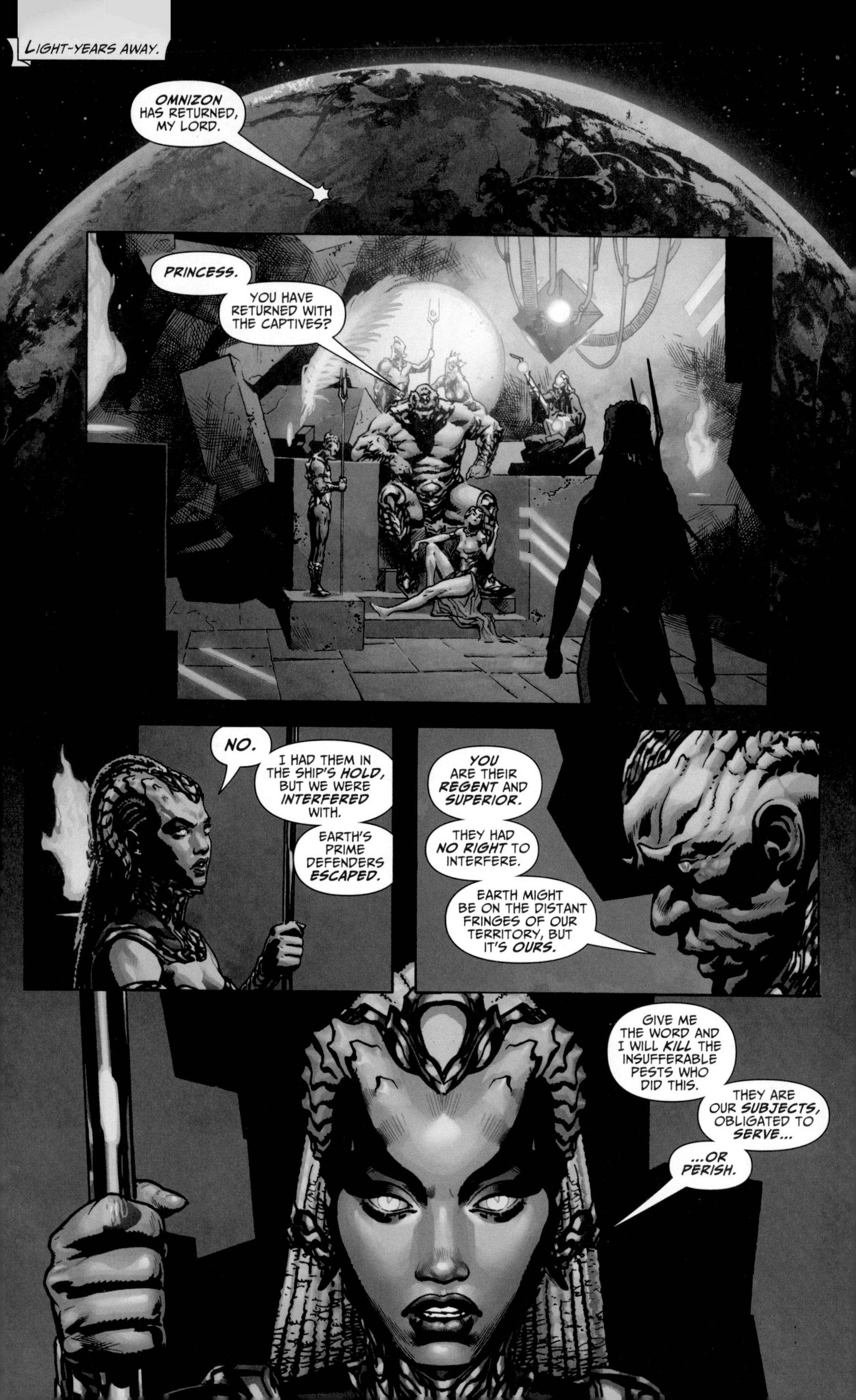
LIGHT-YEARS AWAY.
OMNIZON HAS RETURNED, MY LORD.
PRINCESS.
YOU HAVE RETURNED WITH THE CAPTIVES?
NO.
I HAD THEM IN THE SHIP'S HOLD, BUT WE WERE INTERFERED WITH.
EARTH'S PRIME DEFENDERS ESCAPED.
YOU ARE THEIR REGENT AND SUPERIOR.
THEY HAD NO RIGHT TO INTERFERE.
EARTH MIGHT BE ON THE DISTANT FRINGES OF OUR TERRITORY, BUT IT'S OURS.
GIVE ME THE WORD AND I WILL KILL THE INSUFFERABLE PESTS WHO DID THIS.
THEY ARE OUR SUBJECTS, OBLIGATED TO SERVE...
...OR PERISH.

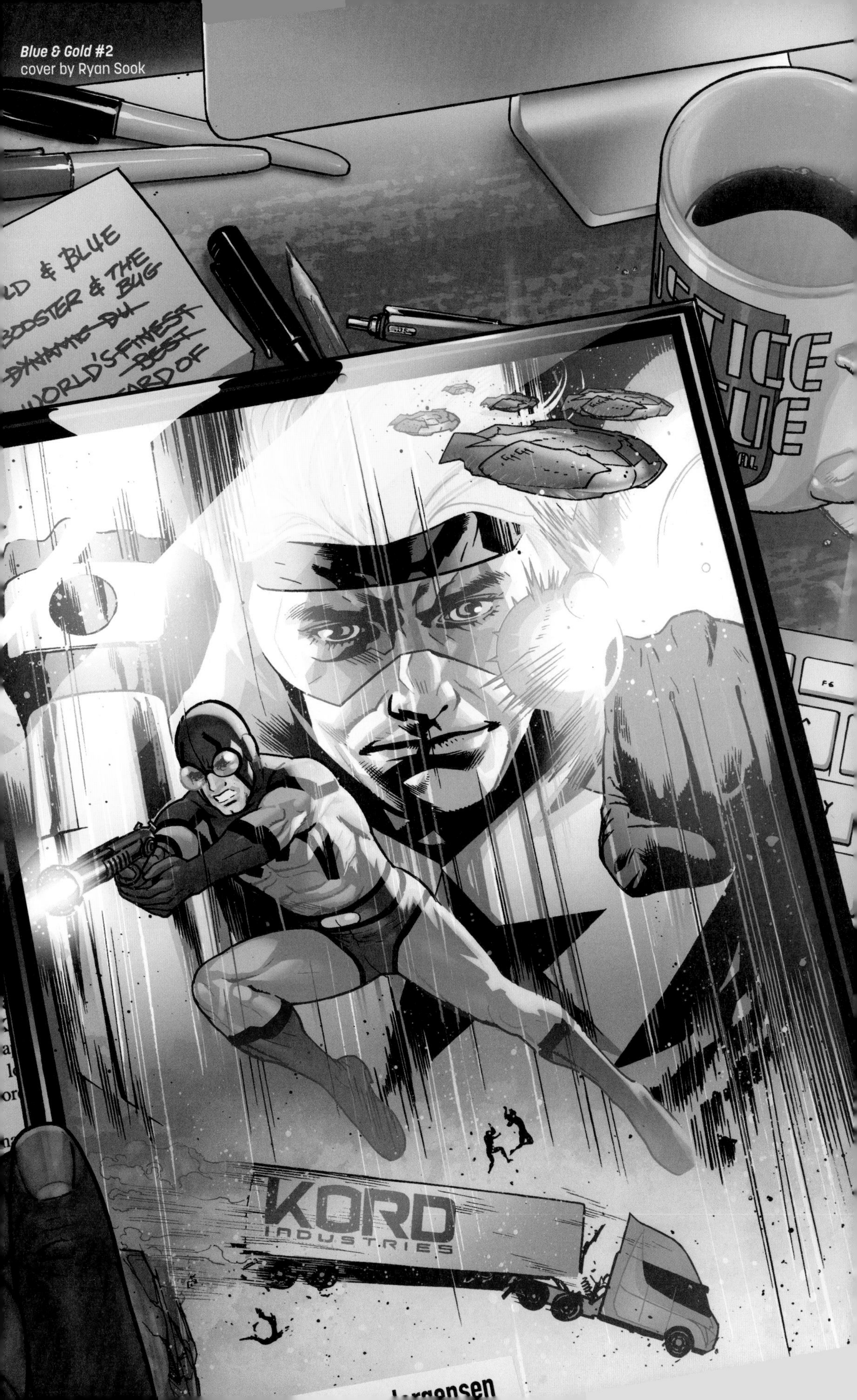
BOOSTER & THE BUG
WORLD'S FINEST
BEST
KORD
INDUSTRIES

Blue & Gold #2
cover by Ryan Sook

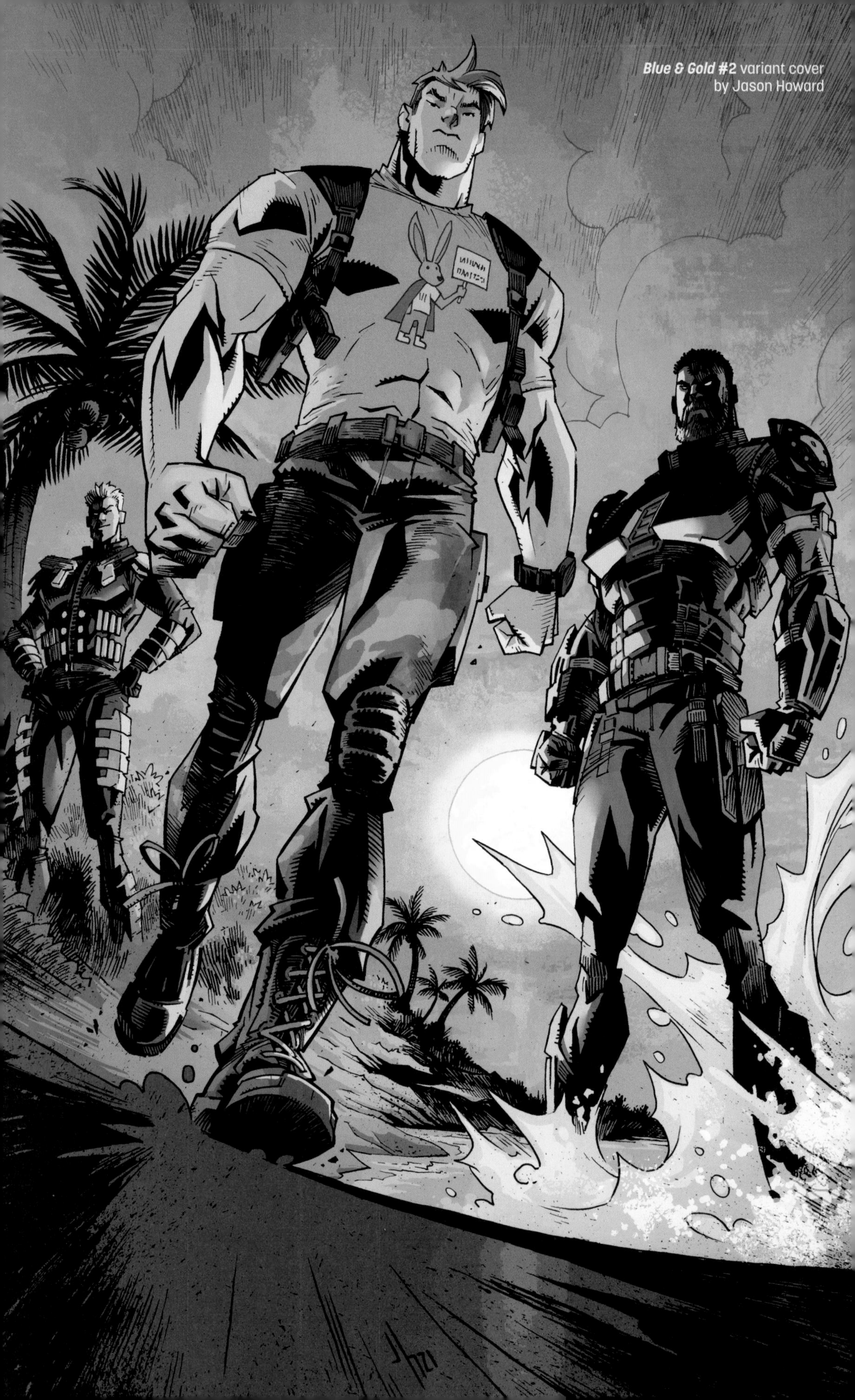

***Blue & Gold* #2** variant cover
by Jason Howard

MY NAME IS TED KORD, OTHERWISE KNOWN AS...

...THE **BLUE BEETLE**.

THAT TRUCK WAYYY OUT IN FRONT OF ME?

IT HAS *MY* NAME ON IT.

SORT OF.

BELONGS TO *KORD* INDUSTRIES, THE COMPANY MY LATE FATHER BUILT.

IT'S *DRIVERLESS,* WHICH MADE IT EASY TO HIJACK AFTER HACKERS TOOK CONTROL...

...LOOTED ITS CARGO, AND SENT IT ON ITS WAY, WHERE IT'S ABOUT TO *HURTLE OFF A CLIFF.*

COMPLICATING ALL OF THIS...

...IS THE DUDE TIED TO THE TOP.

IF I DON'T ACT FAST, I'D SAY HE HAS ABOUT TEN SECONDS LEFT TO LIVE.

HIS NAME IS MICHAEL JON CARTER, THOUGH EVERYONE KNOWS HIM BEST...

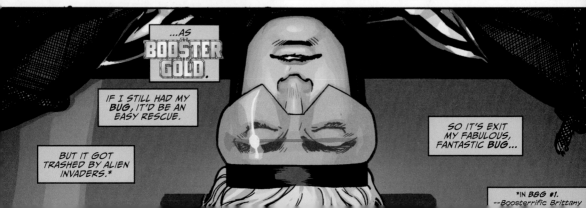

...AS **BOOSTER GOLD.**

IF I STILL HAD MY *BUG,* IT'D BE AN EASY RESCUE.

BUT IT GOT TRASHED BY ALIEN INVADERS.*

SO IT'S EXIT MY FABULOUS, FANTASTIC *BUG...*

*IN BGG #1.
--Boosterrific Brittany

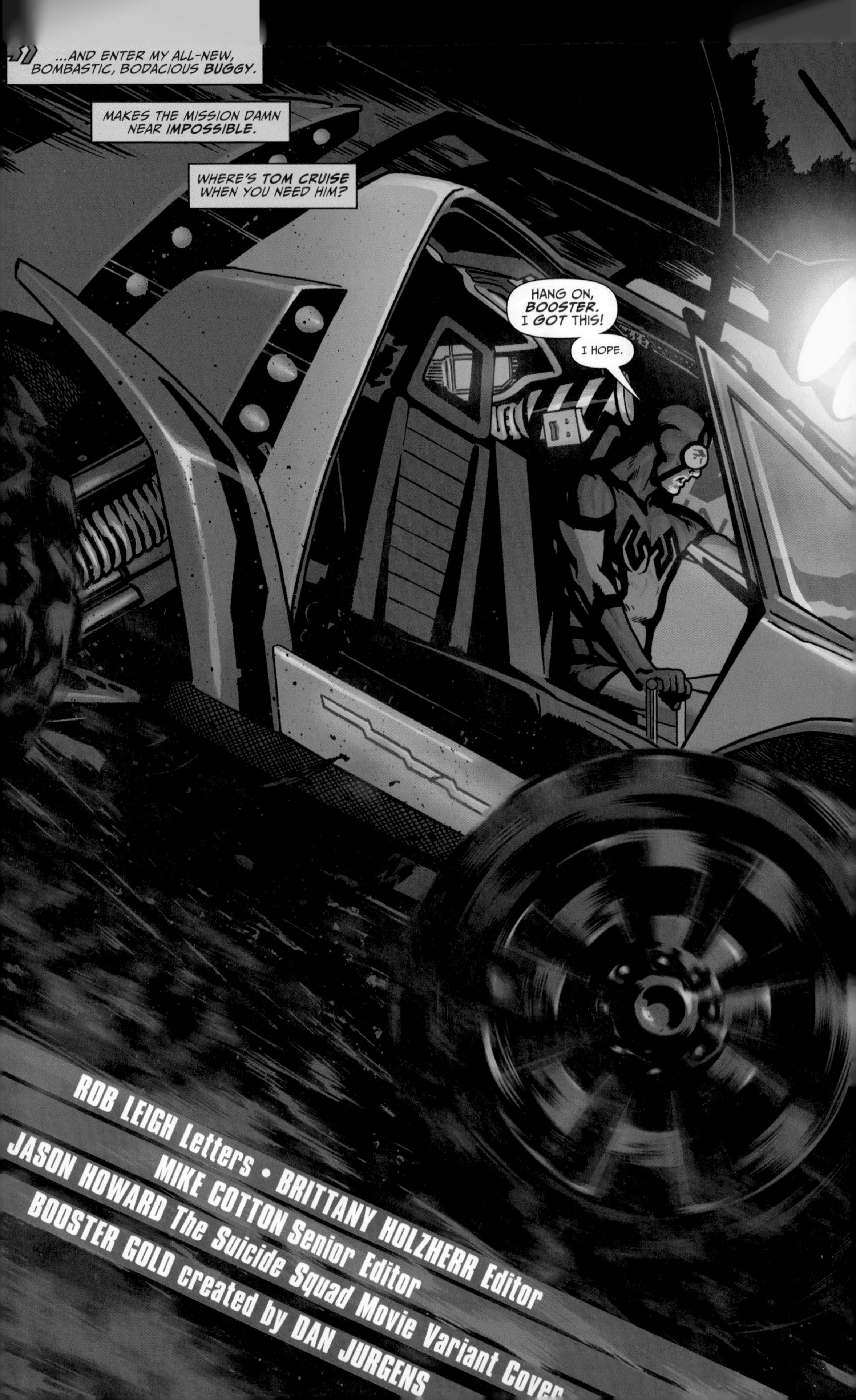
...AND ENTER MY ALL-NEW, BOMBASTIC, BODACIOUS BUGGY.
MAKES THE MISSION DAMN NEAR IMPOSSIBLE.
WHERE'S TOM CRUISE WHEN YOU NEED HIM?
HANG ON, BOOSTER. I GOT THIS!
I HOPE.
ROB LEIGH Letters • BRITTANY HOLZHERR Editor
MIKE COTTON Senior Editor
JASON HOWARD The Suicide Squad Movie Variant Cover
BOOSTER GOLD created by DAN JURGENS

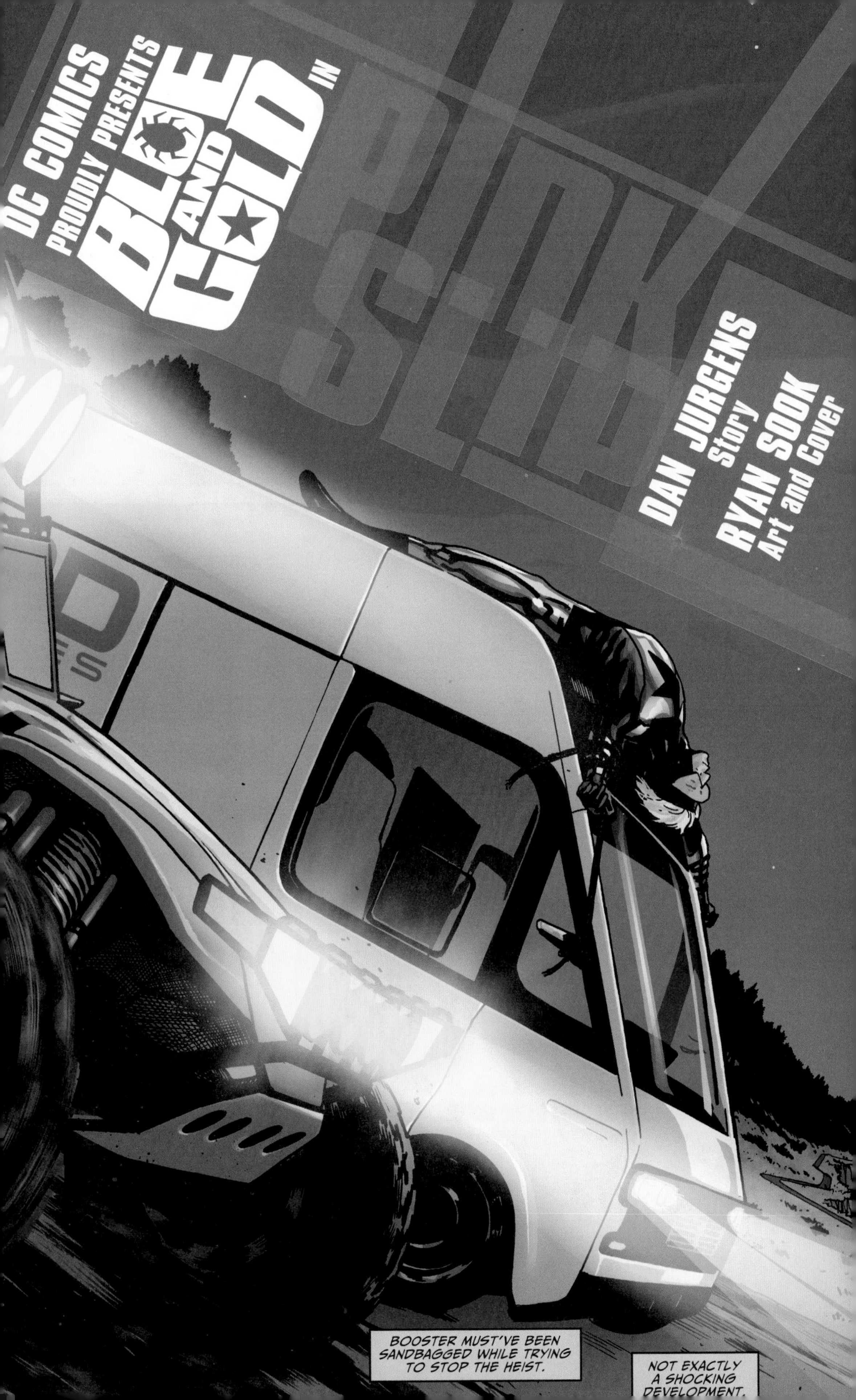
DC COMICS
PROUDLY PRESENTS
BLUE AND GOLD
IN
PINK SLIP
DAN JURGENS
Story
RYAN SOOK
Art and Cover
BOOSTER MUST'VE BEEN SANDBAGGED WHILE TRYING TO STOP THE HEIST.
NOT EXACTLY A SHOCKING DEVELOPMENT.

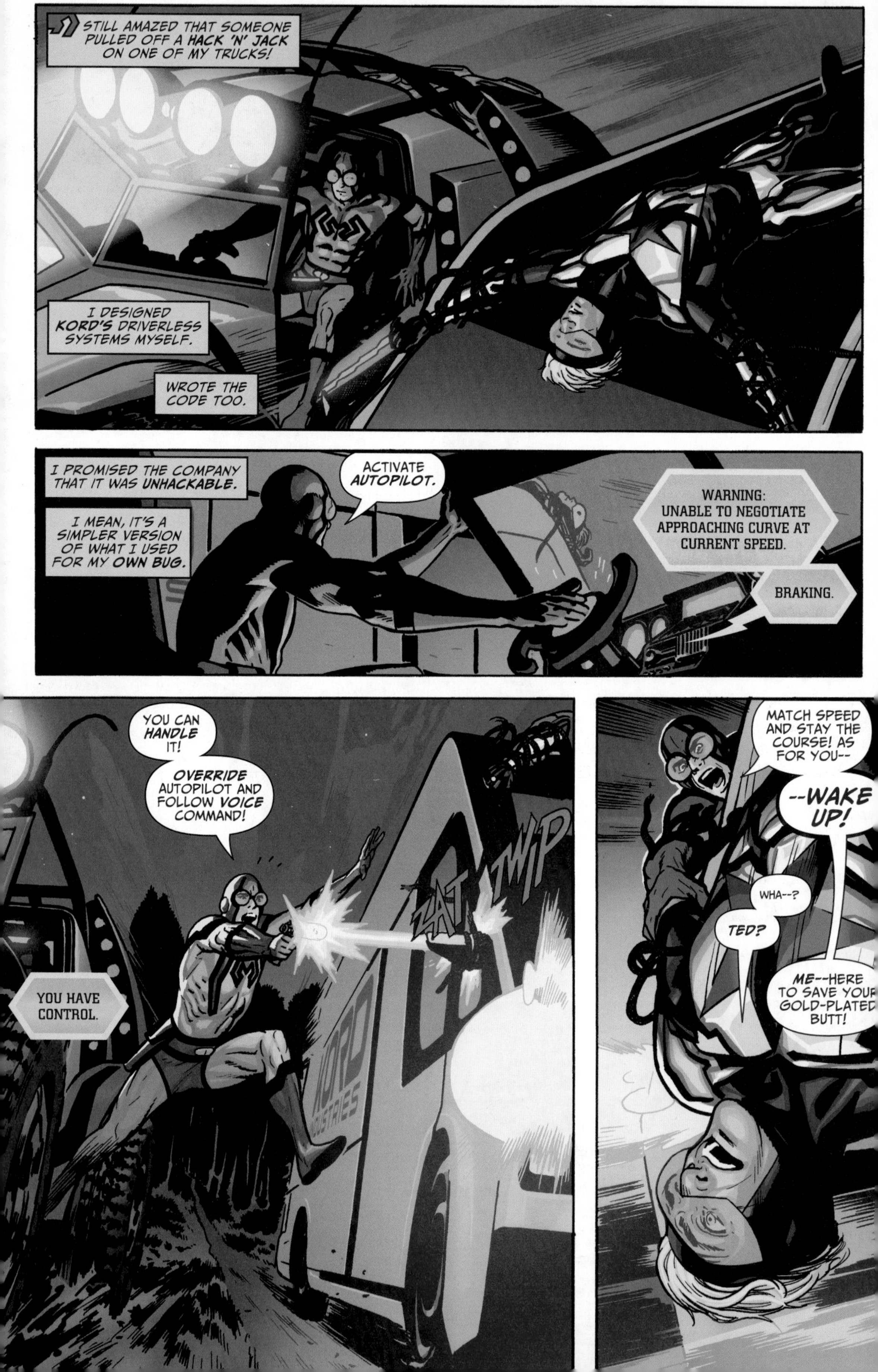
STILL AMAZED THAT SOMEONE PULLED OFF A HACK 'N' JACK ON ONE OF MY TRUCKS!
I DESIGNED KORD'S DRIVERLESS SYSTEMS MYSELF.
WROTE THE CODE TOO.
I PROMISED THE COMPANY THAT IT WAS UNHACKABLE.
I MEAN, IT'S A SIMPLER VERSION OF WHAT I USED FOR MY OWN BUG.
ACTIVATE AUTOPILOT.
WARNING: UNABLE TO NEGOTIATE APPROACHING CURVE AT CURRENT SPEED.
BRAKING.
YOU CAN HANDLE IT!
OVERRIDE AUTOPILOT AND FOLLOW VOICE COMMAND!
ZAT
TWIP
YOU HAVE CONTROL.
KORD INDUSTRIES
MATCH SPEED AND STAY THE COURSE! AS FOR YOU--
--WAKE UP!
WHA--?
TED?
ME--HERE TO SAVE YOUR GOLD-PLATED BUTT!

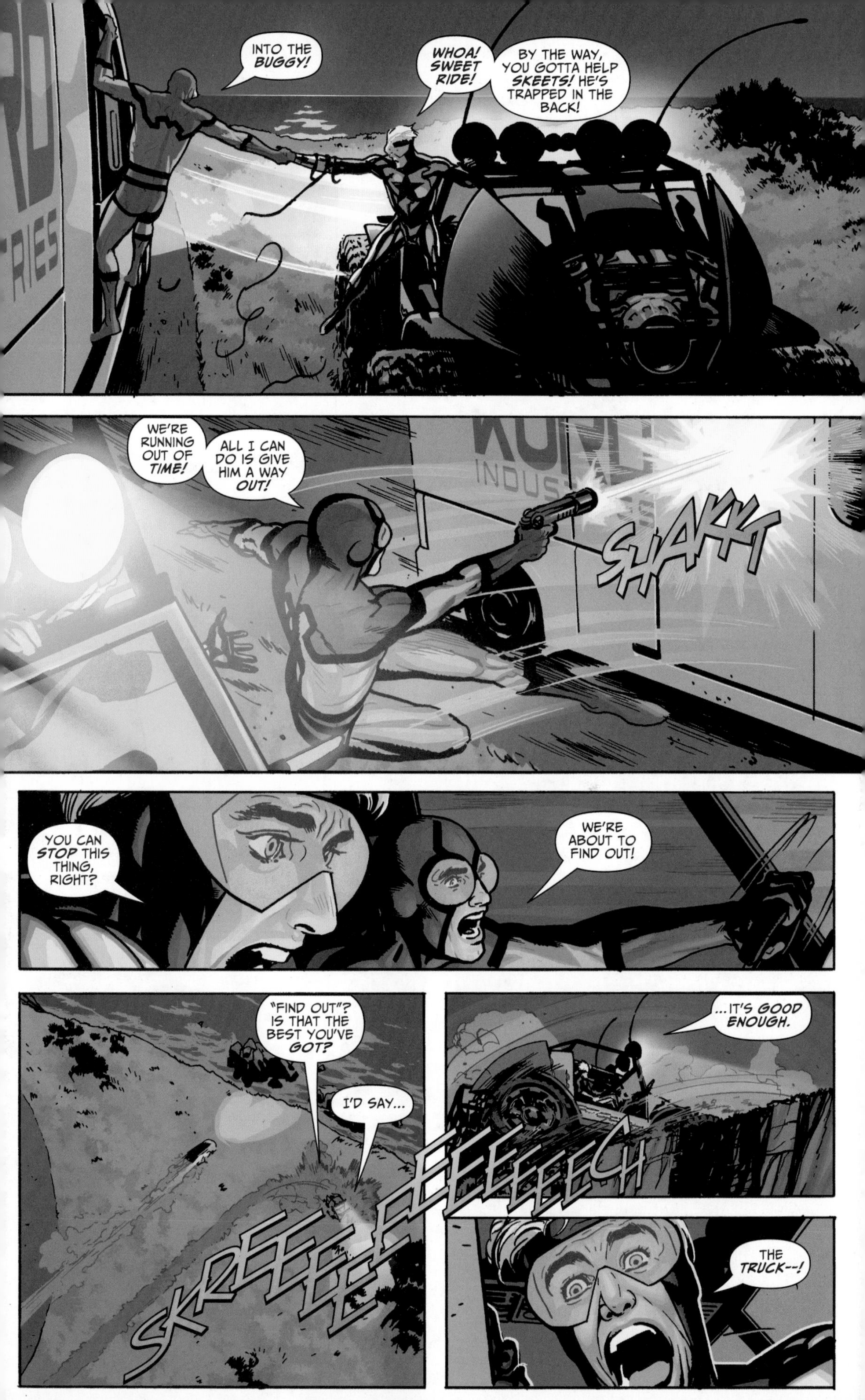
INTO THE BUGGY!
WHOA! SWEET RIDE!
BY THE WAY, YOU GOTTA HELP SKEETS! HE'S TRAPPED IN THE BACK!
WE'RE RUNNING OUT OF TIME!
ALL I CAN DO IS GIVE HIM A WAY OUT!
SHAKKT
YOU CAN STOP THIS THING, RIGHT?
WE'RE ABOUT TO FIND OUT!
"FIND OUT"? IS THAT THE BEST YOU'VE GOT?
I'D SAY...
SKREEEEEEEEEEEEEECH
...IT'S GOOD ENOUGH.
THE TRUCK--!

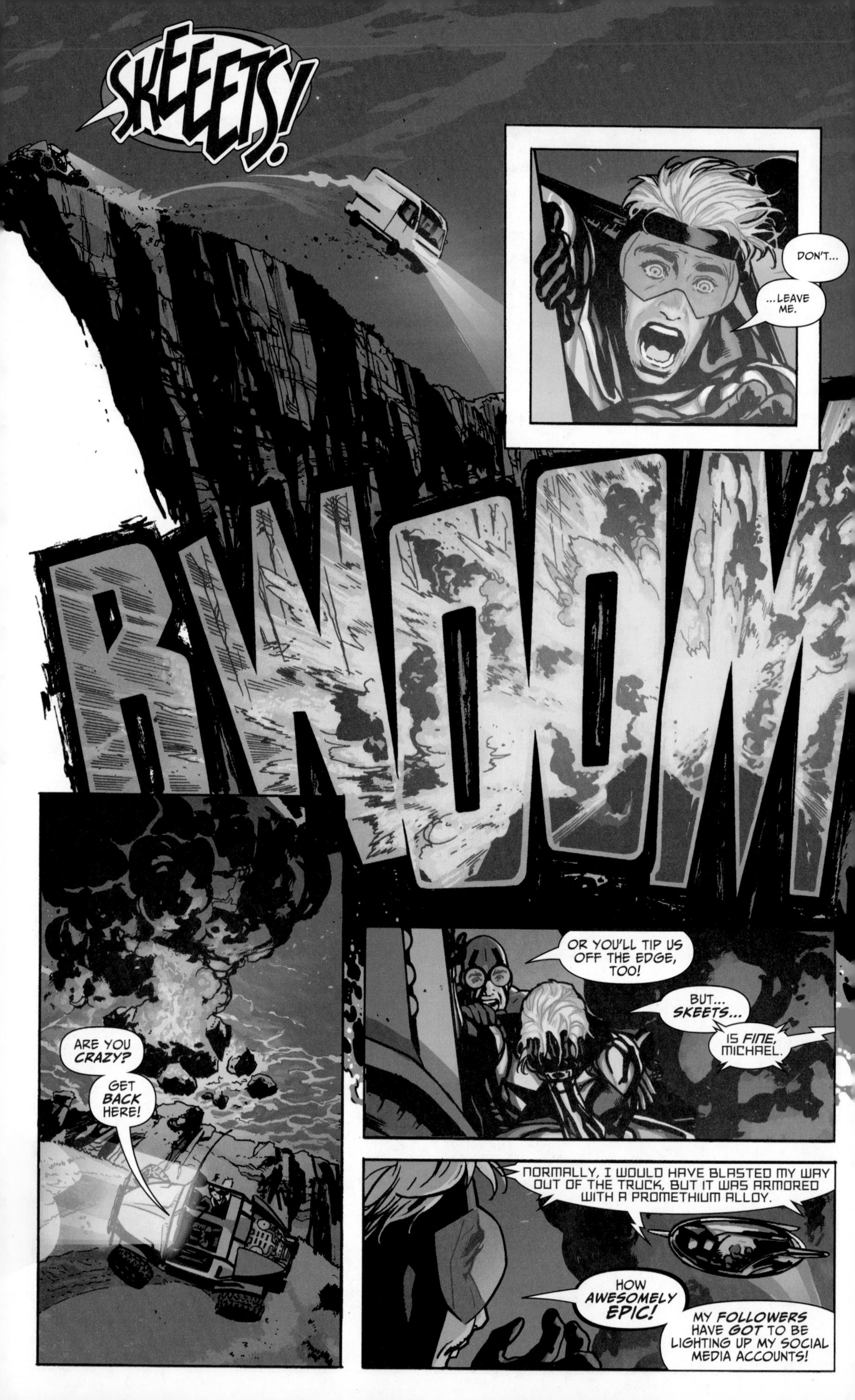
SKEEETS!
DON'T...
...LEAVE ME.
BWOOM
ARE YOU CRAZY?
GET BACK HERE!
OR YOU'LL TIP US OFF THE EDGE, TOO!
BUT... SKEETS...
IS FINE, MICHAEL.
NORMALLY, I WOULD HAVE BLASTED MY WAY OUT OF THE TRUCK, BUT IT WAS ARMORED WITH A PROMETHIUM ALLOY.
HOW AWESOMELY EPIC!
MY FOLLOWERS HAVE GOT TO BE LIGHTING UP MY SOCIAL MEDIA ACCOUNTS!

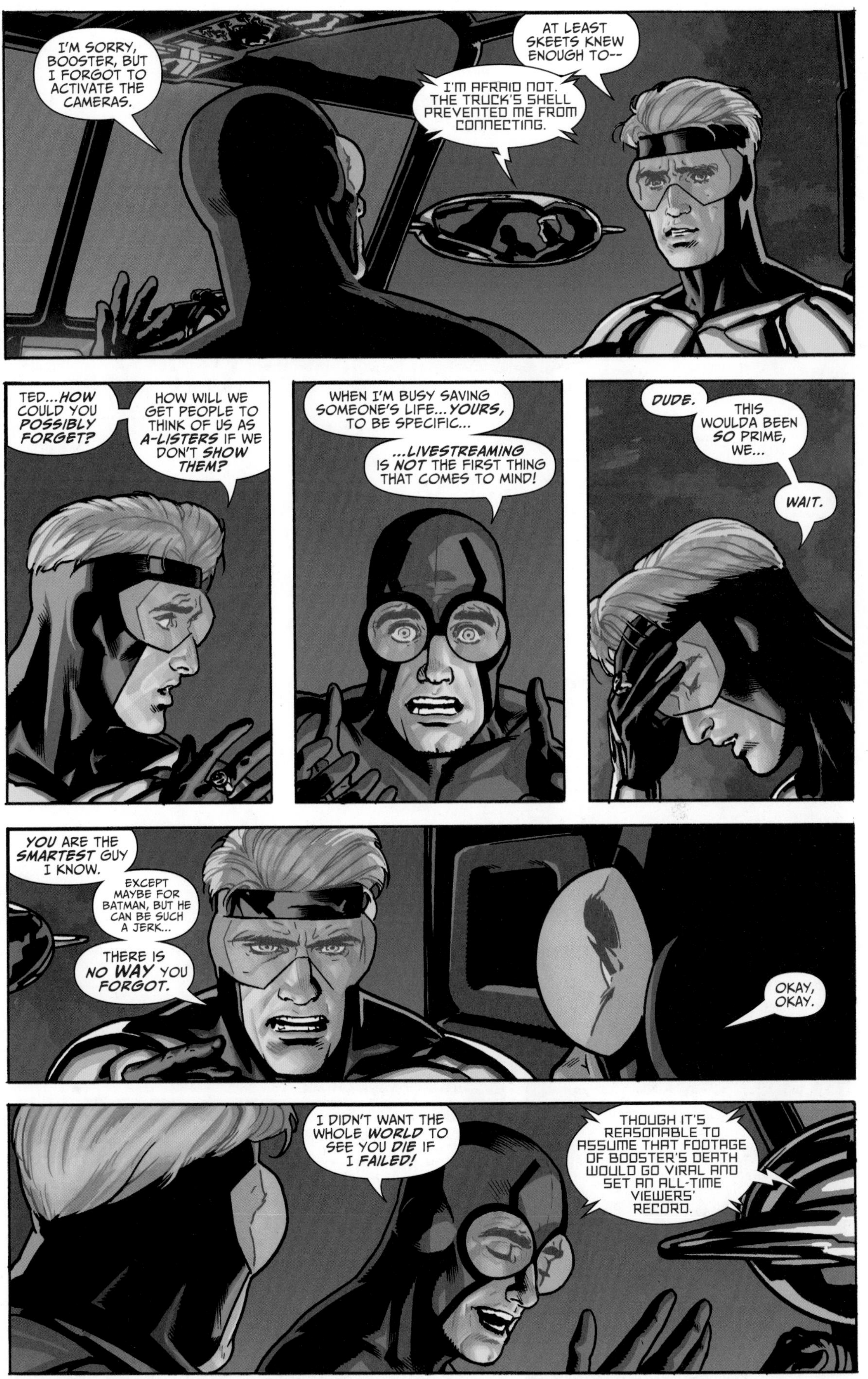
I'M SORRY, BOOSTER, BUT I FORGOT TO ACTIVATE THE CAMERAS.
AT LEAST SKEETS KNEW ENOUGH TO--
I'M AFRAID NOT. THE TRUCK'S SHELL PREVENTED ME FROM CONNECTING.
TED...HOW COULD YOU POSSIBLY FORGET?
HOW WILL WE GET PEOPLE TO THINK OF US AS A-LISTERS IF WE DON'T SHOW THEM?
WHEN I'M BUSY SAVING SOMEONE'S LIFE...YOURS, TO BE SPECIFIC...
...LIVESTREAMING IS NOT THE FIRST THING THAT COMES TO MIND!
DUDE.
THIS WOULDA BEEN SO PRIME, WE...
WAIT.
YOU ARE THE SMARTEST GUY I KNOW.
EXCEPT MAYBE FOR BATMAN, BUT HE CAN BE SUCH A JERK...
THERE IS NO WAY YOU FORGOT.
OKAY, OKAY.
I DIDN'T WANT THE WHOLE WORLD TO SEE YOU DIE IF I FAILED!
THOUGH IT'S REASONABLE TO ASSUME THAT FOOTAGE OF BOOSTER'S DEATH WOULD GO VIRAL AND SET AN ALL-TIME VIEWERS' RECORD.

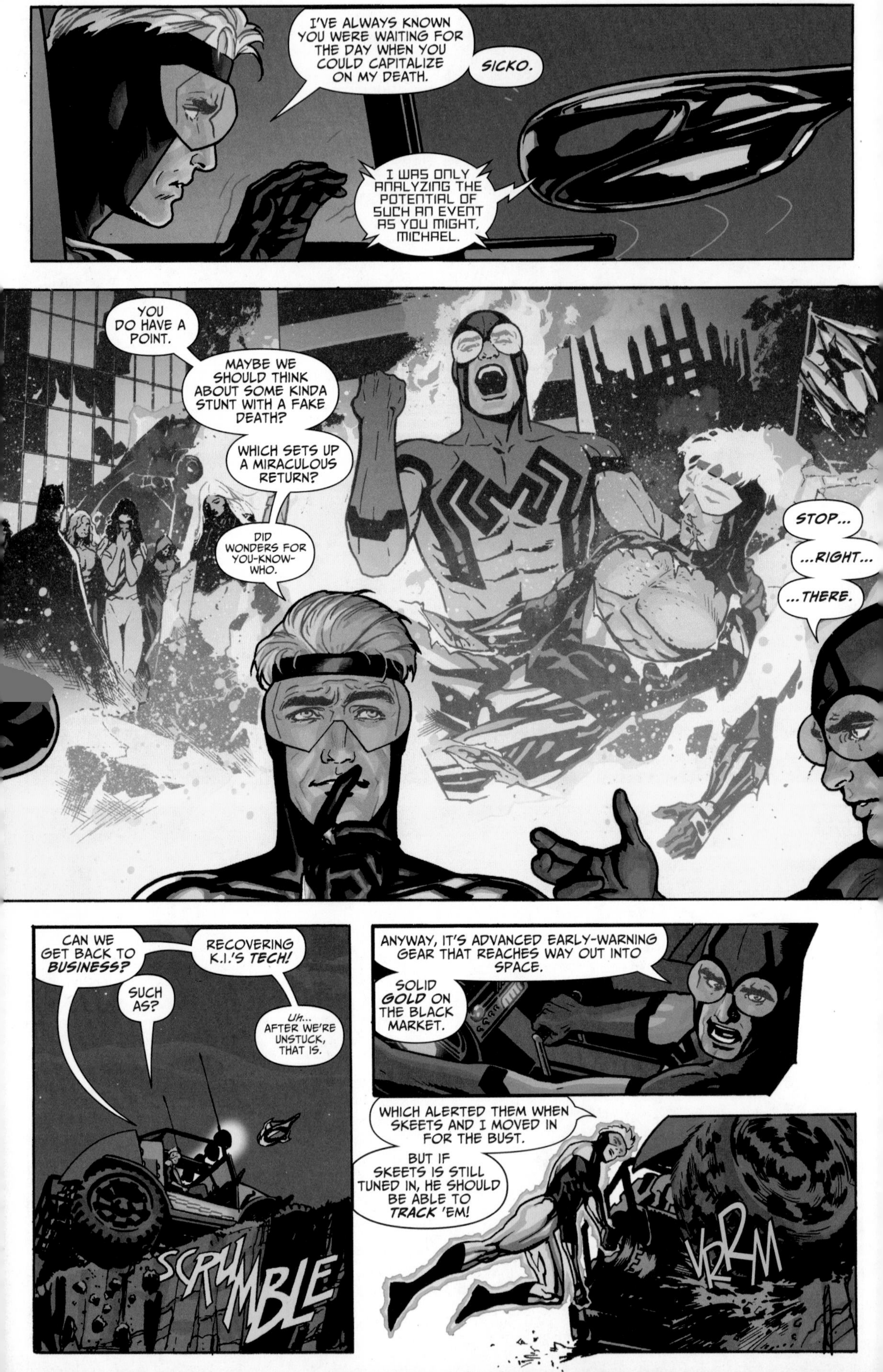

I'VE ALWAYS KNOWN YOU WERE WAITING FOR THE DAY WHEN YOU COULD CAPITALIZE ON MY DEATH.
SICKO.
I WAS ONLY ANALYZING THE POTENTIAL OF SUCH AN EVENT AS YOU MIGHT, MICHAEL.
YOU DO HAVE A POINT.
MAYBE WE SHOULD THINK ABOUT SOME KINDA STUNT WITH A FAKE DEATH?
WHICH SETS UP A MIRACULOUS RETURN?
DID WONDERS FOR YOU-KNOW-WHO.
STOP...
...RIGHT...
...THERE.
CAN WE GET BACK TO BUSINESS?
SUCH AS?
RECOVERING K.I.'S TECH!
Uh... AFTER WE'RE UNSTUCK, THAT IS.
SCRUMBLE
ANYWAY, IT'S ADVANCED EARLY-WARNING GEAR THAT REACHES WAY OUT INTO SPACE.
SOLID GOLD ON THE BLACK MARKET.
WHICH ALERTED THEM WHEN SKEETS AND I MOVED IN FOR THE BUST.
BUT IF SKEETS IS STILL TUNED IN, HE SHOULD BE ABLE TO TRACK 'EM!
VRRM

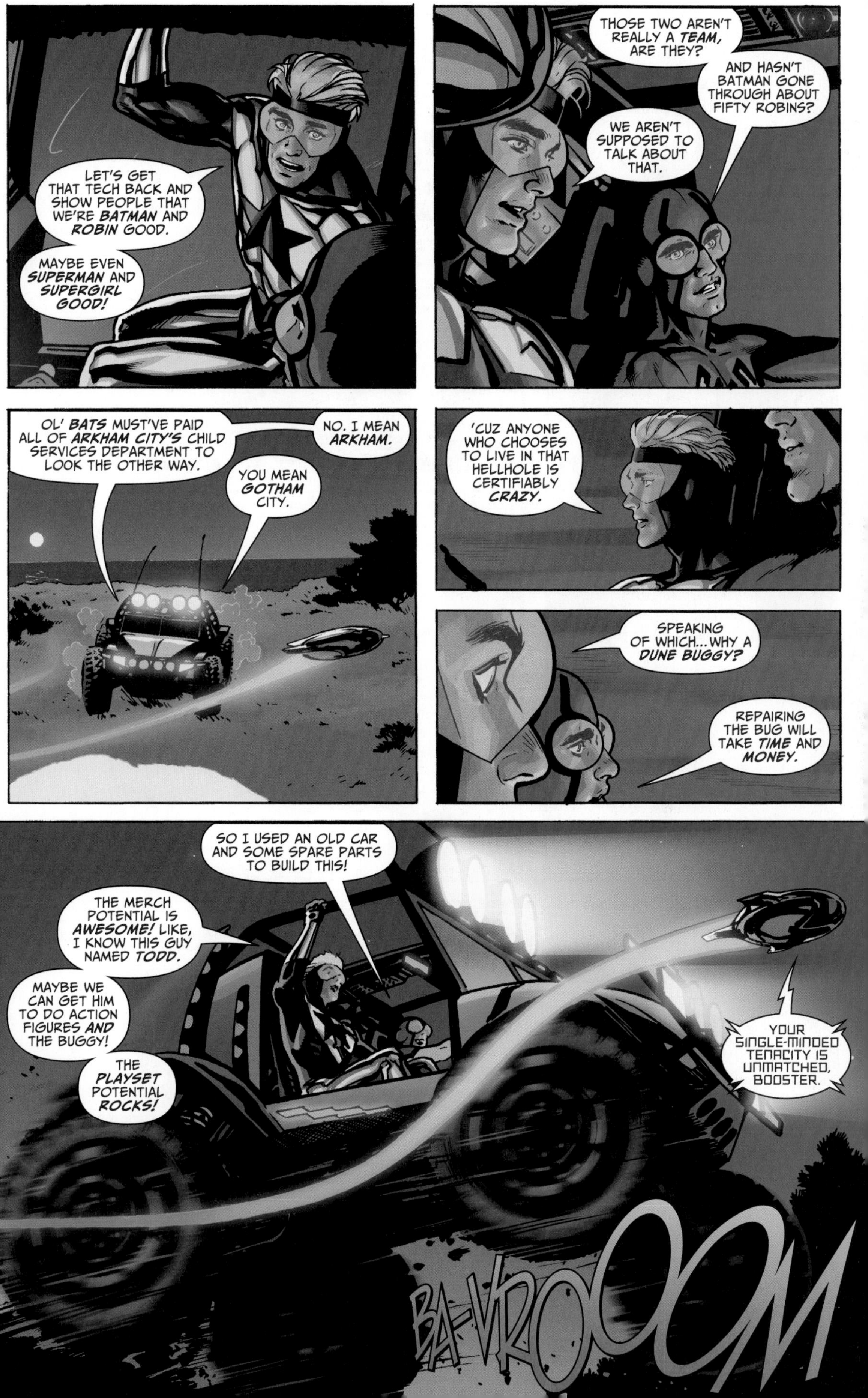
LET'S GET THAT TECH BACK AND SHOW PEOPLE THAT WE'RE BATMAN AND ROBIN GOOD.
MAYBE EVEN SUPERMAN AND SUPERGIRL GOOD!
THOSE TWO AREN'T REALLY A TEAM, ARE THEY?
AND HASN'T BATMAN GONE THROUGH ABOUT FIFTY ROBINS?
WE AREN'T SUPPOSED TO TALK ABOUT THAT.
OL' BATS MUST'VE PAID ALL OF ARKHAM CITY'S CHILD SERVICES DEPARTMENT TO LOOK THE OTHER WAY.
YOU MEAN GOTHAM CITY.
NO. I MEAN ARKHAM.
'CUZ ANYONE WHO CHOOSES TO LIVE IN THAT HELLHOLE IS CERTIFIABLY CRAZY.
SPEAKING OF WHICH...WHY A DUNE BUGGY?
REPAIRING THE BUG WILL TAKE TIME AND MONEY.
SO I USED AN OLD CAR AND SOME SPARE PARTS TO BUILD THIS!
THE MERCH POTENTIAL IS AWESOME! LIKE, I KNOW THIS GUY NAMED TODD.
MAYBE WE CAN GET HIM TO DO ACTION FIGURES AND THE BUGGY!
THE PLAYSET POTENTIAL ROCKS!
YOUR SINGLE-MINDED TENACITY IS UNMATCHED, BOOSTER.
BA-VROOOOM

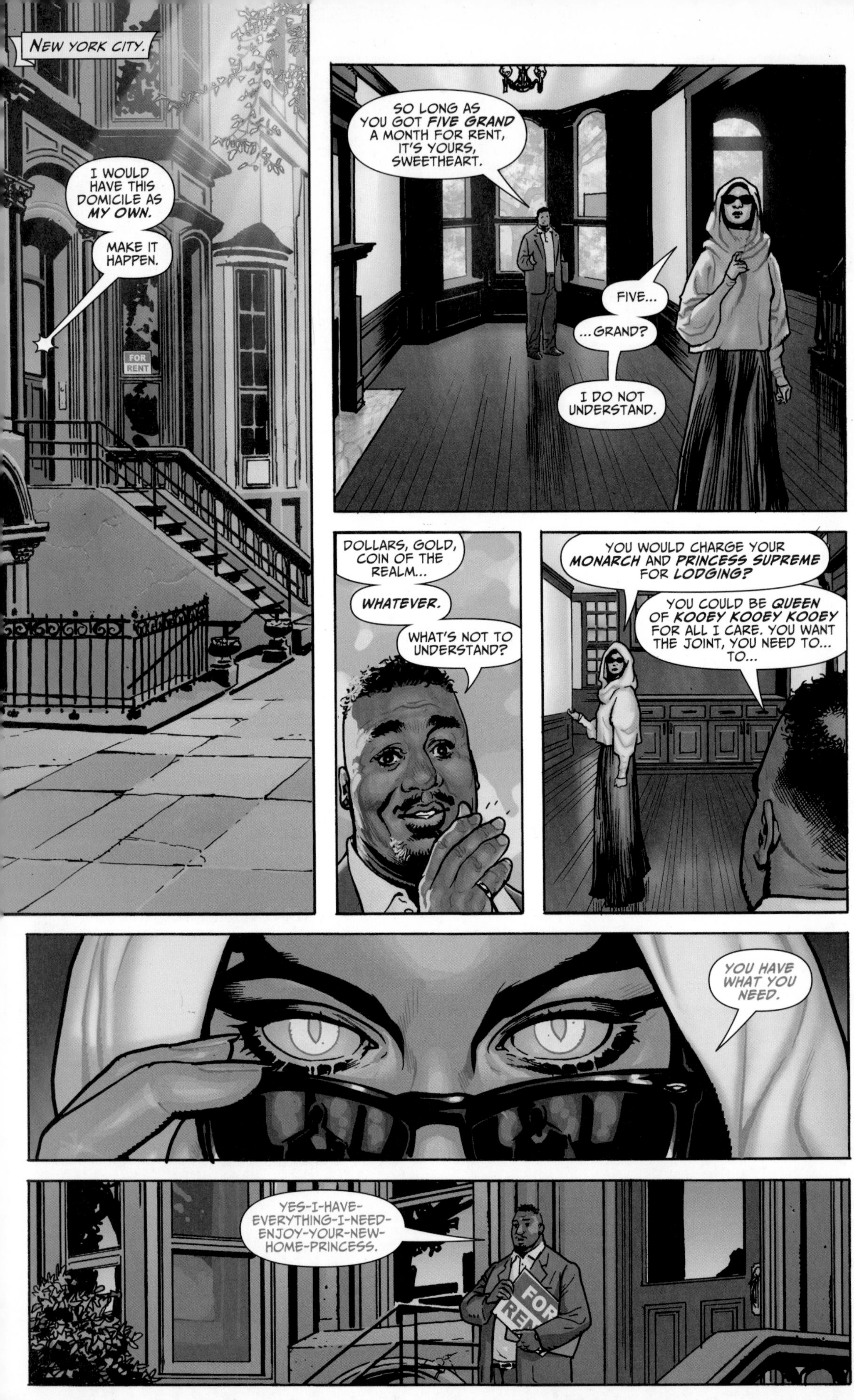
NEW YORK CITY.
I WOULD HAVE THIS DOMICILE AS MY OWN.
MAKE IT HAPPEN.
FOR RENT
SO LONG AS YOU GOT FIVE GRAND A MONTH FOR RENT, IT'S YOURS, SWEETHEART.
FIVE...
...GRAND?
I DO NOT UNDERSTAND.
DOLLARS, GOLD, COIN OF THE REALM...
WHATEVER.
WHAT'S NOT TO UNDERSTAND?
YOU WOULD CHARGE YOUR MONARCH AND PRINCESS SUPREME FOR LODGING?
YOU COULD BE QUEEN OF KOOEY KOOEY KOOEY FOR ALL I CARE. YOU WANT THE JOINT, YOU NEED TO... TO...
YOU HAVE WHAT YOU NEED.
YES-I-HAVE-EVERYTHING-I-NEED-ENJOY-YOUR-NEW-HOME-PRINCESS.

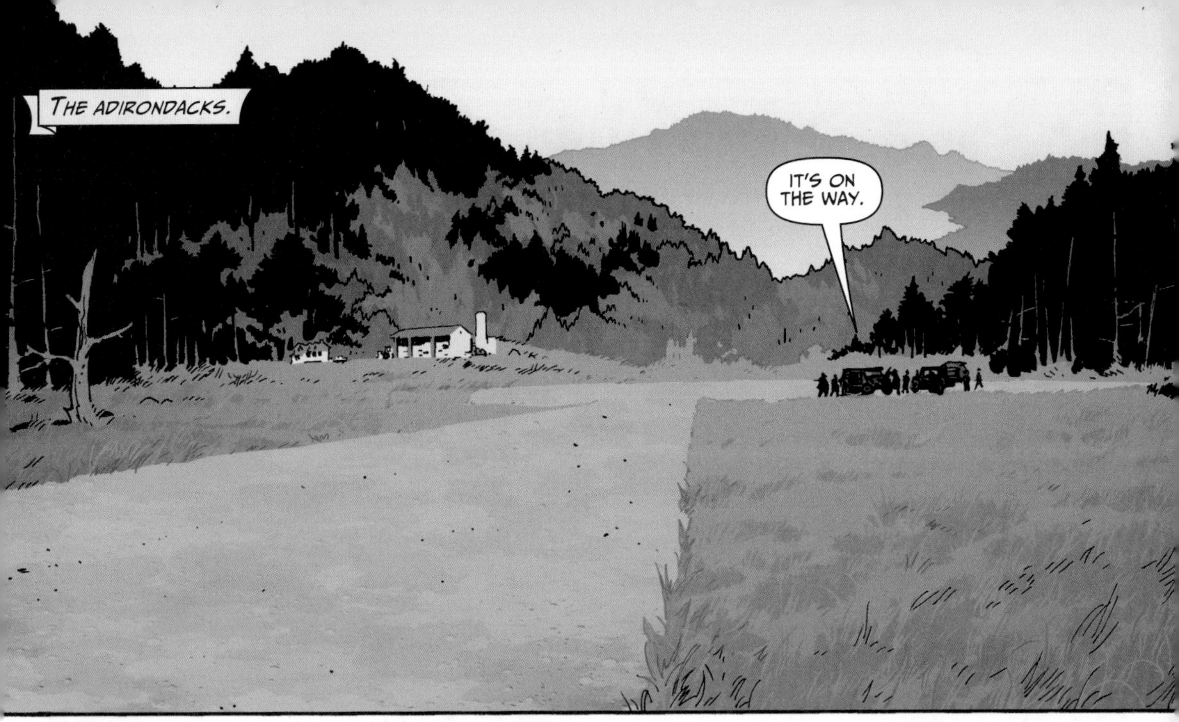
THE ADIRONDACKS.
IT'S ON THE WAY.

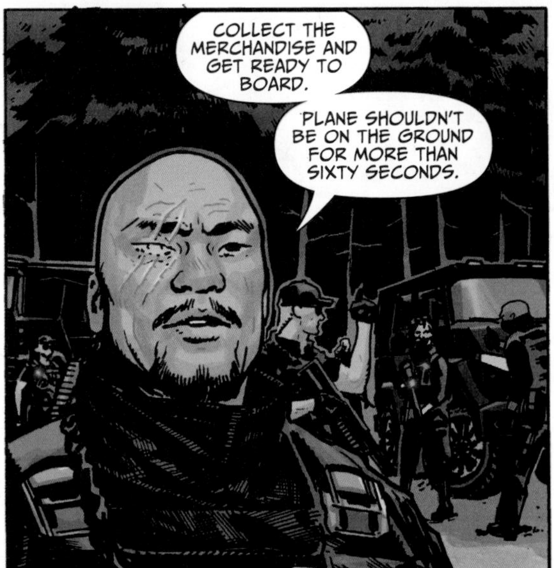
COLLECT THE MERCHANDISE AND GET READY TO BOARD.
PLANE SHOULDN'T BE ON THE GROUND FOR MORE THAN SIXTY SECONDS.

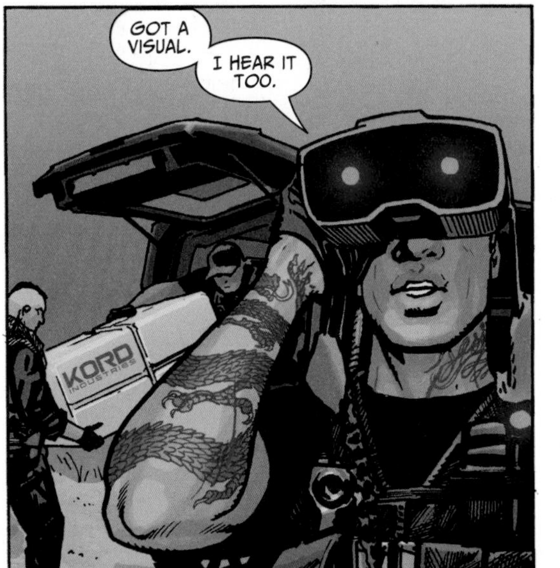
GOT A VISUAL.
I HEAR IT TOO.
KORD INDUSTRIES

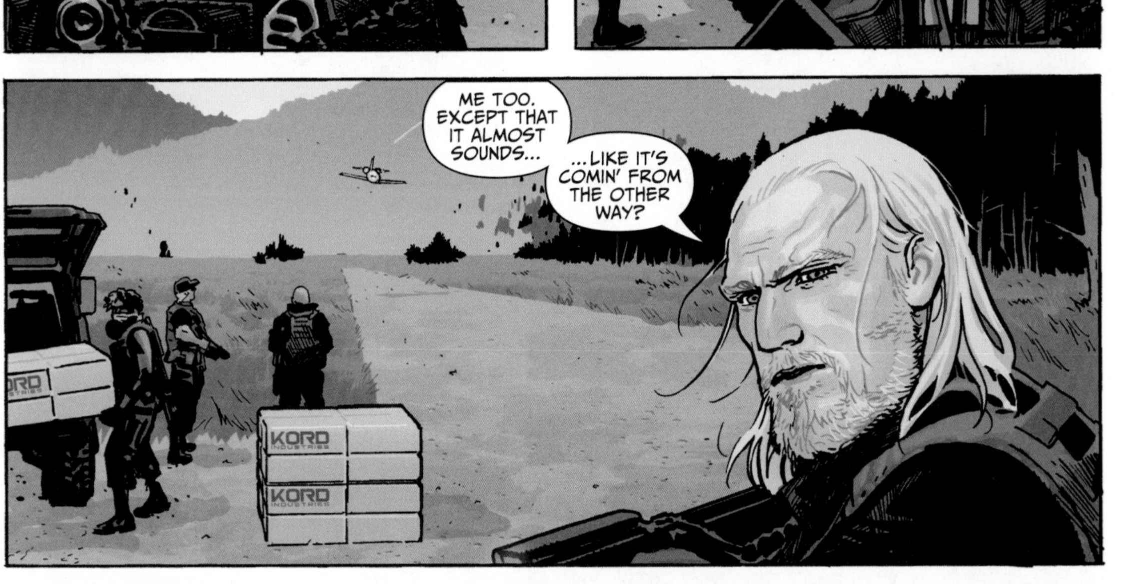
ME TOO. EXCEPT THAT IT ALMOST SOUNDS...
...LIKE IT'S COMIN' FROM THE OTHER WAY?
KORD INDUSTRIES
KORD INDUSTRIES

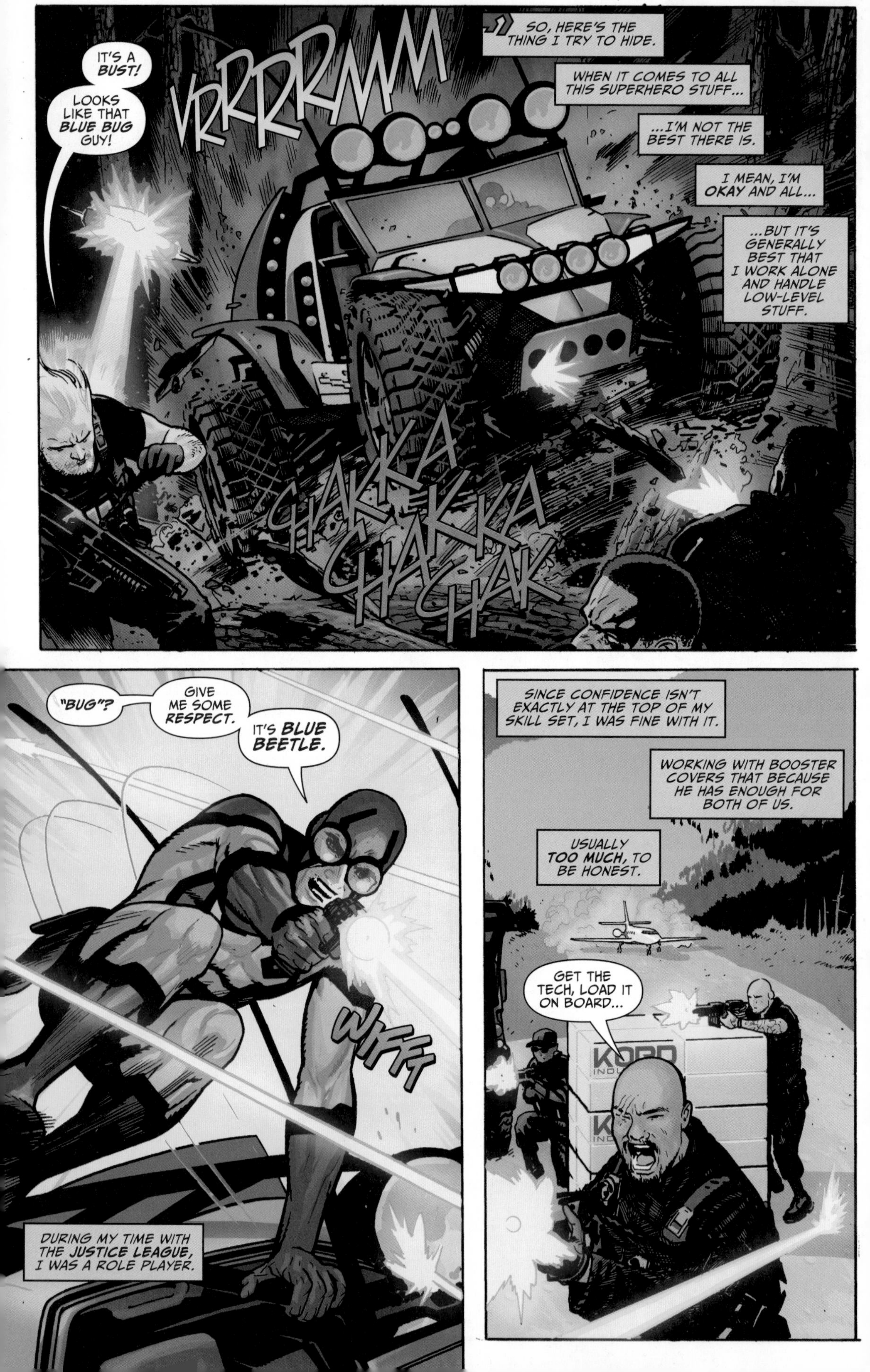

IT'S A BUST!
LOOKS LIKE THAT BLUE BUG GUY!
VRRRRMMM
SO, HERE'S THE THING I TRY TO HIDE.
WHEN IT COMES TO ALL THIS SUPERHERO STUFF...
...I'M NOT THE BEST THERE IS.
I MEAN, I'M OKAY AND ALL...
...BUT IT'S GENERALLY BEST THAT I WORK ALONE AND HANDLE LOW-LEVEL STUFF.
CHAKKA CHAKKA CHAK
"BUG"?
GIVE ME SOME RESPECT.
IT'S BLUE BEETLE.
WIFF
DURING MY TIME WITH THE JUSTICE LEAGUE, I WAS A ROLE PLAYER.
SINCE CONFIDENCE ISN'T EXACTLY AT THE TOP OF MY SKILL SET, I WAS FINE WITH IT.
WORKING WITH BOOSTER COVERS THAT BECAUSE HE HAS ENOUGH FOR BOTH OF US.
USUALLY TOO MUCH, TO BE HONEST.
GET THE TECH, LOAD IT ON BOARD...
KORD

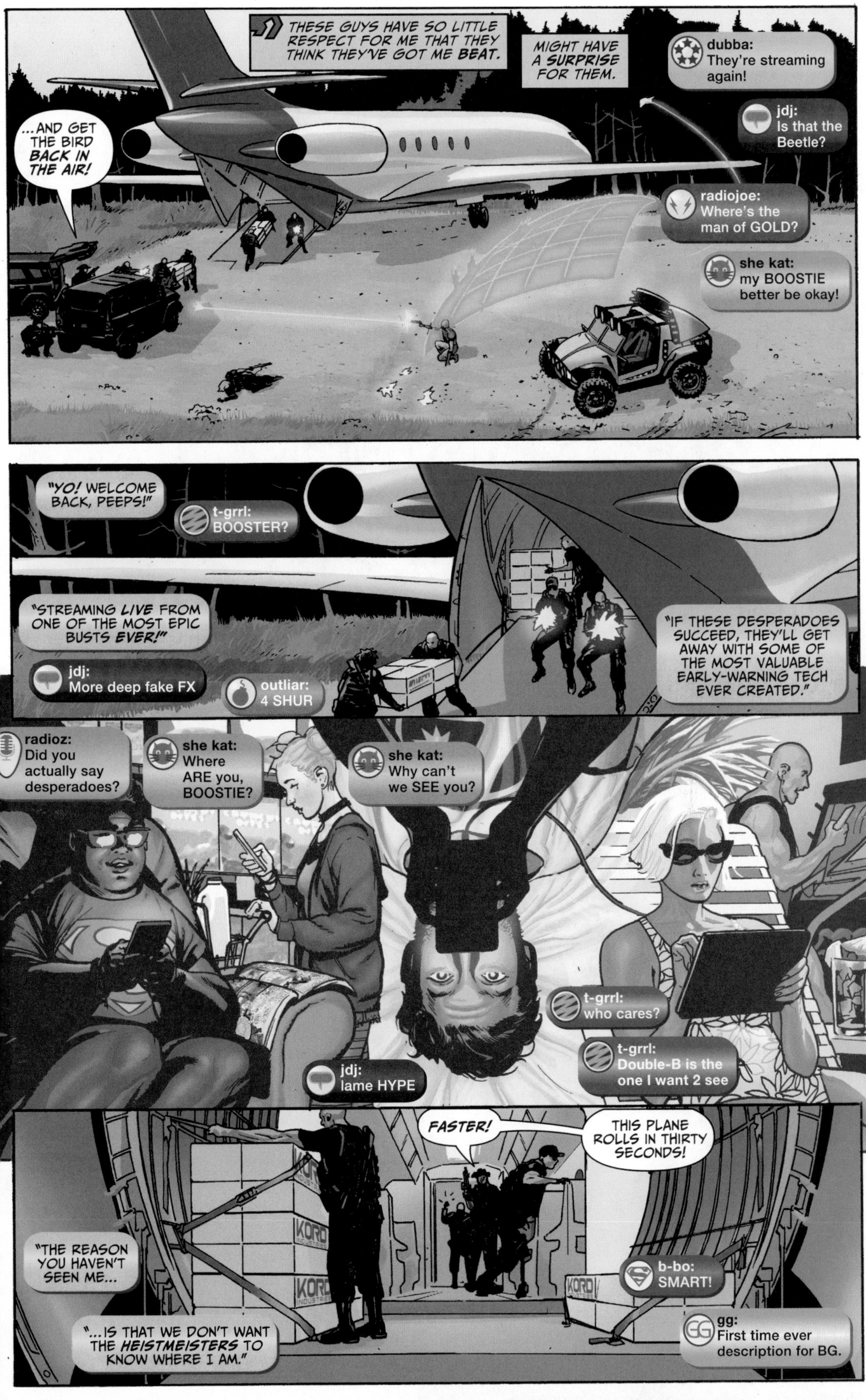
THESE GUYS HAVE SO LITTLE RESPECT FOR ME THAT THEY THINK THEY'VE GOT ME BEAT.
MIGHT HAVE A SURPRISE FOR THEM.
dubba: They're streaming again!
jdj: Is that the Beetle?
...AND GET THE BIRD BACK IN THE AIR!
radiojoe: Where's the man of GOLD?
she kat: my BOOSTIE better be okay!
"YO! WELCOME BACK, PEEPS!"
t-grrl: BOOSTER?
"STREAMING LIVE FROM ONE OF THE MOST EPIC BUSTS EVER!"
jdj: More deep fake FX
outliar: 4 SHUR
"IF THESE DESPERADOES SUCCEED, THEY'LL GET AWAY WITH SOME OF THE MOST VALUABLE EARLY-WARNING TECH EVER CREATED."
radioz: Did you actually say desperadoes?
she kat: Where ARE you, BOOSTIE?
she kat: Why can't we SEE you?
t-grrl: who cares?
t-grrl: Double-B is the one I want 2 see
jdj: lame HYPE
FASTER!
THIS PLANE ROLLS IN THIRTY SECONDS!
KORD
"THE REASON YOU HAVEN'T SEEN ME...
b-bo: SMART!
"...IS THAT WE DON'T WANT THE HEISTMEISTERS TO KNOW WHERE I AM."
gg: First time ever description for BG.

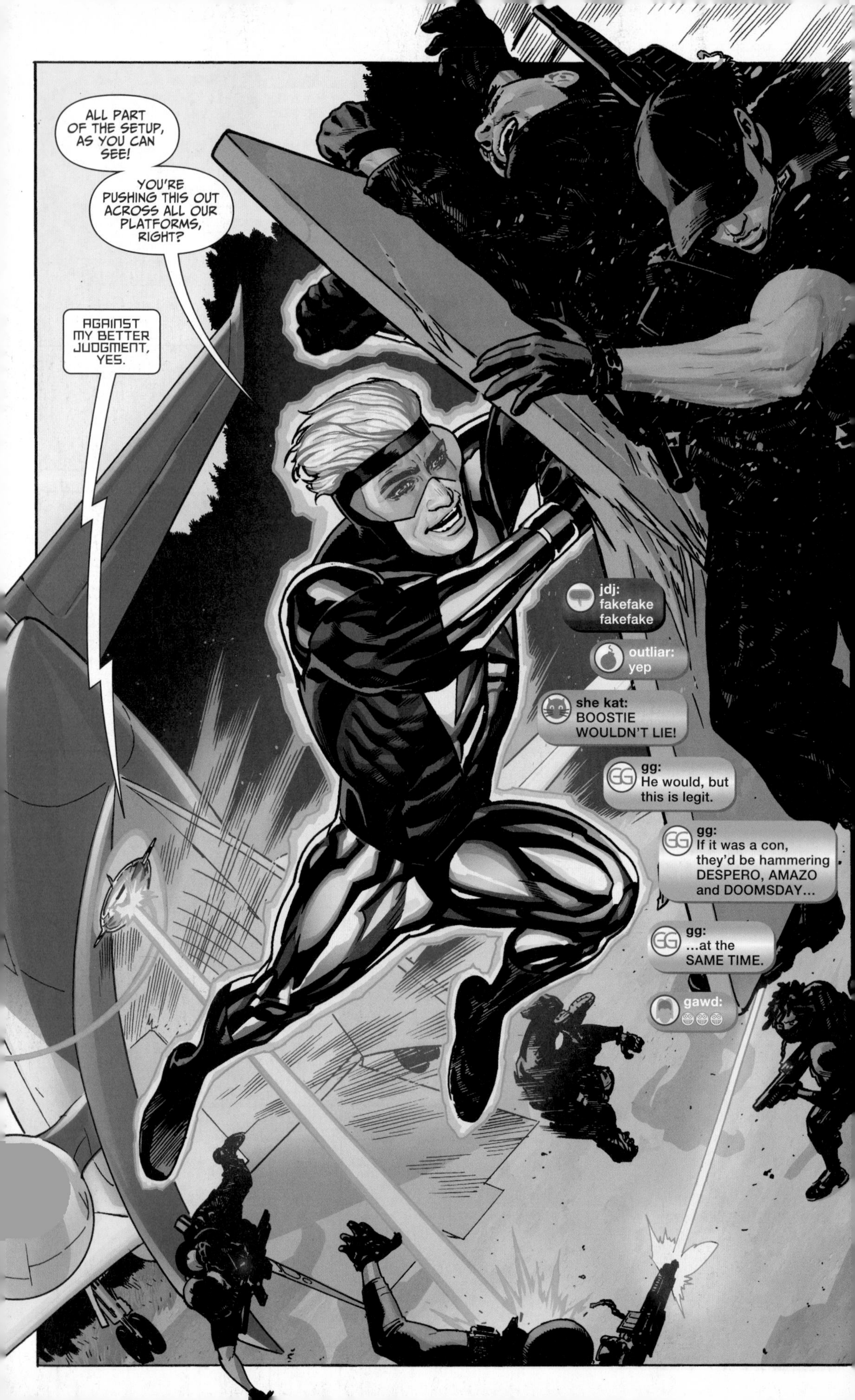
ALL PART OF THE SETUP, AS YOU CAN SEE!
YOU'RE PUSHING THIS OUT ACROSS ALL OUR PLATFORMS, RIGHT?
AGAINST MY BETTER JUDGMENT, YES.
jdj: fakefake fakefake
outliar: yep
she kat: BOOSTIE WOULDN'T LIE!
gg: He would, but this is legit.
gg: If it was a con, they'd be hammering DESPERO, AMAZO and DOOMSDAY...
gg: ...at the SAME TIME.
gawd:

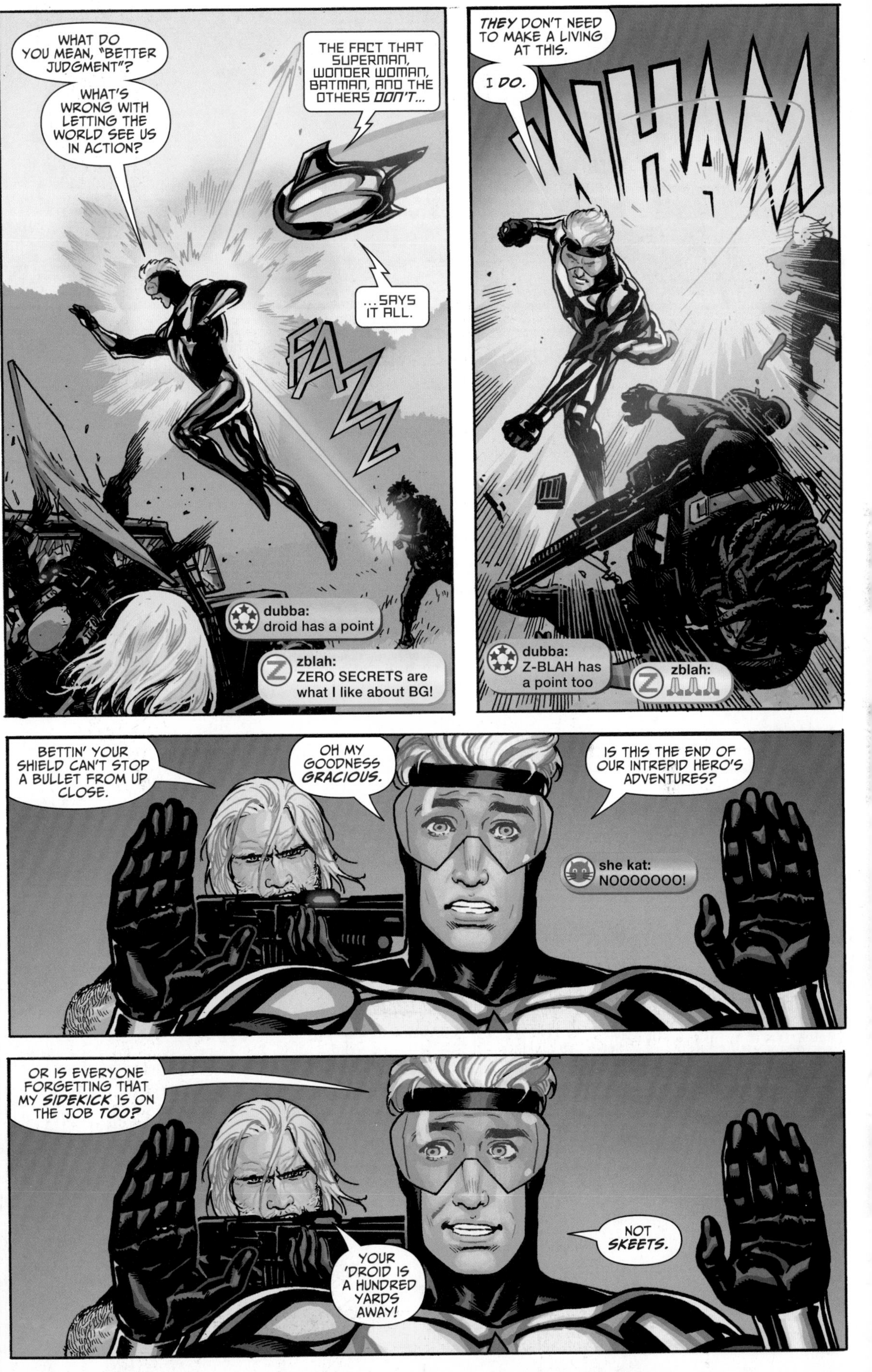

WHAT DO YOU MEAN, "BETTER JUDGMENT"?
WHAT'S WRONG WITH LETTING THE WORLD SEE US IN ACTION?
THE FACT THAT SUPERMAN, WONDER WOMAN, BATMAN, AND THE OTHERS DON'T...
...SAYS IT ALL.
FAZZ
dubba: droid has a point
zblah: ZERO SECRETS are what I like about BG!
THEY DON'T NEED TO MAKE A LIVING AT THIS.
I DO.
WHAM
dubba: Z-BLAH has a point too
zblah:
BETTIN' YOUR SHIELD CAN'T STOP A BULLET FROM UP CLOSE.
OH MY GOODNESS GRACIOUS.
IS THIS THE END OF OUR INTREPID HERO'S ADVENTURES?
she kat: NOOOOOOO!
OR IS EVERYONE FORGETTING THAT MY SIDEKICK IS ON THE JOB TOO?
YOUR 'DROID IS A HUNDRED YARDS AWAY!
NOT SKEETS.

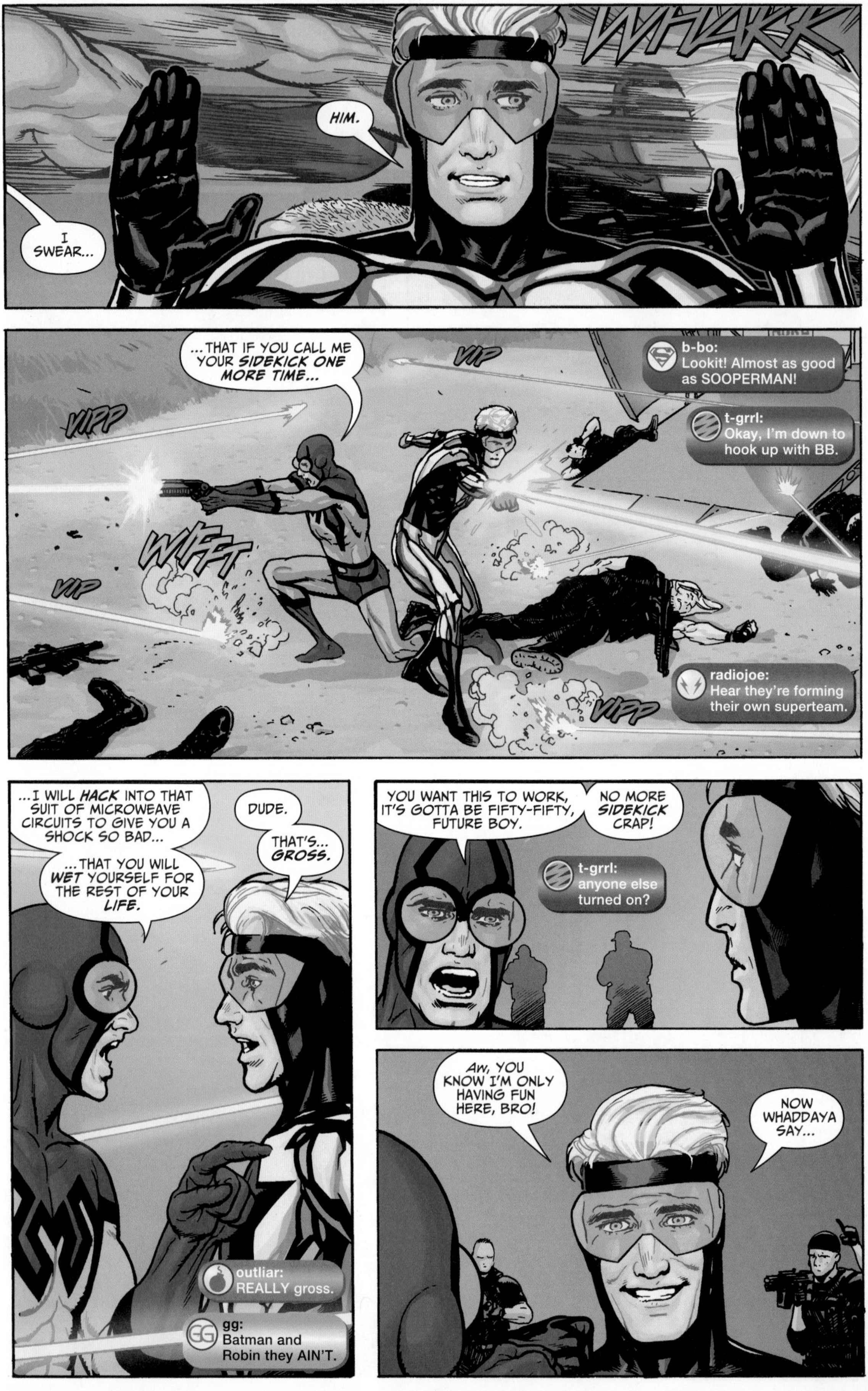
WHAKK
I SWEAR...
HIM.
...THAT IF YOU CALL ME YOUR SIDEKICK ONE MORE TIME...
VIP
b-bo:
Lookit! Almost as good as SOOPERMAN!
VIPP
t-grrl:
Okay, I'm down to hook up with BB.
WIFFT
VIP
radiojoe:
Hear they're forming their own superteam.
VIPP
...I WILL HACK INTO THAT SUIT OF MICROWEAVE CIRCUITS TO GIVE YOU A SHOCK SO BAD...
...THAT YOU WILL WET YOURSELF FOR THE REST OF YOUR LIFE.
DUDE.
THAT'S... GROSS.
outliar:
REALLY gross.
gg:
Batman and Robin they AIN'T.
YOU WANT THIS TO WORK, IT'S GOTTA BE FIFTY-FIFTY, FUTURE BOY.
NO MORE SIDEKICK CRAP!
t-grrl:
anyone else turned on?
AW, YOU KNOW I'M ONLY HAVING FUN HERE, BRO!
NOW WHADDAYA SAY...

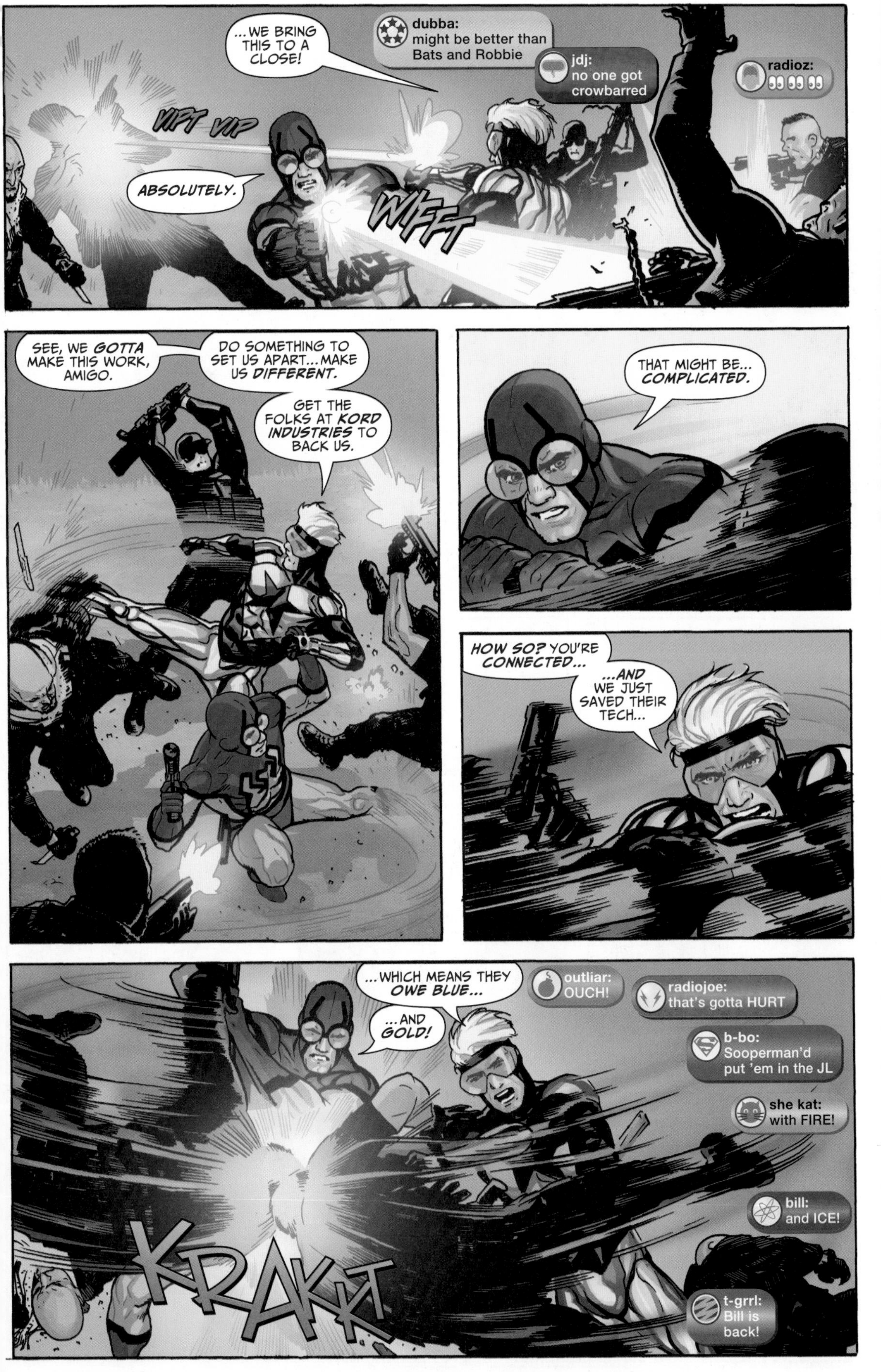
...WE BRING THIS TO A CLOSE!
dubba: might be better than Bats and Robbie
jdj: no one got crowbarred
radioz:
VIPT VIP
ABSOLUTELY.
WIFFT
SEE, WE GOTTA MAKE THIS WORK, AMIGO.
DO SOMETHING TO SET US APART...MAKE US DIFFERENT.
GET THE FOLKS AT KORD INDUSTRIES TO BACK US.
THAT MIGHT BE... COMPLICATED.
HOW SO? YOU'RE CONNECTED...
...AND WE JUST SAVED THEIR TECH...
...WHICH MEANS THEY OWE BLUE...
...AND GOLD!
outliar: OUCH!
radiojoe: that's gotta HURT
b-bo: Sooperman'd put 'em in the JL
she kat: with FIRE!
bill: and ICE!
t-grrl: Bill is back!
KRAKKT

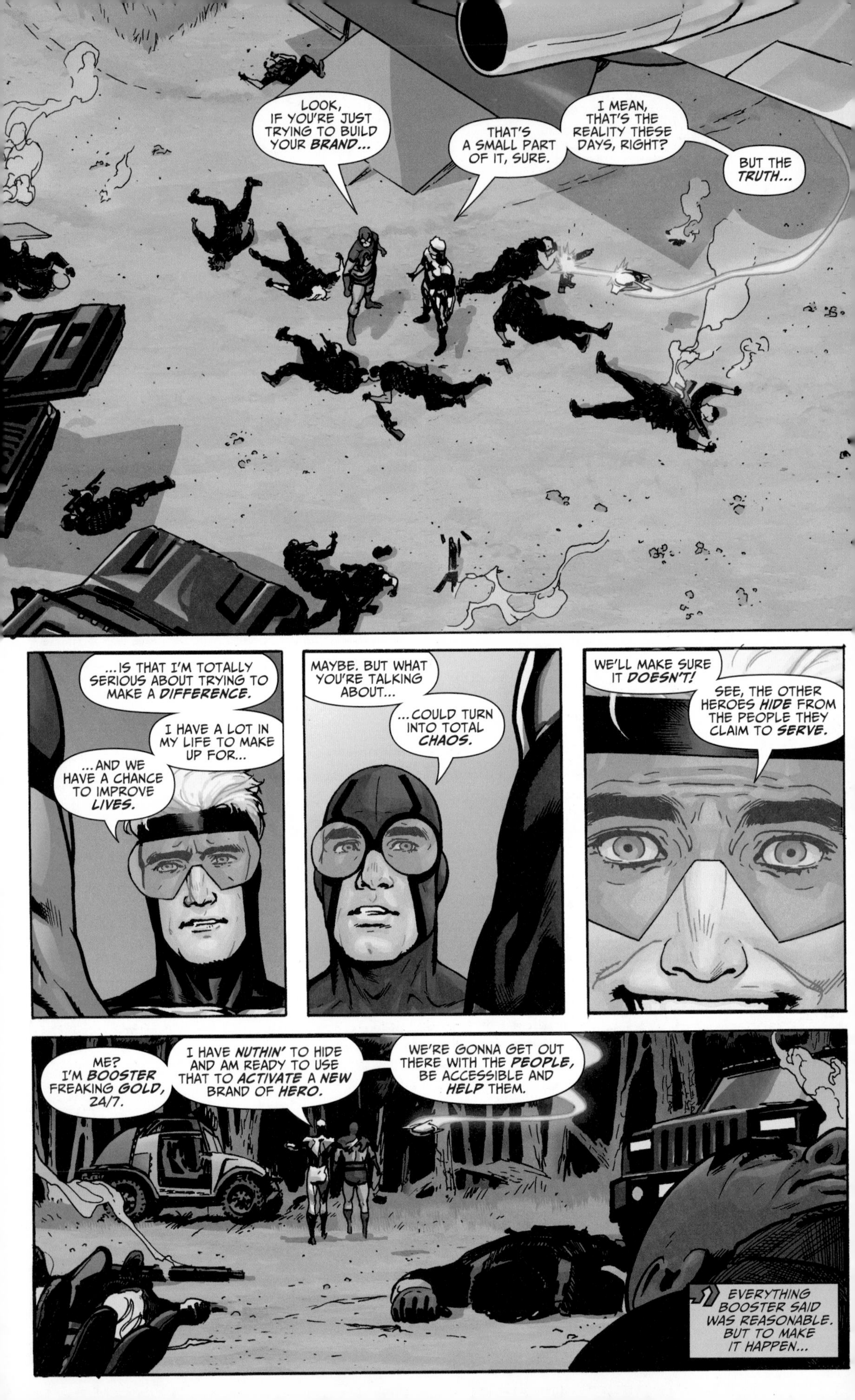
LOOK, IF YOU'RE JUST TRYING TO BUILD YOUR BRAND...
THAT'S A SMALL PART OF IT, SURE.
I MEAN, THAT'S THE REALITY THESE DAYS, RIGHT?
BUT THE TRUTH...
...IS THAT I'M TOTALLY SERIOUS ABOUT TRYING TO MAKE A DIFFERENCE.
I HAVE A LOT IN MY LIFE TO MAKE UP FOR...
...AND WE HAVE A CHANCE TO IMPROVE LIVES.
MAYBE. BUT WHAT YOU'RE TALKING ABOUT...
...COULD TURN INTO TOTAL CHAOS.
WE'LL MAKE SURE IT DOESN'T!
SEE, THE OTHER HEROES HIDE FROM THE PEOPLE THEY CLAIM TO SERVE.
ME? I'M BOOSTER FREAKING GOLD, 24/7.
I HAVE NUTHIN' TO HIDE AND AM READY TO USE THAT TO ACTIVATE A NEW BRAND OF HERO.
WE'RE GONNA GET OUT THERE WITH THE PEOPLE, BE ACCESSIBLE AND HELP THEM.
EVERYTHING BOOSTER SAID WAS REASONABLE. BUT TO MAKE IT HAPPEN...

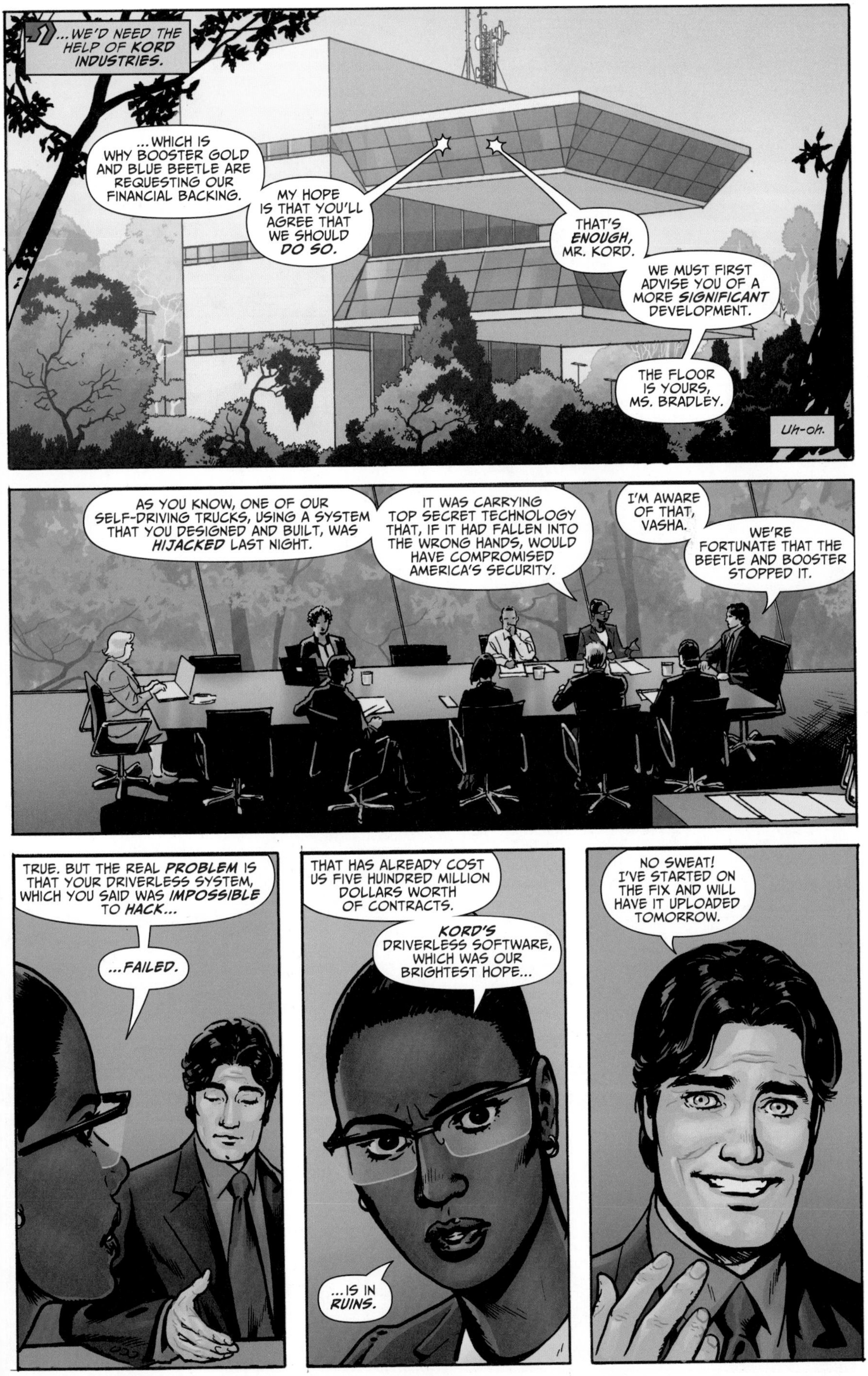
...WE'D NEED THE HELP OF KORD INDUSTRIES.
...WHICH IS WHY BOOSTER GOLD AND BLUE BEETLE ARE REQUESTING OUR FINANCIAL BACKING.
MY HOPE IS THAT YOU'LL AGREE THAT WE SHOULD DO SO.
THAT'S ENOUGH, MR. KORD.
WE MUST FIRST ADVISE YOU OF A MORE SIGNIFICANT DEVELOPMENT.
THE FLOOR IS YOURS, MS. BRADLEY.
Uh-oh.
AS YOU KNOW, ONE OF OUR SELF-DRIVING TRUCKS, USING A SYSTEM THAT YOU DESIGNED AND BUILT, WAS HIJACKED LAST NIGHT.
IT WAS CARRYING TOP SECRET TECHNOLOGY THAT, IF IT HAD FALLEN INTO THE WRONG HANDS, WOULD HAVE COMPROMISED AMERICA'S SECURITY.
I'M AWARE OF THAT, VASHA.
WE'RE FORTUNATE THAT THE BEETLE AND BOOSTER STOPPED IT.
TRUE. BUT THE REAL PROBLEM IS THAT YOUR DRIVERLESS SYSTEM, WHICH YOU SAID WAS IMPOSSIBLE TO HACK...
...FAILED.
THAT HAS ALREADY COST US FIVE HUINDRED MILLION DOLLARS WORTH OF CONTRACTS.
KORD'S DRIVERLESS SOFTWARE, WHICH WAS OUR BRIGHTEST HOPE...
...IS IN RUINS.
NO SWEAT! I'VE STARTED ON THE FIX AND WILL HAVE IT UPLOADED TOMORROW.

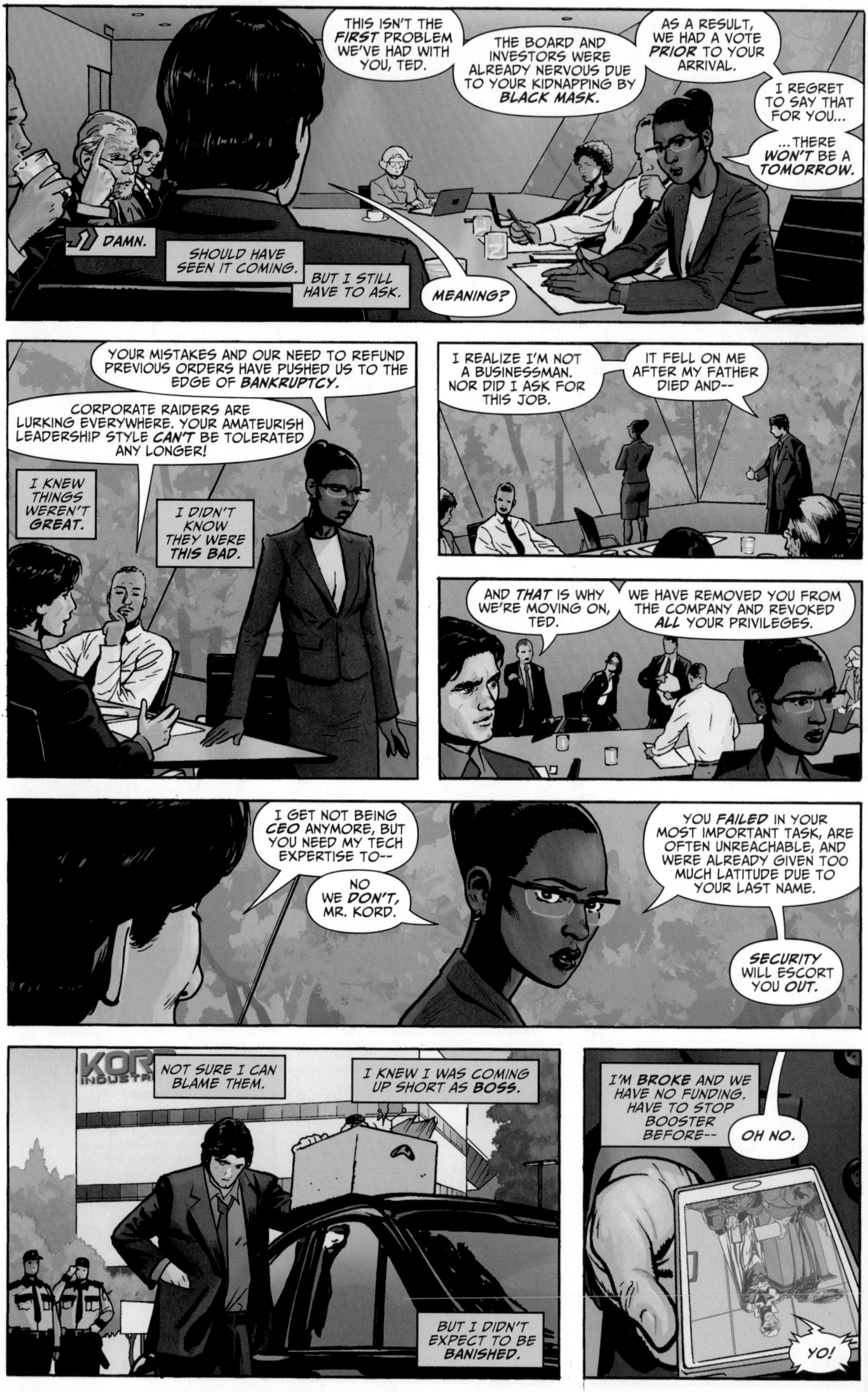
DAMN.
SHOULD HAVE SEEN IT COMING.
BUT I STILL HAVE TO ASK.
THIS ISN'T THE FIRST PROBLEM WE'VE HAD WITH YOU, TED.
THE BOARD AND INVESTORS WERE ALREADY NERVOUS DUE TO YOUR KIDNAPPING BY BLACK MASK.
AS A RESULT, WE HAD A VOTE PRIOR TO YOUR ARRIVAL.
I REGRET TO SAY THAT FOR YOU...
...THERE WON'T BE A TOMORROW.
MEANING?
YOUR MISTAKES AND OUR NEED TO REFUND PREVIOUS ORDERS HAVE PUSHED US TO THE EDGE OF BANKRUPTCY.
CORPORATE RAIDERS ARE LURKING EVERYWHERE. YOUR AMATEURISH LEADERSHIP STYLE CAN'T BE TOLERATED ANY LONGER!
I KNEW THINGS WEREN'T GREAT.
I DIDN'T KNOW THEY WERE THIS BAD.
I REALIZE I'M NOT A BUSINESSMAN. NOR DID I ASK FOR THIS JOB.
IT FELL ON ME AFTER MY FATHER DIED AND--
AND THAT IS WHY WE'RE MOVING ON, TED.
WE HAVE REMOVED YOU FROM THE COMPANY AND REVOKED ALL YOUR PRIVILEGES.
I GET NOT BEING CEO ANYMORE, BUT YOU NEED MY TECH EXPERTISE TO--
NO WE DON'T, MR. KORD.
YOU FAILED IN YOUR MOST IMPORTANT TASK, ARE OFTEN UNREACHABLE, AND WERE ALREADY GIVEN TOO MUCH LATITUDE DUE TO YOUR LAST NAME.
SECURITY WILL ESCORT YOU OUT.
NOT SURE I CAN BLAME THEM.
I KNEW I WAS COMING UP SHORT AS BOSS.
BUT I DIDN'T EXPECT TO BE BANISHED.
I'M BROKE AND WE HAVE NO FUNDING. HAVE TO STOP BOOSTER BEFORE--
OH NO.
YO!

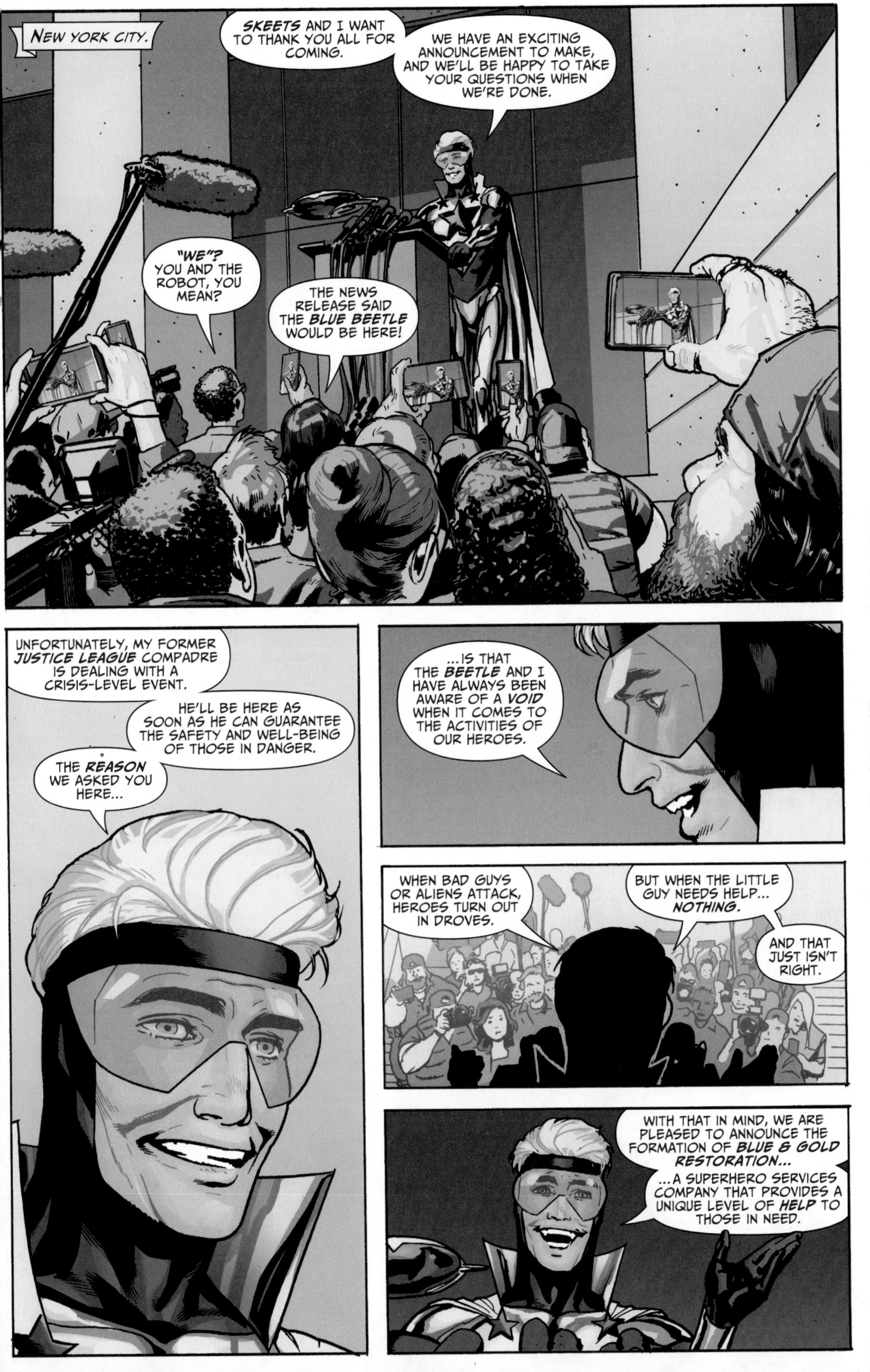
NEW YORK CITY.
SKEETS AND I WANT TO THANK YOU ALL FOR COMING.
WE HAVE AN EXCITING ANNOUNCEMENT TO MAKE, AND WE'LL BE HAPPY TO TAKE YOUR QUESTIONS WHEN WE'RE DONE.
"WE"? YOU AND THE ROBOT, YOU MEAN?
THE NEWS RELEASE SAID THE BLUE BEETLE WOULD BE HERE!
UNFORTUNATELY, MY FORMER JUSTICE LEAGUE COMPADRE IS DEALING WITH A CRISIS-LEVEL EVENT.
HE'LL BE HERE AS SOON AS HE CAN GUARANTEE THE SAFETY AND WELL-BEING OF THOSE IN DANGER.
THE REASON WE ASKED YOU HERE...
...IS THAT THE BEETLE AND I HAVE ALWAYS BEEN AWARE OF A VOID WHEN IT COMES TO THE ACTIVITIES OF OUR HEROES.
WHEN BAD GUYS OR ALIENS ATTACK, HEROES TURN OUT IN DROVES.
BUT WHEN THE LITTLE GUY NEEDS HELP... NOTHING.
AND THAT JUST ISN'T RIGHT.
WITH THAT IN MIND, WE ARE PLEASED TO ANNOUNCE THE FORMATION OF BLUE & GOLD RESTORATION...
...A SUPERHERO SERVICES COMPANY THAT PROVIDES A UNIQUE LEVEL OF HELP TO THOSE IN NEED.

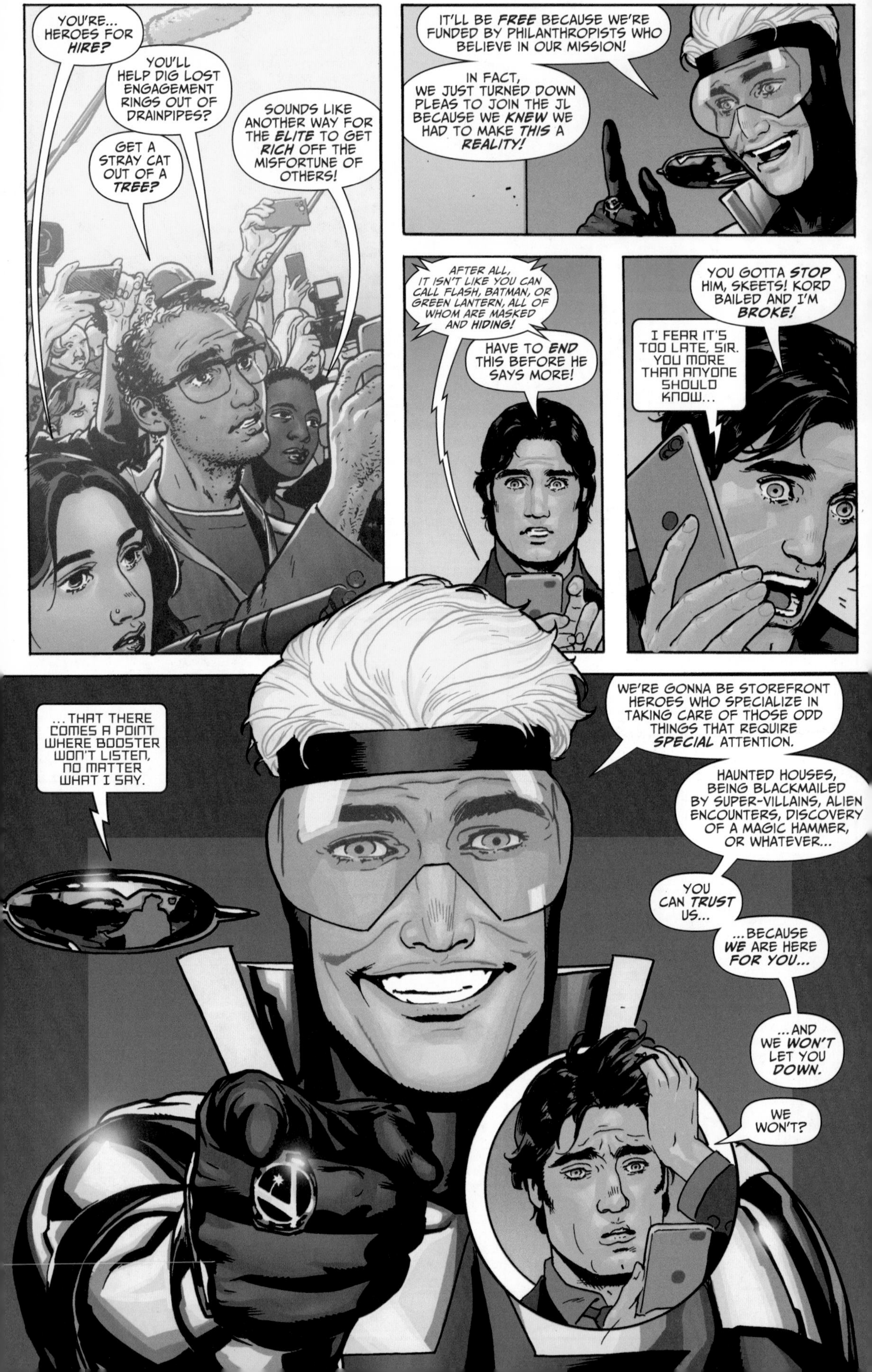
YOU'RE... HEROES FOR HIRE?
YOU'LL HELP DIG LOST ENGAGEMENT RINGS OUT OF DRAINPIPES?
GET A STRAY CAT OUT OF A TREE?
SOUNDS LIKE ANOTHER WAY FOR THE ELITE TO GET RICH OFF THE MISFORTUNE OF OTHERS!
IT'LL BE FREE BECAUSE WE'RE FUNDED BY PHILANTHROPISTS WHO BELIEVE IN OUR MISSION!
IN FACT, WE JUST TURNED DOWN PLEAS TO JOIN THE JL BECAUSE WE KNEW WE HAD TO MAKE THIS A REALITY!
AFTER ALL, IT ISN'T LIKE YOU CAN CALL FLASH, BATMAN, OR GREEN LANTERN, ALL OF WHOM ARE MASKED AND HIDING!
HAVE TO END THIS BEFORE HE SAYS MORE!
YOU GOTTA STOP HIM, SKEETS! KORD BAILED AND I'M BROKE!
I FEAR IT'S TOO LATE, SIR. YOU MORE THAN ANYONE SHOULD KNOW...
...THAT THERE COMES A POINT WHERE BOOSTER WON'T LISTEN, NO MATTER WHAT I SAY.
WE'RE GONNA BE STOREFRONT HEROES WHO SPECIALIZE IN TAKING CARE OF THOSE ODD THINGS THAT REQUIRE SPECIAL ATTENTION.
HAUNTED HOUSES, BEING BLACKMAILED BY SUPER-VILLAINS, ALIEN ENCOUNTERS, DISCOVERY OF A MAGIC HAMMER, OR WHATEVER...
YOU CAN TRUST US...
...BECAUSE WE ARE HERE FOR YOU...
...AND WE WON'T LET YOU DOWN.
WE WON'T?

Blue & Gold #3
cover by Ryan Sook

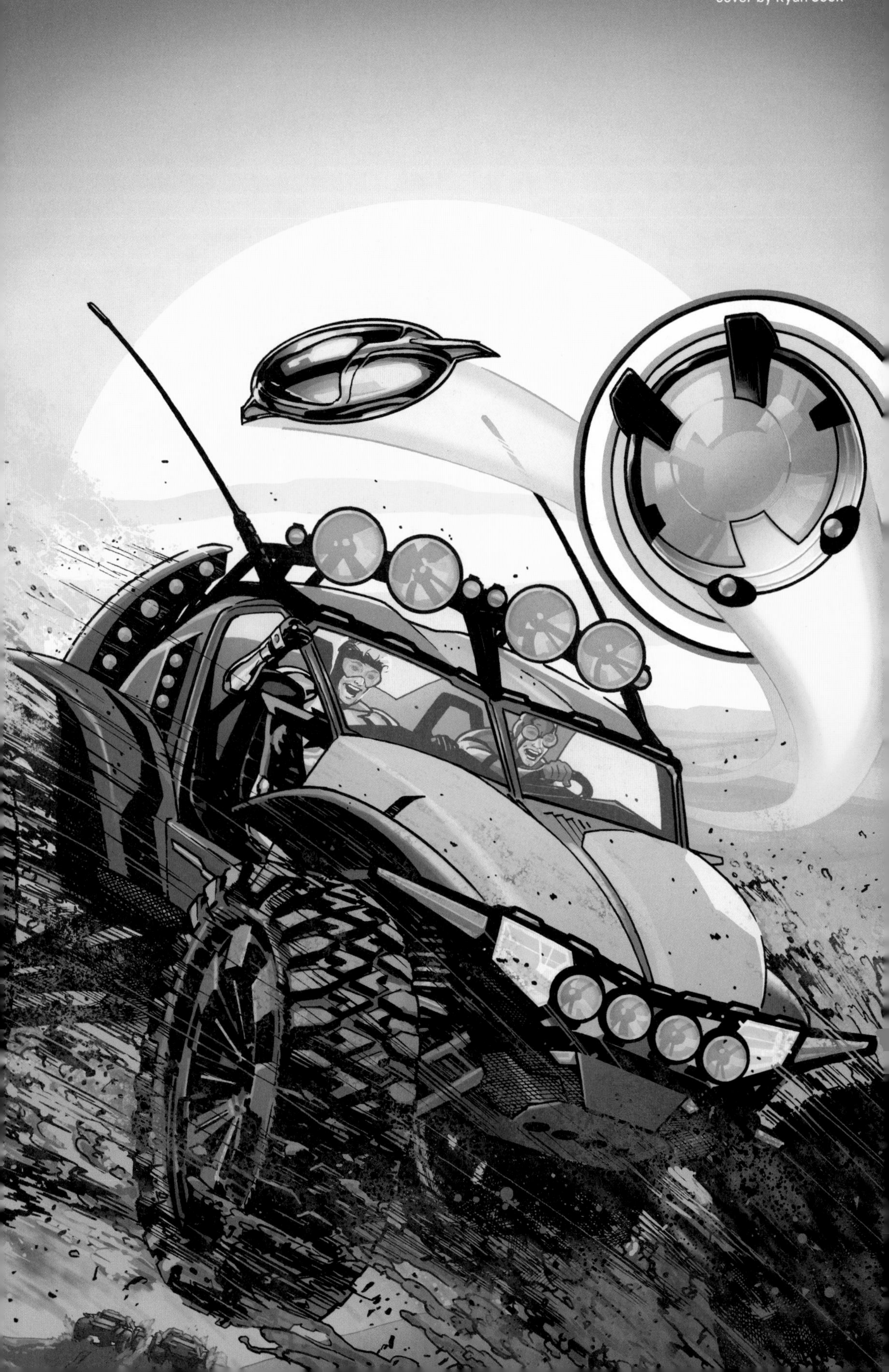

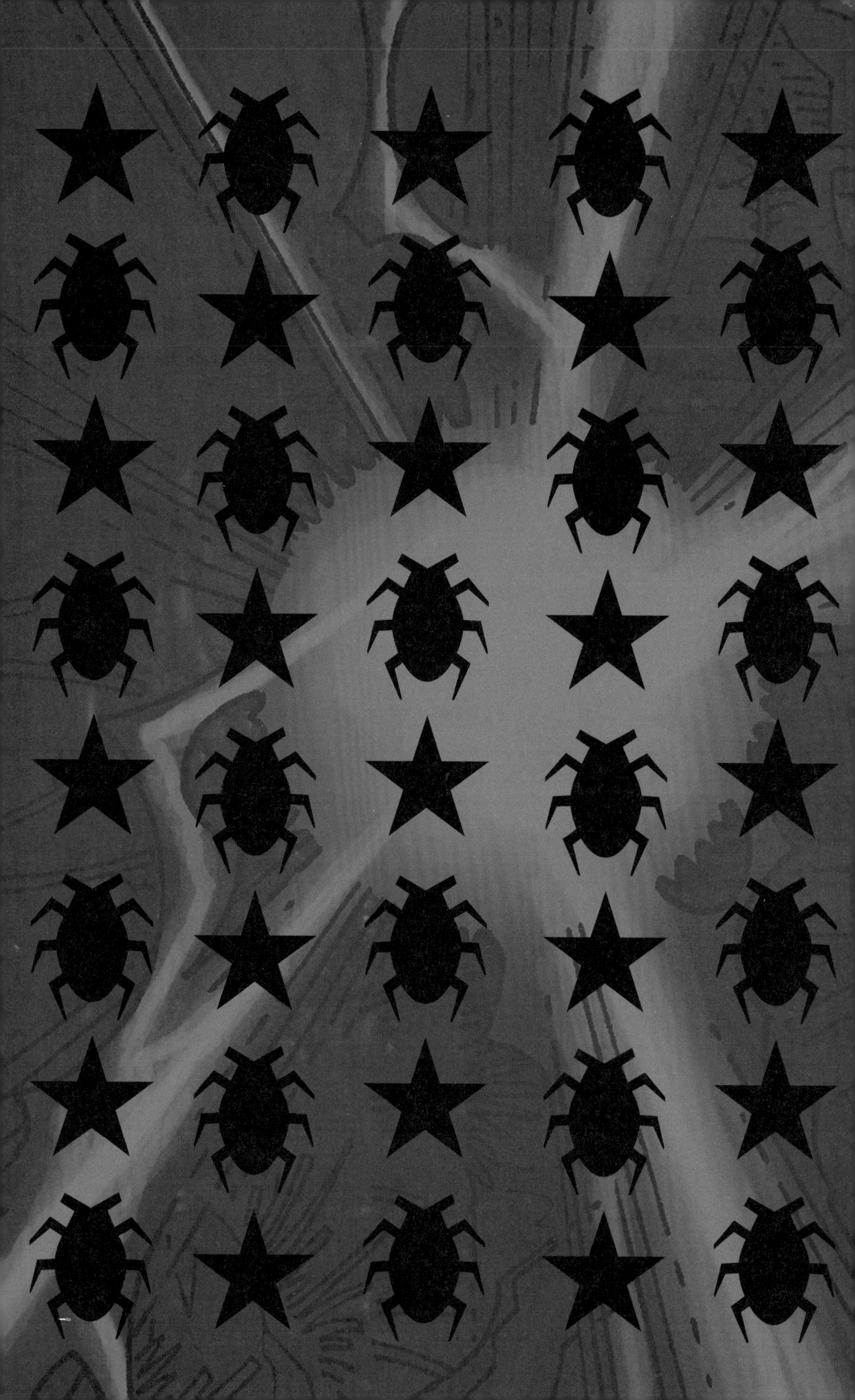

OMNIZON

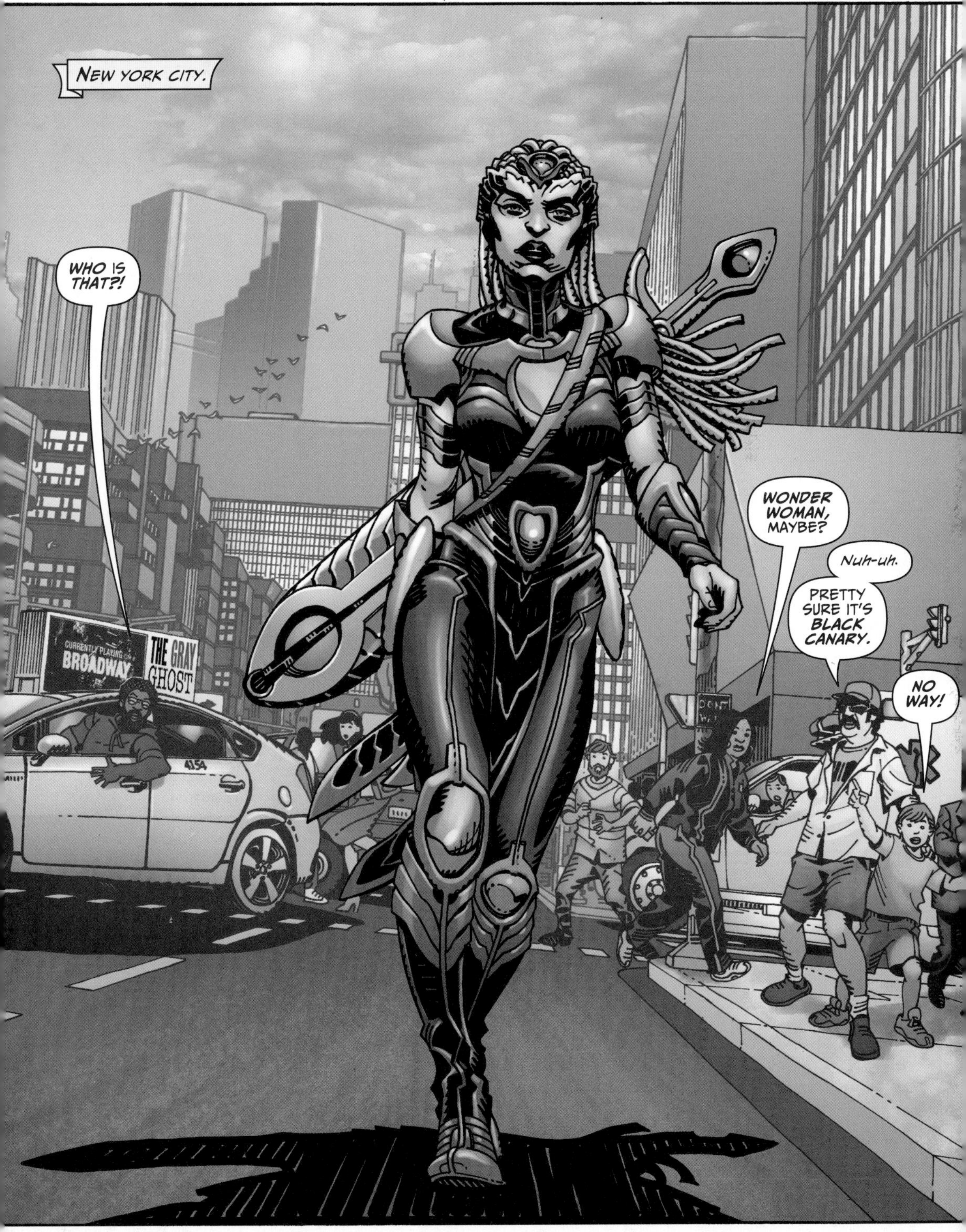
New York City.
WHO IS THAT?!
CURRENTLY PLAYING ON BROADWAY
THE GRAY GHOST
WONDER WOMAN, MAYBE?
Nuh-uh.
PRETTY SURE IT'S BLACK CANARY.
NO WAY!

DAN JURGENS STORY · CULLY HAMNER ART · CHRIS SOTOMAYOR COLORS · ROB LEIGH LETTERS · RYAN SOOK COVER · BRITTANY HOLZHERR EDITOR · MIKE COTTON SENIOR EDITOR

BOOSTER GOLD CREATED BY DAN JURGENS

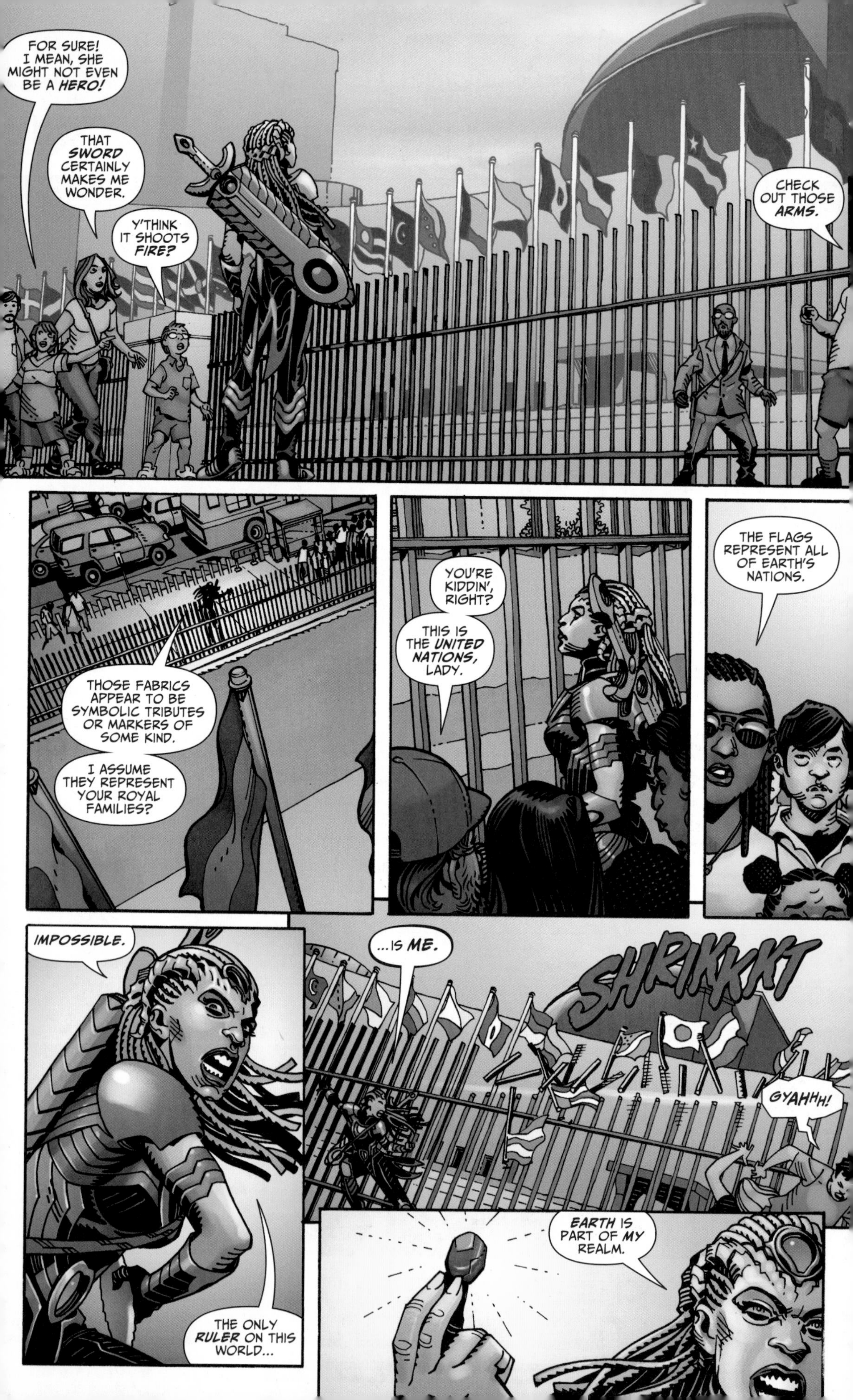
FOR SURE! I MEAN, SHE MIGHT NOT EVEN BE A HERO!
THAT SWORD CERTAINLY MAKES ME WONDER.
Y'THINK IT SHOOTS FIRE?
CHECK OUT THOSE ARMS.
THOSE FABRICS APPEAR TO BE SYMBOLIC TRIBUTES OR MARKERS OF SOME KIND.
I ASSUME THEY REPRESENT YOUR ROYAL FAMILIES?
YOU'RE KIDDIN', RIGHT?
THIS IS THE UNITED NATIONS, LADY.
THE FLAGS REPRESENT ALL OF EARTH'S NATIONS.
IMPOSSIBLE.
THE ONLY RULER ON THIS WORLD...
...IS ME.
SHRIKKKT
GYAHHH!
EARTH IS PART OF MY REALM.

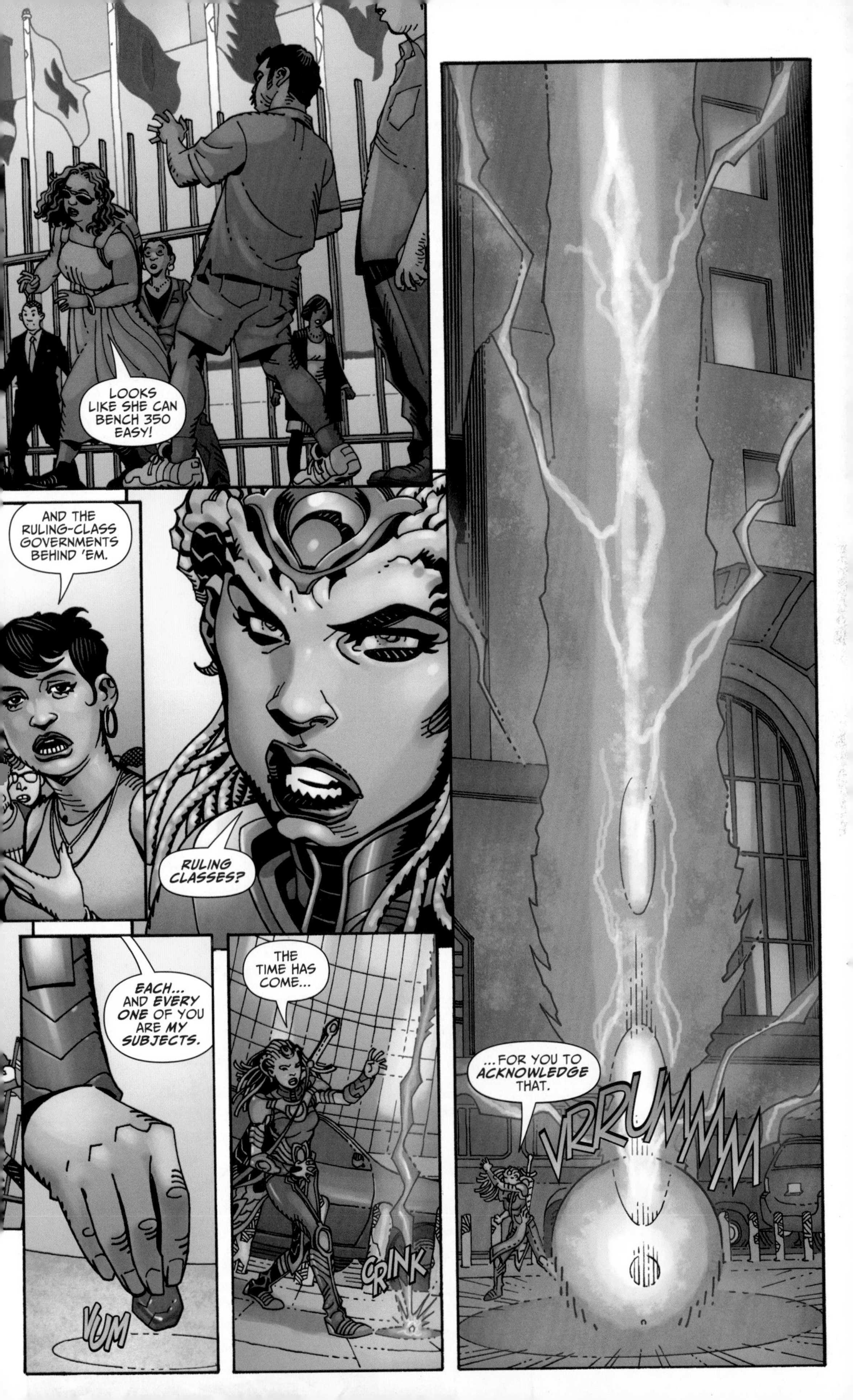
LOOKS LIKE SHE CAN BENCH 350 EASY!
AND THE RULING-CLASS GOVERNMENTS BEHIND 'EM.
RULING CLASSES?
EACH... AND EVERY ONE OF YOU ARE MY SUBJECTS.
VUM
THE TIME HAS COME...
CRINK
...FOR YOU TO ACKNOWLEDGE THAT.
VRRUMMM

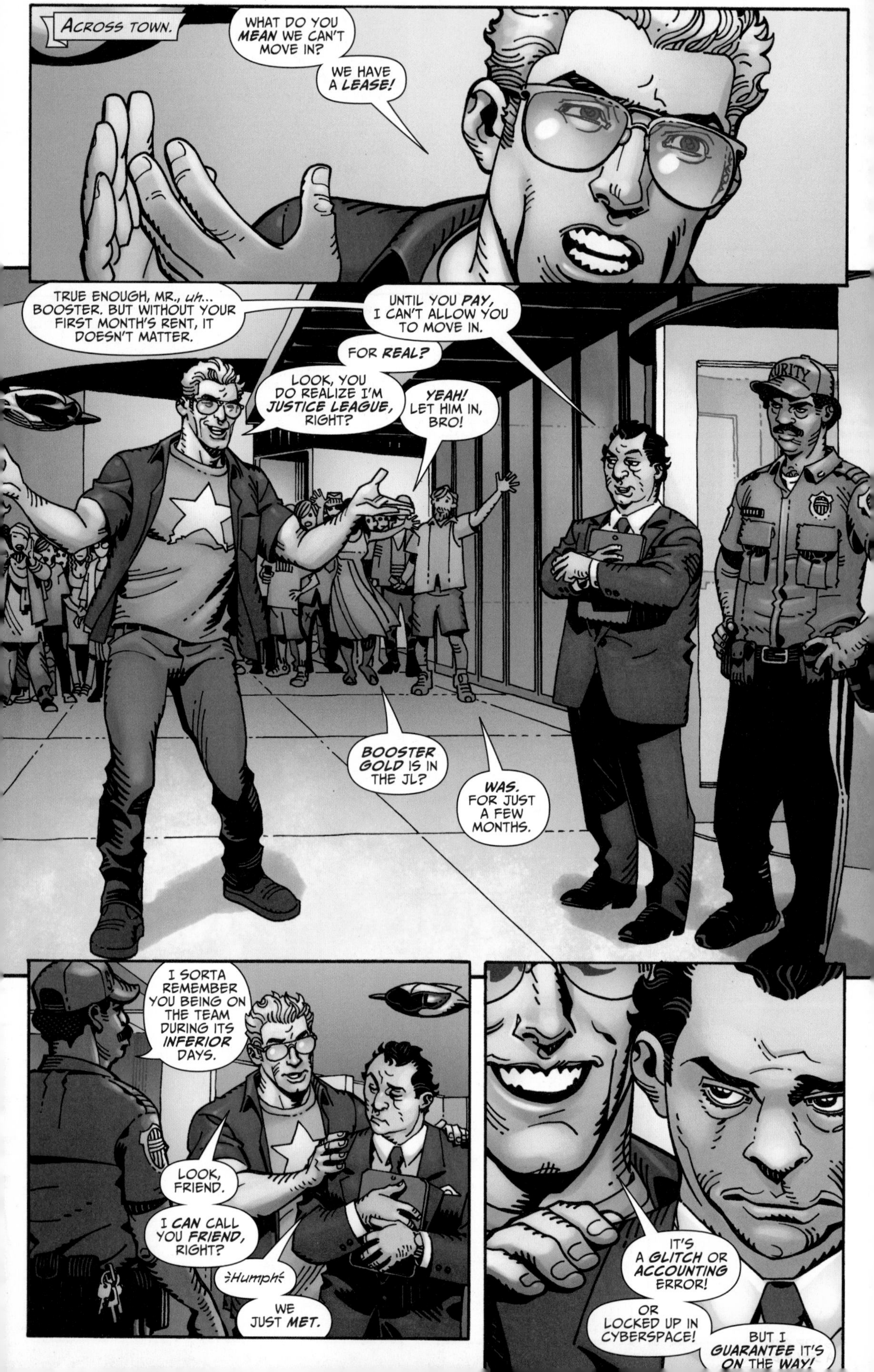
ACROSS TOWN.
WHAT DO YOU MEAN WE CAN'T MOVE IN?
WE HAVE A LEASE!
TRUE ENOUGH, MR., uh... BOOSTER. BUT WITHOUT YOUR FIRST MONTH'S RENT, IT DOESN'T MATTER.
UNTIL YOU PAY, I CAN'T ALLOW YOU TO MOVE IN.
FOR REAL?
LOOK, YOU DO REALIZE I'M JUSTICE LEAGUE, RIGHT?
YEAH! LET HIM IN, BRO!
BOOSTER GOLD IS IN THE JL?
WAS. FOR JUST A FEW MONTHS.
I SORTA REMEMBER YOU BEING ON THE TEAM DURING ITS INFERIOR DAYS.
LOOK, FRIEND.
I CAN CALL YOU FRIEND, RIGHT?
Humph
WE JUST MET.
IT'S A GLITCH OR ACCOUNTING ERROR!
OR LOCKED UP IN CYBERSPACE!
BUT I GUARANTEE IT'S ON THE WAY!

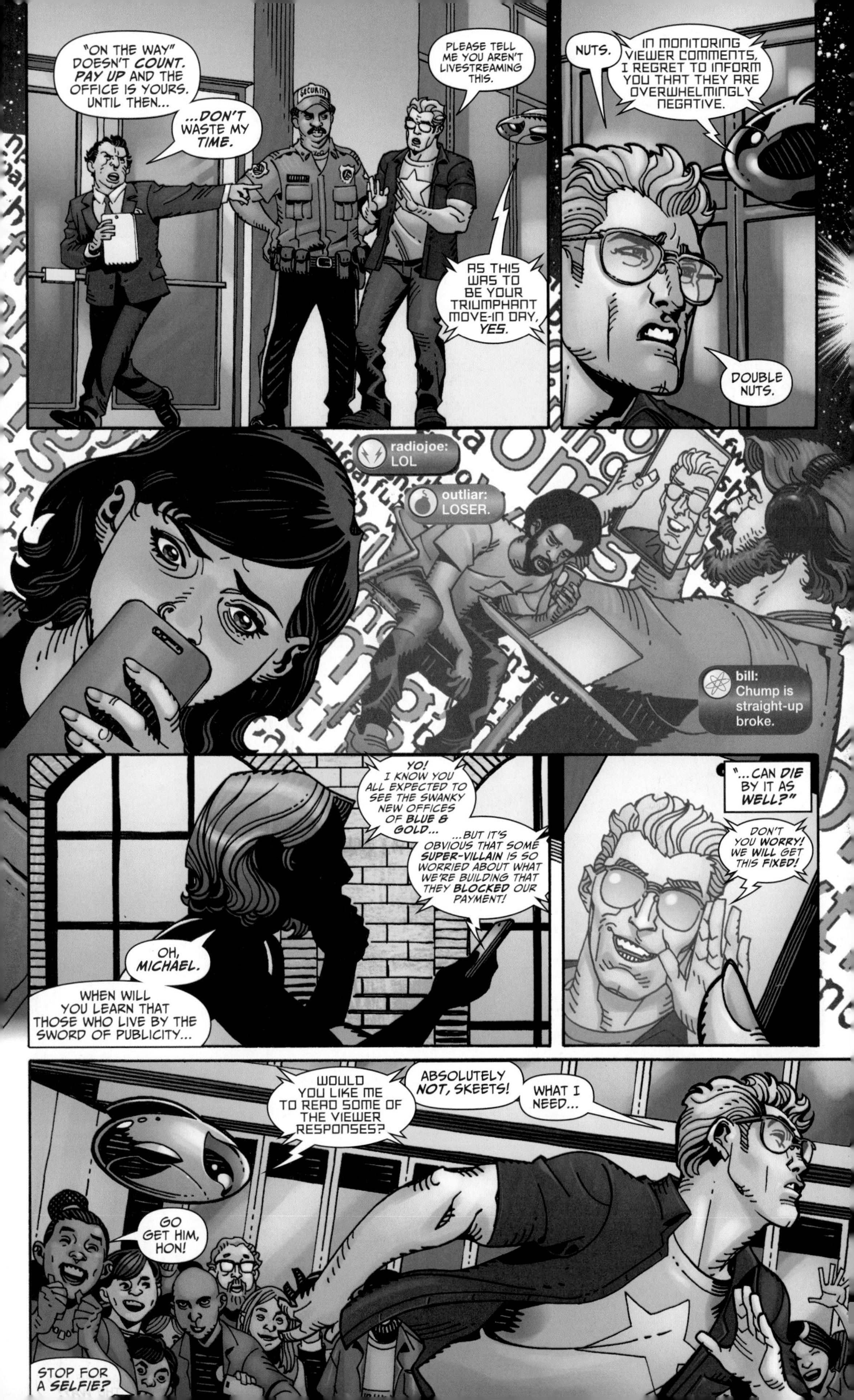

"ON THE WAY" DOESN'T COUNT. PAY UP AND THE OFFICE IS YOURS. UNTIL THEN...
...DON'T WASTE MY TIME.
PLEASE TELL ME YOU AREN'T LIVESTREAMING THIS.
AS THIS WAS TO BE YOUR TRIUMPHANT MOVE-IN DAY, YES.
NUTS.
IN MONITORING VIEWER COMMENTS, I REGRET TO INFORM YOU THAT THEY ARE OVERWHELMINGLY NEGATIVE.
DOUBLE NUTS.
radiojoe: LOL
outliar: LOSER.
bill: Chump is straight-up broke.
YO! I KNOW YOU ALL EXPECTED TO SEE THE SWANKY NEW OFFICES OF BLUE & GOLD...
...BUT IT'S OBVIOUS THAT SOME SUPER-VILLAIN IS SO WORRIED ABOUT WHAT WE'RE BUILDING THAT THEY BLOCKED OUR PAYMENT!
OH, MICHAEL.
WHEN WILL YOU LEARN THAT THOSE WHO LIVE BY THE SWORD OF PUBLICITY...
"...CAN DIE BY IT AS WELL?"
DON'T YOU WORRY! WE WILL GET THIS FIXED!
WOULD YOU LIKE ME TO READ SOME OF THE VIEWER RESPONSES?
ABSOLUTELY NOT, SKEETS!
WHAT I NEED...
GO GET HIM, HON!
STOP FOR A SELFIE?

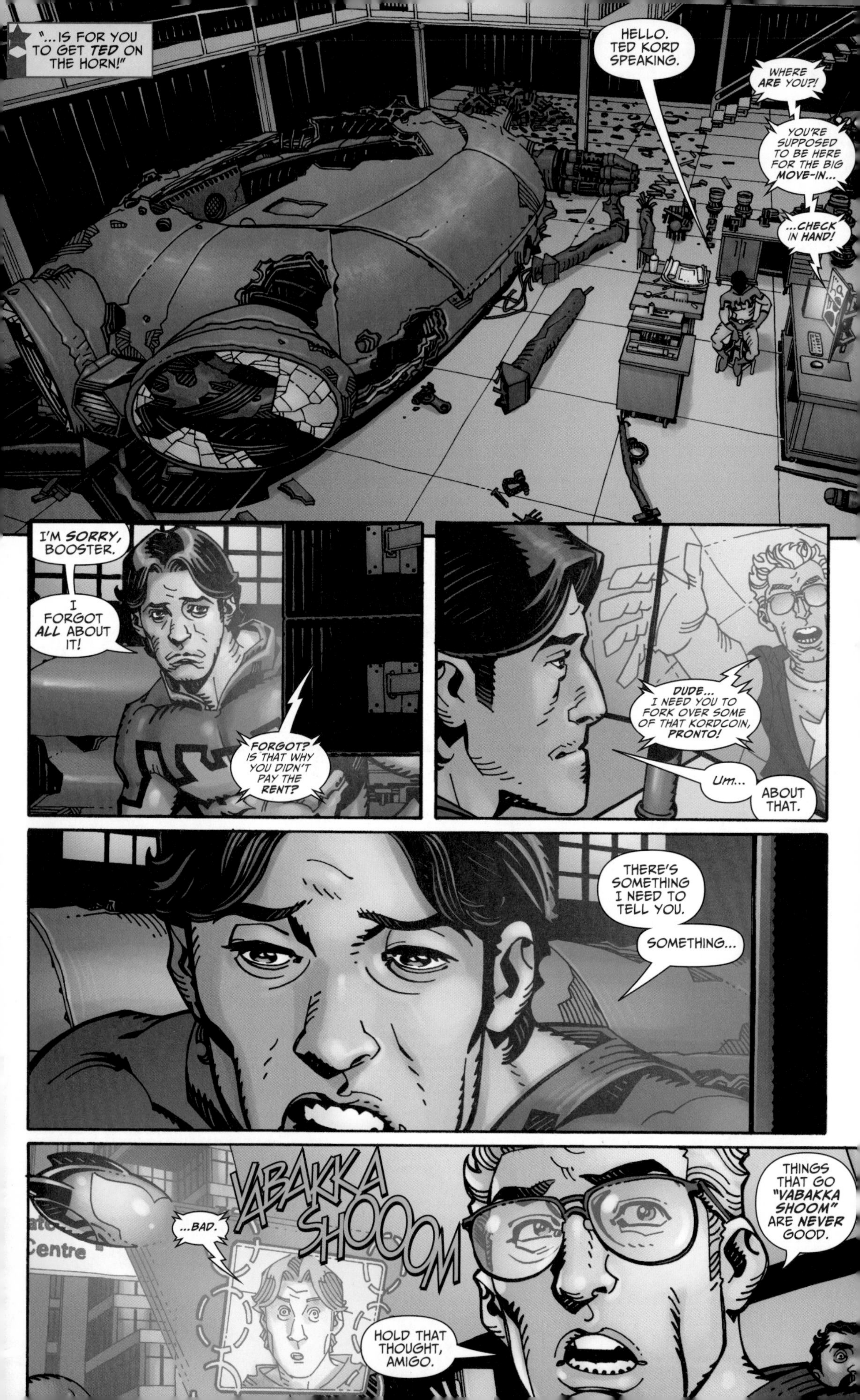
"...IS FOR YOU TO GET TED ON THE HORN!"
HELLO. TED KORD SPEAKING.
WHERE ARE YOU?!
YOU'RE SUPPOSED TO BE HERE FOR THE BIG MOVE-IN...
...CHECK IN HAND!
I'M SORRY, BOOSTER.
I FORGOT ALL ABOUT IT!
FORGOT? IS THAT WHY YOU DIDN'T PAY THE RENT?
DUDE... I NEED YOU TO FORK OVER SOME OF THAT KORDCOIN, PRONTO!
Um...
ABOUT THAT.
THERE'S SOMETHING I NEED TO TELL YOU.
SOMETHING...
VABAKKA SHOOOM
...BAD.
THINGS THAT GO "VABAKKA SHOOM" ARE NEVER GOOD.
HOLD THAT THOUGHT, AMIGO.

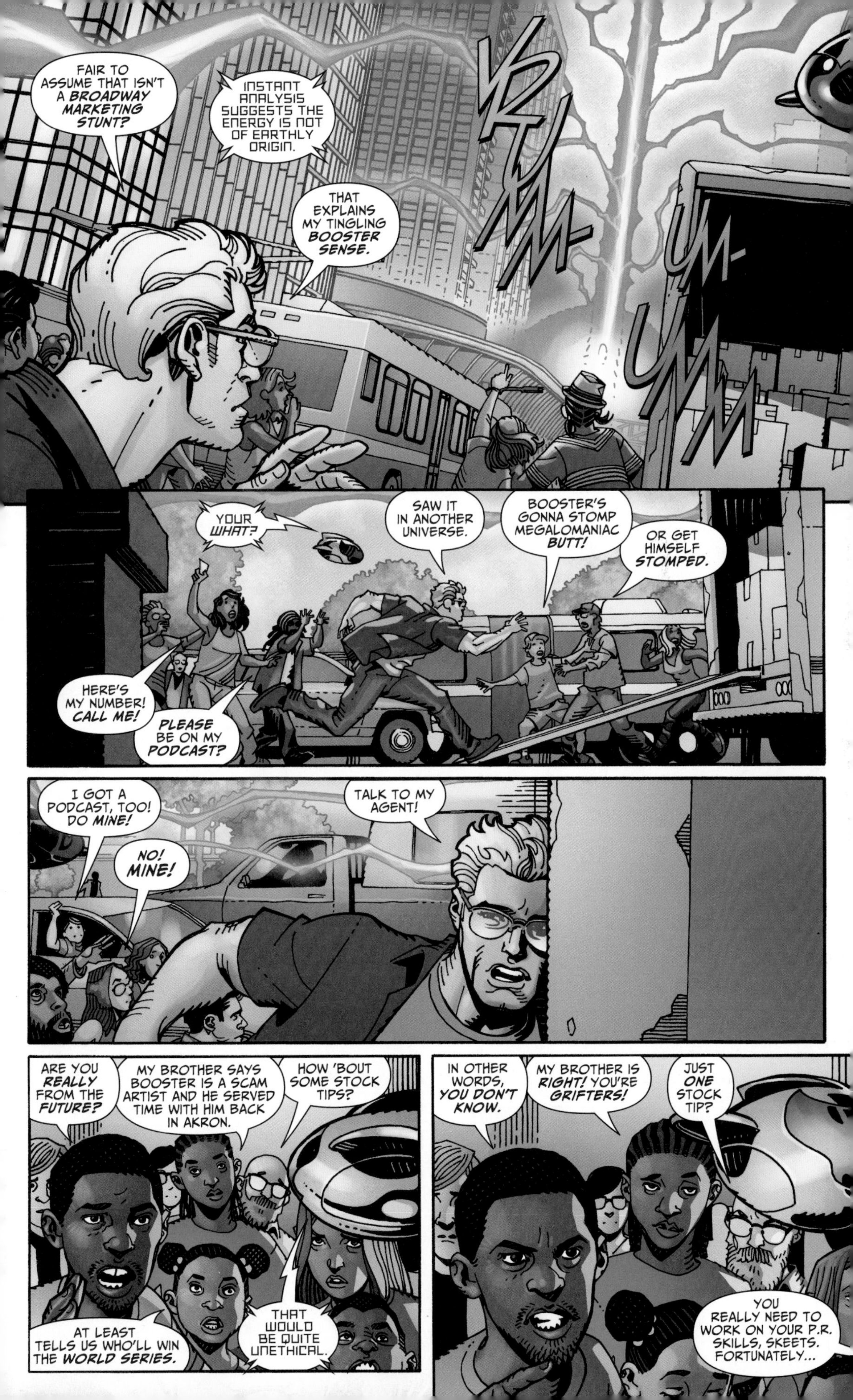
FAIR TO ASSUME THAT ISN'T A BROADWAY MARKETING STUNT?
INSTANT ANALYSIS SUGGESTS THE ENERGY IS NOT OF EARTHLY ORIGIN.
THAT EXPLAINS MY TINGLING BOOSTER SENSE.
VRUMMMUMMM
YOUR WHAT?
SAW IT IN ANOTHER UNIVERSE.
BOOSTER'S GONNA STOMP MEGALOMANIAC BUTT!
OR GET HIMSELF STOMPED.
HERE'S MY NUMBER! CALL ME!
PLEASE BE ON MY PODCAST?
I GOT A PODCAST, TOO! DO MINE!
NO! MINE!
TALK TO MY AGENT!
ARE YOU REALLY FROM THE FUTURE?
MY BROTHER SAYS BOOSTER IS A SCAM ARTIST AND HE SERVED TIME WITH HIM BACK IN AKRON.
HOW 'BOUT SOME STOCK TIPS?
AT LEAST TELLS US WHO'LL WIN THE WORLD SERIES.
THAT WOULD BE QUITE UNETHICAL.
IN OTHER WORDS, YOU DON'T KNOW.
MY BROTHER IS RIGHT! YOU'RE GRIFTERS!
JUST ONE STOCK TIP?
YOU REALLY NEED TO WORK ON YOUR P.R. SKILLS, SKEETS. FORTUNATELY...

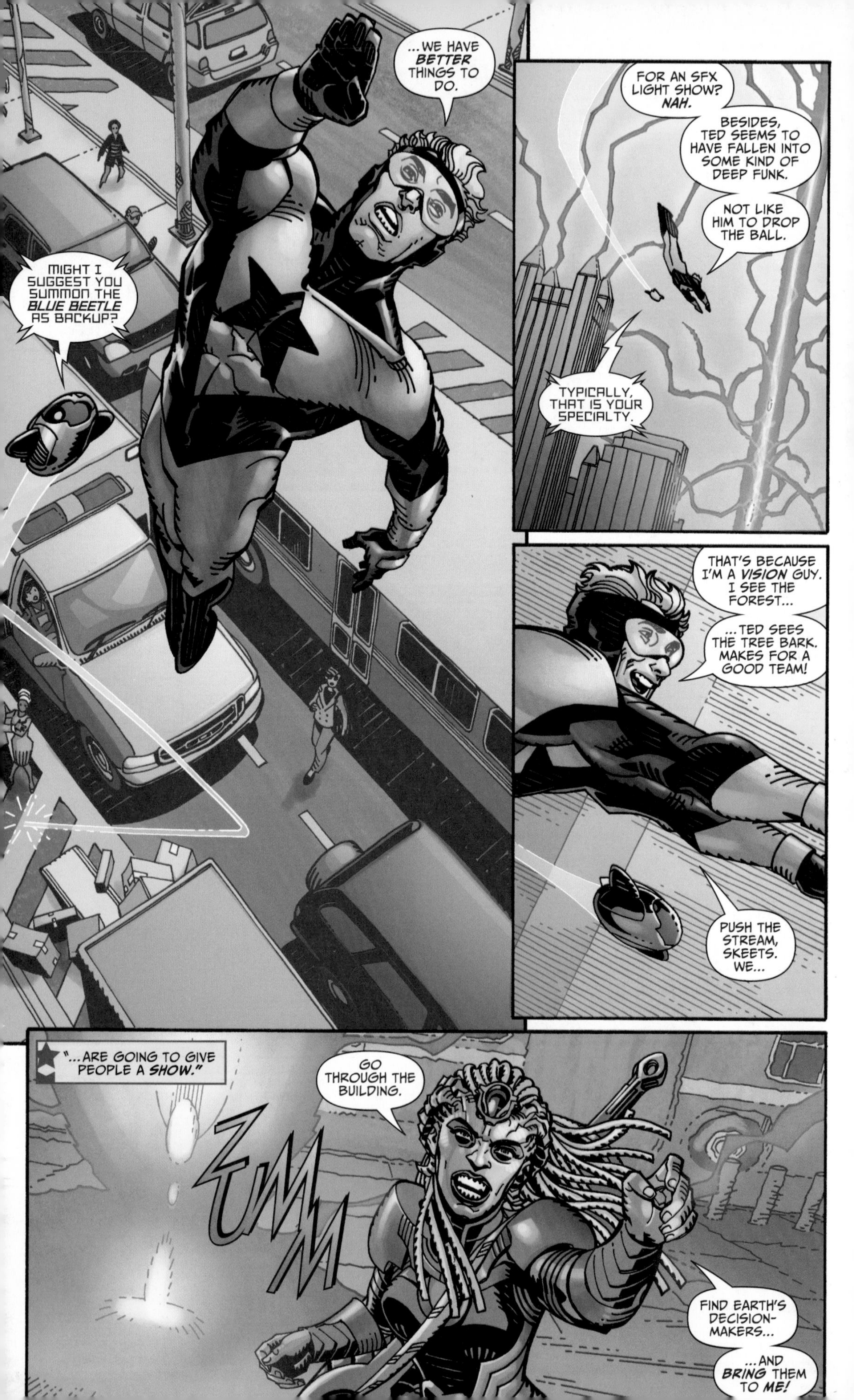

...WE HAVE BETTER THINGS TO DO.
MIGHT I SUGGEST YOU SUMMON THE BLUE BEETLE AS BACKUP?
FOR AN SFX LIGHT SHOW? NAH.
BESIDES, TED SEEMS TO HAVE FALLEN INTO SOME KIND OF DEEP FUNK.
NOT LIKE HIM TO DROP THE BALL.
TYPICALLY, THAT IS YOUR SPECIALTY.
THAT'S BECAUSE I'M A VISION GUY. I SEE THE FOREST...
...TED SEES THE TREE BARK. MAKES FOR A GOOD TEAM!
PUSH THE STREAM, SKEETS. WE...
"...ARE GOING TO GIVE PEOPLE A SHOW."
GO THROUGH THE BUILDING.
ZUMM
FIND EARTH'S DECISION-MAKERS...
...AND BRING THEM TO ME!

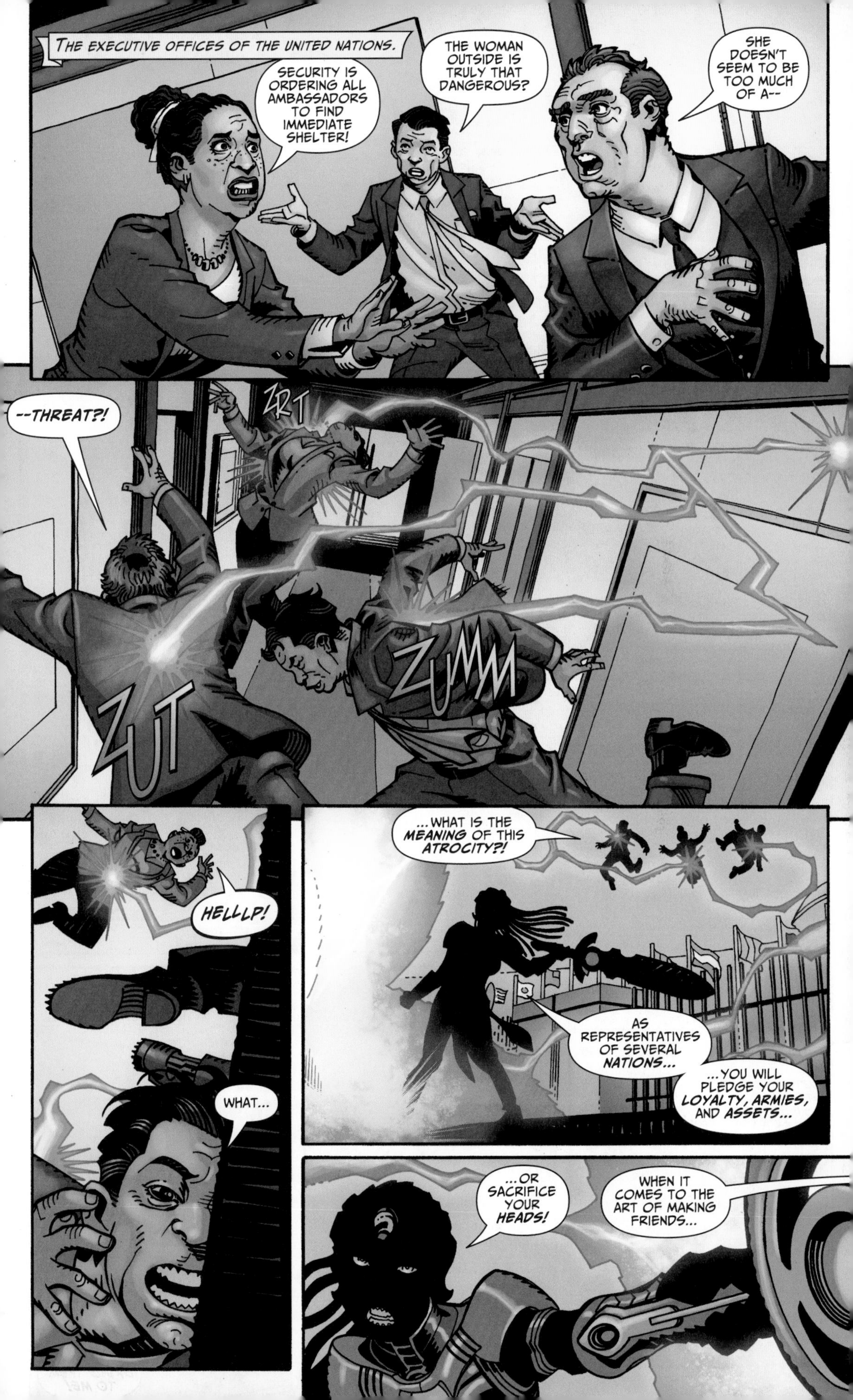
THE EXECUTIVE OFFICES OF THE UNITED NATIONS.
SECURITY IS ORDERING ALL AMBASSADORS TO FIND IMMEDIATE SHELTER!
THE WOMAN OUTSIDE IS TRULY THAT DANGEROUS?
SHE DOESN'T SEEM TO BE TOO MUCH OF A--
--THREAT?!
ZRT
ZUMM
ZUT
HELLLP!
WHAT...
...WHAT IS THE MEANING OF THIS ATROCITY?!
AS REPRESENTATIVES OF SEVERAL NATIONS...
...YOU WILL PLEDGE YOUR LOYALTY, ARMIES, AND ASSETS...
...OR SACRIFICE YOUR HEADS!
WHEN IT COMES TO THE ART OF MAKING FRIENDS...

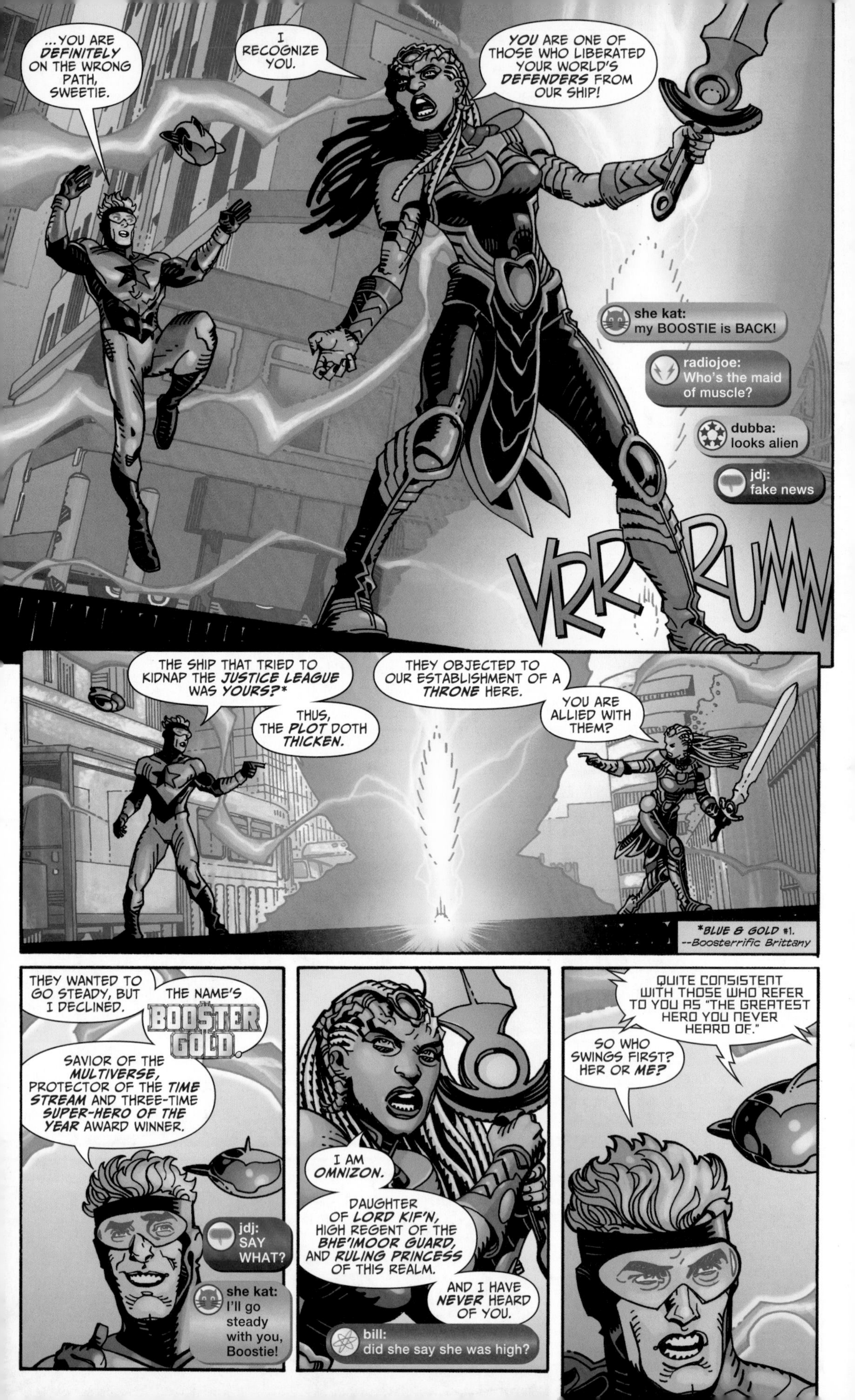
...YOU ARE DEFINITELY ON THE WRONG PATH, SWEETIE.
I RECOGNIZE YOU.
YOU ARE ONE OF THOSE WHO LIBERATED YOUR WORLD'S DEFENDERS FROM OUR SHIP!
she kat: my BOOSTIE is BACK!
radiojoe: Who's the maid of muscle?
dubba: looks alien
jdj: fake news
VRRRUMM
THE SHIP THAT TRIED TO KIDNAP THE JUSTICE LEAGUE WAS YOURS?*
THUS, THE PLOT DOTH THICKEN.
THEY OBJECTED TO OUR ESTABLISHMENT OF A THRONE HERE.
YOU ARE ALLIED WITH THEM?
*BLUE & GOLD #1. --Boosterrific Brittany
THEY WANTED TO GO STEADY, BUT I DECLINED.
THE NAME'S BOOSTER GOLD.
SAVIOR OF THE MULTIVERSE, PROTECTOR OF THE TIME STREAM AND THREE-TIME SUPER-HERO OF THE YEAR AWARD WINNER.
jdj: SAY WHAT?
she kat: I'll go steady with you, Boostie!
I AM OMNIZON.
DAUGHTER OF LORD KIF'N, HIGH REGENT OF THE BHE'IMOOR GUARD, AND RULING PRINCESS OF THIS REALM.
AND I HAVE NEVER HEARD OF YOU.
bill: did she say she was high?
QUITE CONSISTENT WITH THOSE WHO REFER TO YOU AS "THE GREATEST HERO YOU NEVER HEARD OF."
SO WHO SWINGS FIRST? HER OR ME?

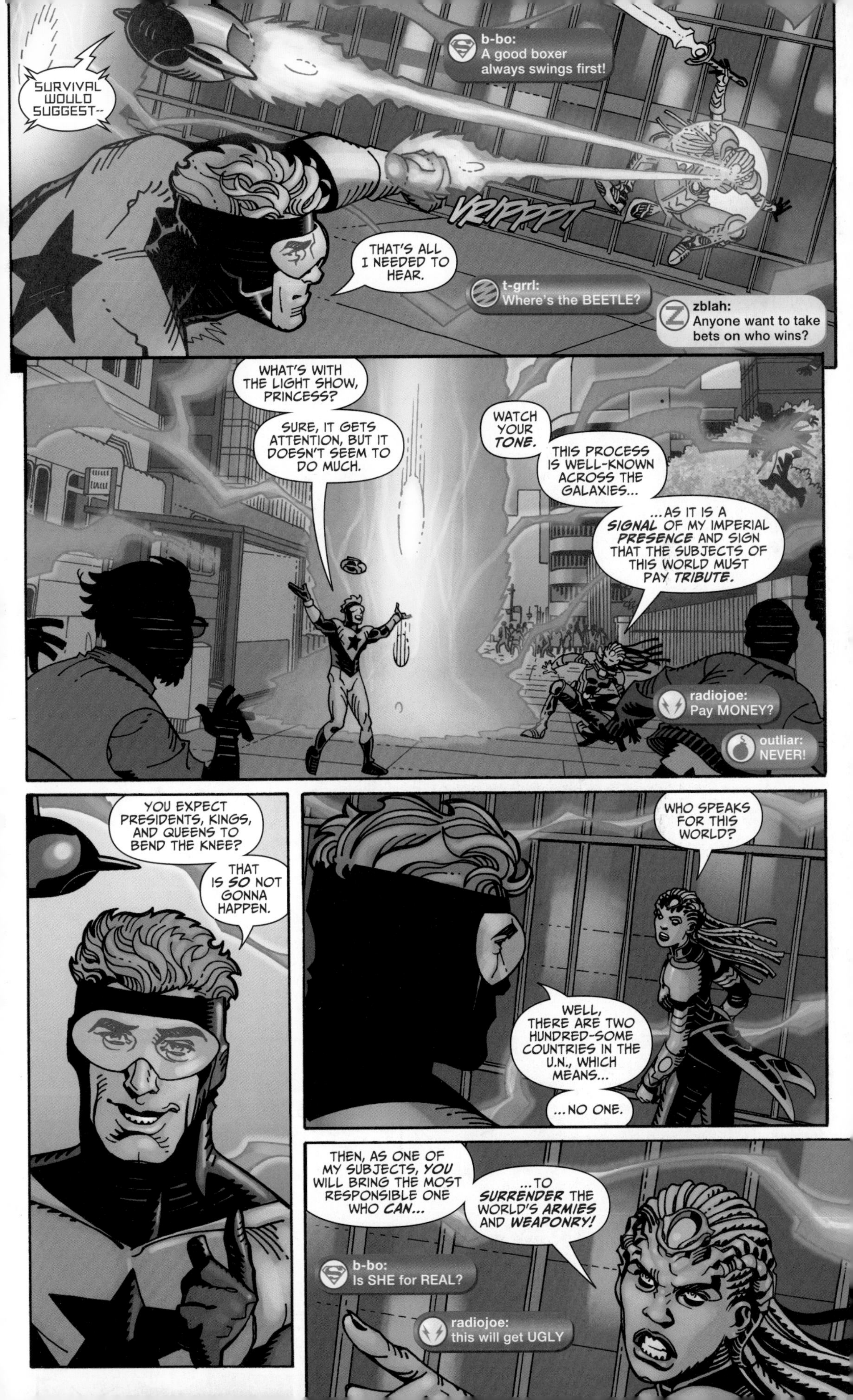
SURVIVAL WOULD SUGGEST--
b-bo: A good boxer always swings first!
VRIPPPT
THAT'S ALL I NEEDED TO HEAR.
t-grrl: Where's the BEETLE?
zblah: Anyone want to take bets on who wins?
WHAT'S WITH THE LIGHT SHOW, PRINCESS?
SURE, IT GETS ATTENTION, BUT IT DOESN'T SEEM TO DO MUCH.
WATCH YOUR TONE.
THIS PROCESS IS WELL-KNOWN ACROSS THE GALAXIES...
...AS IT IS A SIGNAL OF MY IMPERIAL PRESENCE AND SIGN THAT THE SUBJECTS OF THIS WORLD MUST PAY TRIBUTE.
radiojoe: Pay MONEY?
outliar: NEVER!
YOU EXPECT PRESIDENTS, KINGS, AND QUEENS TO BEND THE KNEE?
THAT IS SO NOT GONNA HAPPEN.
WHO SPEAKS FOR THIS WORLD?
WELL, THERE ARE TWO HUNDRED-SOME COUNTRIES IN THE U.N., WHICH MEANS...
...NO ONE.
THEN, AS ONE OF MY SUBJECTS, YOU WILL BRING THE MOST RESPONSIBLE ONE WHO CAN...
...TO SURRENDER THE WORLD'S ARMIES AND WEAPONRY!
b-bo: Is SHE for REAL?
radiojoe: this will get UGLY

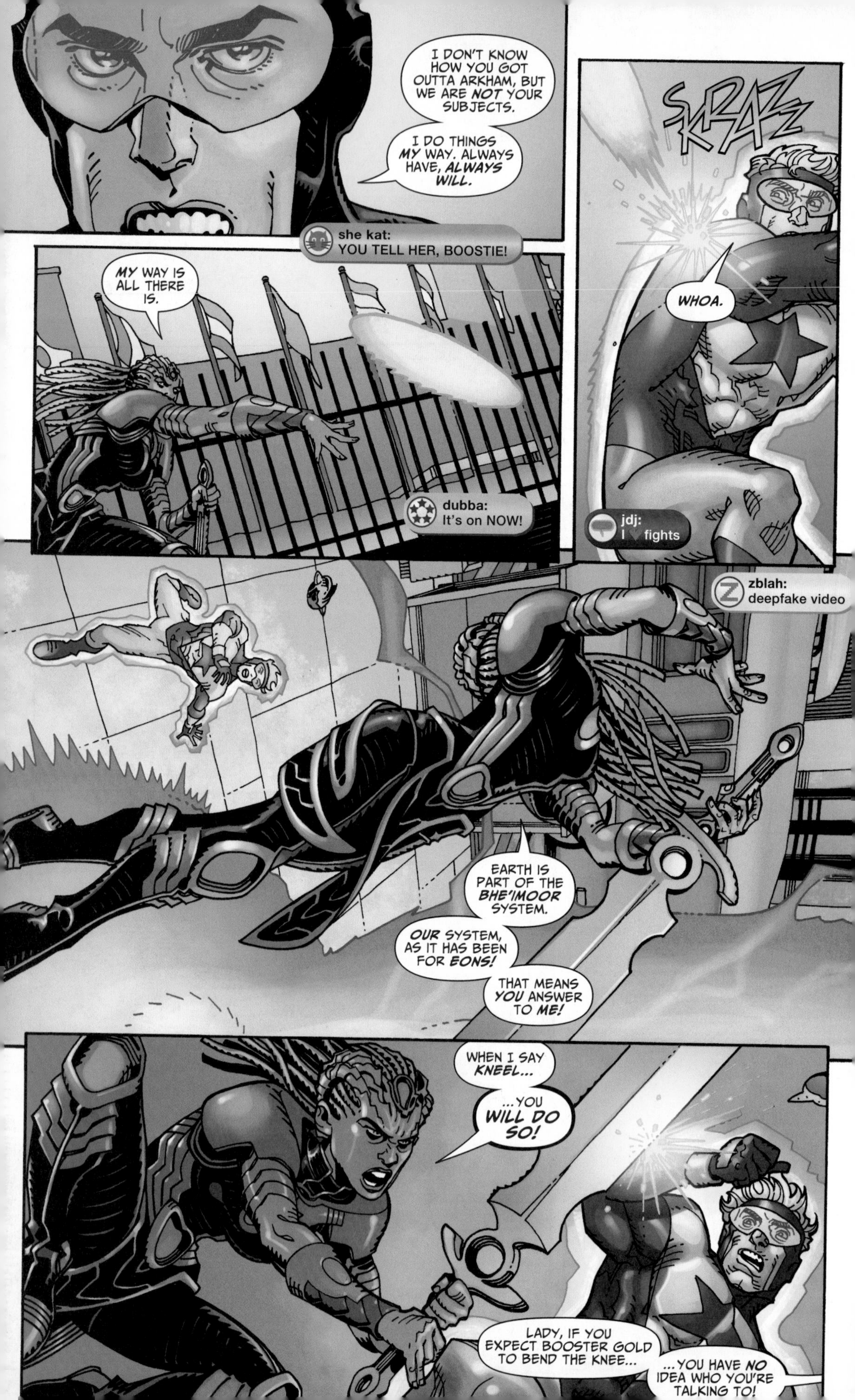
I DON'T KNOW HOW YOU GOT OUTTA ARKHAM, BUT WE ARE *NOT* YOUR SUBJECTS.
I DO THINGS *MY* WAY. ALWAYS HAVE, *ALWAYS WILL.*
she kat:
YOU TELL HER, BOOSTIE!
MY WAY IS ALL THERE IS.
dubba:
It's on NOW!
SKRAZZ
WHOA.
jdj:
I ♥ fights
zblah:
deepfake video
EARTH IS PART OF THE *BHE'IMOOR* SYSTEM.
OUR SYSTEM, AS IT HAS BEEN FOR *EONS!*
THAT MEANS *YOU* ANSWER TO *ME!*
WHEN I SAY *KNEEL...*
...YOU *WILL DO SO!*
LADY, IF YOU EXPECT BOOSTER GOLD TO BEND THE KNEE...
...YOU HAVE *NO* IDEA WHO YOU'RE TALKING TO!

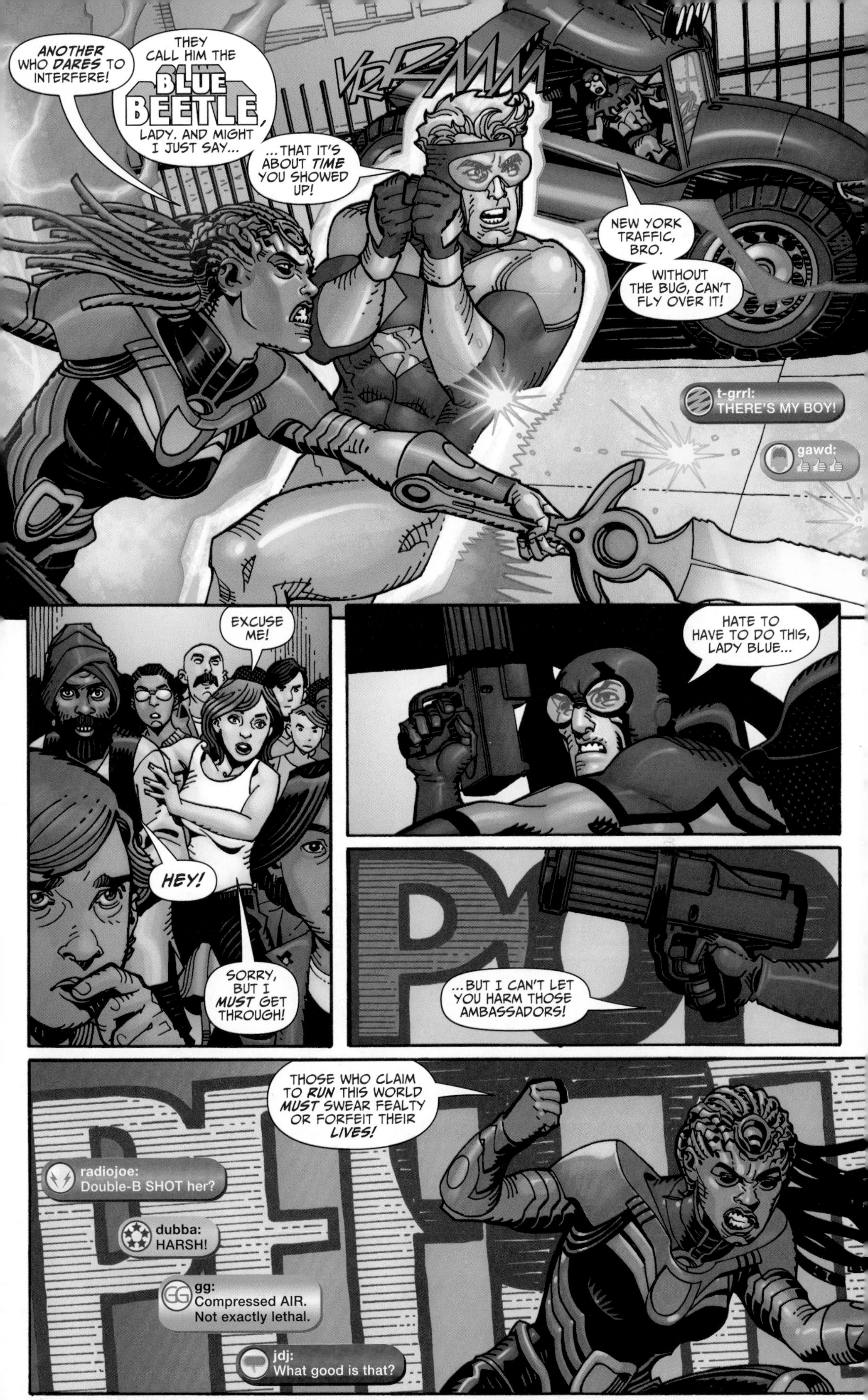
VRRMMM
ANOTHER WHO DARES TO INTERFERE!
THEY CALL HIM THE BLUE BEETLE, LADY. AND MIGHT I JUST SAY...
...THAT IT'S ABOUT TIME YOU SHOWED UP!
NEW YORK TRAFFIC, BRO.
WITHOUT THE BUG, CAN'T FLY OVER IT!
t-grrl: THERE'S MY BOY!
gawd:
EXCUSE ME!
HEY!
SORRY, BUT I MUST GET THROUGH!
HATE TO HAVE TO DO THIS, LADY BLUE...
...BUT I CAN'T LET YOU HARM THOSE AMBASSADORS!
THOSE WHO CLAIM TO RUN THIS WORLD MUST SWEAR FEALTY OR FORFEIT THEIR LIVES!
radiojoe: Double-B SHOT her?
dubba: HARSH!
gg: Compressed AIR. Not exactly lethal.
jdj: What good is that?

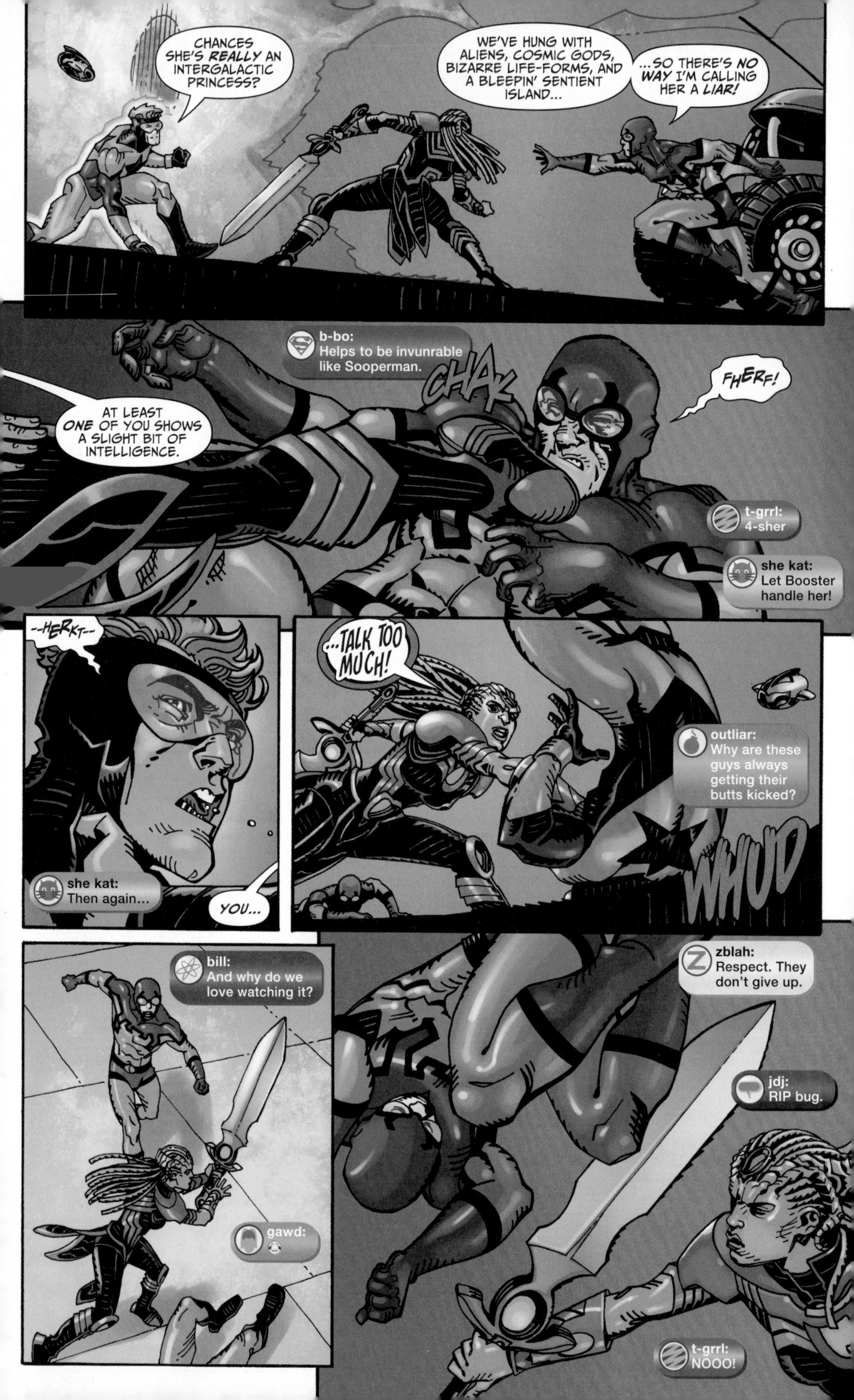

CHANCES SHE'S REALLY AN INTERGALACTIC PRINCESS?
WE'VE HUNG WITH ALIENS, COSMIC GODS, BIZARRE LIFE-FORMS, AND A BLEEPIN' SENTIENT ISLAND...
...SO THERE'S NO WAY I'M CALLING HER A LIAR!
b-bo: Helps to be invunrable like Sooperman.
CHAK
FHERF!
AT LEAST ONE OF YOU SHOWS A SLIGHT BIT OF INTELLIGENCE.
t-grrl: 4-sher
she kat: Let Booster handle her!
--HERKT--
she kat: Then again...
YOU...
...TALK TOO MUCH!
outliar: Why are these guys always getting their butts kicked?
WHUD
bill: And why do we love watching it?
gawd:
zblah: Respect. They don't give up.
jdj: RIP bug.
t-grrl: NOOO!

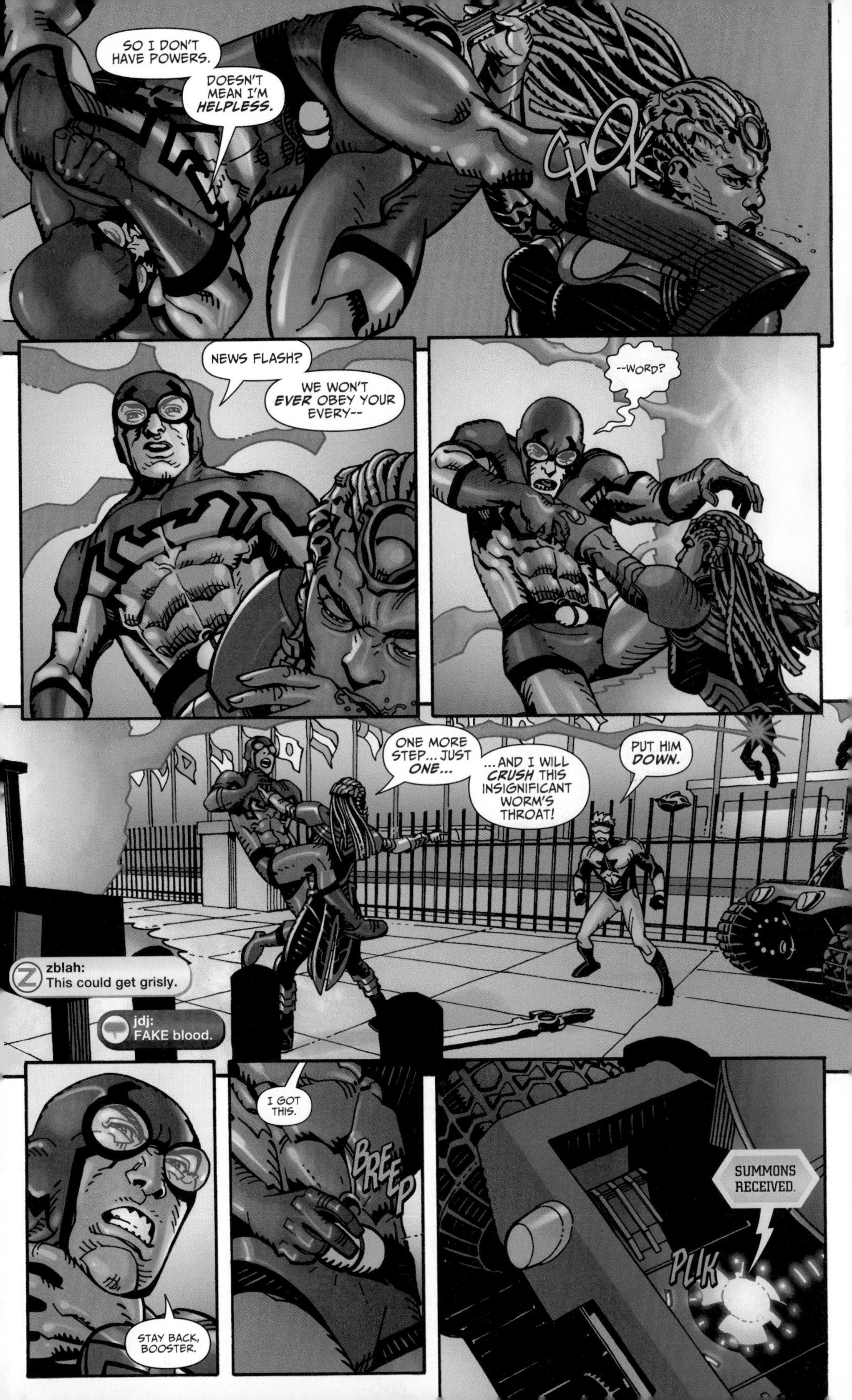

SO I DON'T HAVE POWERS.
DOESN'T MEAN I'M HELPLESS.
CHOK
NEWS FLASH?
WE WON'T EVER OBEY YOUR EVERY--
--WORD?
ONE MORE STEP... JUST ONE...
...AND I WILL CRUSH THIS INSIGNIFICANT WORM'S THROAT!
PUT HIM DOWN.
zblah:
This could get grisly.
jdj:
FAKE blood.
STAY BACK, BOOSTER.
I GOT THIS.
BREEP
SUMMONS RECEIVED.
PLIK

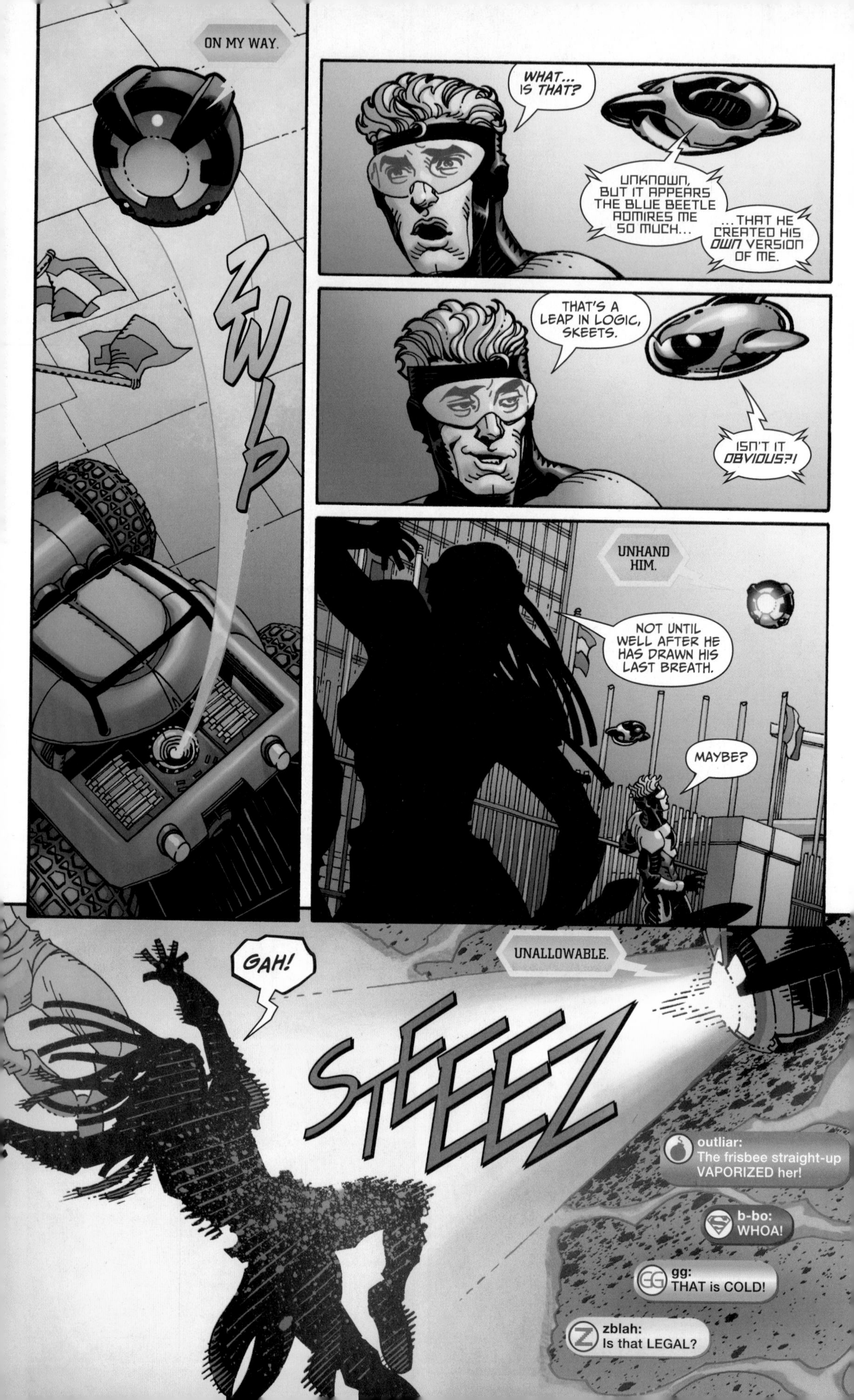
ON MY WAY.
ZWIP
WHAT... IS THAT?
UNKNOWN, BUT IT APPEARS THE BLUE BEETLE ADMIRES ME SO MUCH...
...THAT HE CREATED HIS OWN VERSION OF ME.
THAT'S A LEAP IN LOGIC, SKEETS.
ISN'T IT OBVIOUS?!
UNHAND HIM.
NOT UNTIL WELL AFTER HE HAS DRAWN HIS LAST BREATH.
MAYBE?
GAH!
UNALLOWABLE.
STEEEZ
outliar: The frisbee straight-up VAPORIZED her!
b-bo: WHOA!
gg: THAT is COLD!
zblah: Is that LEGAL?

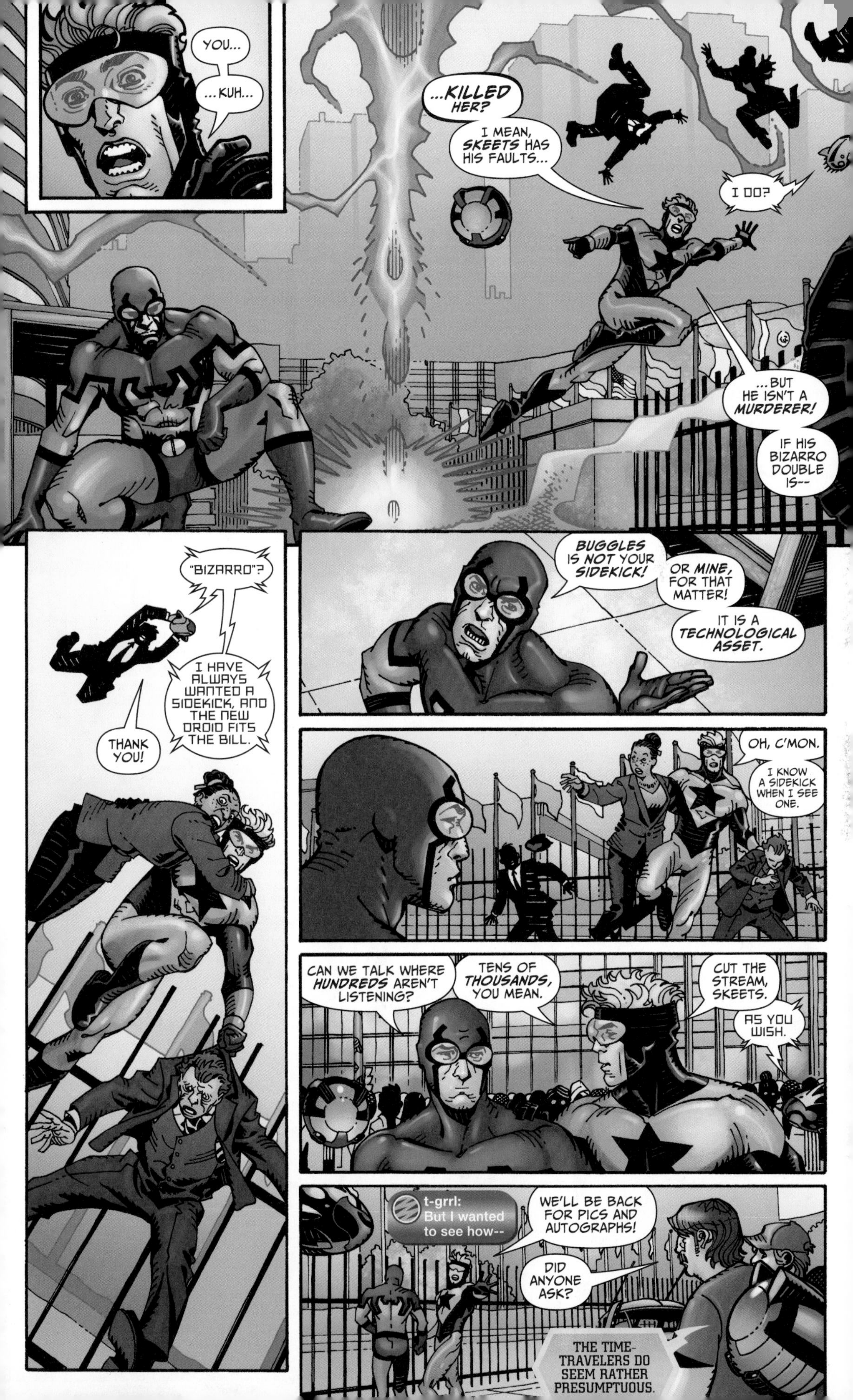
YOU...
...KUH...
...KILLED HER?
I MEAN, SKEETS HAS HIS FAULTS...
I DO?
...BUT HE ISN'T A MURDERER!
IF HIS BIZARRO DOUBLE IS--
"BIZARRO"?
I HAVE ALWAYS WANTED A SIDEKICK, AND THE NEW DROID FITS THE BILL.
THANK YOU!
BUGGLES IS NOT YOUR SIDEKICK!
OR MINE, FOR THAT MATTER!
IT IS A TECHNOLOGICAL ASSET.
OH, C'MON.
I KNOW A SIDEKICK WHEN I SEE ONE.
CAN WE TALK WHERE HUNDREDS AREN'T LISTENING?
TENS OF THOUSANDS, YOU MEAN.
CUT THE STREAM, SKEETS.
AS YOU WISH.
t-grrl:
But I wanted to see how--
WE'LL BE BACK FOR PICS AND AUTOGRAPHS!
DID ANYONE ASK?
THE TIME-TRAVELERS DO SEEM RATHER PRESUMPTUOUS.

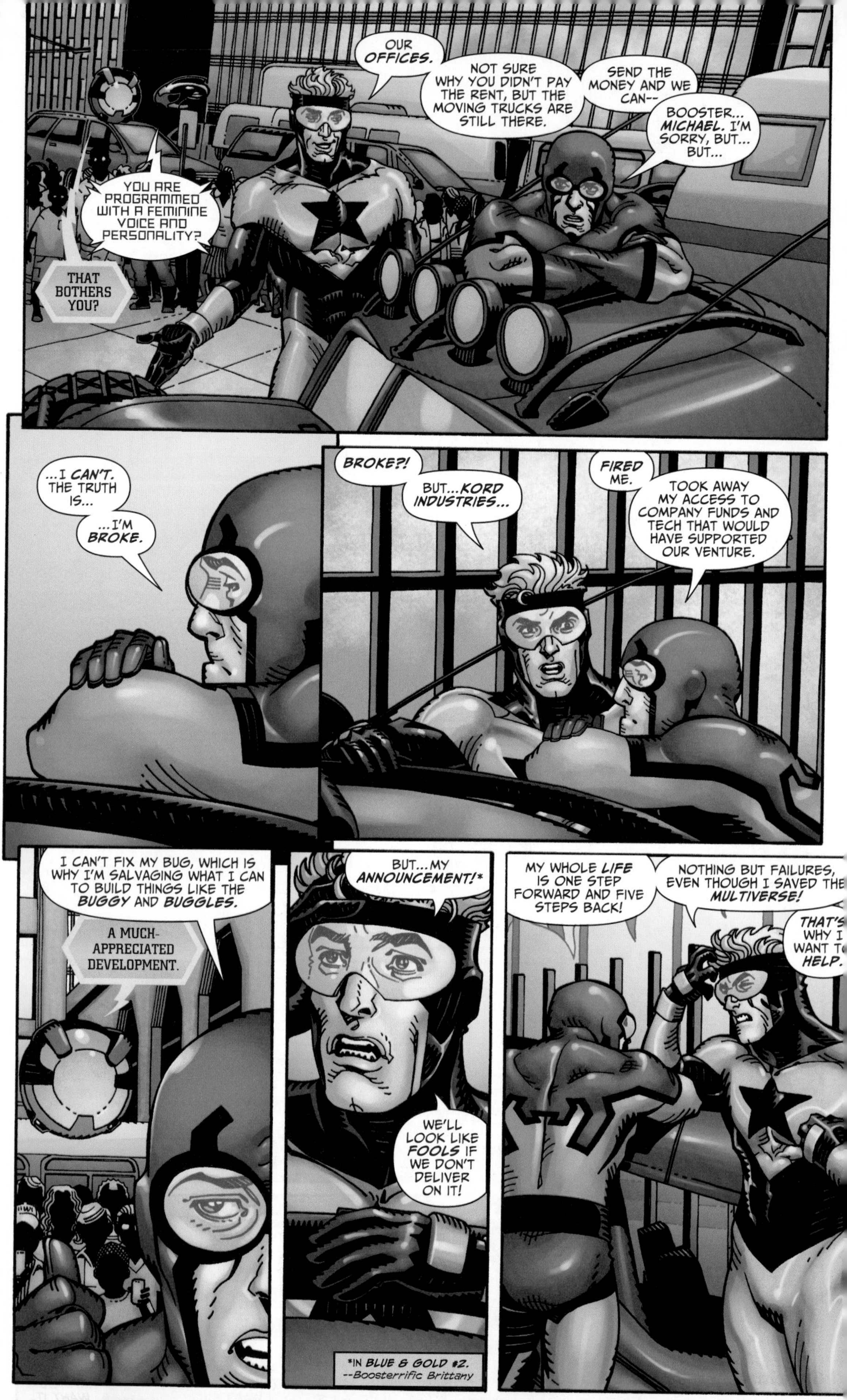
OUR OFFICES.
NOT SURE WHY YOU DIDN'T PAY THE RENT, BUT THE MOVING TRUCKS ARE STILL THERE.
SEND THE MONEY AND WE CAN--
BOOSTER... MICHAEL. I'M SORRY, BUT... BUT...
YOU ARE PROGRAMMED WITH A FEMININE VOICE AND PERSONALITY?
THAT BOTHERS YOU?
...I CAN'T. THE TRUTH IS...
...I'M BROKE.
BROKE?!
BUT...KORD INDUSTRIES...
FIRED ME.
TOOK AWAY MY ACCESS TO COMPANY FUNDS AND TECH THAT WOULD HAVE SUPPORTED OUR VENTURE.
I CAN'T FIX MY BUG, WHICH IS WHY I'M SALVAGING WHAT I CAN TO BUILD THINGS LIKE THE BUGGY AND BUGGLES.
A MUCH-APPRECIATED DEVELOPMENT.
BUT...MY ANNOUNCEMENT!*
WE'LL LOOK LIKE FOOLS IF WE DON'T DELIVER ON IT!
*IN BLUE & GOLD #2. --Boosterrific Brittany
MY WHOLE LIFE IS ONE STEP FORWARD AND FIVE STEPS BACK!
NOTHING BUT FAILURES, EVEN THOUGH I SAVED THE MULTIVERSE!
THAT'S WHY I WANT TO HELP.

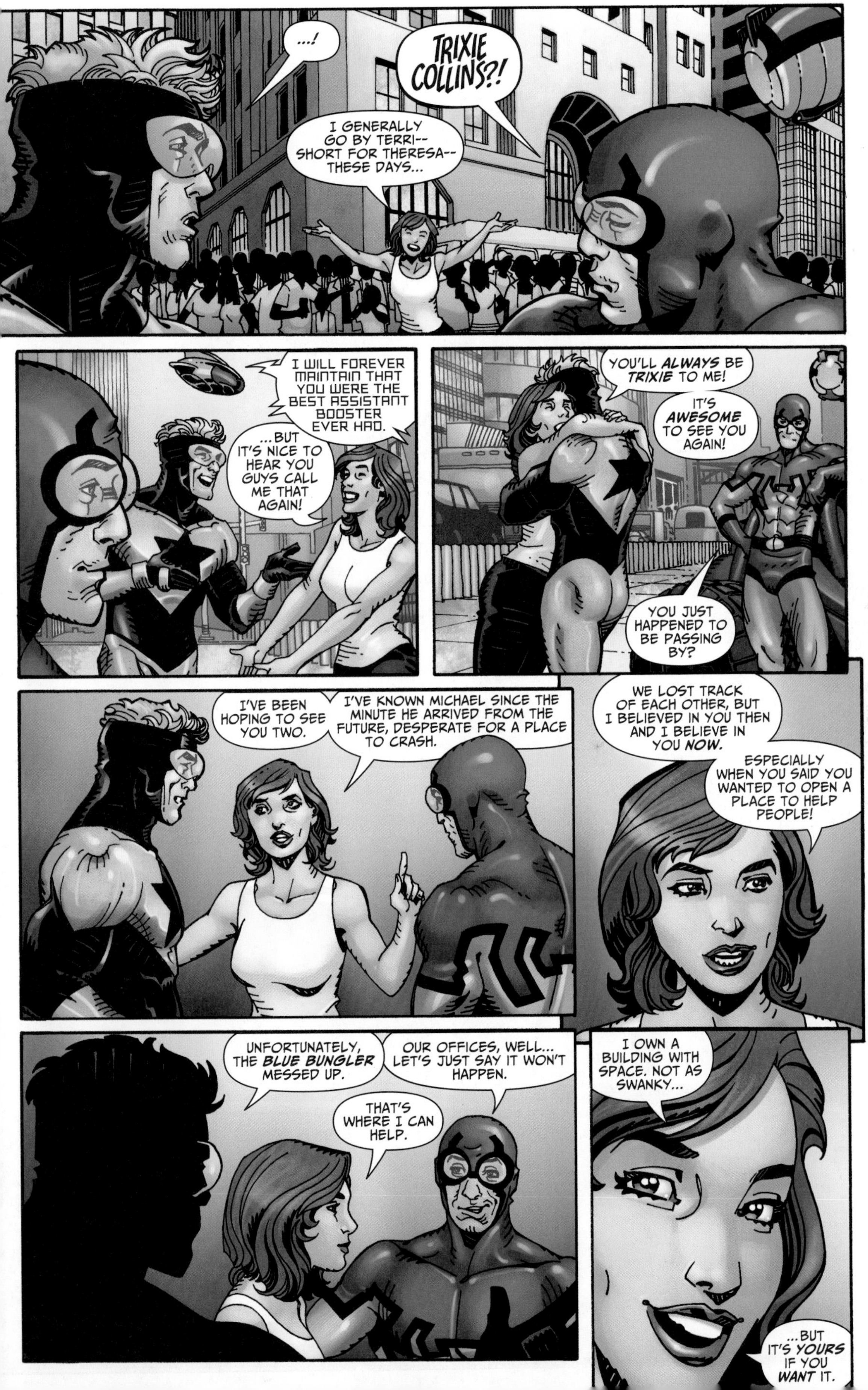

...!
TRIXIE COLLINS?!
I GENERALLY GO BY TERRI-- SHORT FOR THERESA-- THESE DAYS...
I WILL FOREVER MAINTAIN THAT YOU WERE THE BEST ASSISTANT BOOSTER EVER HAD.
...BUT IT'S NICE TO HEAR YOU GUYS CALL ME THAT AGAIN!
YOU'LL ALWAYS BE TRIXIE TO ME!
IT'S AWESOME TO SEE YOU AGAIN!
YOU JUST HAPPENED TO BE PASSING BY?
I'VE BEEN HOPING TO SEE YOU TWO.
I'VE KNOWN MICHAEL SINCE THE MINUTE HE ARRIVED FROM THE FUTURE, DESPERATE FOR A PLACE TO CRASH.
WE LOST TRACK OF EACH OTHER, BUT I BELIEVED IN YOU THEN AND I BELIEVE IN YOU NOW.
ESPECIALLY WHEN YOU SAID YOU WANTED TO OPEN A PLACE TO HELP PEOPLE!
UNFORTUNATELY, THE BLUE BUNGLER MESSED UP.
OUR OFFICES, WELL... LET'S JUST SAY IT WON'T HAPPEN.
THAT'S WHERE I CAN HELP.
I OWN A BUILDING WITH SPACE. NOT AS SWANKY...
...BUT IT'S YOURS IF YOU WANT IT.

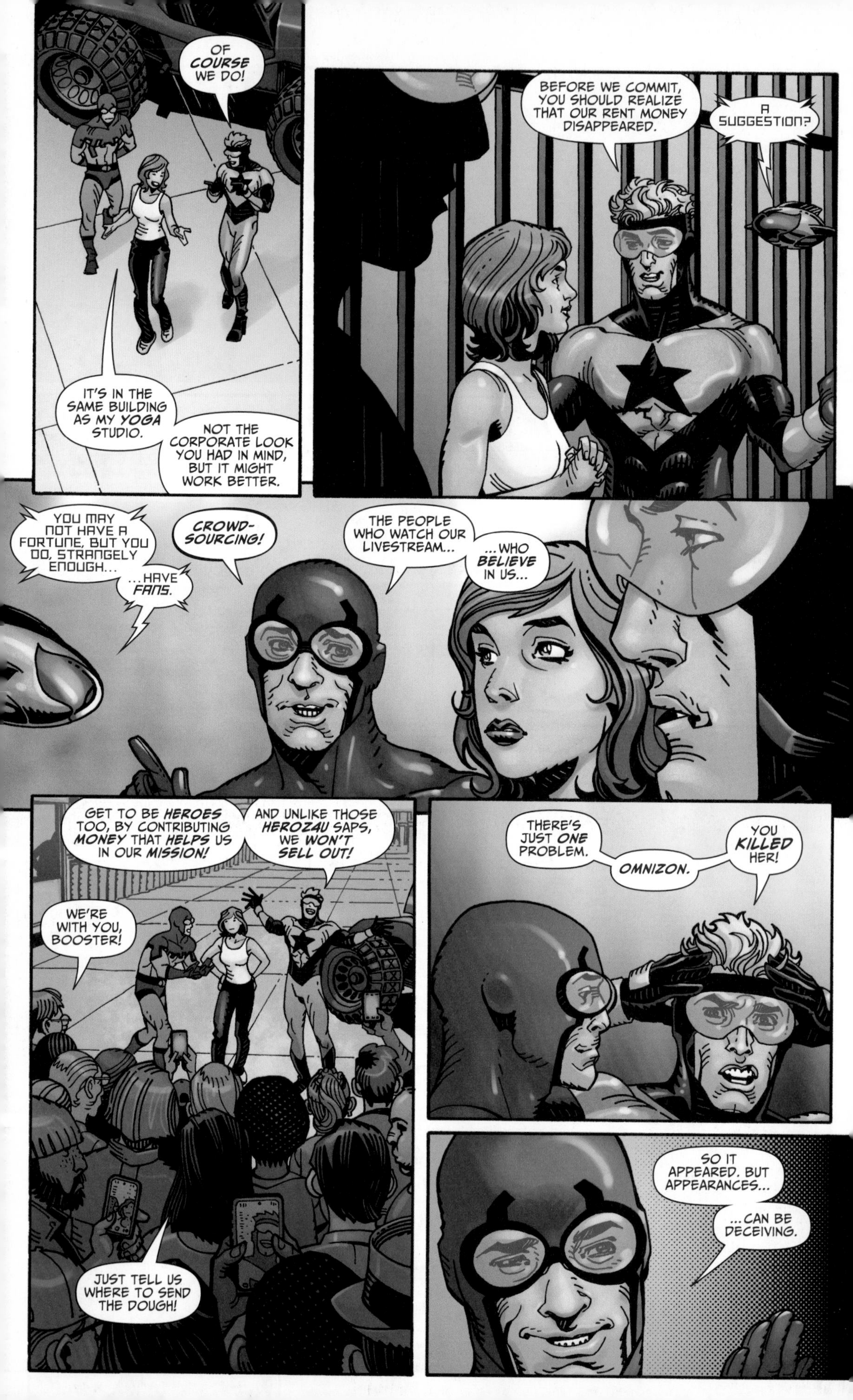
OF COURSE WE DO!
IT'S IN THE SAME BUILDING AS MY YOGA STUDIO.
NOT THE CORPORATE LOOK YOU HAD IN MIND, BUT IT MIGHT WORK BETTER.
BEFORE WE COMMIT, YOU SHOULD REALIZE THAT OUR RENT MONEY DISAPPEARED.
A SUGGESTION?
YOU MAY NOT HAVE A FORTUNE, BUT YOU DO, STRANGELY ENOUGH...
...HAVE FANS.
CROWD-SOURCING!
THE PEOPLE WHO WATCH OUR LIVESTREAM...
...WHO BELIEVE IN US...
GET TO BE HEROES TOO, BY CONTRIBUTING MONEY THAT HELPS US IN OUR MISSION!
AND UNLIKE THOSE HEROZ4U SAPS, WE WON'T SELL OUT!
WE'RE WITH YOU, BOOSTER!
JUST TELL US WHERE TO SEND THE DOUGH!
THERE'S JUST ONE PROBLEM.
OMNIZON.
YOU KILLED HER!
SO IT APPEARED. BUT APPEARANCES...
...CAN BE DECEIVING.

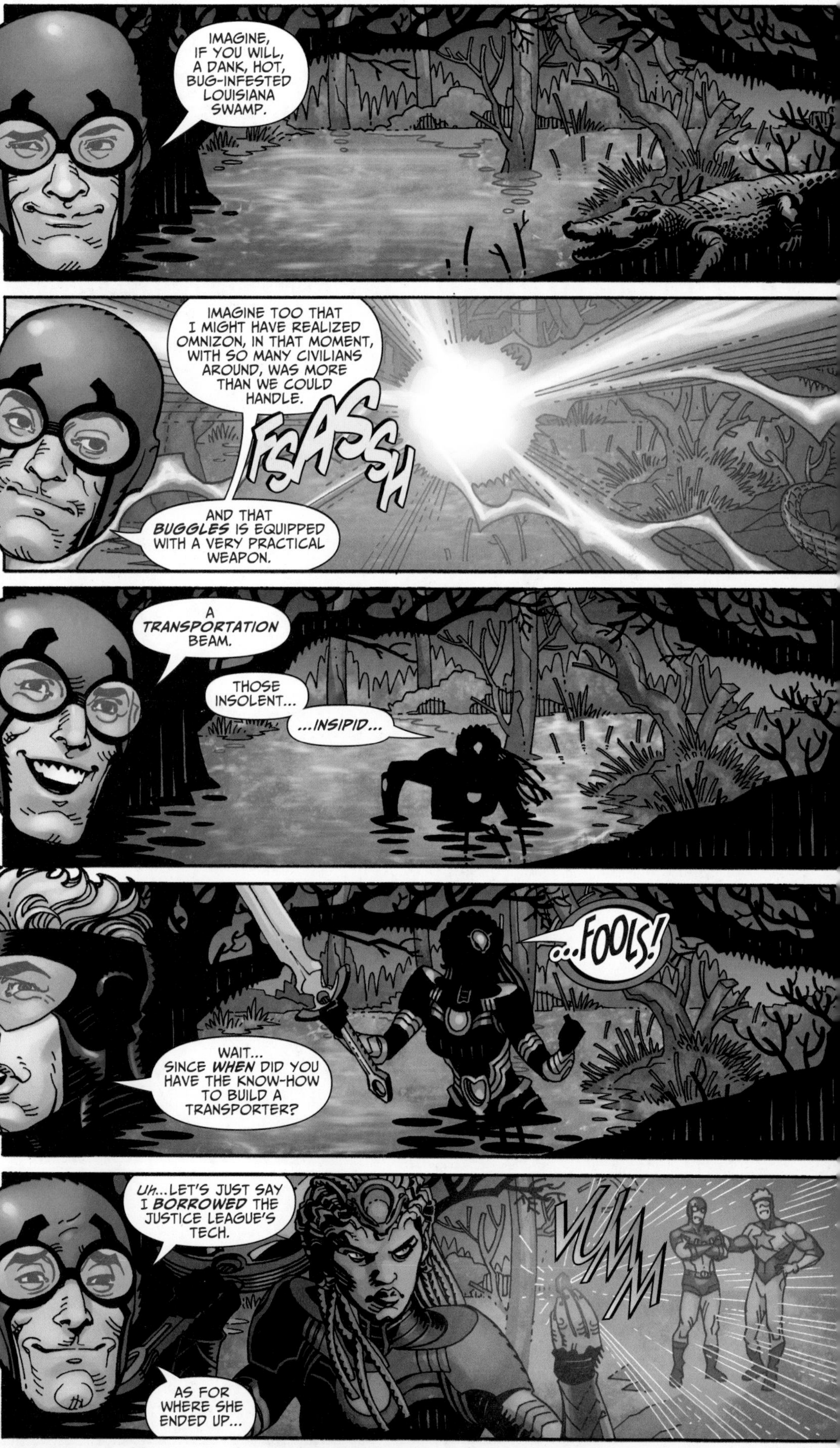
IMAGINE, IF YOU WILL, A DANK, HOT, BUG-INFESTED LOUISIANA SWAMP.
IMAGINE TOO THAT I MIGHT HAVE REALIZED OMNIZON, IN THAT MOMENT, WITH SO MANY CIVILIANS AROUND, WAS MORE THAN WE COULD HANDLE.
FSASSH
AND THAT *BUGGLES* IS EQUIPPED WITH A VERY PRACTICAL WEAPON.
A *TRANSPORTATION* BEAM.
THOSE INSOLENT...
...*INSIPID*...
...FOOLS!
WAIT... SINCE *WHEN* DID YOU HAVE THE KNOW-HOW TO BUILD A TRANSPORTER?
Uh...LET'S JUST SAY I *BORROWED* THE JUSTICE LEAGUE'S TECH.
VUMM
AS FOR WHERE SHE ENDED UP...

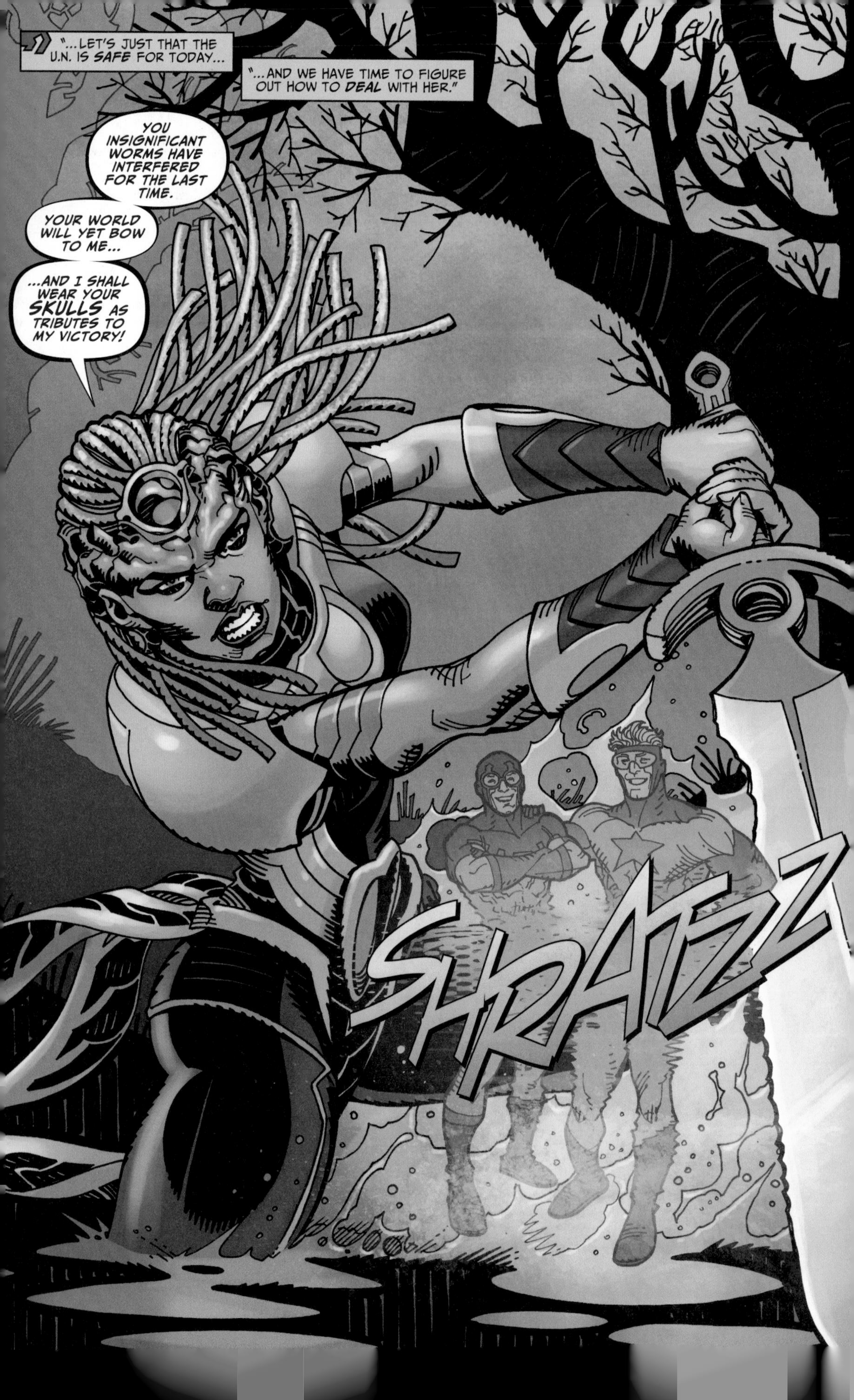
"...LET'S JUST THAT THE U.N. IS SAFE FOR TODAY...
"...AND WE HAVE TIME TO FIGURE OUT HOW TO DEAL WITH HER."
YOU INSIGNIFICANT WORMS HAVE INTERFERED FOR THE LAST TIME.
YOUR WORLD WILL YET BOW TO ME...
...AND I SHALL WEAR YOUR SKULLS AS TRIBUTES TO MY VICTORY!
SHRATZZ

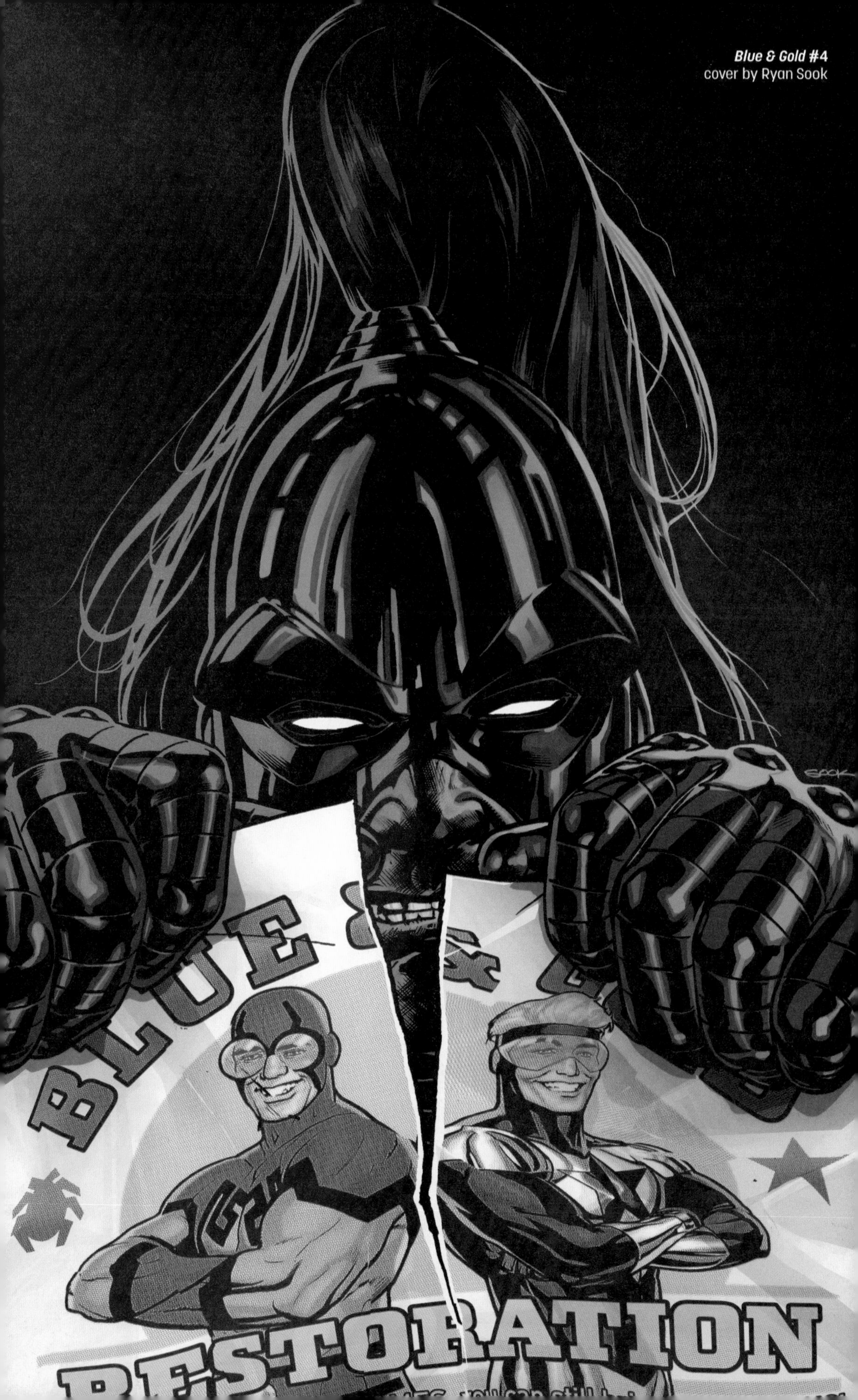
SOOK
BLUE &
RESTORATION

Blue & Gold **#4**
cover by Ryan Sook

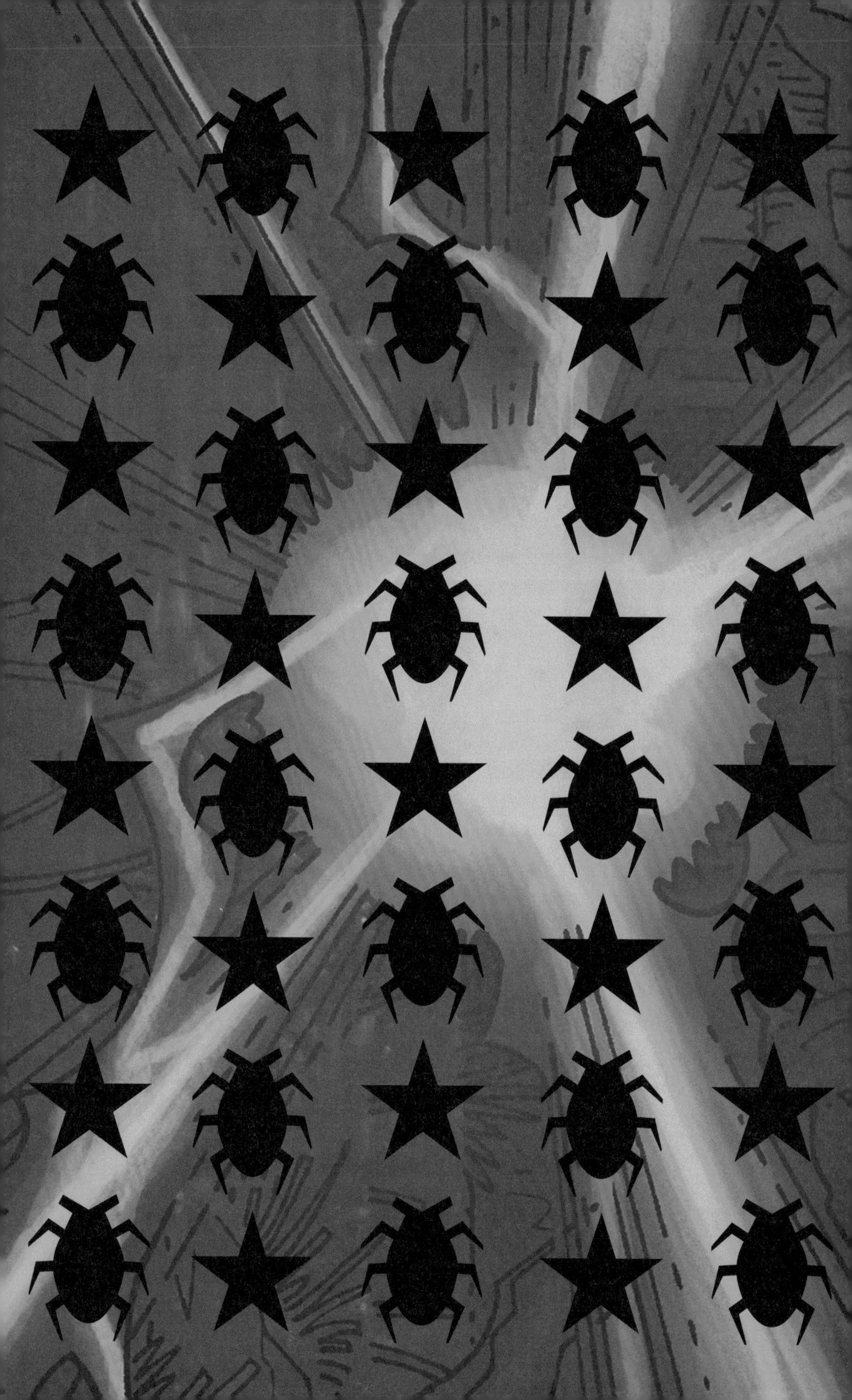

SPLITTIN' IMAGE

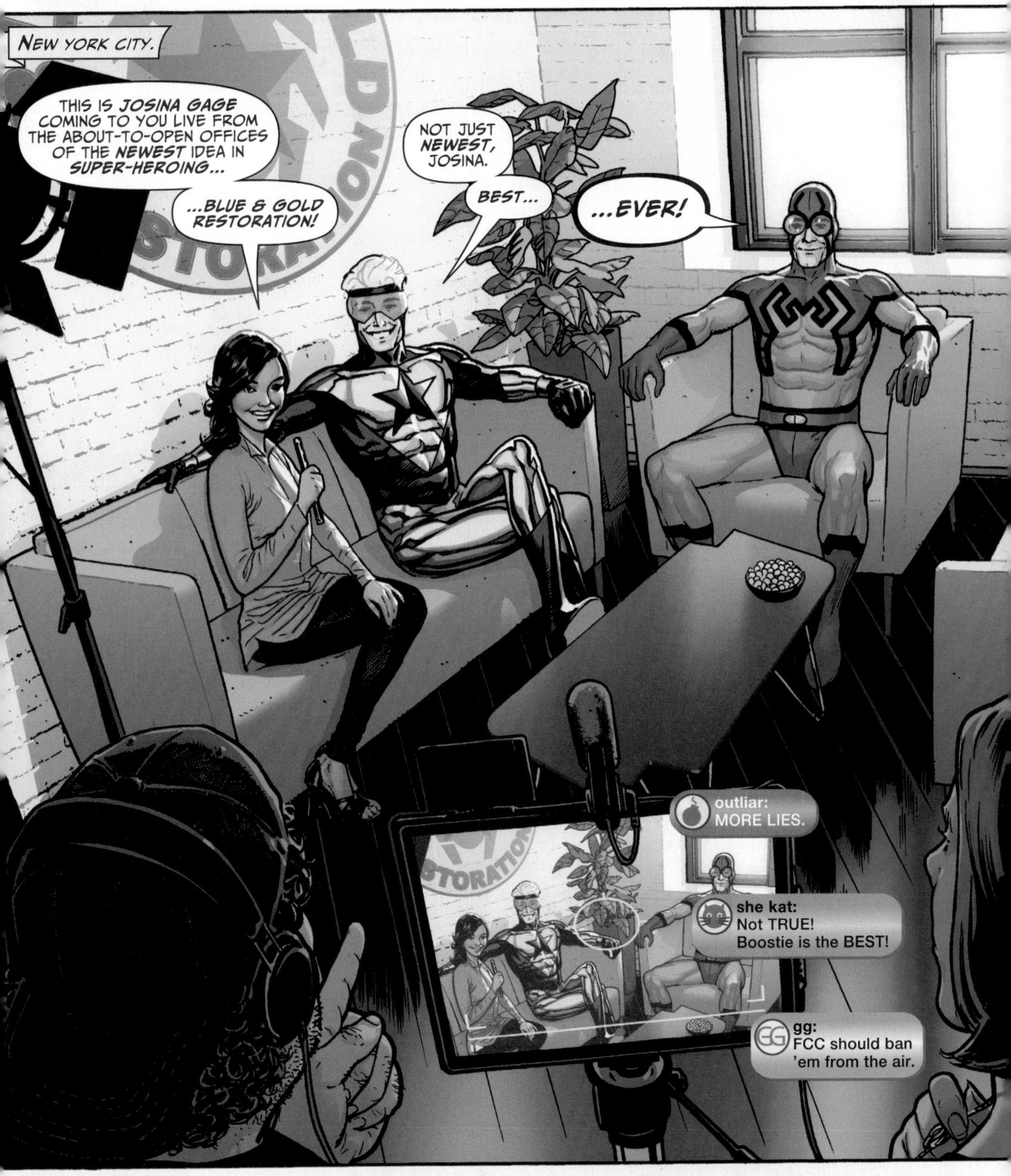

NEW YORK CITY.
THIS IS JOSINA GAGE COMING TO YOU LIVE FROM THE ABOUT-TO-OPEN OFFICES OF THE NEWEST IDEA IN SUPER-HEROING...
...BLUE & GOLD RESTORATION!
NOT JUST NEWEST, JOSINA.
BEST...
...EVER!
outliar: MORE LIES.
she kat: Not TRUE! Boostie is the BEST!
gg: FCC should ban 'em from the air.

DAN JURGENS STORY | RYAN SOOK ART, PRESENT DAY | KEVIN MAGUIRE ART, BLUE BEETLE'S SEQUENCE | DAN JURGENS AND NORM RAPMUND ART, BOOSTER GOLD'S SEQUENCE

RYAN SOOK COLORS | ROB LEIGH LETTERS | RYAN SOOK COVER | BRITTANY HOLZHERR EDITOR | MIKE COTTON SENIOR EDITOR

BOOSTER GOLD CREATED BY DAN JURGENS

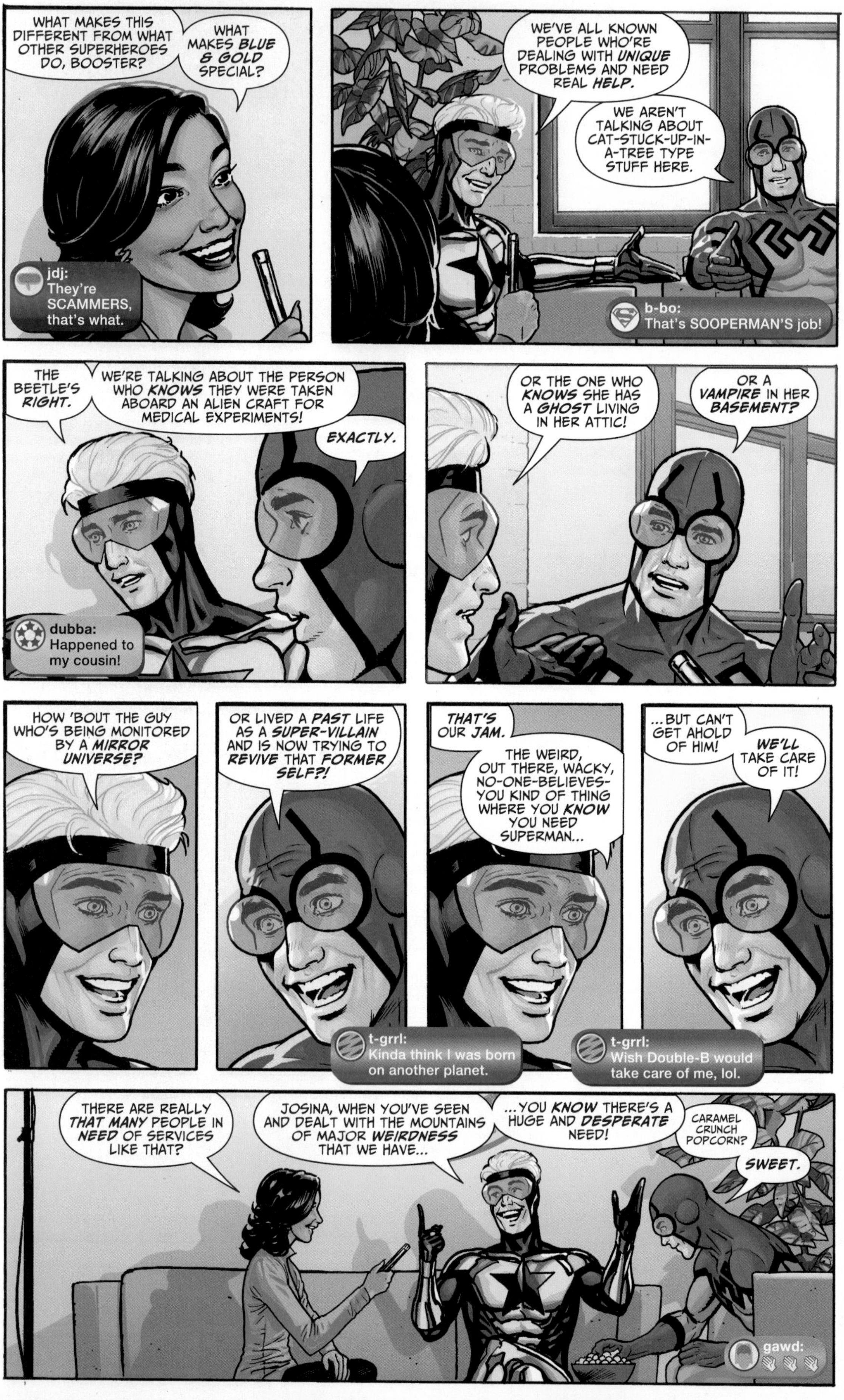

WHAT MAKES THIS DIFFERENT FROM WHAT OTHER SUPERHEROES DO, BOOSTER?
WHAT MAKES BLUE & GOLD SPECIAL?
jdj: They're SCAMMERS, that's what.
WE'VE ALL KNOWN PEOPLE WHO'RE DEALING WITH UNIQUE PROBLEMS AND NEED REAL HELP.
WE AREN'T TALKING ABOUT CAT-STUCK-UP-IN-A-TREE TYPE STUFF HERE.
b-bo: That's SOOPERMAN'S job!
THE BEETLE'S RIGHT.
WE'RE TALKING ABOUT THE PERSON WHO KNOWS THEY WERE TAKEN ABOARD AN ALIEN CRAFT FOR MEDICAL EXPERIMENTS!
EXACTLY.
dubba: Happened to my cousin!
OR THE ONE WHO KNOWS SHE HAS A GHOST LIVING IN HER ATTIC!
OR A VAMPIRE IN HER BASEMENT?
HOW 'BOUT THE GUY WHO'S BEING MONITORED BY A MIRROR UNIVERSE?
OR LIVED A PAST LIFE AS A SUPER-VILLAIN AND IS NOW TRYING TO REVIVE THAT FORMER SELF?!
t-grrl: Kinda think I was born on another planet.
THAT'S OUR JAM.
THE WEIRD, OUT THERE, WACKY, NO-ONE-BELIEVES-YOU KIND OF THING WHERE YOU KNOW YOU NEED SUPERMAN...
...BUT CAN'T GET AHOLD OF HIM!
WE'LL TAKE CARE OF IT!
t-grrl: Wish Double-B would take care of me, lol.
THERE ARE REALLY THAT MANY PEOPLE IN NEED OF SERVICES LIKE THAT?
JOSINA, WHEN YOU'VE SEEN AND DEALT WITH THE MOUNTAINS OF MAJOR WEIRDNESS THAT WE HAVE...
...YOU KNOW THERE'S A HUGE AND DESPERATE NEED!
CARAMEL CRUNCH POPCORN?
SWEET.
gawd:

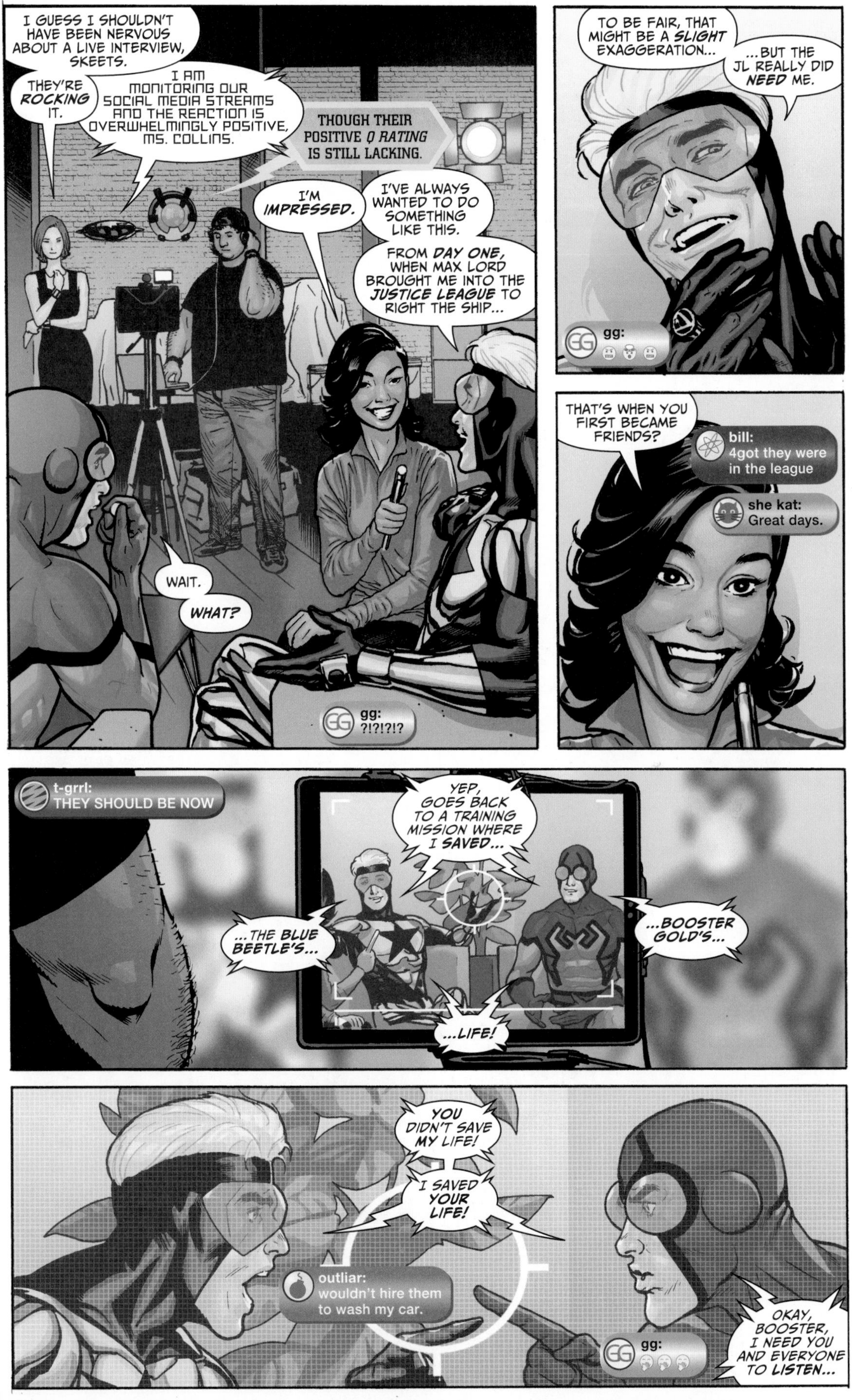
I GUESS I SHOULDN'T HAVE BEEN NERVOUS ABOUT A LIVE INTERVIEW, SKEETS.
THEY'RE ROCKING IT.
I AM MONITORING OUR SOCIAL MEDIA STREAMS AND THE REACTION IS OVERWHELMINGLY POSITIVE, MS. COLLINS.
THOUGH THEIR POSITIVE Q RATING IS STILL LACKING.
I'M IMPRESSED.
I'VE ALWAYS WANTED TO DO SOMETHING LIKE THIS.
FROM DAY ONE, WHEN MAX LORD BROUGHT ME INTO THE JUSTICE LEAGUE TO RIGHT THE SHIP...
WAIT.
WHAT?
gg: ?!?!?!?
TO BE FAIR, THAT MIGHT BE A SLIGHT EXAGGERATION...
...BUT THE JL REALLY DID NEED ME.
gg:
THAT'S WHEN YOU FIRST BECAME FRIENDS?
bill: 4got they were in the league
she kat: Great days.
t-grrl: THEY SHOULD BE NOW
YEP, GOES BACK TO A TRAINING MISSION WHERE I SAVED...
...THE BLUE BEETLE'S...
...BOOSTER GOLD'S...
...LIFE!
YOU DIDN'T SAVE MY LIFE!
I SAVED YOUR LIFE!
outliar: wouldn't hire them to wash my car.
gg:
OKAY, BOOSTER, I NEED YOU AND EVERYONE TO LISTEN...

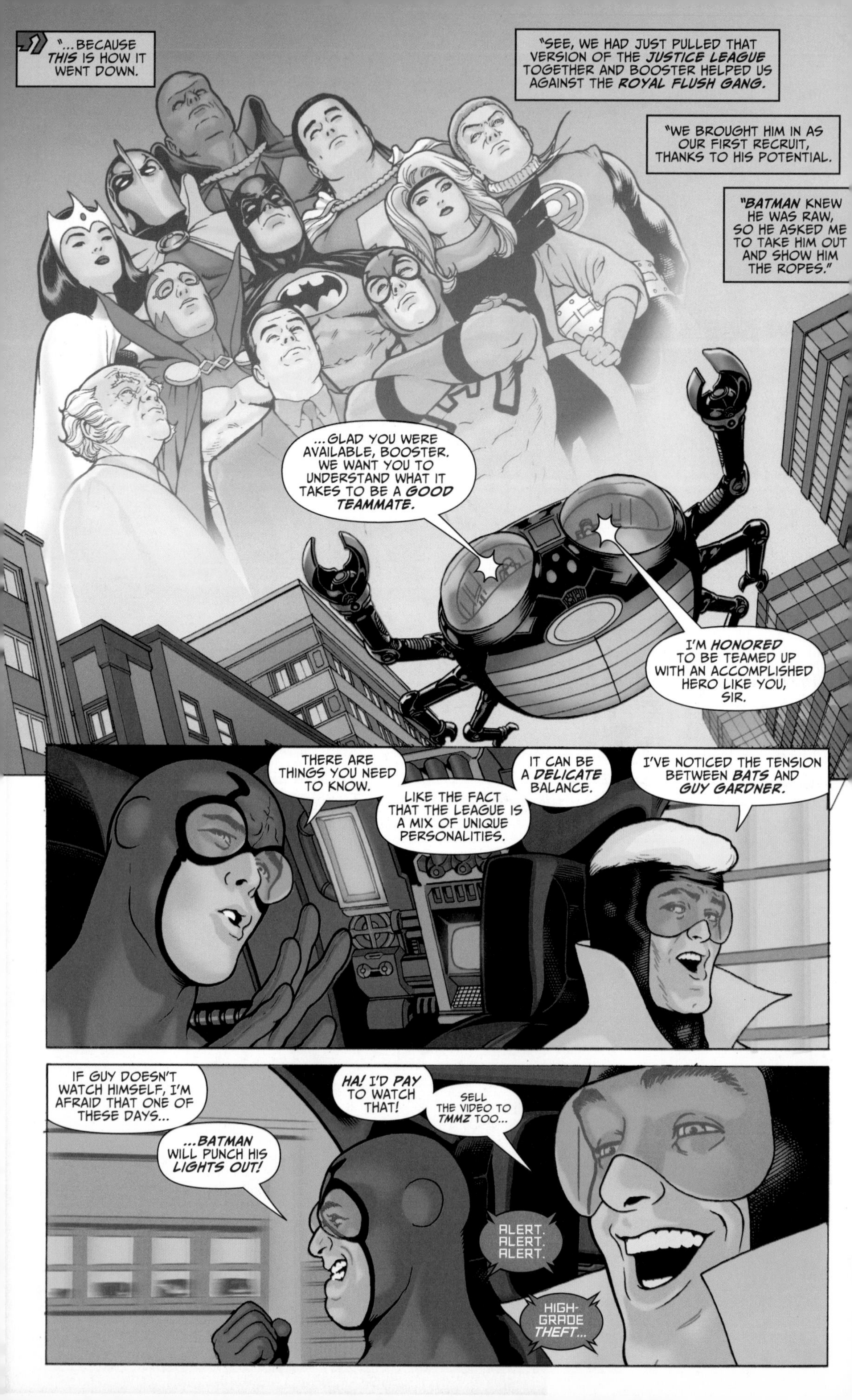
"...BECAUSE THIS IS HOW IT WENT DOWN.
"SEE, WE HAD JUST PULLED THAT VERSION OF THE JUSTICE LEAGUE TOGETHER AND BOOSTER HELPED US AGAINST THE ROYAL FLUSH GANG.
"WE BROUGHT HIM IN AS OUR FIRST RECRUIT, THANKS TO HIS POTENTIAL.
"BATMAN KNEW HE WAS RAW, SO HE ASKED ME TO TAKE HIM OUT AND SHOW HIM THE ROPES."
...GLAD YOU WERE AVAILABLE, BOOSTER. WE WANT YOU TO UNDERSTAND WHAT IT TAKES TO BE A GOOD TEAMMATE.
I'M HONORED TO BE TEAMED UP WITH AN ACCOMPLISHED HERO LIKE YOU, SIR.
THERE ARE THINGS YOU NEED TO KNOW.
LIKE THE FACT THAT THE LEAGUE IS A MIX OF UNIQUE PERSONALITIES.
IT CAN BE A DELICATE BALANCE.
I'VE NOTICED THE TENSION BETWEEN BATS AND GUY GARDNER.
IF GUY DOESN'T WATCH HIMSELF, I'M AFRAID THAT ONE OF THESE DAYS...
...BATMAN WILL PUNCH HIS LIGHTS OUT!
HA! I'D PAY TO WATCH THAT!
SELL THE VIDEO TO TMMZ TOO...
ALERT. ALERT. ALERT.
HIGH-GRADE THEFT...

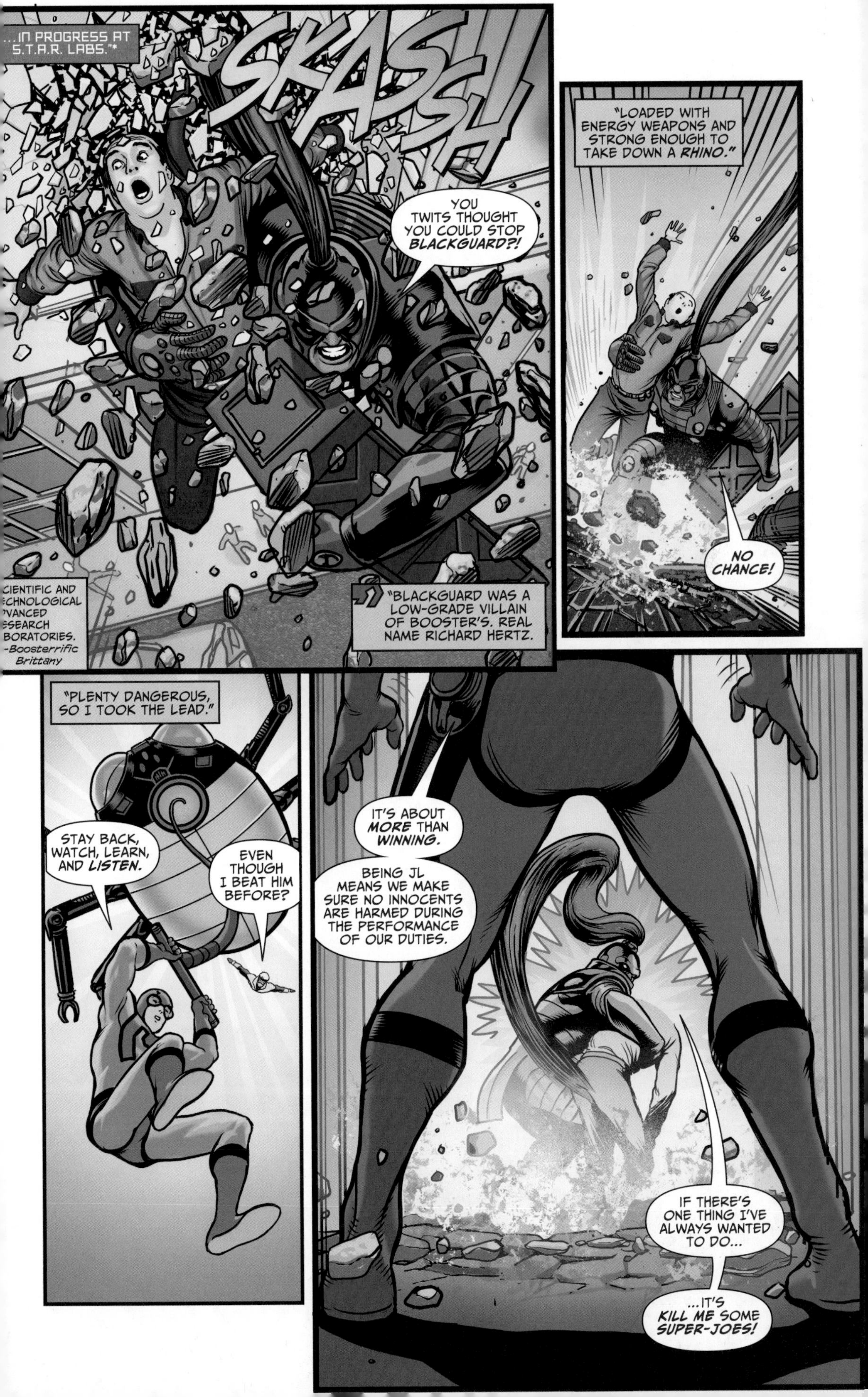
...IN PROGRESS AT S.T.A.R. LABS."*
SKASH
YOU TWITS THOUGHT YOU COULD STOP BLACKGUARD?!
CIENTIFIC AND ECHNOLOGICAL DVANCED ESEARCH BORATORIES. –Boosterrific Brittany
"BLACKGUARD WAS A LOW-GRADE VILLAIN OF BOOSTER'S. REAL NAME RICHARD HERTZ.
"LOADED WITH ENERGY WEAPONS AND STRONG ENOUGH TO TAKE DOWN A RHINO."
NO CHANCE!
"PLENTY DANGEROUS, SO I TOOK THE LEAD."
STAY BACK, WATCH, LEARN, AND LISTEN.
EVEN THOUGH I BEAT HIM BEFORE?
IT'S ABOUT MORE THAN WINNING.
BEING JL MEANS WE MAKE SURE NO INNOCENTS ARE HARMED DURING THE PERFORMANCE OF OUR DUTIES.
IF THERE'S ONE THING I'VE ALWAYS WANTED TO DO...
...IT'S KILL ME SOME SUPER-JOES!

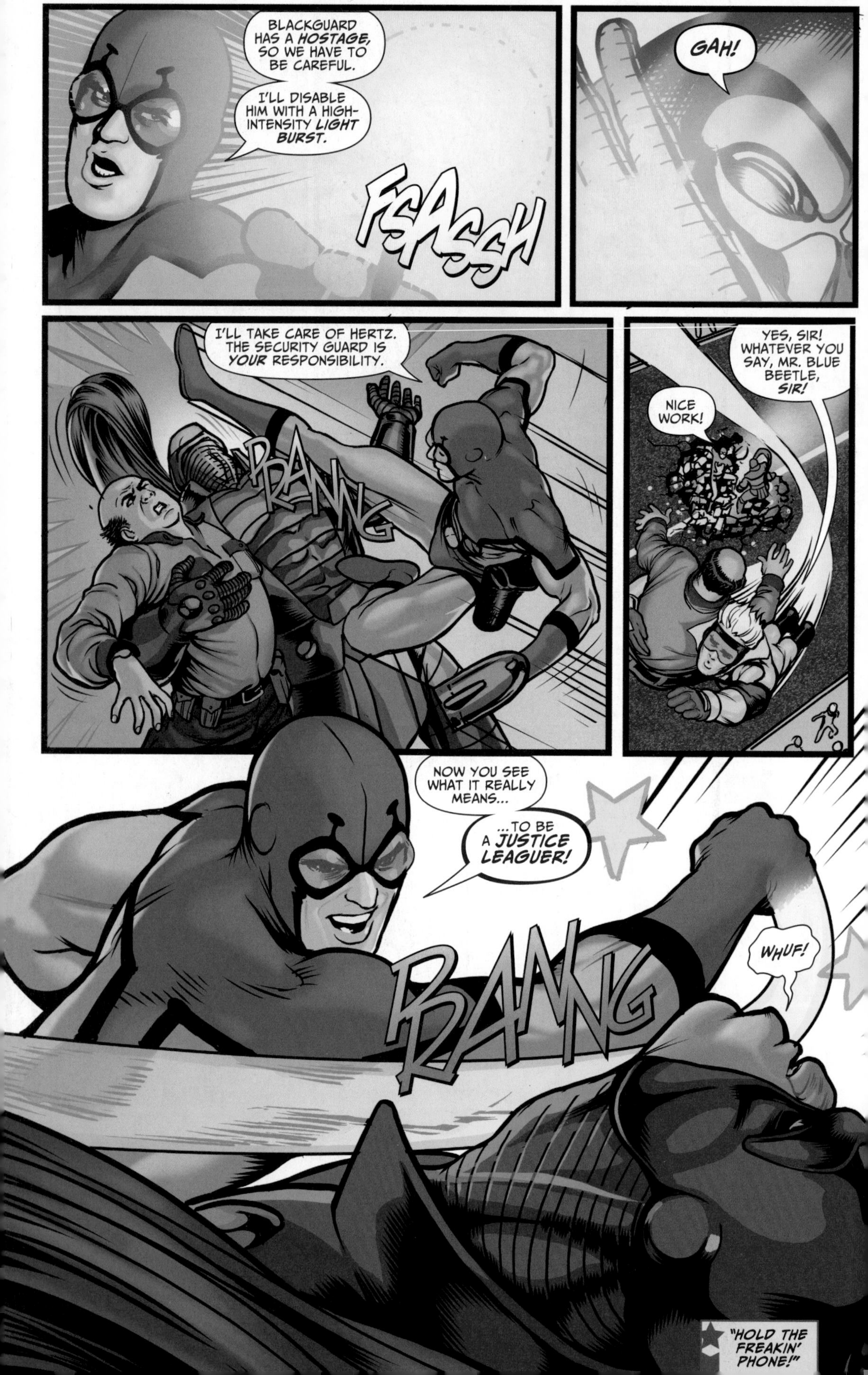
BLACKGUARD HAS A HOSTAGE, SO WE HAVE TO BE CAREFUL.
I'LL DISABLE HIM WITH A HIGH-INTENSITY LIGHT BURST.
FSASSH
GAH!
I'LL TAKE CARE OF HERTZ. THE SECURITY GUARD IS YOUR RESPONSIBILITY.
BRANNG
YES, SIR! WHATEVER YOU SAY, MR. BLUE BEETLE, SIR!
NICE WORK!
NOW YOU SEE WHAT IT REALLY MEANS...
...TO BE A JUSTICE LEAGUER!
BRANNG
WHUF!
"HOLD THE FREAKIN' PHONE!"

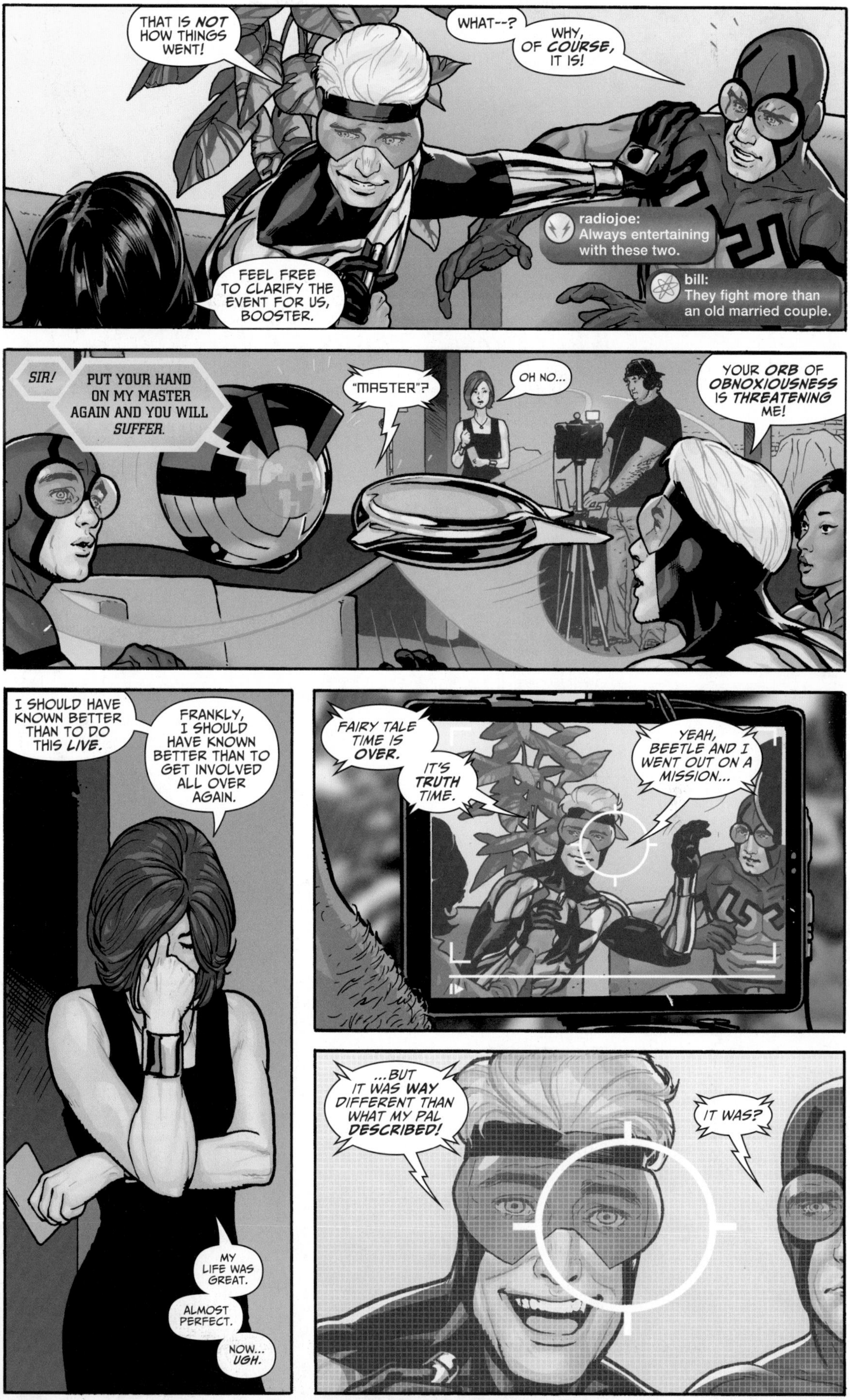
THAT IS NOT HOW THINGS WENT!
WHAT--?
WHY, OF COURSE, IT IS!
radiojoe:
Always entertaining with these two.
FEEL FREE TO CLARIFY THE EVENT FOR US, BOOSTER.
bill:
They fight more than an old married couple.
SIR!
PUT YOUR HAND ON MY MASTER AGAIN AND YOU WILL SUFFER.
"MASTER"?
OH NO...
YOUR ORB OF OBNOXIOUSNESS IS THREATENING ME!
I SHOULD HAVE KNOWN BETTER THAN TO DO THIS LIVE.
FRANKLY, I SHOULD HAVE KNOWN BETTER THAN TO GET INVOLVED ALL OVER AGAIN.
MY LIFE WAS GREAT.
ALMOST PERFECT.
NOW... UGH.
FAIRY TALE TIME IS OVER.
IT'S TRUTH TIME.
YEAH, BEETLE AND I WENT OUT ON A MISSION...
...BUT IT WAS WAY DIFFERENT THAN WHAT MY PAL DESCRIBED!
IT WAS?

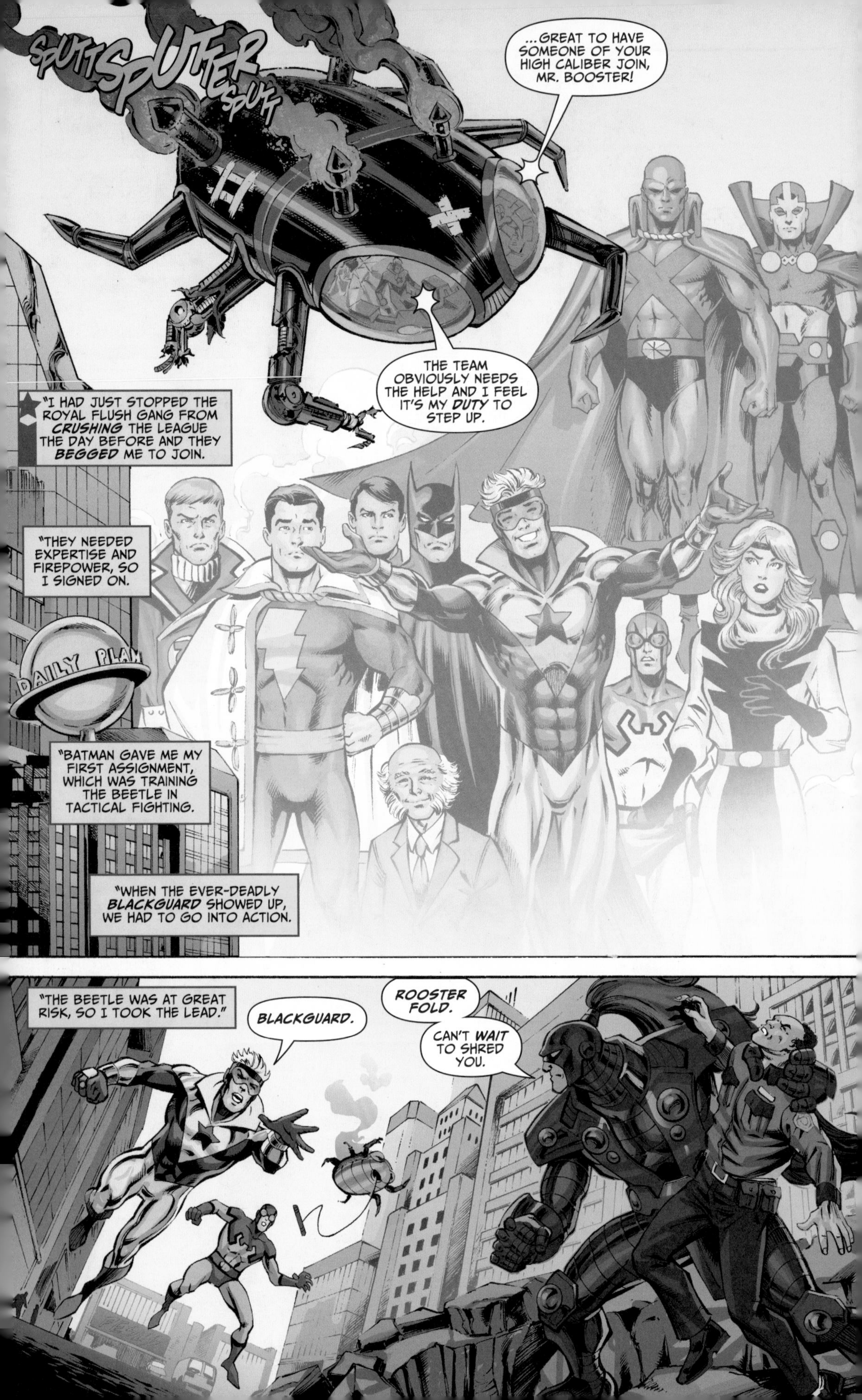

SPUTT SPUTTER SPUTT
...GREAT TO HAVE SOMEONE OF YOUR HIGH CALIBER JOIN, MR. BOOSTER!
THE TEAM OBVIOUSLY NEEDS THE HELP AND I FEEL IT'S MY DUTY TO STEP UP.
"I HAD JUST STOPPED THE ROYAL FLUSH GANG FROM CRUSHING THE LEAGUE THE DAY BEFORE AND THEY BEGGED ME TO JOIN.
"THEY NEEDED EXPERTISE AND FIREPOWER, SO I SIGNED ON.
DAILY PLAN
"BATMAN GAVE ME MY FIRST ASSIGNMENT, WHICH WAS TRAINING THE BEETLE IN TACTICAL FIGHTING.
"WHEN THE EVER-DEADLY BLACKGUARD SHOWED UP, WE HAD TO GO INTO ACTION.
"THE BEETLE WAS AT GREAT RISK, SO I TOOK THE LEAD."
BLACKGUARD.
ROOSTER FOLD.
CAN'T WAIT TO SHRED YOU.

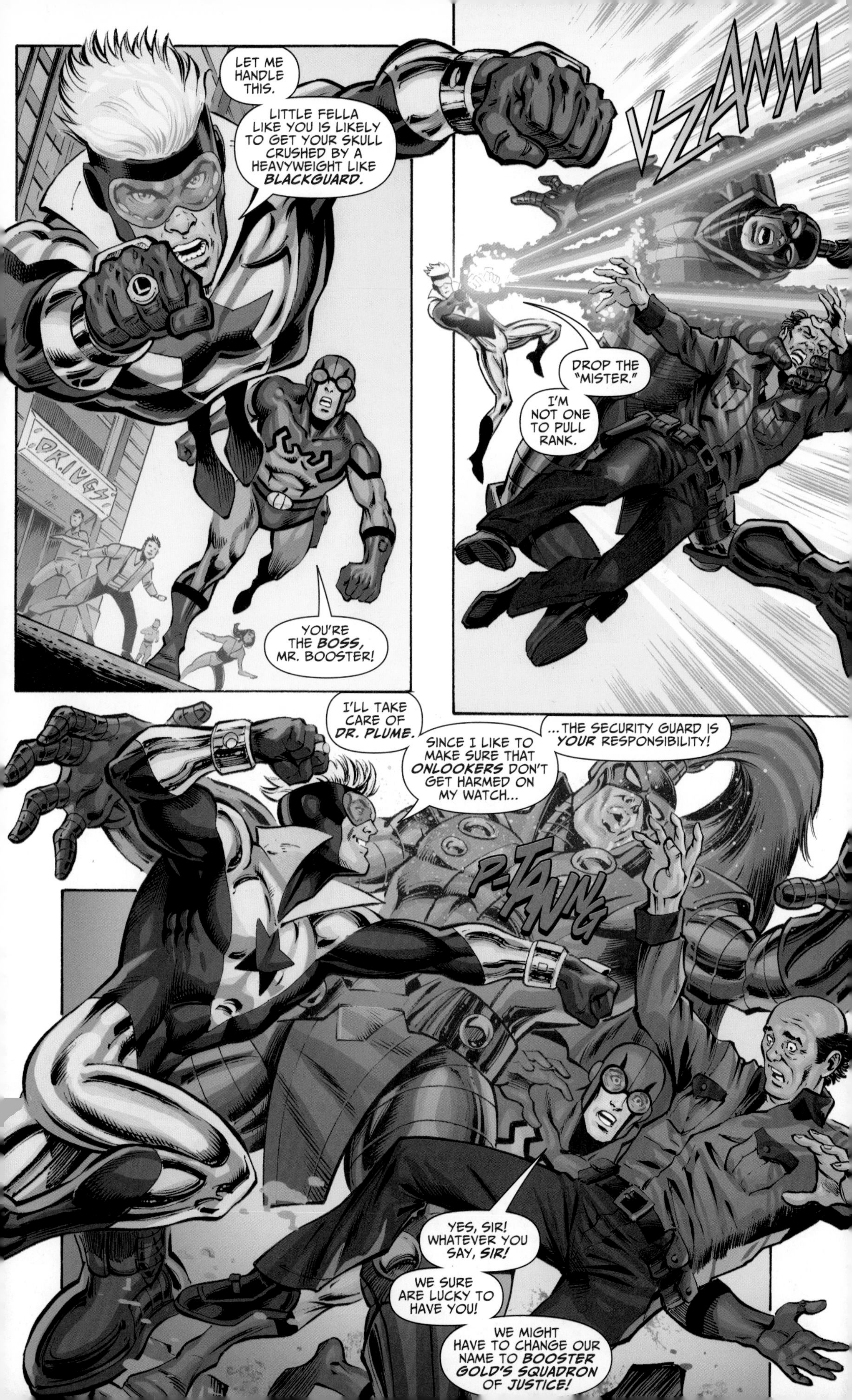
LET ME HANDLE THIS.
LITTLE FELLA LIKE YOU IS LIKELY TO GET YOUR SKULL CRUSHED BY A HEAVYWEIGHT LIKE ***BLACKGUARD.***
DRUGS
YOU'RE THE ***BOSS***, MR. BOOSTER!
V-ZZAMM
DROP THE "MISTER."
I'M NOT ONE TO PULL RANK.
I'LL TAKE CARE OF ***DR. PLUME.***
SINCE I LIKE TO MAKE SURE THAT ***ONLOOKERS*** DON'T GET HARMED ON MY WATCH...
...THE SECURITY GUARD IS ***YOUR*** RESPONSIBILITY!
P-TANNG
YES, SIR! WHATEVER YOU SAY, ***SIR!***
WE SURE ARE LUCKY TO HAVE YOU!
WE MIGHT HAVE TO CHANGE OUR NAME TO ***BOOSTER GOLD'S SQUADRON OF JUSTICE!***

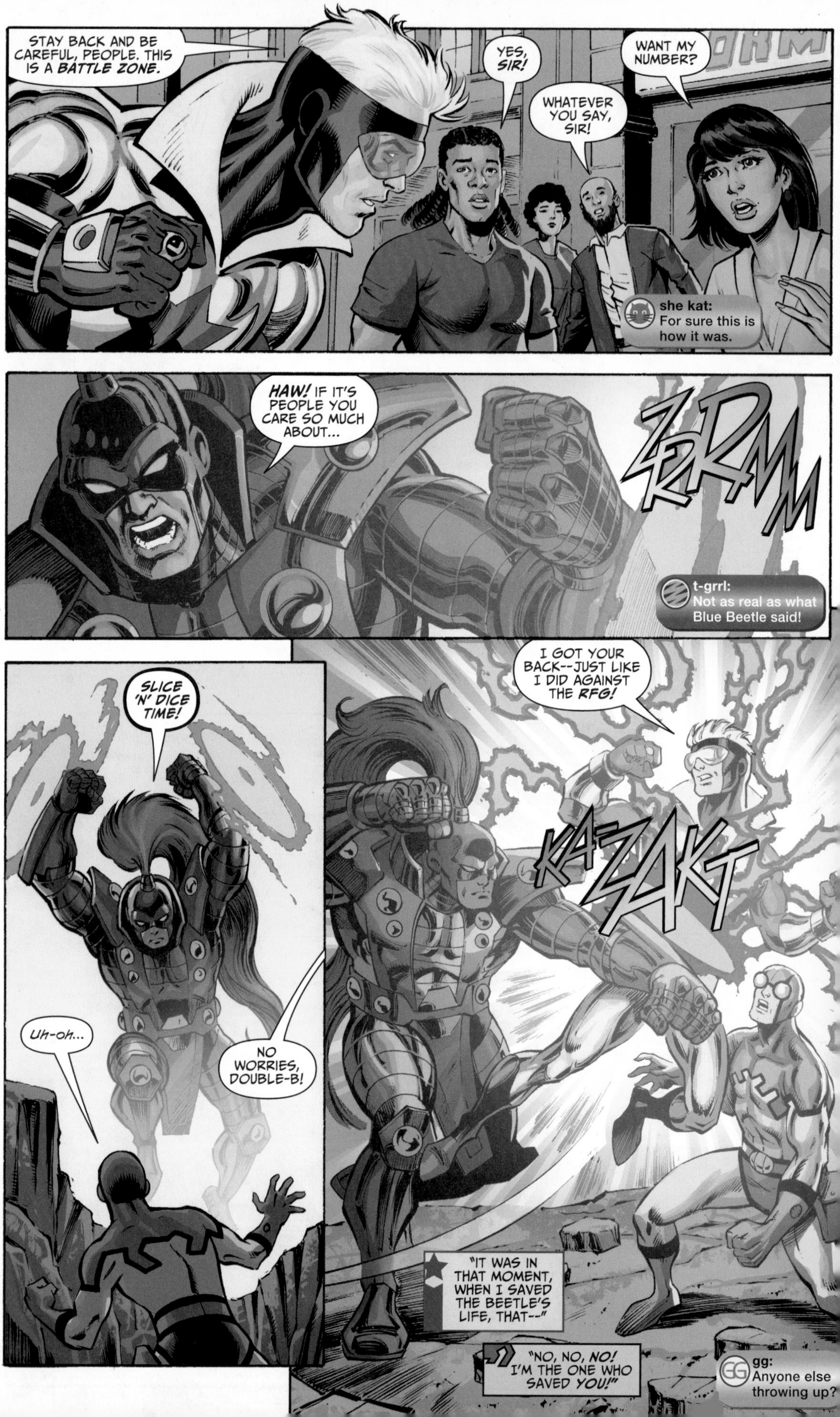
STAY BACK AND BE CAREFUL, PEOPLE. THIS IS A BATTLE ZONE.
YES, SIR!
WANT MY NUMBER?
WHATEVER YOU SAY, SIR!
she kat:
For sure this is how it was.
HAW! IF IT'S PEOPLE YOU CARE SO MUCH ABOUT...
ZZRRMMM
t-grrl:
Not as real as what Blue Beetle said!
SLICE 'N' DICE TIME!
Uh-oh...
NO WORRIES, DOUBLE-B!
I GOT YOUR BACK--JUST LIKE I DID AGAINST THE RFG!
KAZAKT
"IT WAS IN THAT MOMENT, WHEN I SAVED THE BEETLE'S LIFE, THAT--"
"NO, NO, NO! I'M THE ONE WHO SAVED YOU!"
gg:
Anyone else throwing up?

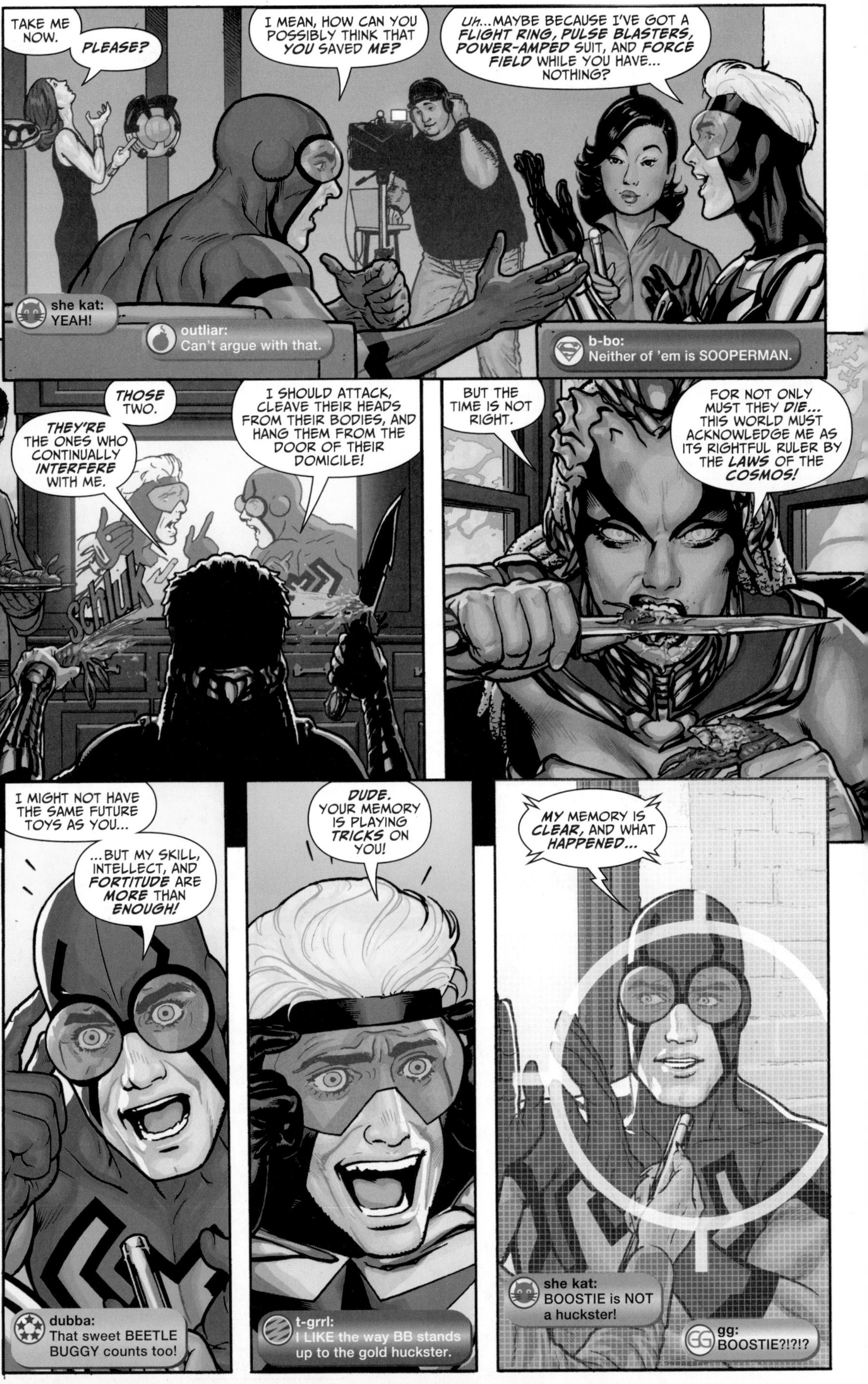

TAKE ME NOW.
PLEASE?
I MEAN, HOW CAN YOU POSSIBLY THINK THAT YOU SAVED ME?
UH...MAYBE BECAUSE I'VE GOT A FLIGHT RING, PULSE BLASTERS, POWER-AMPED SUIT, AND FORCE FIELD WHILE YOU HAVE... NOTHING?
she kat: YEAH!
outliar: Can't argue with that.
b-bo: Neither of 'em is SOOPERMAN.
THOSE TWO.
THEY'RE THE ONES WHO CONTINUALLY INTERFERE WITH ME.
I SHOULD ATTACK, CLEAVE THEIR HEADS FROM THEIR BODIES, AND HANG THEM FROM THE DOOR OF THEIR DOMICILE!
SCHLUK
BUT THE TIME IS NOT RIGHT.
FOR NOT ONLY MUST THEY DIE... THIS WORLD MUST ACKNOWLEDGE ME AS ITS RIGHTFUL RULER BY THE LAWS OF THE COSMOS!
I MIGHT NOT HAVE THE SAME FUTURE TOYS AS YOU...
...BUT MY SKILL, INTELLECT, AND FORTITUDE ARE MORE THAN ENOUGH!
dubba: That sweet BEETLE BUGGY counts too!
DUDE. YOUR MEMORY IS PLAYING TRICKS ON YOU!
t-grrl: I LIKE the way BB stands up to the gold huckster.
MY MEMORY IS CLEAR, AND WHAT HAPPENED...
she kat: BOOSTIE is NOT a huckster!
gg: BOOSTIE?!?!?

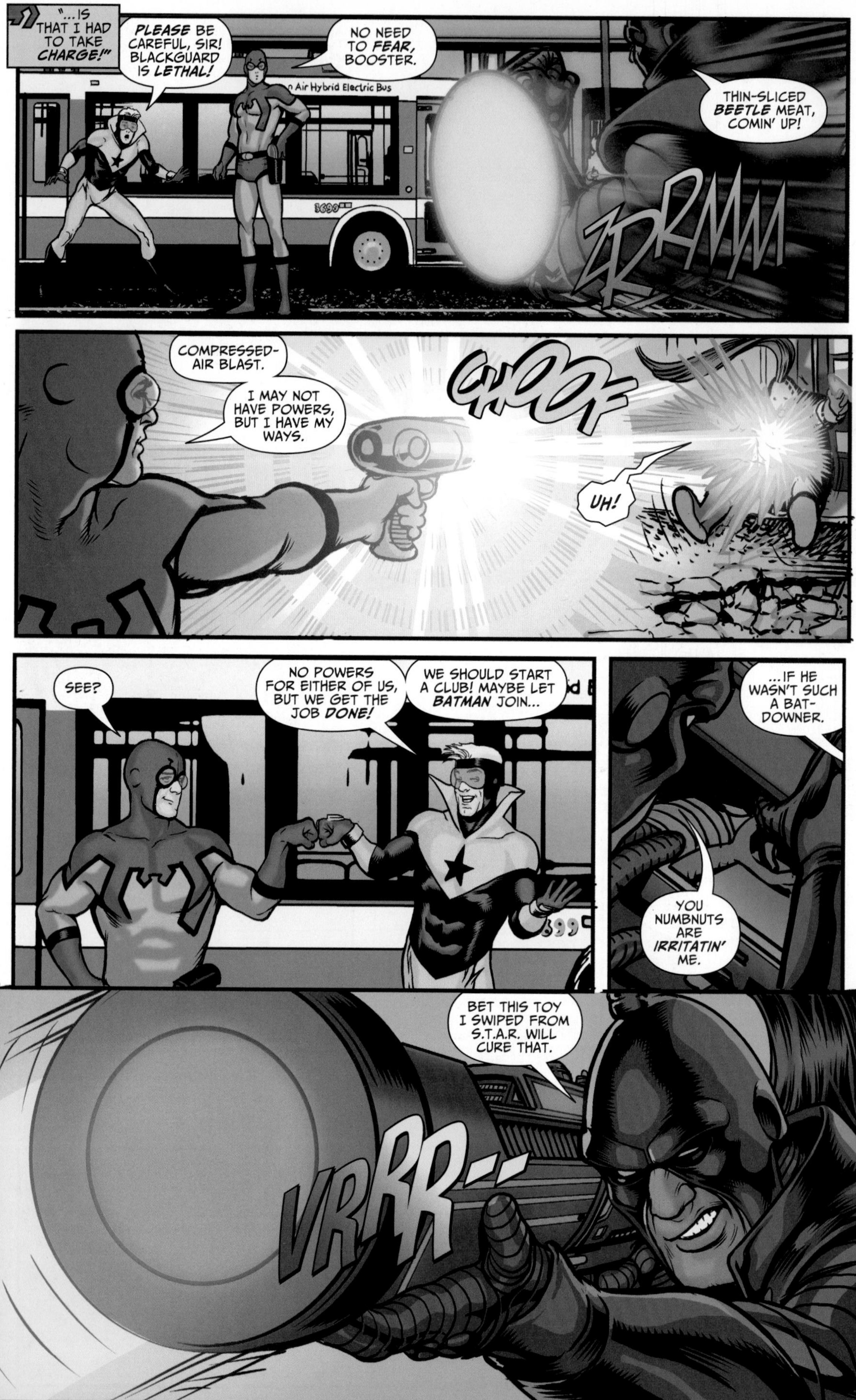
"...IS THAT I HAD TO TAKE CHARGE!"
PLEASE BE CAREFUL, SIR! BLACKGUARD IS LETHAL!
NO NEED TO FEAR, BOOSTER.
THIN-SLICED BEETLE MEAT, COMIN' UP!
ZZRMMM
COMPRESSED-AIR BLAST.
I MAY NOT HAVE POWERS, BUT I HAVE MY WAYS.
CHOOOF
UH!
SEE?
NO POWERS FOR EITHER OF US, BUT WE GET THE JOB DONE!
WE SHOULD START A CLUB! MAYBE LET BATMAN JOIN...
...IF HE WASN'T SUCH A BAT-DOWNER.
YOU NUMBNUTS ARE IRRITATIN' ME.
BET THIS TOY I SWIPED FROM S.T.A.R. WILL CURE THAT.
VRRR--

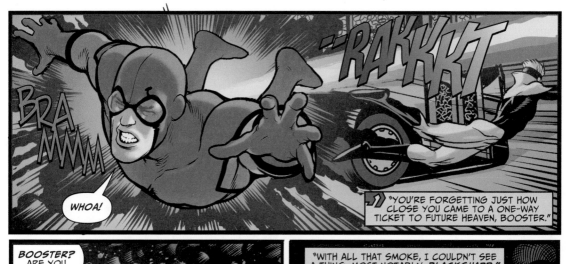

BRAMMM

--RAKKKT

WHOA!

"YOU'RE FORGETTING JUST HOW CLOSE YOU CAME TO A ONE-WAY TICKET TO FUTURE HEAVEN, BOOSTER."

BOOSTER? ARE YOU OKAY?

"WITH ALL THAT SMOKE, I COULDN'T SEE A THING. MOST NOTABLY, BLACKGUARD."

BOOSTER?

CHAK

HAW!

BEETLE? WAS THAT YOU?

I'M FINE, BUT I CAN'T SEE--

BOOSTER.

Erp.

DUMB NAME.

HOW 'BOUT HEADLESS NUTCASE?

ZRRM

"AGAIN, THE BLUE BEETLE'S MEMORY IS FAULTY!"

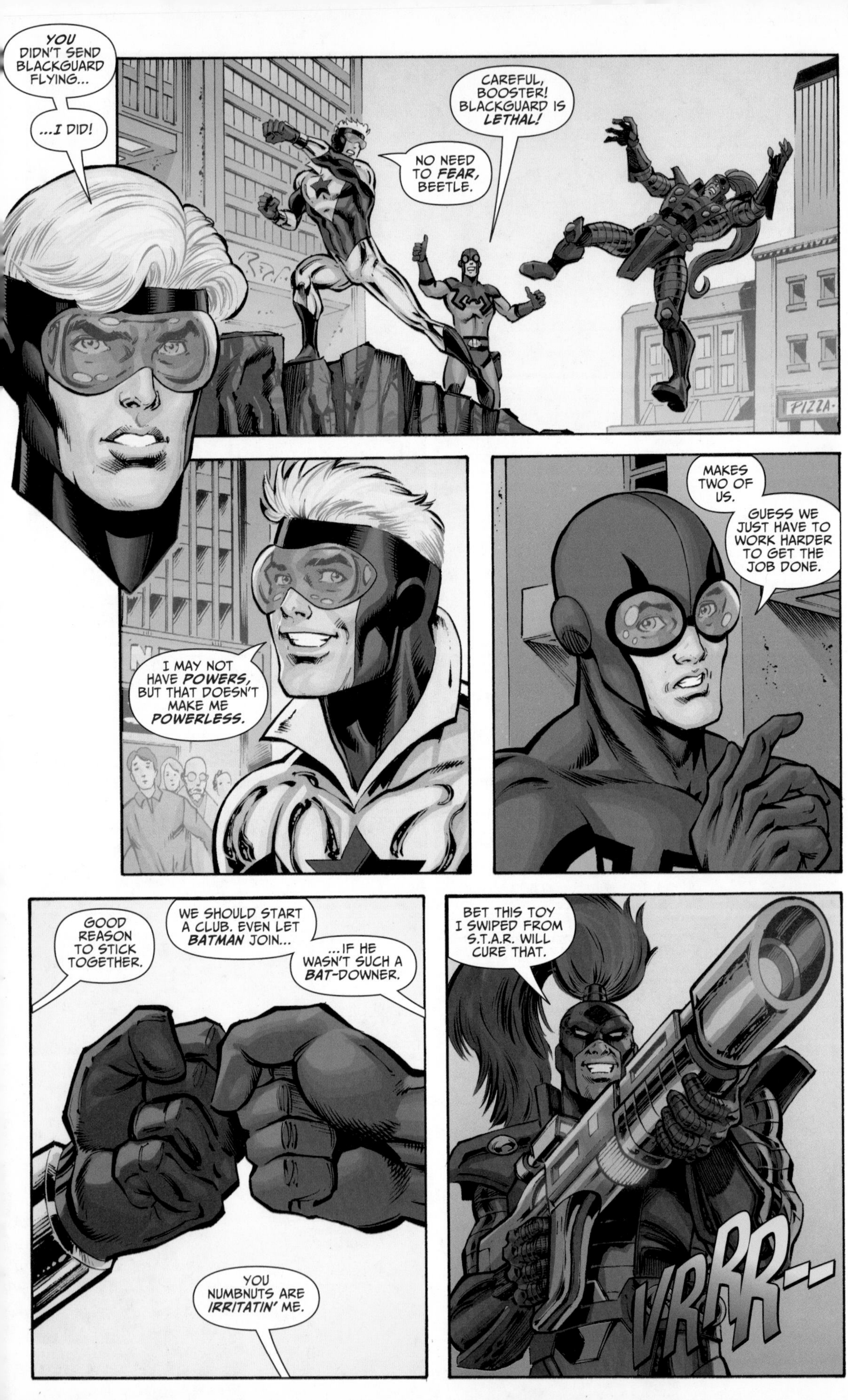
YOU DIDN'T SEND BLACKGUARD FLYING...
...I DID!
NO NEED TO FEAR, BEETLE.
CAREFUL, BOOSTER! BLACKGUARD IS LETHAL!
PIZZA
I MAY NOT HAVE POWERS, BUT THAT DOESN'T MAKE ME POWERLESS.
MAKES TWO OF US.
GUESS WE JUST HAVE TO WORK HARDER TO GET THE JOB DONE.
GOOD REASON TO STICK TOGETHER.
WE SHOULD START A CLUB. EVEN LET BATMAN JOIN...
...IF HE WASN'T SUCH A BAT-DOWNER.
YOU NUMBNUTS ARE IRRITATIN' ME.
BET THIS TOY I SWIPED FROM S.T.A.R. WILL CURE THAT.
VRRR--

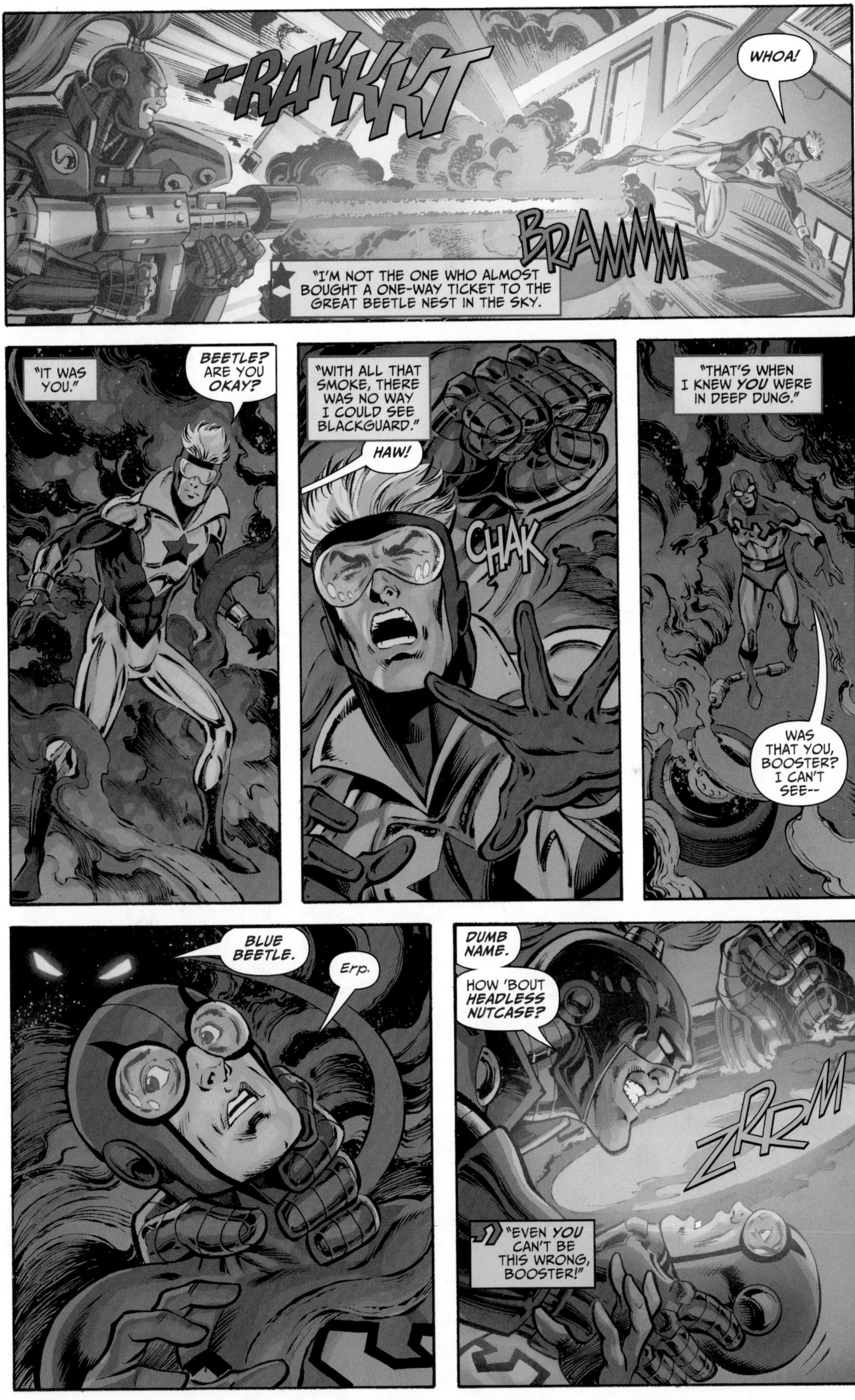

--RAKKKKT
WHOA!
BRAMMMM
"I'M NOT THE ONE WHO ALMOST BOUGHT A ONE-WAY TICKET TO THE GREAT BEETLE NEST IN THE SKY.
"IT WAS YOU."
BEETLE? ARE YOU OKAY?
"WITH ALL THAT SMOKE, THERE WAS NO WAY I COULD SEE BLACKGUARD."
HAW!
CHAK
"THAT'S WHEN I KNEW YOU WERE IN DEEP DUNG."
WAS THAT YOU, BOOSTER? I CAN'T SEE--
BLUE BEETLE.
Erp.
DUMB NAME.
HOW 'BOUT HEADLESS NUTCASE?
ZRRM
"EVEN YOU CAN'T BE THIS WRONG, BOOSTER!"

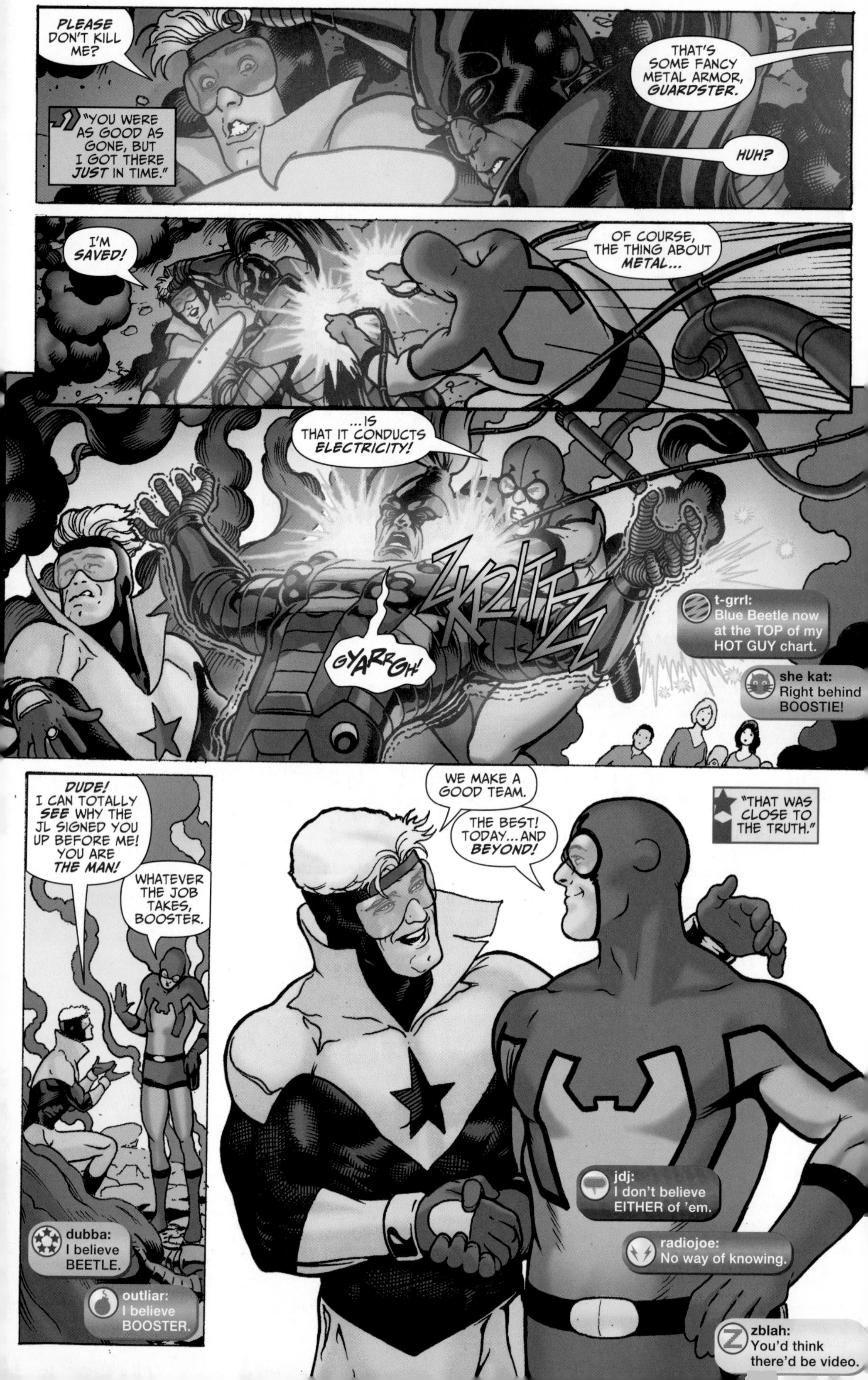
PLEASE DON'T KILL ME?
"YOU WERE AS GOOD AS GONE, BUT I GOT THERE JUST IN TIME."
THAT'S SOME FANCY METAL ARMOR, GUARDSTER.
HUH?
I'M SAVED!
OF COURSE, THE THING ABOUT METAL...
...IS THAT IT CONDUCTS ELECTRICITY!
ZKRITZZZ
GYARRGH!
t-grrl: Blue Beetle now at the TOP of my HOT GUY chart.
she kat: Right behind BOOSTIE!
DUDE! I CAN TOTALLY SEE WHY THE JL SIGNED YOU UP BEFORE ME! YOU ARE THE MAN!
WHATEVER THE JOB TAKES, BOOSTER.
dubba: I believe BEETLE.
outliar: I believe BOOSTER.
WE MAKE A GOOD TEAM.
THE BEST! TODAY...AND BEYOND!
"THAT WAS CLOSE TO THE TRUTH."
jdj: I don't believe EITHER of 'em.
radiojoe: No way of knowing.
zblah: You'd think there'd be video.

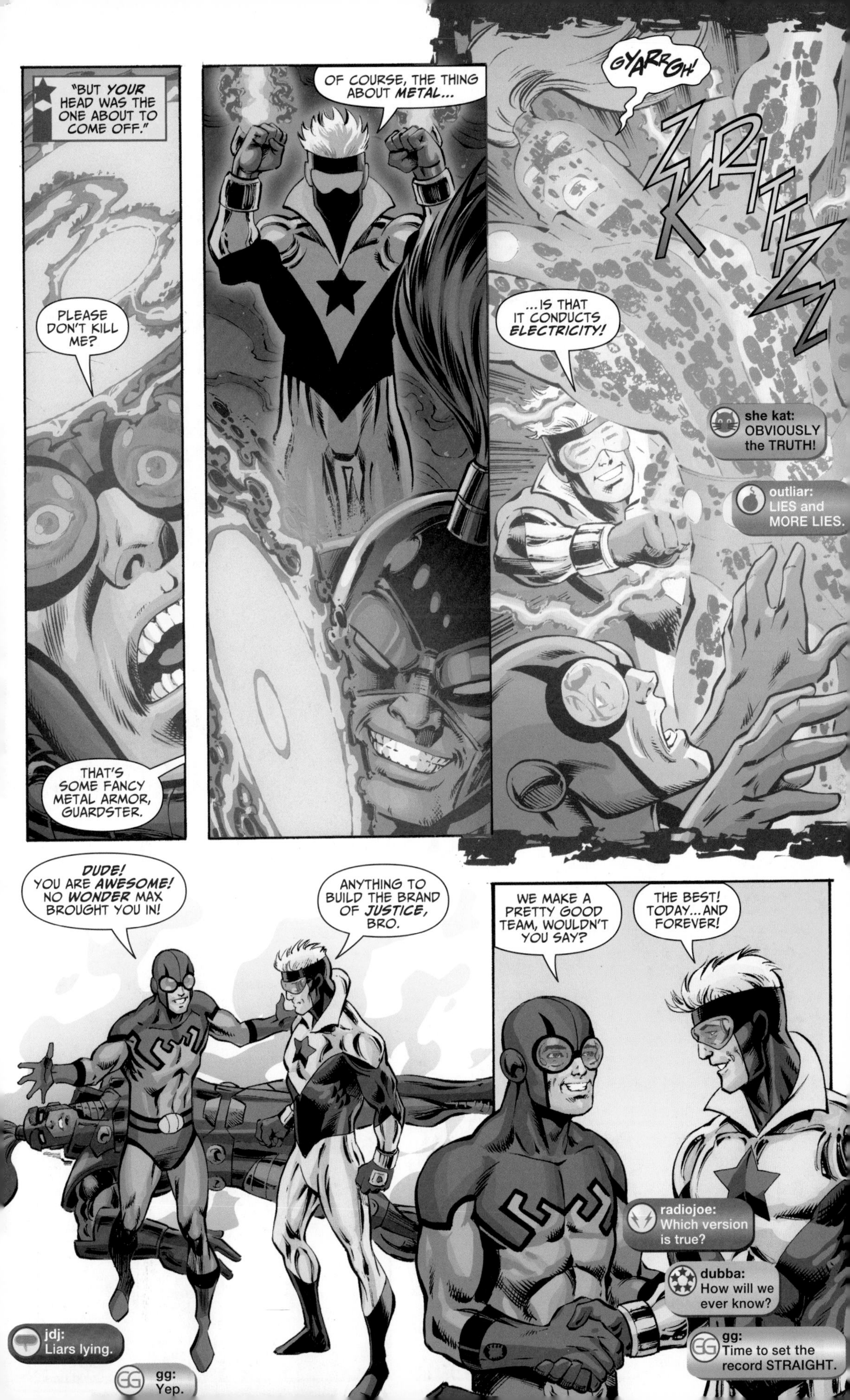

"BUT YOUR HEAD WAS THE ONE ABOUT TO COME OFF."
PLEASE DON'T KILL ME?
THAT'S SOME FANCY METAL ARMOR, GUARDSTER.
OF COURSE, THE THING ABOUT METAL...
GYARRGH!
ZZRRTTZZ
...IS THAT IT CONDUCTS ELECTRICITY!
she kat: OBVIOUSLY the TRUTH!
outliar: LIES and MORE LIES.
DUDE! YOU ARE AWESOME! NO WONDER MAX BROUGHT YOU IN!
ANYTHING TO BUILD THE BRAND OF JUSTICE, BRO.
WE MAKE A PRETTY GOOD TEAM, WOULDN'T YOU SAY?
THE BEST! TODAY...AND FOREVER!
radiojoe: Which version is true?
dubba: How will we ever know?
jdj: Liars lying.
gg: Yep.
gg: Time to set the record STRAIGHT.

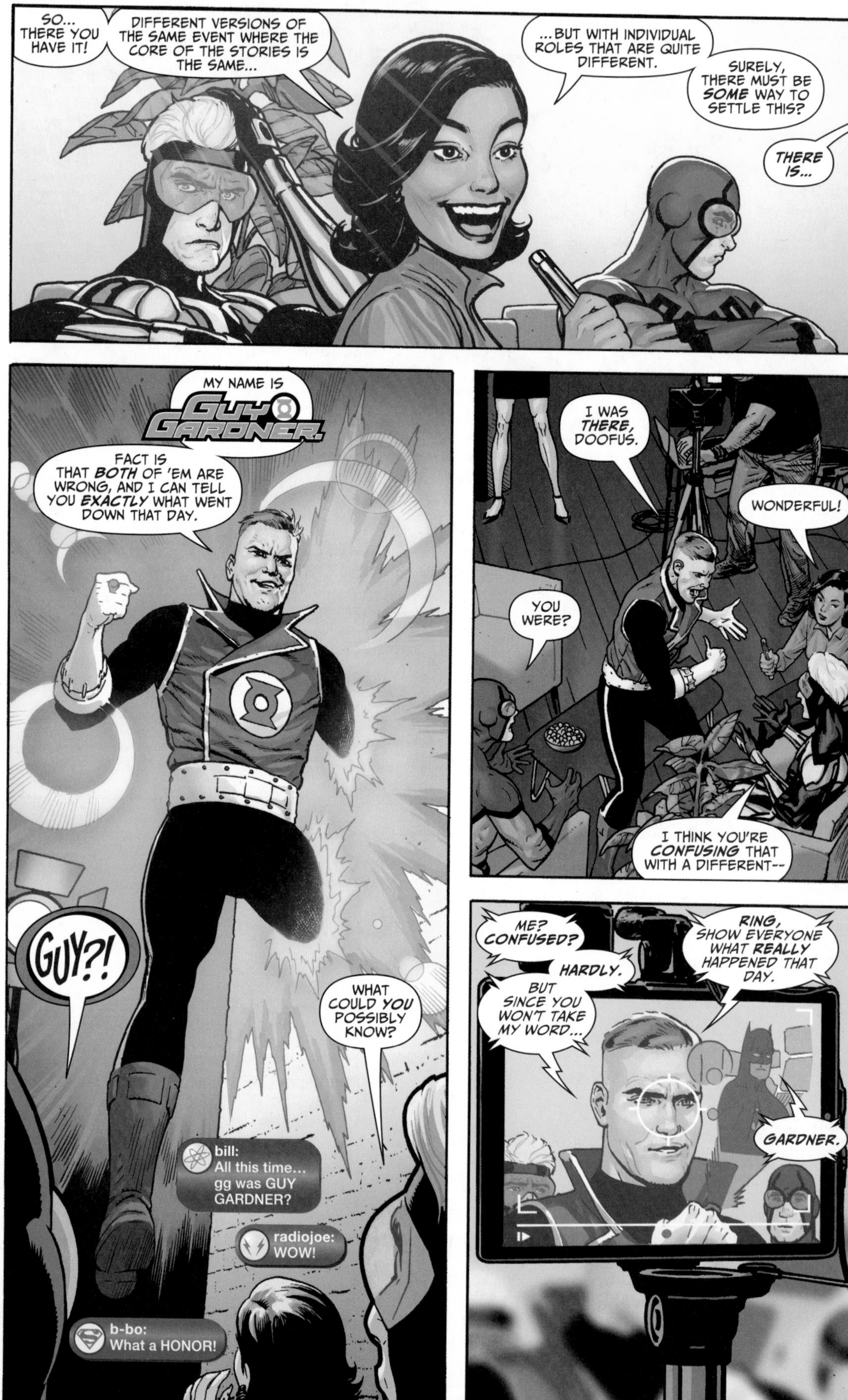
SO... THERE YOU HAVE IT!
DIFFERENT VERSIONS OF THE SAME EVENT WHERE THE CORE OF THE STORIES IS THE SAME...
...BUT WITH INDIVIDUAL ROLES THAT ARE QUITE DIFFERENT.
SURELY, THERE MUST BE SOME WAY TO SETTLE THIS?
THERE IS...
MY NAME IS
GUY GARDNER.
FACT IS THAT BOTH OF 'EM ARE WRONG, AND I CAN TELL YOU EXACTLY WHAT WENT DOWN THAT DAY.
GUY?!
WHAT COULD YOU POSSIBLY KNOW?
bill: All this time... gg was GUY GARDNER?
radiojoe: WOW!
b-bo: What a HONOR!
I WAS THERE, DOOFUS.
WONDERFUL!
YOU WERE?
I THINK YOU'RE CONFUSING THAT WITH A DIFFERENT--
ME? CONFUSED?
HARDLY.
BUT SINCE YOU WON'T TAKE MY WORD...
RING, SHOW EVERYONE WHAT REALLY HAPPENED THAT DAY.
GARDNER.

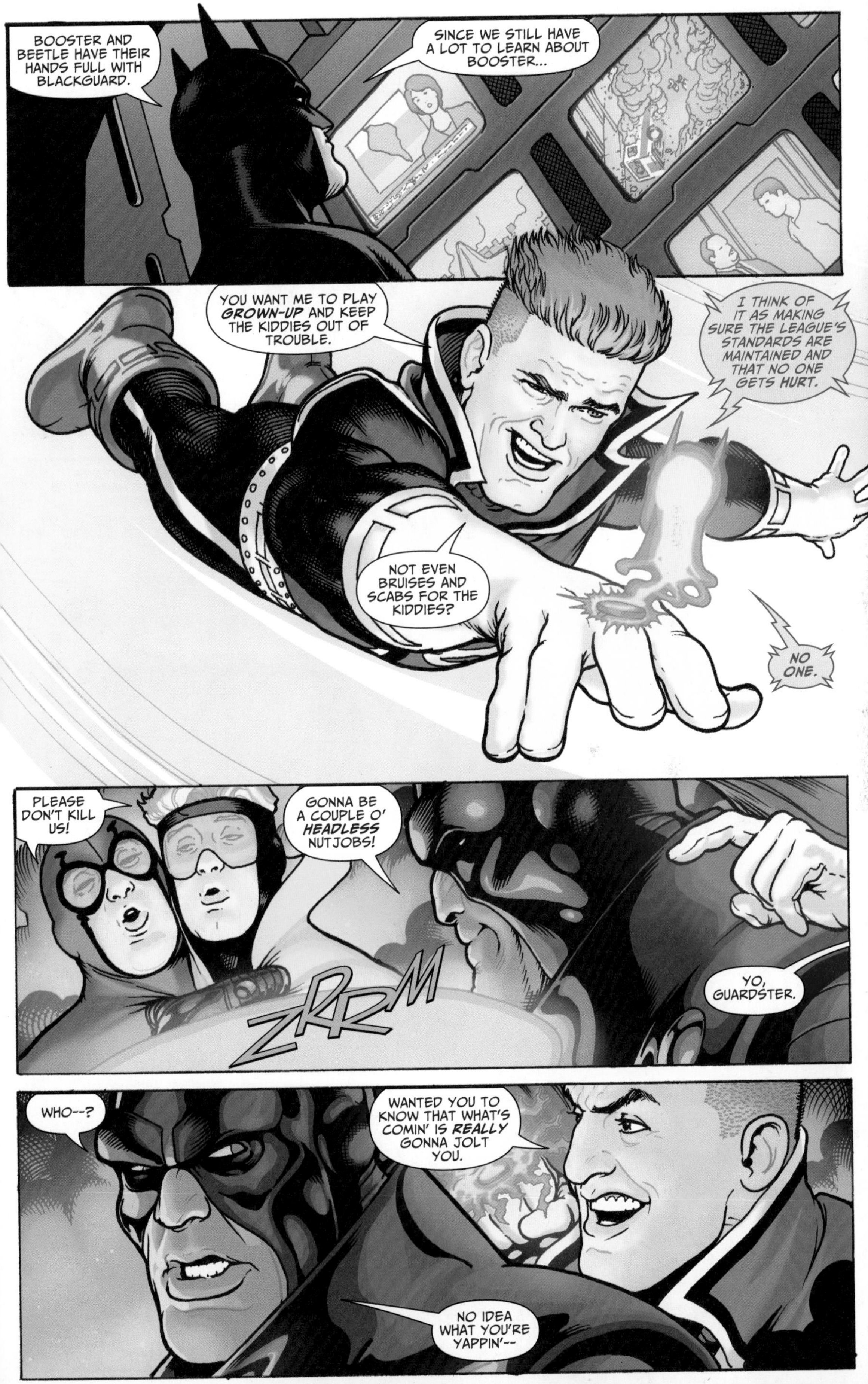
BOOSTER AND BEETLE HAVE THEIR HANDS FULL WITH BLACKGUARD.
SINCE WE STILL HAVE A LOT TO LEARN ABOUT BOOSTER...
YOU WANT ME TO PLAY GROWN-UP AND KEEP THE KIDDIES OUT OF TROUBLE.
I THINK OF IT AS MAKING SURE THE LEAGUE'S STANDARDS ARE MAINTAINED AND THAT NO ONE GETS HURT.
NOT EVEN BRUISES AND SCABS FOR THE KIDDIES?
NO ONE.
PLEASE DON'T KILL US!
GONNA BE A COUPLE O' HEADLESS NUTJOBS!
ZRRM
YO, GUARDSTER.
WHO--?
WANTED YOU TO KNOW THAT WHAT'S COMIN' IS REALLY GONNA JOLT YOU.
NO IDEA WHAT YOU'RE YAPPIN'--

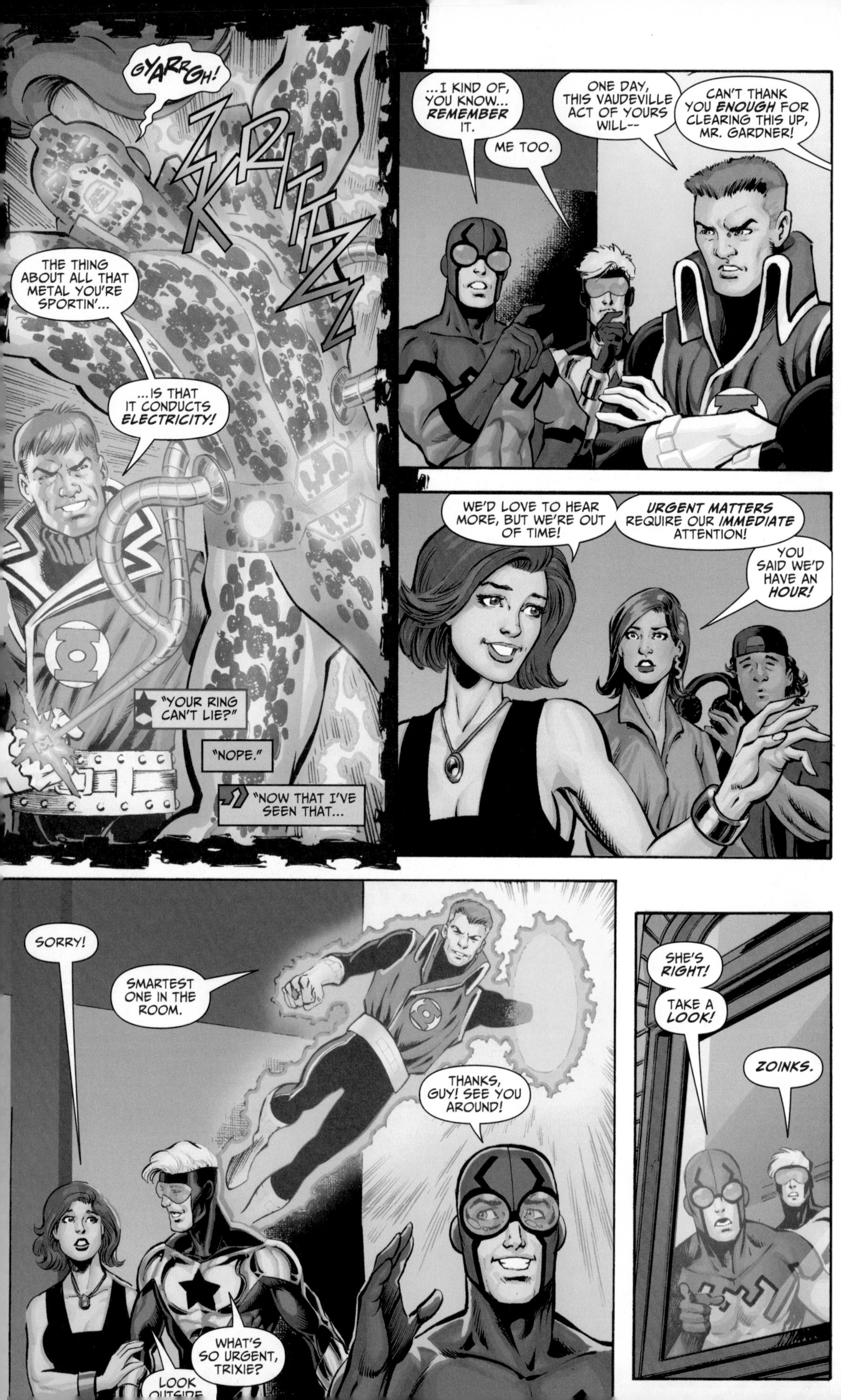

GYARRGH!
THE THING ABOUT ALL THAT METAL YOU'RE SPORTIN'...
...IS THAT IT CONDUCTS ELECTRICITY!
"YOUR RING CAN'T LIE?"
"NOPE."
"NOW THAT I'VE SEEN THAT...
...I KIND OF, YOU KNOW... REMEMBER IT.
ME TOO.
ONE DAY, THIS VAUDEVILLE ACT OF YOURS WILL--
CAN'T THANK YOU ENOUGH FOR CLEARING THIS UP, MR. GARDNER!
WE'D LOVE TO HEAR MORE, BUT WE'RE OUT OF TIME!
URGENT MATTERS REQUIRE OUR IMMEDIATE ATTENTION!
YOU SAID WE'D HAVE AN HOUR!
SORRY!
SMARTEST ONE IN THE ROOM.
THANKS, GUY! SEE YOU AROUND!
WHAT'S SO URGENT, TRIXIE?
LOOK
SHE'S RIGHT!
TAKE A LOOK!
ZOINKS.

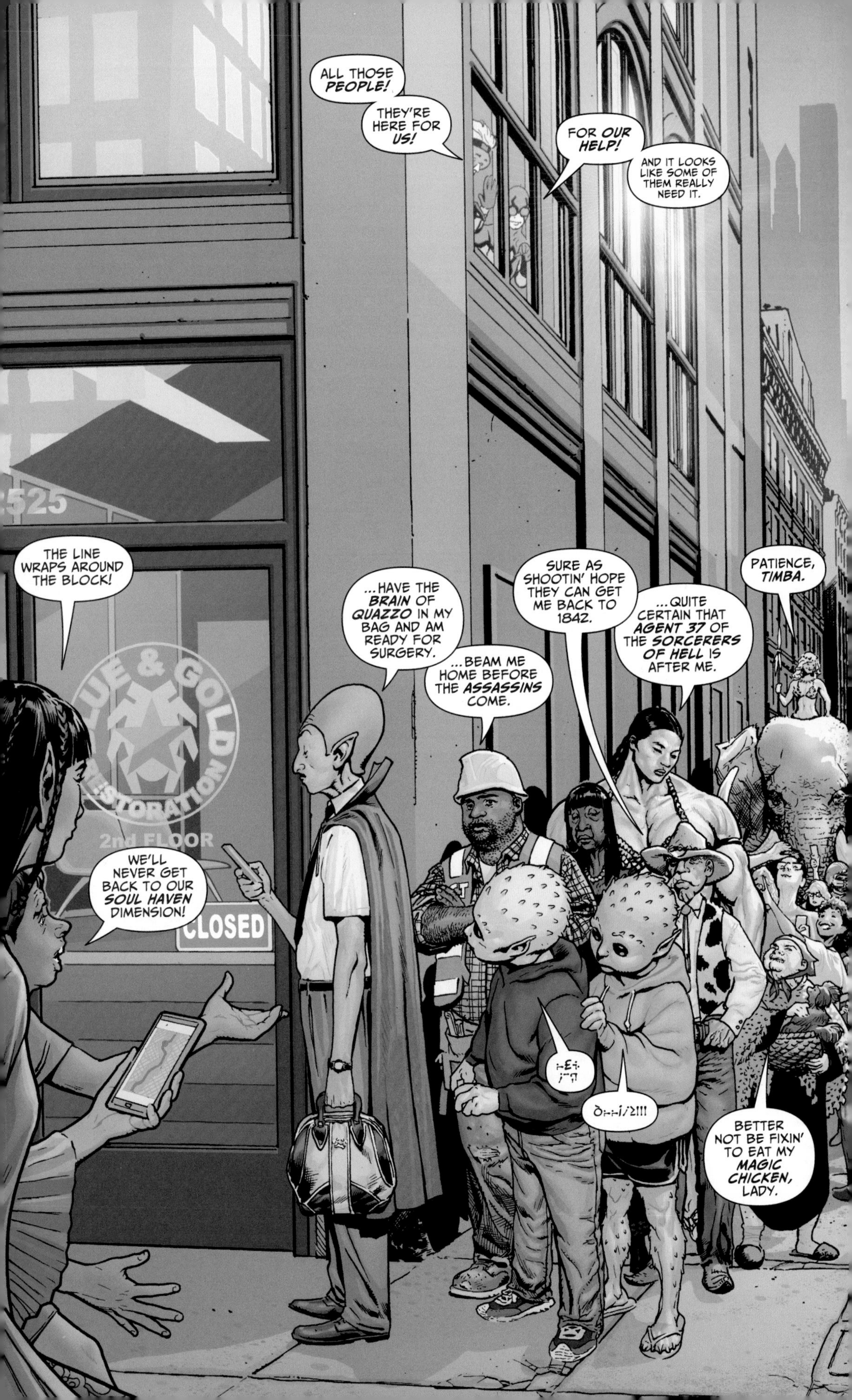

ALL THOSE PEOPLE!
THEY'RE HERE FOR US!
FOR OUR HELP!
AND IT LOOKS LIKE SOME OF THEM REALLY NEED IT.
525
THE LINE WRAPS AROUND THE BLOCK!
LUE & GOLD RESTORATION
2nd FLOOR
WE'LL NEVER GET BACK TO OUR SOUL HAVEN DIMENSION!
CLOSED
...HAVE THE BRAIN OF QUAZZO IN MY BAG AND AM READY FOR SURGERY.
...BEAM ME HOME BEFORE THE ASSASSINS COME.
SURE AS SHOOTIN' HOPE THEY CAN GET ME BACK TO 1842.
...QUITE CERTAIN THAT AGENT 37 OF THE SORCERERS OF HELL IS AFTER ME.
PATIENCE, TIMBA.
BETTER NOT BE FIXIN' TO EAT MY MAGIC CHICKEN, LADY.

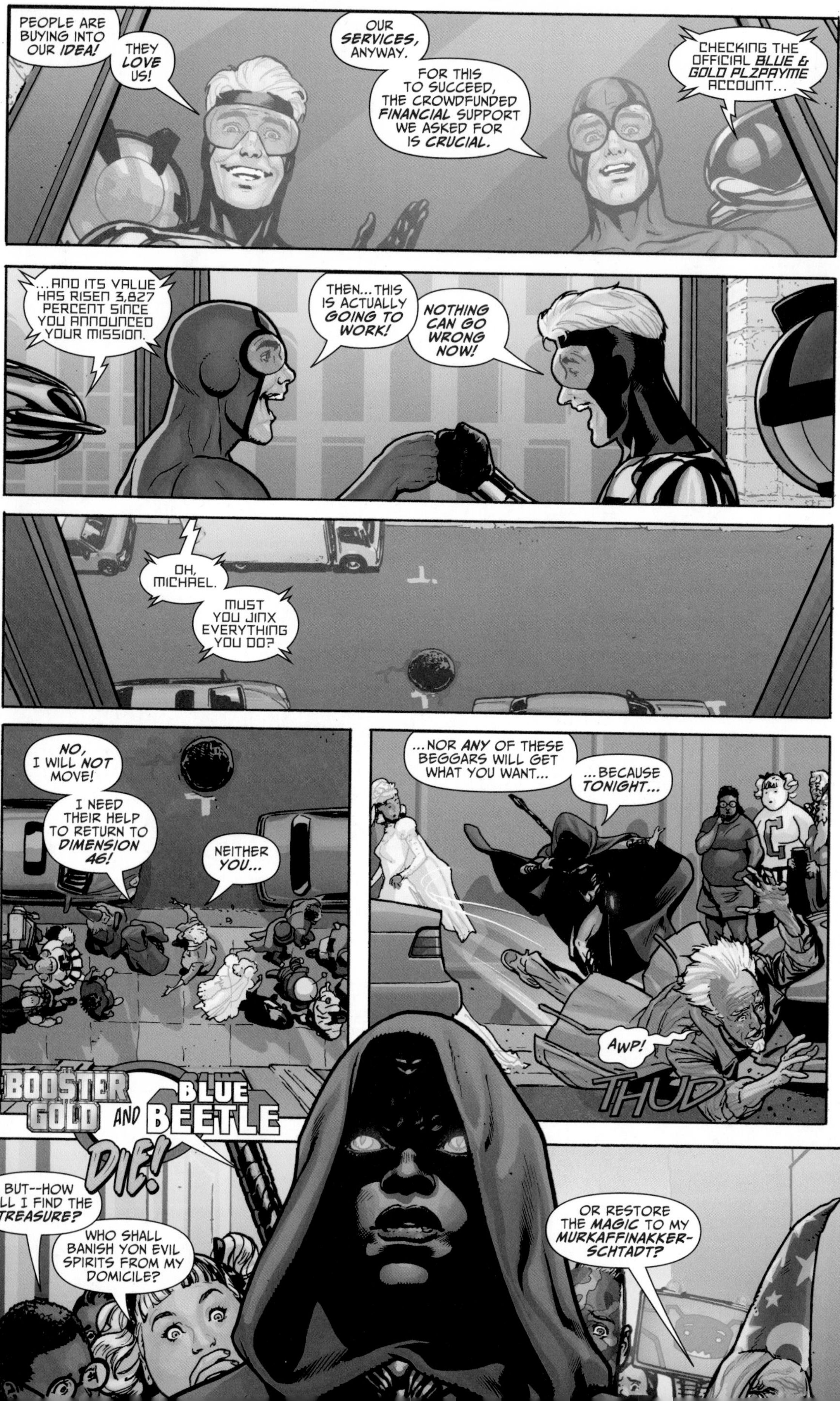
PEOPLE ARE BUYING INTO OUR IDEA!
THEY LOVE US!
OUR SERVICES, ANYWAY.
FOR THIS TO SUCCEED, THE CROWDFUNDED FINANCIAL SUPPORT WE ASKED FOR IS CRUCIAL.
CHECKING THE OFFICIAL BLUE & GOLD PLZPAYME ACCOUNT...
...AND ITS VALUE HAS RISEN 3,827 PERCENT SINCE YOU ANNOUNCED YOUR MISSION.
THEN... THIS IS ACTUALLY GOING TO WORK!
NOTHING CAN GO WRONG NOW!
OH, MICHAEL.
MUST YOU JINX EVERYTHING YOU DO?
NO, I WILL NOT MOVE!
I NEED THEIR HELP TO RETURN TO DIMENSION 46!
NEITHER YOU...
...NOR ANY OF THESE BEGGARS WILL GET WHAT YOU WANT...
...BECAUSE TONIGHT...
AWP!
THUD
...BOO$TER GOLD AND BLUE BEETLE DIE!
BUT--HOW WILL I FIND THE TREASURE?
WHO SHALL BANISH YON EVIL SPIRITS FROM MY DOMICILE?
OR RESTORE THE MAGIC TO MY MURKAFFINAKKER-SCHTADT?

***Blue & Gold* #5**
cover by Ryan Sook

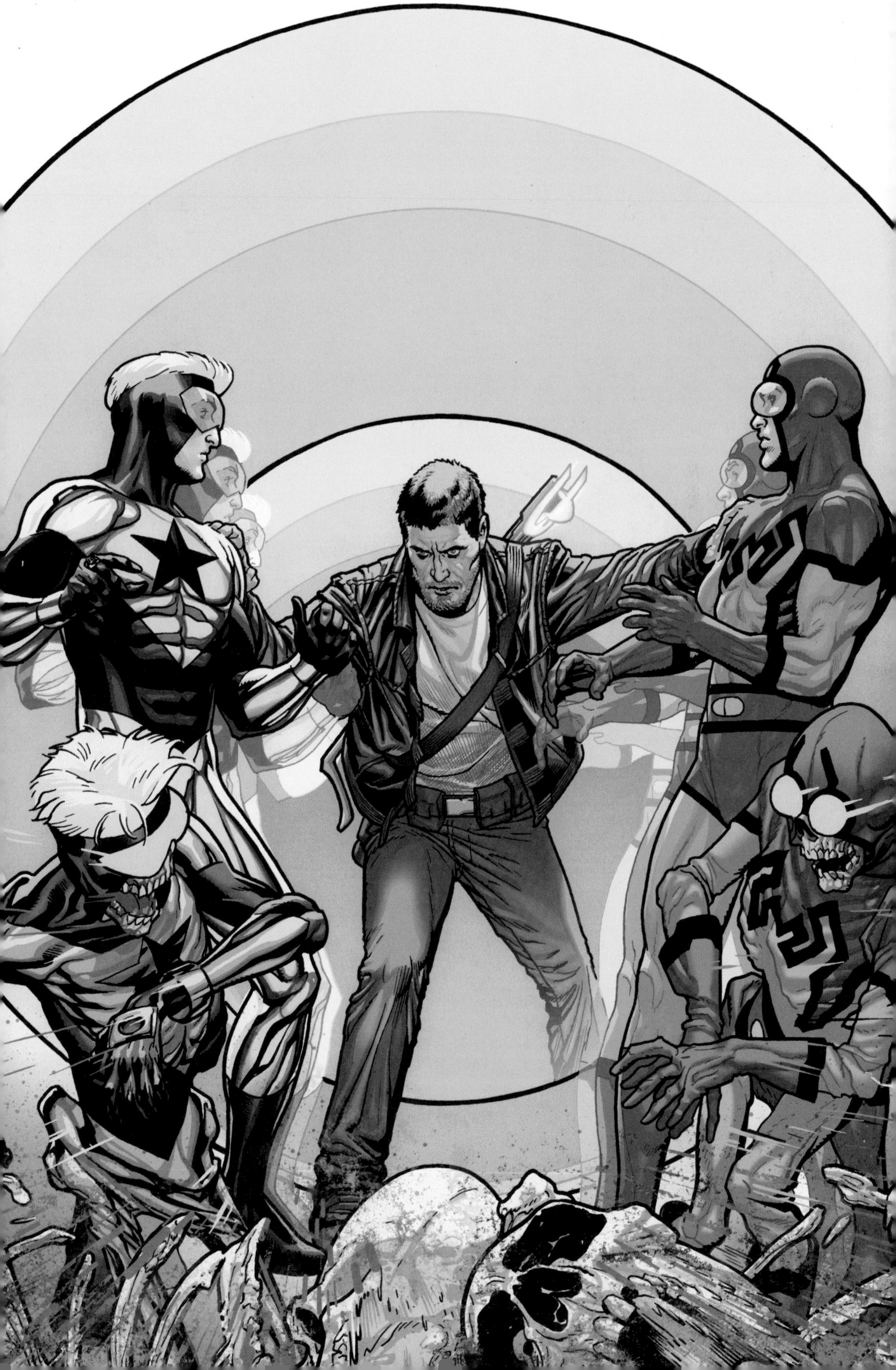

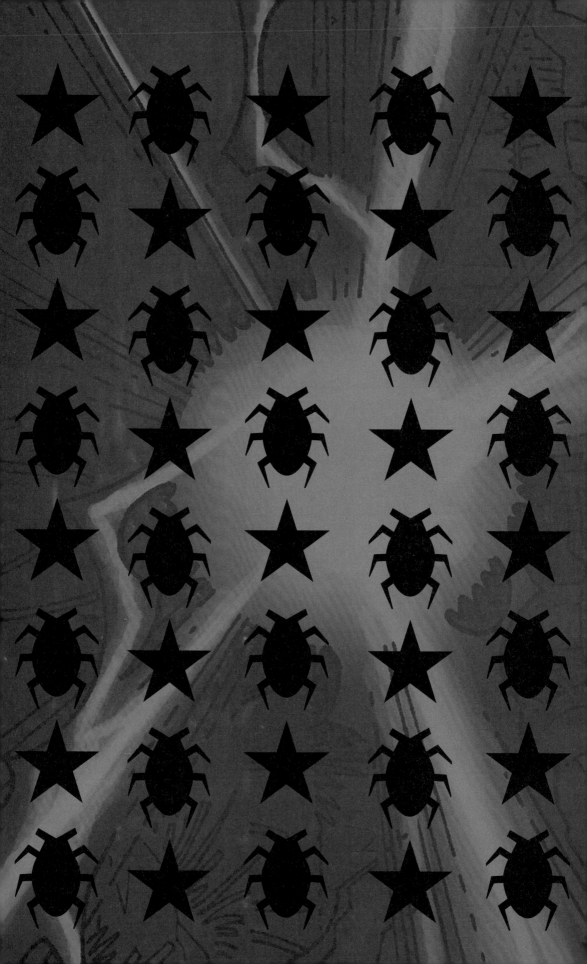

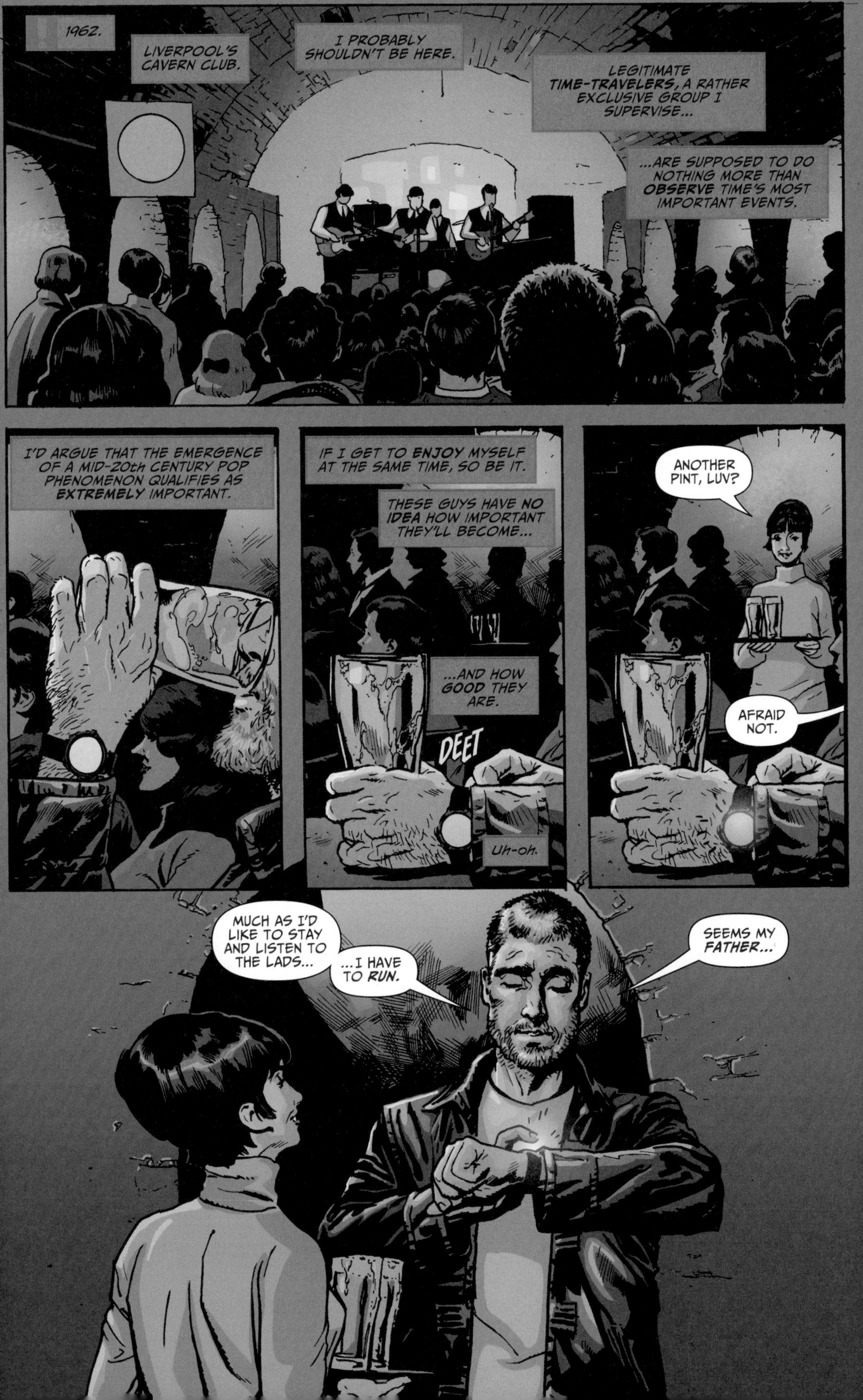
1962.
LIVERPOOL'S CAVERN CLUB.
I PROBABLY SHOULDN'T BE HERE.
LEGITIMATE TIME-TRAVELERS, A RATHER EXCLUSIVE GROUP I SUPERVISE...
...ARE SUPPOSED TO DO NOTHING MORE THAN OBSERVE TIME'S MOST IMPORTANT EVENTS.
I'D ARGUE THAT THE EMERGENCE OF A MID-20th CENTURY POP PHENOMENON QUALIFIES AS EXTREMELY IMPORTANT.
IF I GET TO ENJOY MYSELF AT THE SAME TIME, SO BE IT.
THESE GUYS HAVE NO IDEA HOW IMPORTANT THEY'LL BECOME...
...AND HOW GOOD THEY ARE.
DEET
Uh-oh.
ANOTHER PINT, LUV?
AFRAID NOT.
MUCH AS I'D LIKE TO STAY AND LISTEN TO THE LADS...
...I HAVE TO RUN.
SEEMS MY FATHER...

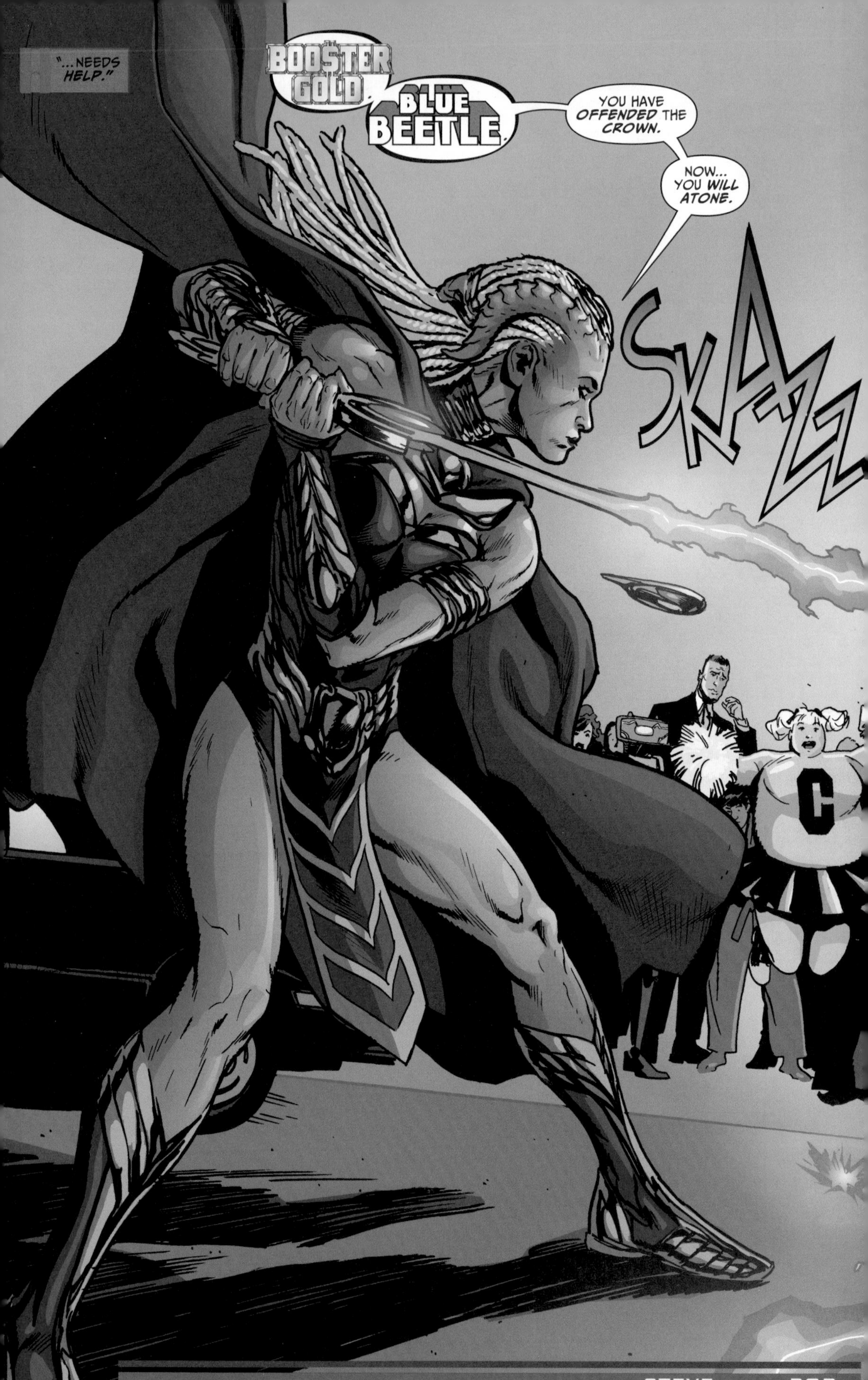
"...NEEDS HELP."
BOOSTER GOLD
BLUE BEETLE
YOU HAVE OFFENDED THE CROWN.
NOW... YOU WILL ATONE.
SKAZZ

DAN JURGENS STORY
RYAN SOOK ART AND COVER
STEVE BUCCELLATO COLORS
ROB LEIGH LETTERS

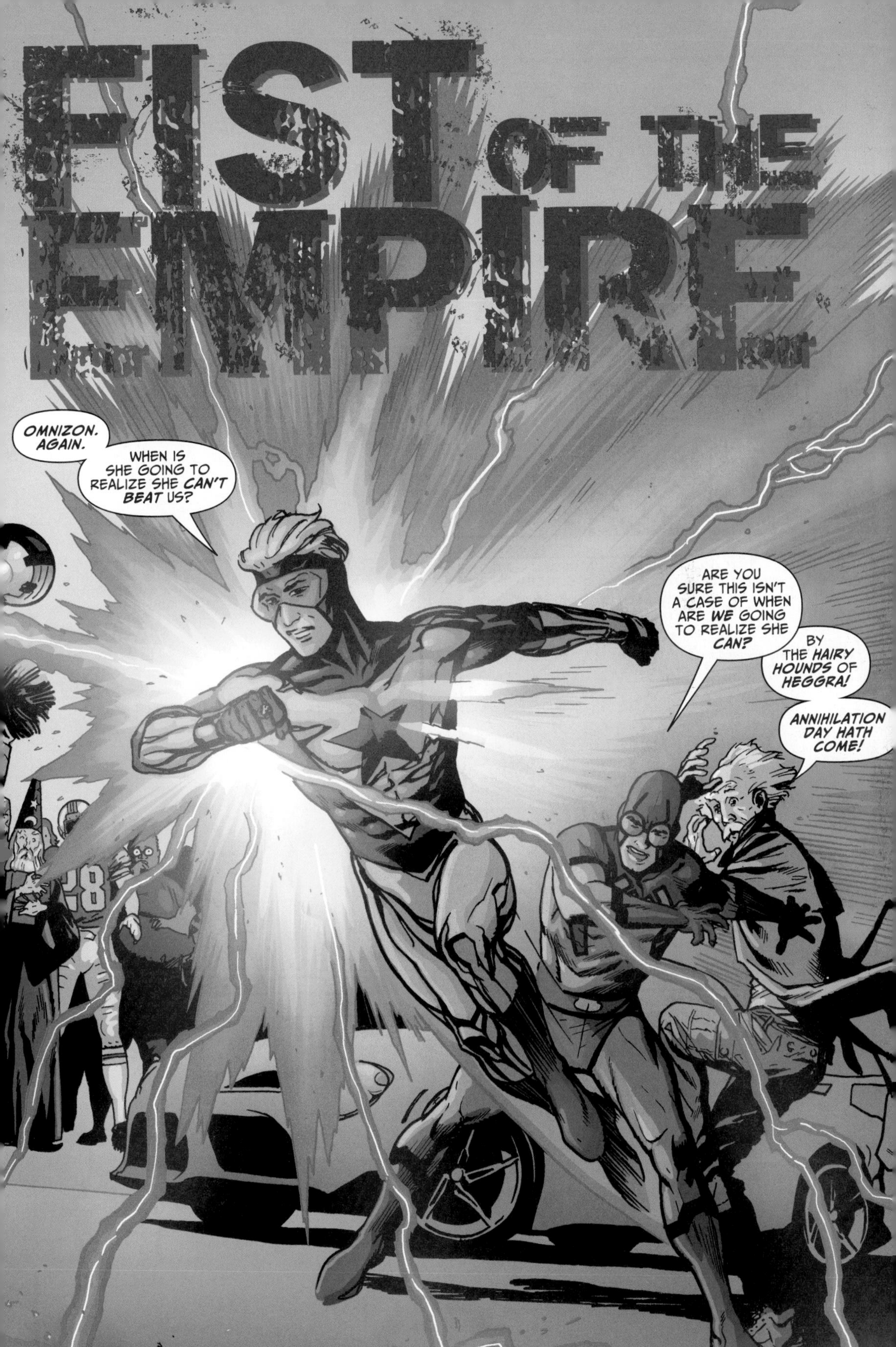
FIST OF THE EMPIRE
OMNIZON. AGAIN.
WHEN IS SHE GOING TO REALIZE SHE CAN'T BEAT US?
ARE YOU SURE THIS ISN'T A CASE OF WHEN ARE WE GOING TO REALIZE SHE CAN?
BY THE HAIRY HOUNDS OF HEGGRA!
ANNIHILATION DAY HATH COME!

SIMONE DI MEO
PEACEMAKER
VARIANT COVER

CHRIS
ROSA
ASSOC. EDITOR

BRITTANY
HOLZHERR
EDITOR

PAUL
KAMINSKI
SENIOR EDITOR

BOOSTER GOLD
CREATED BY
DAN JURGENS

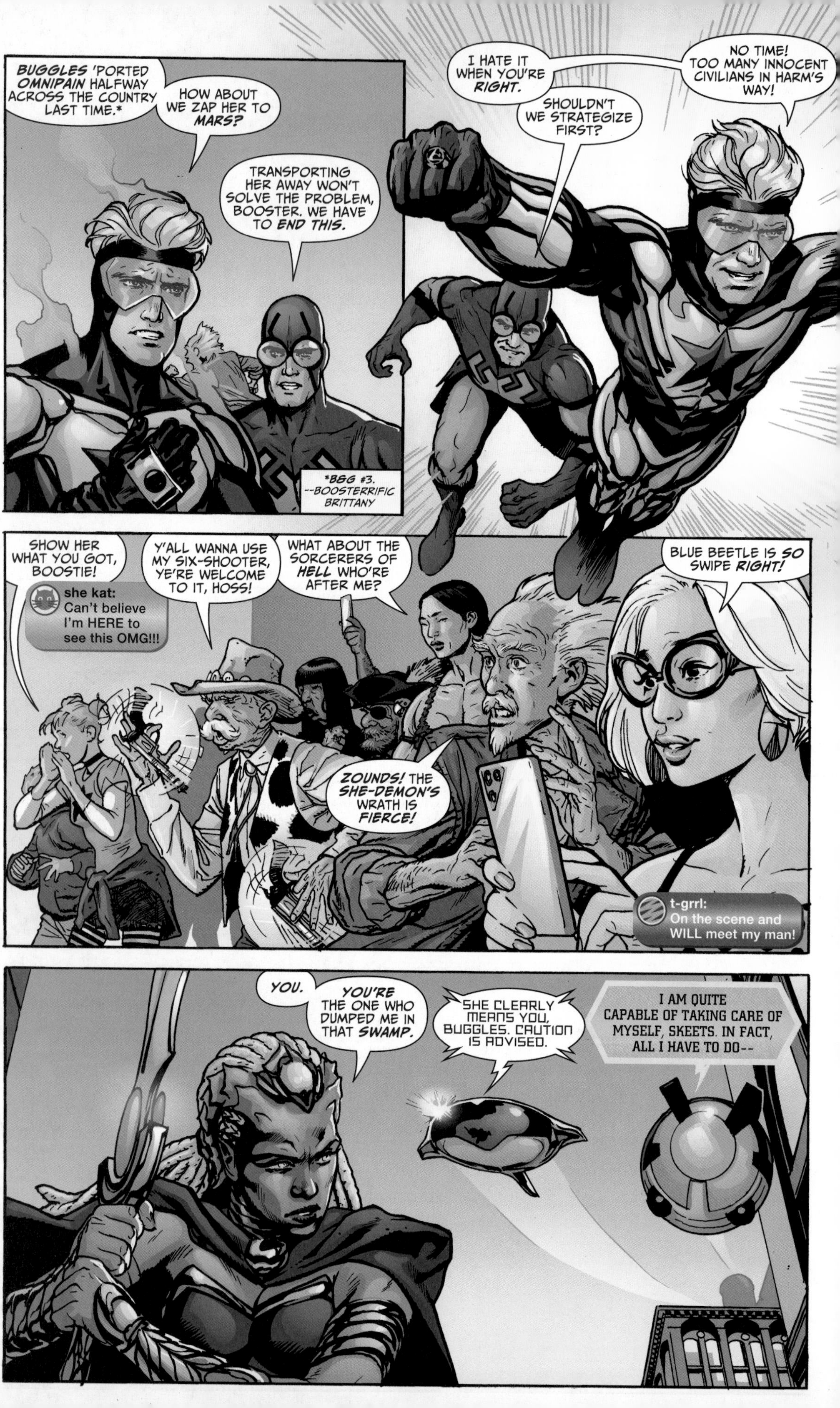
BUGGLES 'PORTED OMNIPAIN HALFWAY ACROSS THE COUNTRY LAST TIME.*
HOW ABOUT WE ZAP HER TO MARS?
TRANSPORTING HER AWAY WON'T SOLVE THE PROBLEM, BOOSTER. WE HAVE TO END THIS.
*BSG #3. --BOOSTERRIFIC BRITTANY
I HATE IT WHEN YOU'RE RIGHT.
NO TIME! TOO MANY INNOCENT CIVILIANS IN HARM'S WAY!
SHOULDN'T WE STRATEGIZE FIRST?
SHOW HER WHAT YOU GOT, BOOSTIE!
she kat: Can't believe I'm HERE to see this OMG!!!
Y'ALL WANNA USE MY SIX-SHOOTER, YE'RE WELCOME TO IT, HOSS!
WHAT ABOUT THE SORCERERS OF HELL WHO'RE AFTER ME?
BLUE BEETLE IS SO SWIPE RIGHT!
ZOUNDS! THE SHE-DEMON'S WRATH IS FIERCE!
t-grrl: On the scene and WILL meet my man!
YOU.
YOU'RE THE ONE WHO DUMPED ME IN THAT SWAMP.
SHE CLEARLY MEANS YOU, BUGGLES. CAUTION IS ADVISED.
I AM QUITE CAPABLE OF TAKING CARE OF MYSELF, SKEETS. IN FACT, ALL I HAVE TO DO--

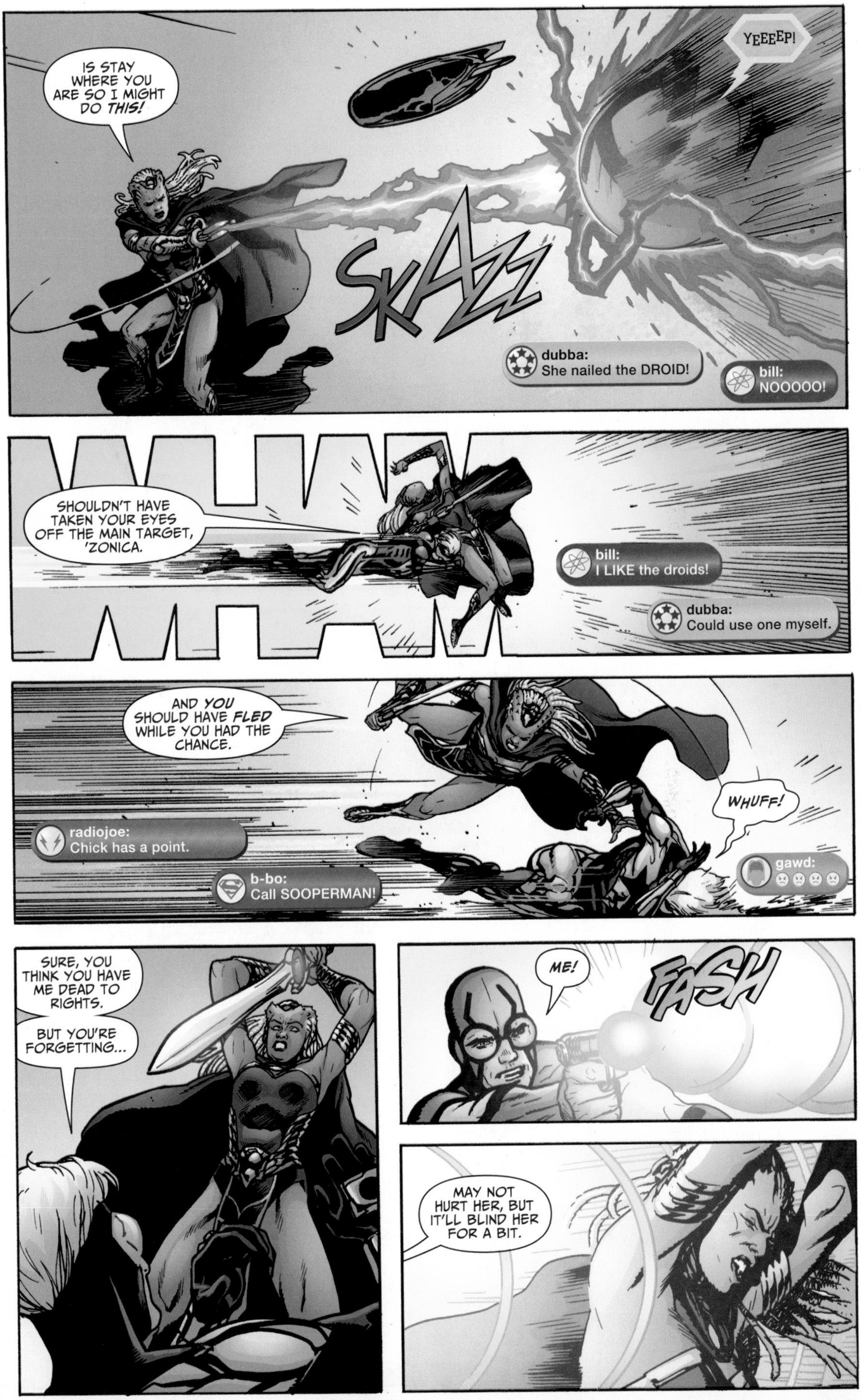
IS STAY WHERE YOU ARE SO I MIGHT DO THIS!
YEEEEP!
SKAZZ
dubba: She nailed the DROID!
bill: NOOOOO!
WHAM
SHOULDN'T HAVE TAKEN YOUR EYES OFF THE MAIN TARGET, 'ZONICA.
bill: I LIKE the droids!
dubba: Could use one myself.
AND YOU SHOULD HAVE FLED WHILE YOU HAD THE CHANCE.
WHUFF!
radiojoe: Chick has a point.
b-bo: Call SOOPERMAN!
gawd:
SURE, YOU THINK YOU HAVE ME DEAD TO RIGHTS.
BUT YOU'RE FORGETTING...
ME!
FASH
MAY NOT HURT HER, BUT IT'LL BLIND HER FOR A BIT.

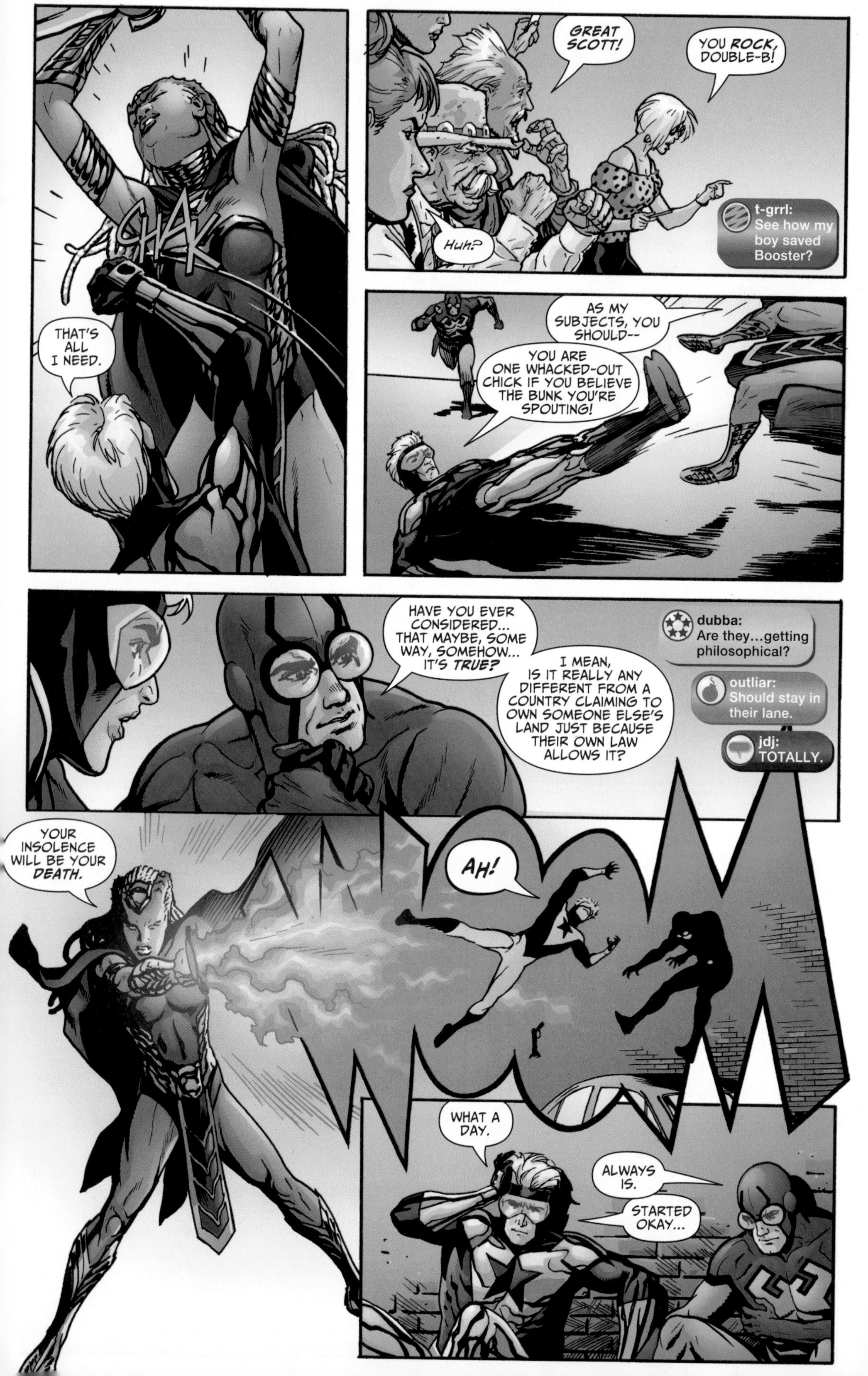
CHAK
THAT'S ALL I NEED.
GREAT SCOTT!
YOU ROCK, DOUBLE-B!
Huh?
t-grrl: See how my boy saved Booster?
AS MY SUBJECTS, YOU SHOULD--
YOU ARE ONE WHACKED-OUT CHICK IF YOU BELIEVE THE BUNK YOU'RE SPOUTING!
HAVE YOU EVER CONSIDERED... THAT MAYBE, SOME WAY, SOMEHOW... IT'S TRUE?
I MEAN, IS IT REALLY ANY DIFFERENT FROM A COUNTRY CLAIMING TO OWN SOMEONE ELSE'S LAND JUST BECAUSE THEIR OWN LAW ALLOWS IT?
dubba: Are they...getting philosophical?
outliar: Should stay in their lane.
jdj: TOTALLY.
YOUR INSOLENCE WILL BE YOUR DEATH.
AH!
WHAT A DAY.
ALWAYS IS.
STARTED OKAY...

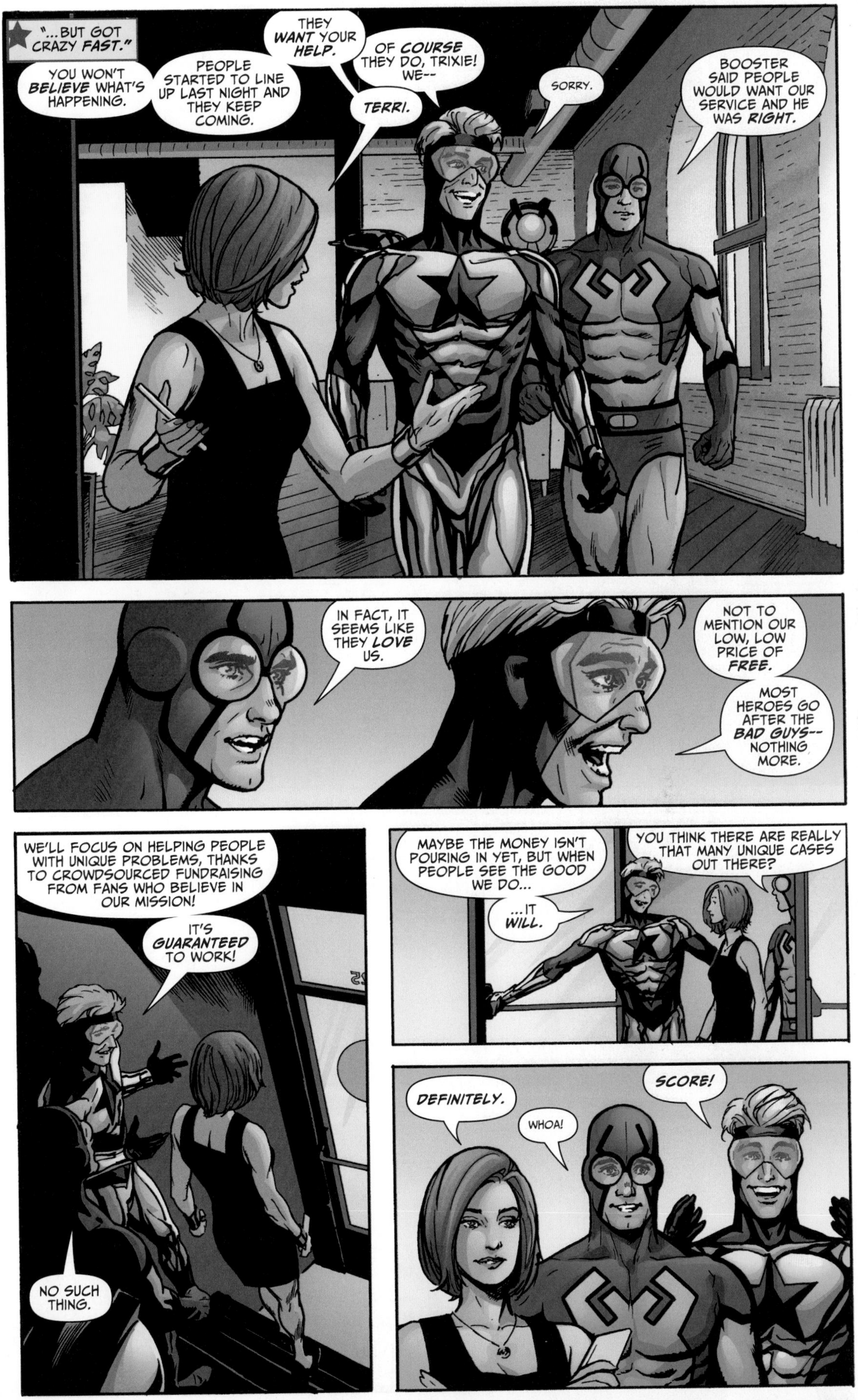
"...BUT GOT CRAZY FAST."
YOU WON'T BELIEVE WHAT'S HAPPENING.
PEOPLE STARTED TO LINE UP LAST NIGHT AND THEY KEEP COMING.
THEY WANT YOUR HELP.
OF COURSE THEY DO, TRIXIE! WE--
TERRI.
SORRY.
BOOSTER SAID PEOPLE WOULD WANT OUR SERVICE AND HE WAS RIGHT.
IN FACT, IT SEEMS LIKE THEY LOVE US.
NOT TO MENTION OUR LOW, LOW PRICE OF FREE.
MOST HEROES GO AFTER THE BAD GUYS--NOTHING MORE.
WE'LL FOCUS ON HELPING PEOPLE WITH UNIQUE PROBLEMS, THANKS TO CROWDSOURCED FUNDRAISING FROM FANS WHO BELIEVE IN OUR MISSION!
IT'S GUARANTEED TO WORK!
NO SUCH THING.
MAYBE THE MONEY ISN'T POURING IN YET, BUT WHEN PEOPLE SEE THE GOOD WE DO...
...IT WILL.
YOU THINK THERE ARE REALLY THAT MANY UNIQUE CASES OUT THERE?
DEFINITELY.
WHOA!
SCORE!

GOOD MORNING!

LADIES AND GENTLEMEN, *WELCOME* TO THE FIRST-EVER DAY OF OPERATIONS FOR *BLUE & GOLD RESTORATION!*

WE'LL START BY DOCUMENTING YOUR REQUESTS AND WILL ADDRESS THEM IN ORDER OF IMPORTANCE.

QUITE EXCELLENT, AS I MUST HAVE THE *BRAIN* OF *QUAZZO* TRANSPLANTED IN PLACE OF MY OWN.

AN' I HAS TO BE GETTIN' ON BACK TO 1842, I DOES.

...WILL BE *KILLED* IF AGENT 37 FINDS ME!

AVAST, MATEY! CAN YE HELP AN OLD *PIRATE* FIND HIS LOST *TREASURE?*

...MUST BE RETURNED TO DIMENSION X AS SOON AS *POSSIBLE!*

...*PLEASE* GET MY KITTY OUT OF OUR TREE?

MISSING MISTER WHISKERS

...*PLEASE* GET BOOSTIE'S AUTOGRAPH?!

...RETURN TO THE CORNFIELD OUTSIDE PEAKSVILLE, PLEASE.

...FEAR I AM COMPOSED OF UNSTABLE COMPOUNDS AND ABOUT TO *EXPLODE.*

ᔑᓭᑫ ᔑᓭᒷ ᒲᔑᓭ ᒷᓵᔑᒲᓵᒲᒷᓵᒲ ᒷᑑ ᔑᒲᓭᑑ

...ENTIRE *LEGION* OF MICROSCOPIC PEOPLE LIVING IN MY GLOVE COMPARTMENT!

...WAS SECRETLY WED TO SUPERMAN TEN YEARS AGO, BUT HE *REFUSES* TO ADMIT IT!

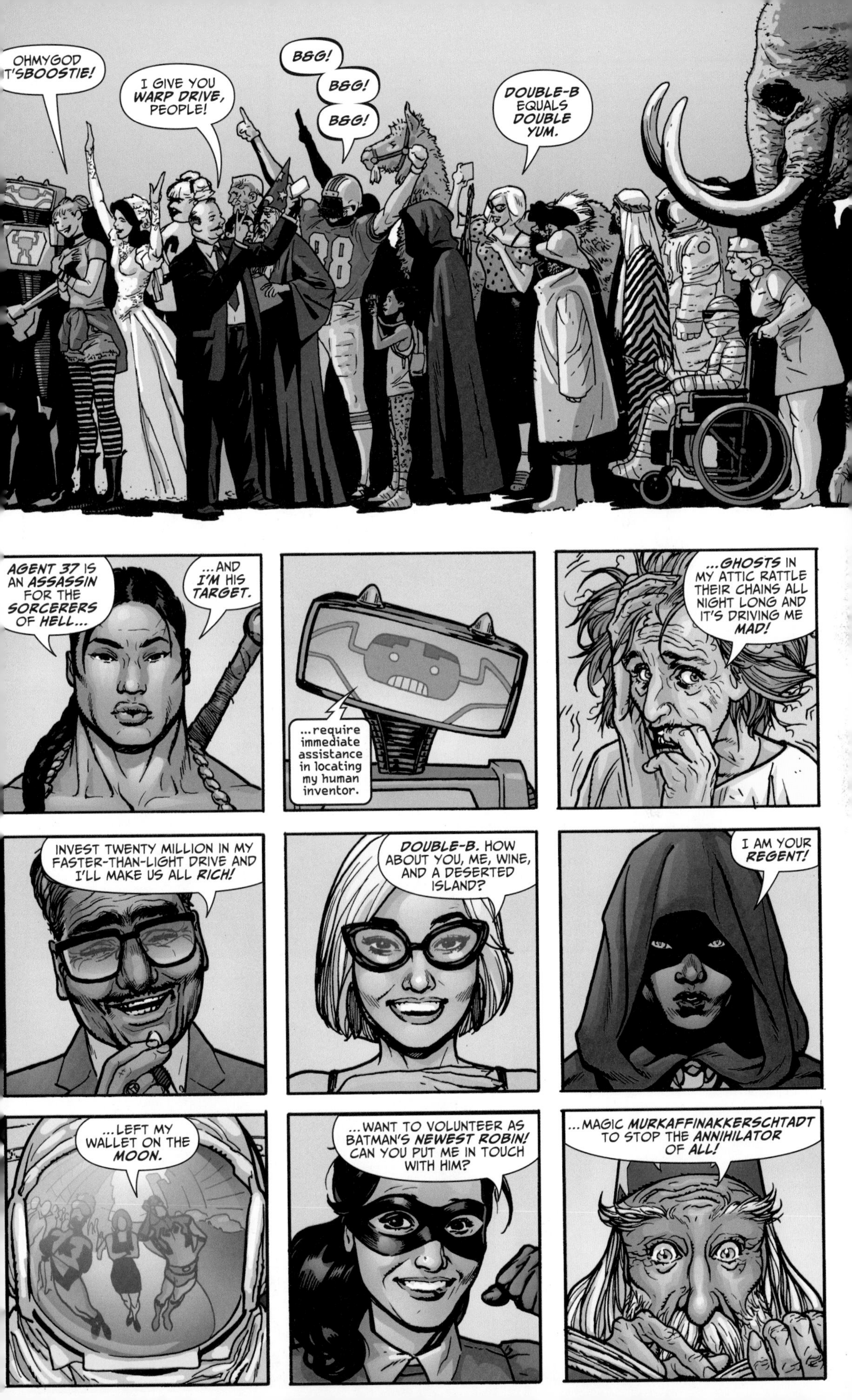
OHMYGOD IT'SBOOSTIE!
I GIVE YOU WARP DRIVE, PEOPLE!
B&G!
B&G!
B&G!
DOUBLE-B EQUALS DOUBLE YUM.
AGENT 37 IS AN ASSASSIN FOR THE SORCERERS OF HELL...
...AND I'M HIS TARGET.
...require immediate assistance in locating my human inventor.
...GHOSTS IN MY ATTIC RATTLE THEIR CHAINS ALL NIGHT LONG AND IT'S DRIVING ME MAD!
INVEST TWENTY MILLION IN MY FASTER-THAN-LIGHT DRIVE AND I'LL MAKE US ALL RICH!
DOUBLE-B. HOW ABOUT YOU, ME, WINE, AND A DESERTED ISLAND?
I AM YOUR REGENT!
...LEFT MY WALLET ON THE MOON.
...WANT TO VOLUNTEER AS BATMAN'S NEWEST ROBIN! CAN YOU PUT ME IN TOUCH WITH HIM?
...MAGIC MURKAFFINAKKERSCHTADT TO STOP THE ANNIHILATOR OF ALL!

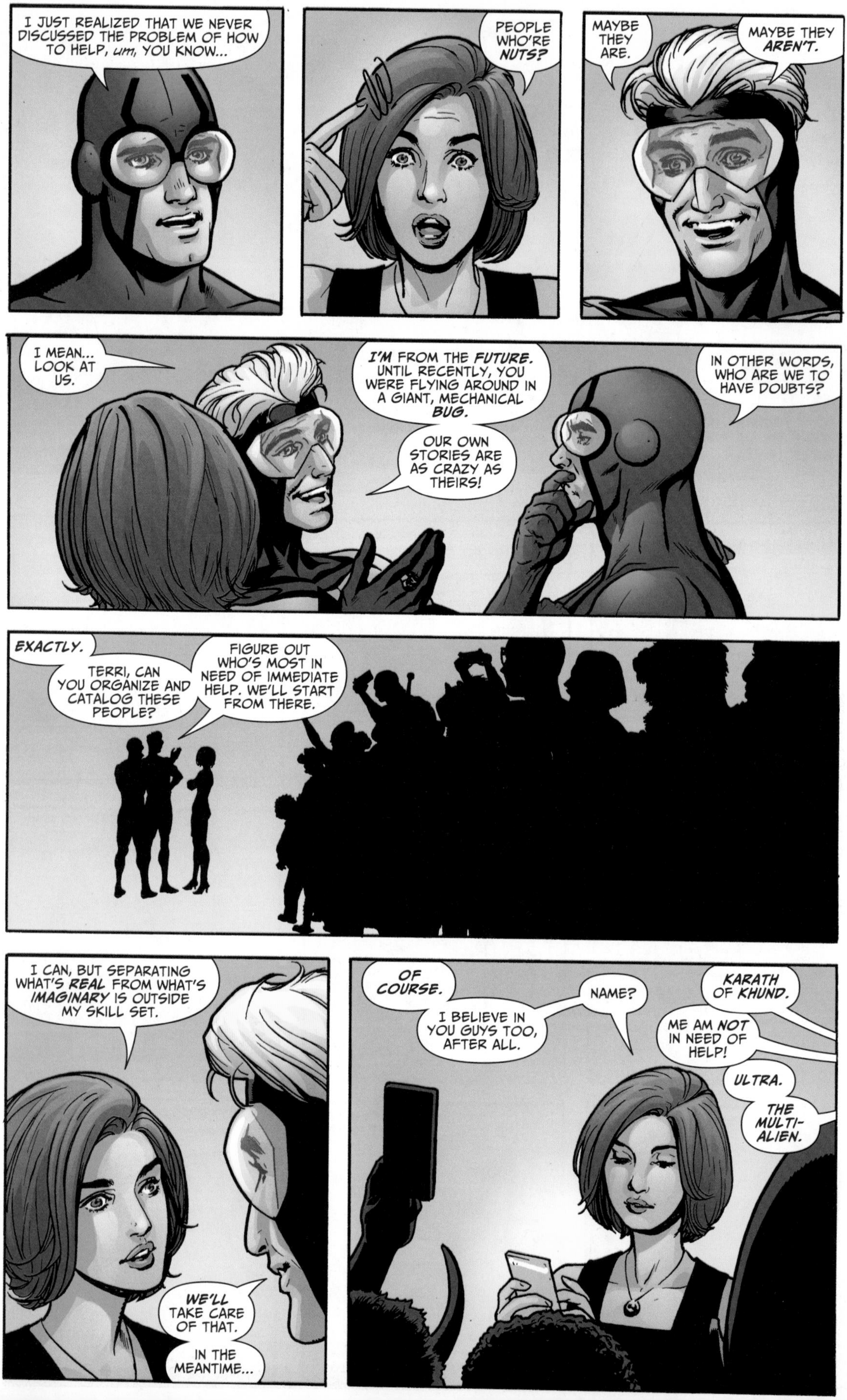
I JUST REALIZED THAT WE NEVER DISCUSSED THE PROBLEM OF HOW TO HELP, *um*, YOU KNOW...
PEOPLE WHO'RE *NUTS?*
MAYBE THEY ARE.
MAYBE THEY *AREN'T.*
I MEAN... LOOK AT US.
I'M FROM THE *FUTURE.* UNTIL RECENTLY, YOU WERE FLYING AROUND IN A GIANT, MECHANICAL *BUG.*
OUR OWN STORIES ARE AS CRAZY AS THEIRS!
IN OTHER WORDS, WHO ARE WE TO HAVE DOUBTS?
EXACTLY.
TERRI, CAN YOU ORGANIZE AND CATALOG THESE PEOPLE?
FIGURE OUT WHO'S MOST IN NEED OF IMMEDIATE HELP. WE'LL START FROM THERE.
I CAN, BUT SEPARATING WHAT'S *REAL* FROM WHAT'S *IMAGINARY* IS OUTSIDE MY SKILL SET.
WE'LL TAKE CARE OF THAT.
IN THE MEANTIME...
OF COURSE.
I BELIEVE IN YOU GUYS TOO, AFTER ALL.
NAME?
KARATH OF KHUND.
ME AM *NOT* IN NEED OF HELP!
ULTRA.
THE MULTI-ALIEN.

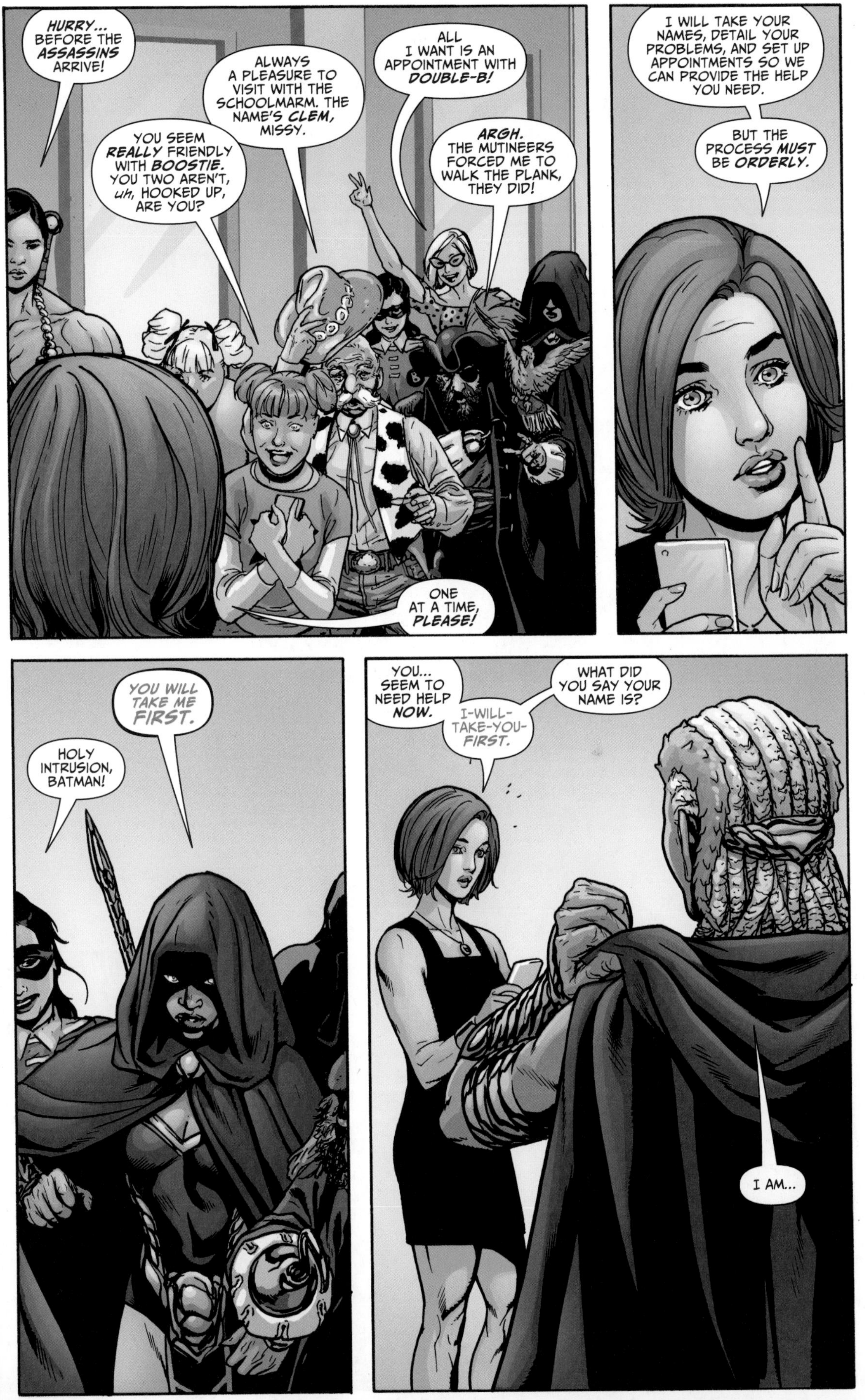
HURRY... BEFORE THE ASSASSINS ARRIVE!
ALWAYS A PLEASURE TO VISIT WITH THE SCHOOLMARM. THE NAME'S CLEM, MISSY.
ALL I WANT IS AN APPOINTMENT WITH DOUBLE-B!
YOU SEEM REALLY FRIENDLY WITH BOOSTIE. YOU TWO AREN'T, uh, HOOKED UP, ARE YOU?
ARGH. THE MUTINEERS FORCED ME TO WALK THE PLANK, THEY DID!
ONE AT A TIME, PLEASE!
I WILL TAKE YOUR NAMES, DETAIL YOUR PROBLEMS, AND SET UP APPOINTMENTS SO WE CAN PROVIDE THE HELP YOU NEED.
BUT THE PROCESS MUST BE ORDERLY.
YOU WILL TAKE ME FIRST.
HOLY INTRUSION, BATMAN!
YOU... SEEM TO NEED HELP NOW.
WHAT DID YOU SAY YOUR NAME IS?
I-WILL-TAKE-YOU-FIRST.
I AM...

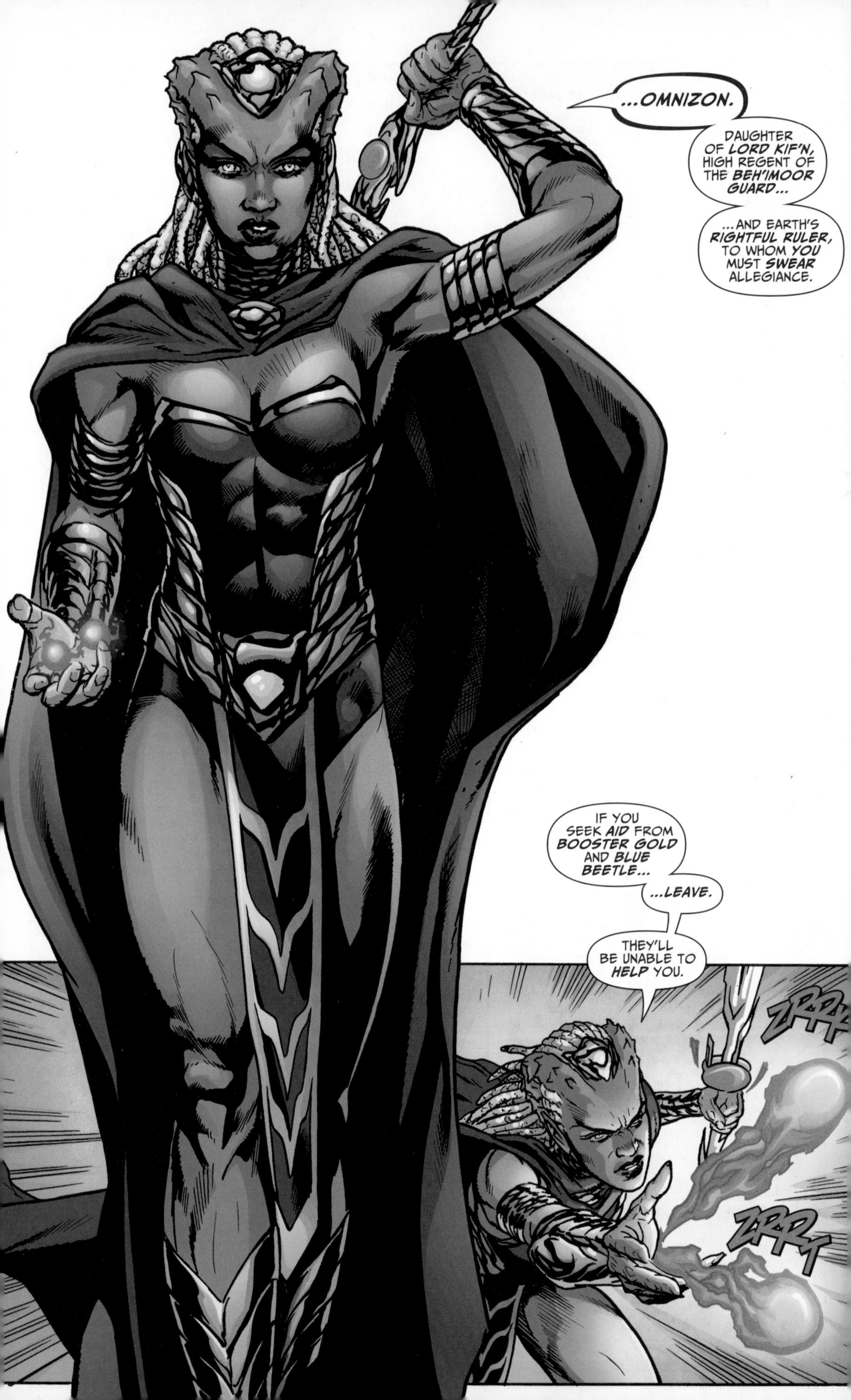
...OMNIZON.
DAUGHTER OF LORD KIF'N, HIGH REGENT OF THE BEH'IMOOR GUARD...
...AND EARTH'S RIGHTFUL RULER, TO WHOM YOU MUST SWEAR ALLEGIANCE.
IF YOU SEEK AID FROM BOOSTER GOLD AND BLUE BEETLE...
...LEAVE.
THEY'LL BE UNABLE TO HELP YOU.
ZRRK
ZRRRT

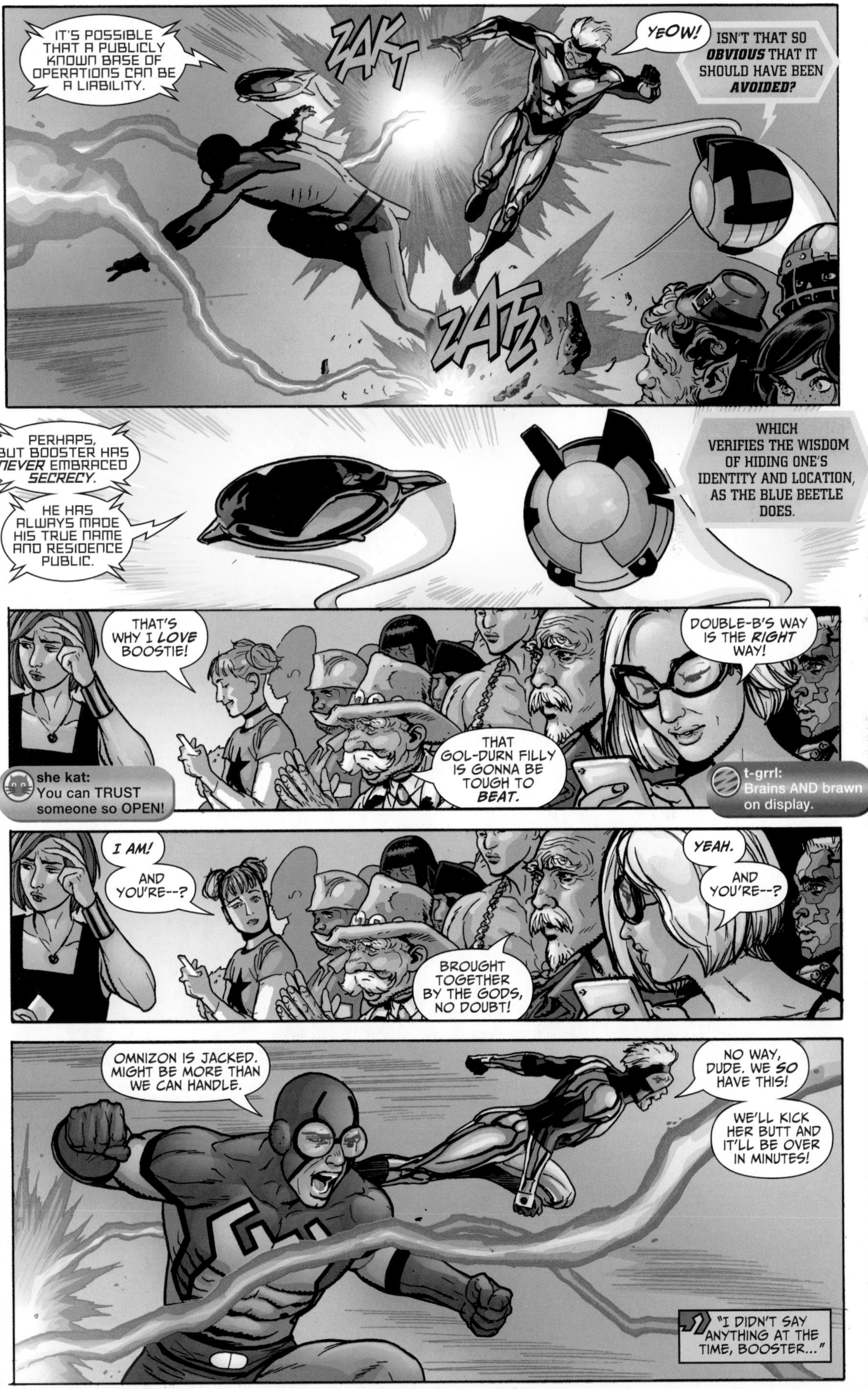
IT'S POSSIBLE THAT A PUBLICLY KNOWN BASE OF OPERATIONS CAN BE A LIABILITY.
ZAK
YEOW!
ISN'T THAT SO OBVIOUS THAT IT SHOULD HAVE BEEN AVOIDED?
ZAK
PERHAPS, BUT BOOSTER HAS NEVER EMBRACED SECRECY.
HE HAS ALWAYS MADE HIS TRUE NAME AND RESIDENCE PUBLIC.
WHICH VERIFIES THE WISDOM OF HIDING ONE'S IDENTITY AND LOCATION, AS THE BLUE BEETLE DOES.
THAT'S WHY I LOVE BOOSTIE!
DOUBLE-B'S WAY IS THE RIGHT WAY!
THAT GOL-DURN FILLY IS GONNA BE TOUGH TO BEAT.
she kat:
You can TRUST someone so OPEN!
t-grrl:
Brains AND brawn on display.
I AM!
AND YOU'RE--?
YEAH.
AND YOU'RE--?
BROUGHT TOGETHER BY THE GODS, NO DOUBT!
OMNIZON IS JACKED. MIGHT BE MORE THAN WE CAN HANDLE.
NO WAY, DUDE. WE SO HAVE THIS!
WE'LL KICK HER BUTT AND IT'LL BE OVER IN MINUTES!
"I DIDN'T SAY ANYTHING AT THE TIME, BOOSTER..."

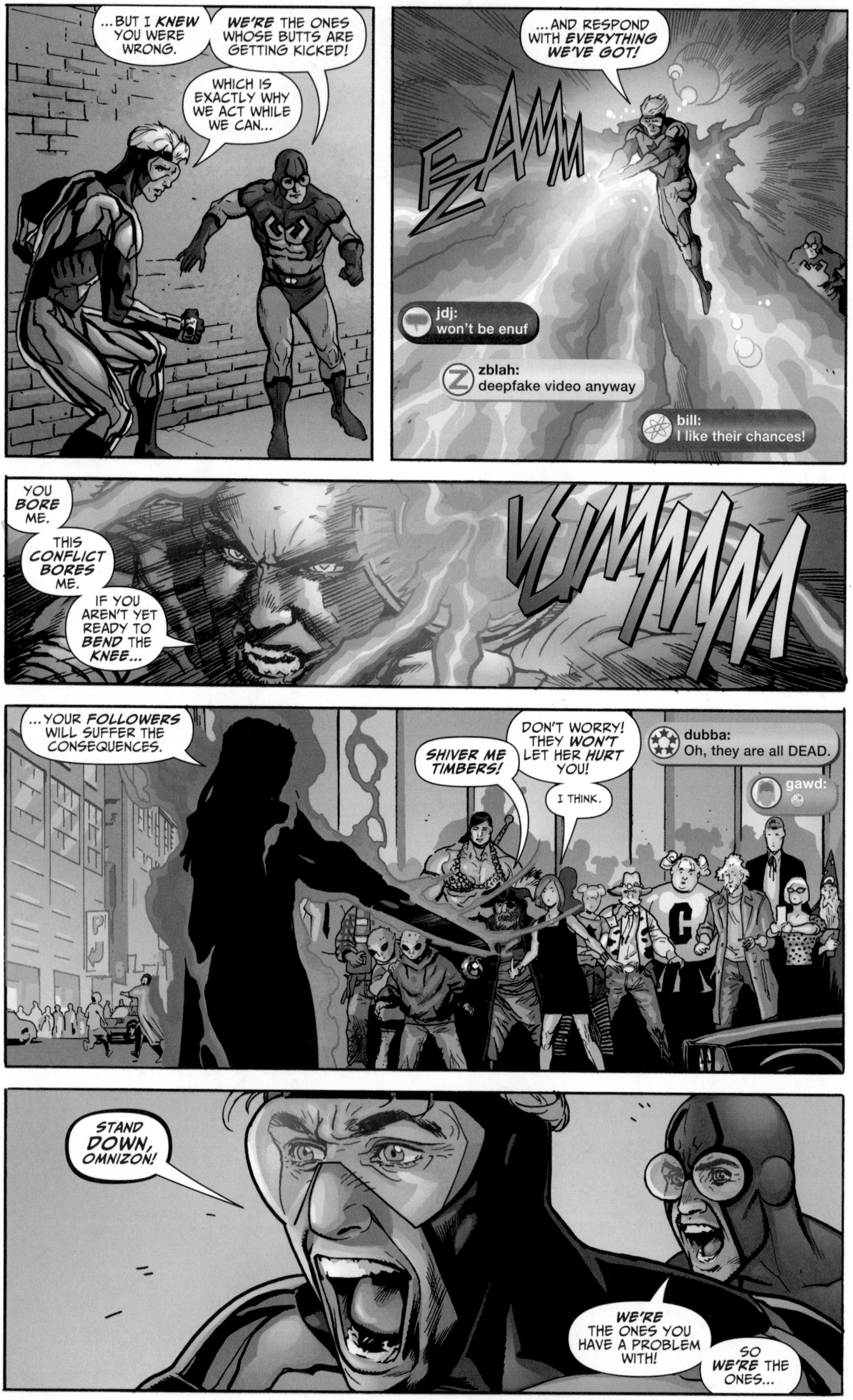
...BUT I KNEW YOU WERE WRONG.
WE'RE THE ONES WHOSE BUTTS ARE GETTING KICKED!
WHICH IS EXACTLY WHY WE ACT WHILE WE CAN...
...AND RESPOND WITH EVERYTHING WE'VE GOT!
FZAMM
jdj: won't be enuf
zblah: deepfake video anyway
bill: I like their chances!
YOU BORE ME.
THIS CONFLICT BORES ME.
IF YOU AREN'T YET READY TO BEND THE KNEE...
VVMMM
...YOUR FOLLOWERS WILL SUFFER THE CONSEQUENCES.
SHIVER ME TIMBERS!
DON'T WORRY! THEY WON'T LET HER HURT YOU!
I THINK.
dubba: Oh, they are all DEAD.
gawd:
STAND DOWN, OMNIZON!
WE'RE THE ONES YOU HAVE A PROBLEM WITH!
SO WE'RE THE ONES...

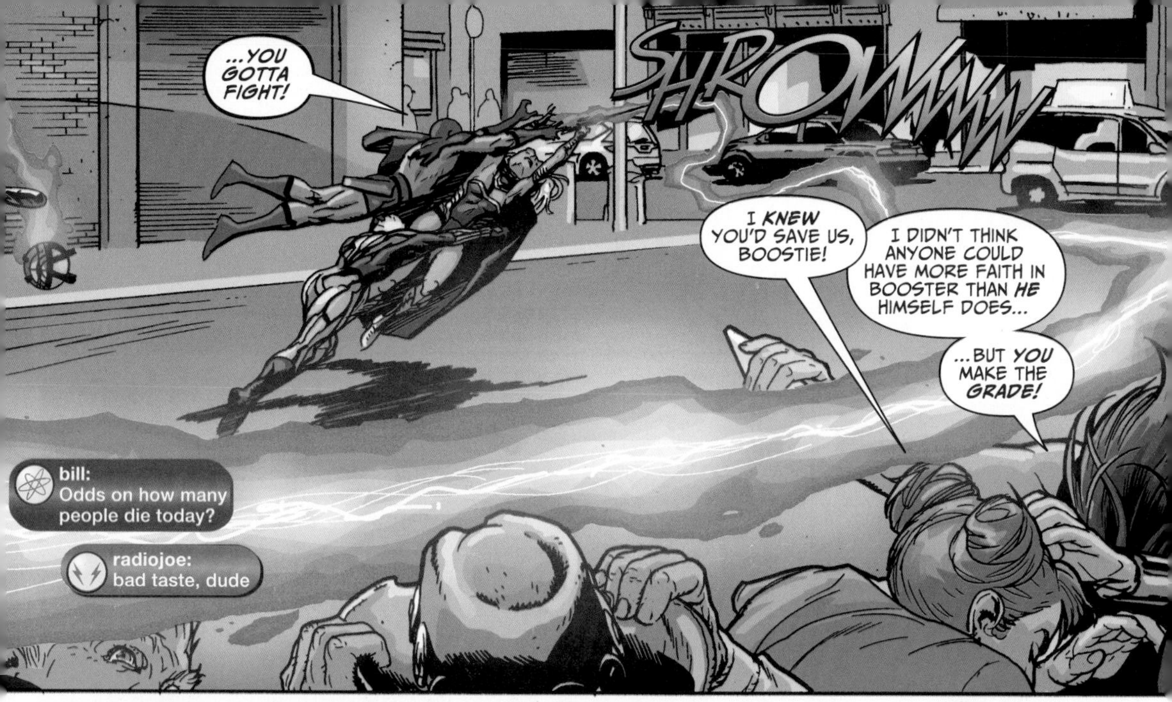
...YOU GOTTA FIGHT!
SHROWWW
I KNEW YOU'D SAVE US, BOOSTIE!
I DIDN'T THINK ANYONE COULD HAVE MORE FAITH IN BOOSTER THAN HE HIMSELF DOES...
...BUT YOU MAKE THE GRADE!
bill:
Odds on how many people die today?
radiojoe:
bad taste, dude

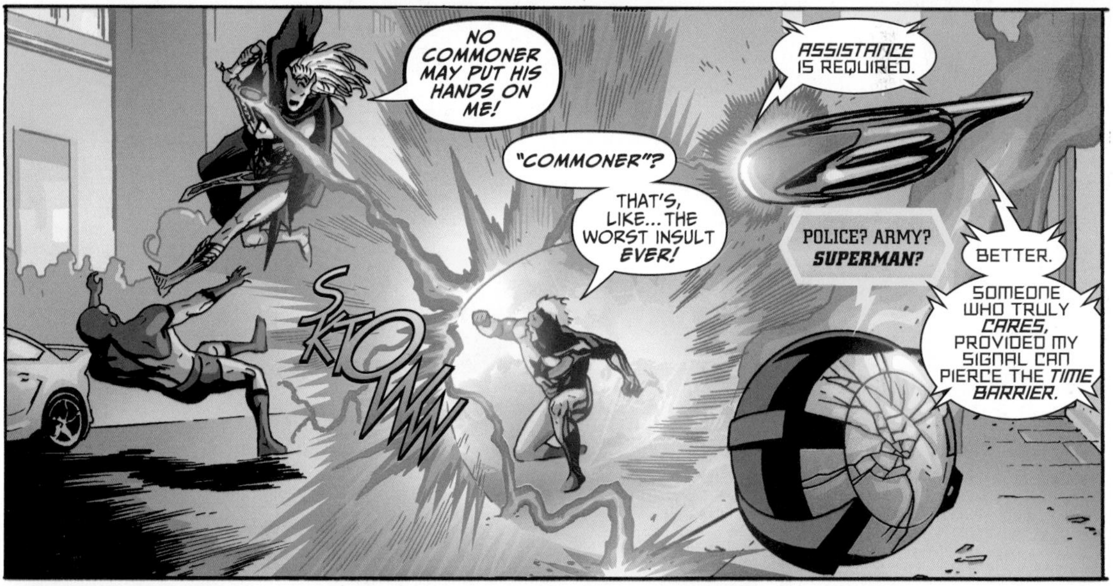
NO COMMONER MAY PUT HIS HANDS ON ME!
"COMMONER"?
THAT'S, LIKE... THE WORST INSULT EVER!
SKTOWW
ASSISTANCE IS REQUIRED.
POLICE? ARMY? SUPERMAN?
BETTER.
SOMEONE WHO TRULY CARES, PROVIDED MY SIGNAL CAN PIERCE THE TIME BARRIER.

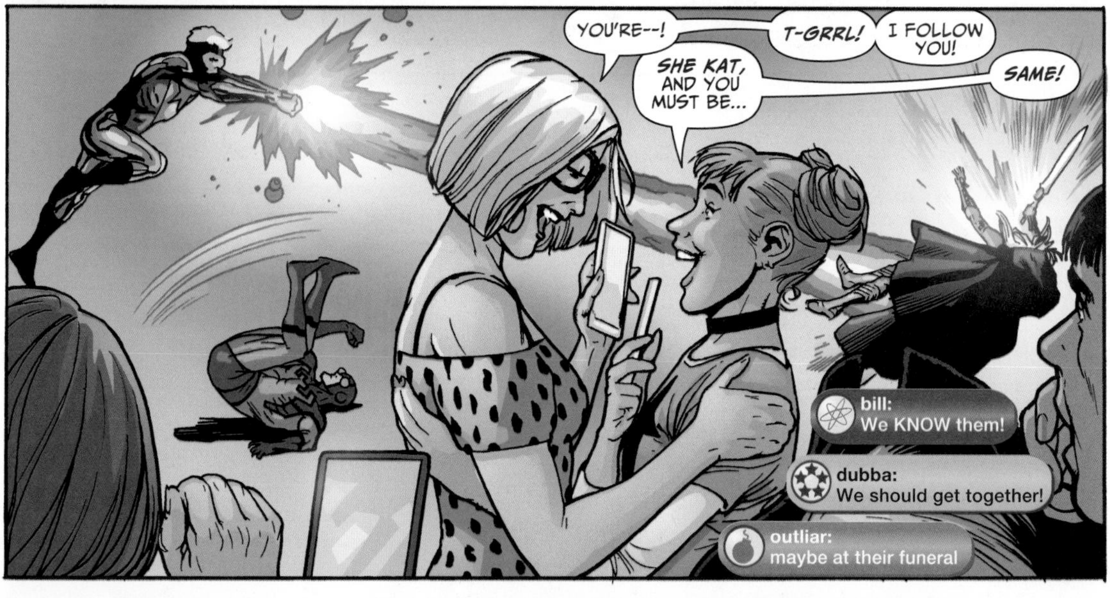
YOU'RE--!
T-GRRL!
I FOLLOW YOU!
SHE KAT, AND YOU MUST BE...
SAME!
bill:
We KNOW them!
dubba:
We should get together!
outliar:
maybe at their funeral

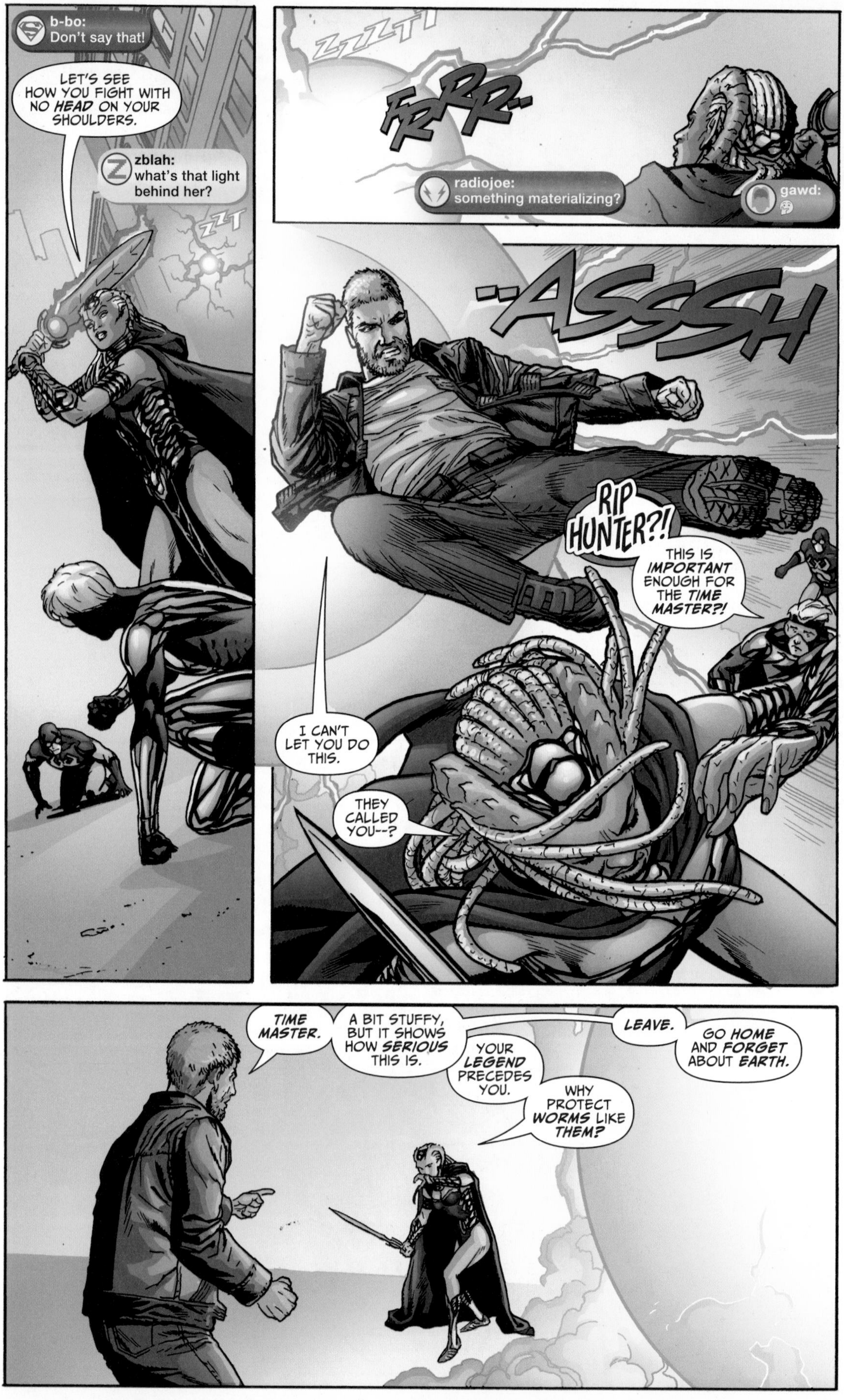
b-bo:
Don't say that!
LET'S SEE HOW YOU FIGHT WITH NO HEAD ON YOUR SHOULDERS.
zblah:
what's that light behind her?
ZZT
ZZZZT!
FRRR-
radiojoe:
something materializing?
gawd:
--ASSSH
RIP HUNTER?!
THIS IS IMPORTANT ENOUGH FOR THE TIME MASTER?!
I CAN'T LET YOU DO THIS.
THEY CALLED YOU--?
TIME MASTER.
A BIT STUFFY, BUT IT SHOWS HOW SERIOUS THIS IS.
YOUR LEGEND PRECEDES YOU.
WHY PROTECT WORMS LIKE THEM?
LEAVE.
GO HOME AND FORGET ABOUT EARTH.

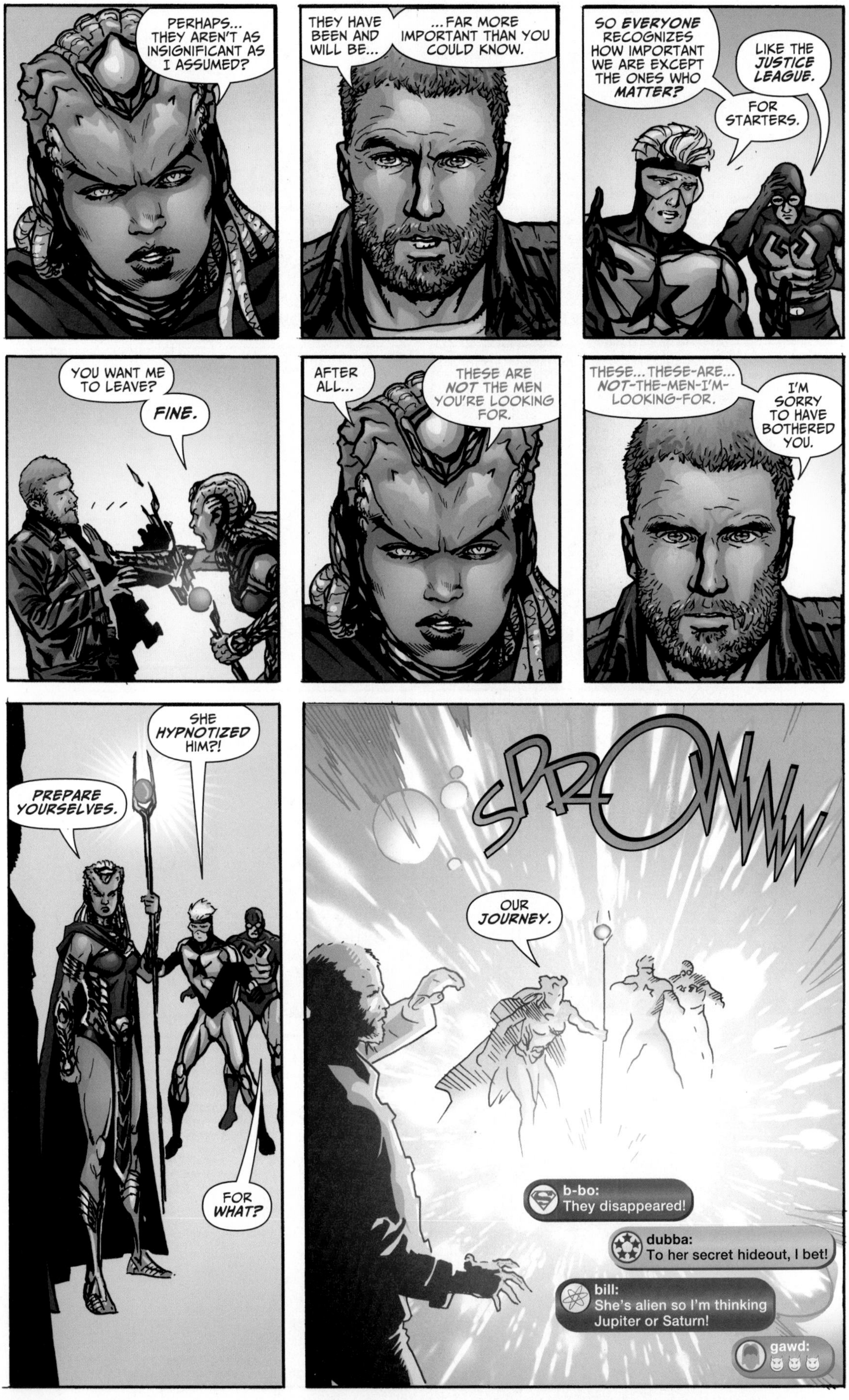
PERHAPS... THEY AREN'T AS INSIGNIFICANT AS I ASSUMED?
THEY HAVE BEEN AND WILL BE...
...FAR MORE IMPORTANT THAN YOU COULD KNOW.
SO EVERYONE RECOGNIZES HOW IMPORTANT WE ARE EXCEPT THE ONES WHO MATTER?
LIKE THE JUSTICE LEAGUE.
FOR STARTERS.
YOU WANT ME TO LEAVE?
FINE.
AFTER ALL...
THESE ARE NOT THE MEN YOU'RE LOOKING FOR.
THESE... THESE-ARE... NOT-THE-MEN-I'M-LOOKING-FOR.
I'M SORRY TO HAVE BOTHERED YOU.
SHE HYPNOTIZED HIM?!
PREPARE YOURSELVES.
FOR WHAT?
SPROWWW
OUR JOURNEY.
b-bo:
They disappeared!
dubba:
To her secret hideout, I bet!
bill:
She's alien so I'm thinking Jupiter or Saturn!
gawd:

WHAT IN *TARNATION* IS GOIN' ON HERE?

Buh... *BOOSTIE?*

DON'T WORRY. DOUBLE-B WILL PROTECT HIM.

THOSE TWO ARE ABOUT TO BE *KEELHAULED*, I FEAR. THEY'RE NOTHIN' BUT *SHARK BAIT* NOW!

WITHOUT THEIR *PROTECTION*, I'M AS GOOD AS *DEAD.*

I shall do what I can, fair maiden.

NOT HOW I WANTED THIS TO GO.

RIP? IS IT REALLY *YOU?!*

TRIXIE?!

TERRI NOW, BUT... NEVER MIND.

I WONDERED IF YOU AND MICHAEL STAYED IN TOUCH!

I'M *NEVER* FAR AWAY.

ANY IDEA WHERE OMNIZON TOOK THEM?

I'M AFRAID SO, AND IT'S ABOUT TO GET *COMPLICATED.*

SHE CLAIMS TO BE OUR *RULER.*

SAYS EARTH IS PART OF HER REALM AND WE'RE SUPPOSED TO *OBEY* HER EVERY ORDER!

CRAZY, RIGHT?

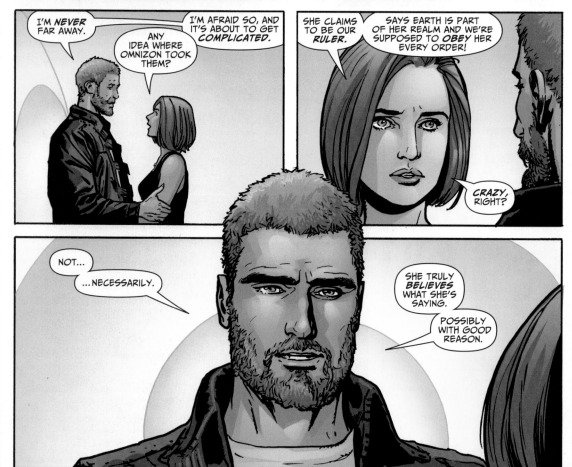

NOT...

...NECESSARILY.

SHE TRULY *BELIEVES* WHAT SHE'S SAYING.

POSSIBLY WITH GOOD REASON.

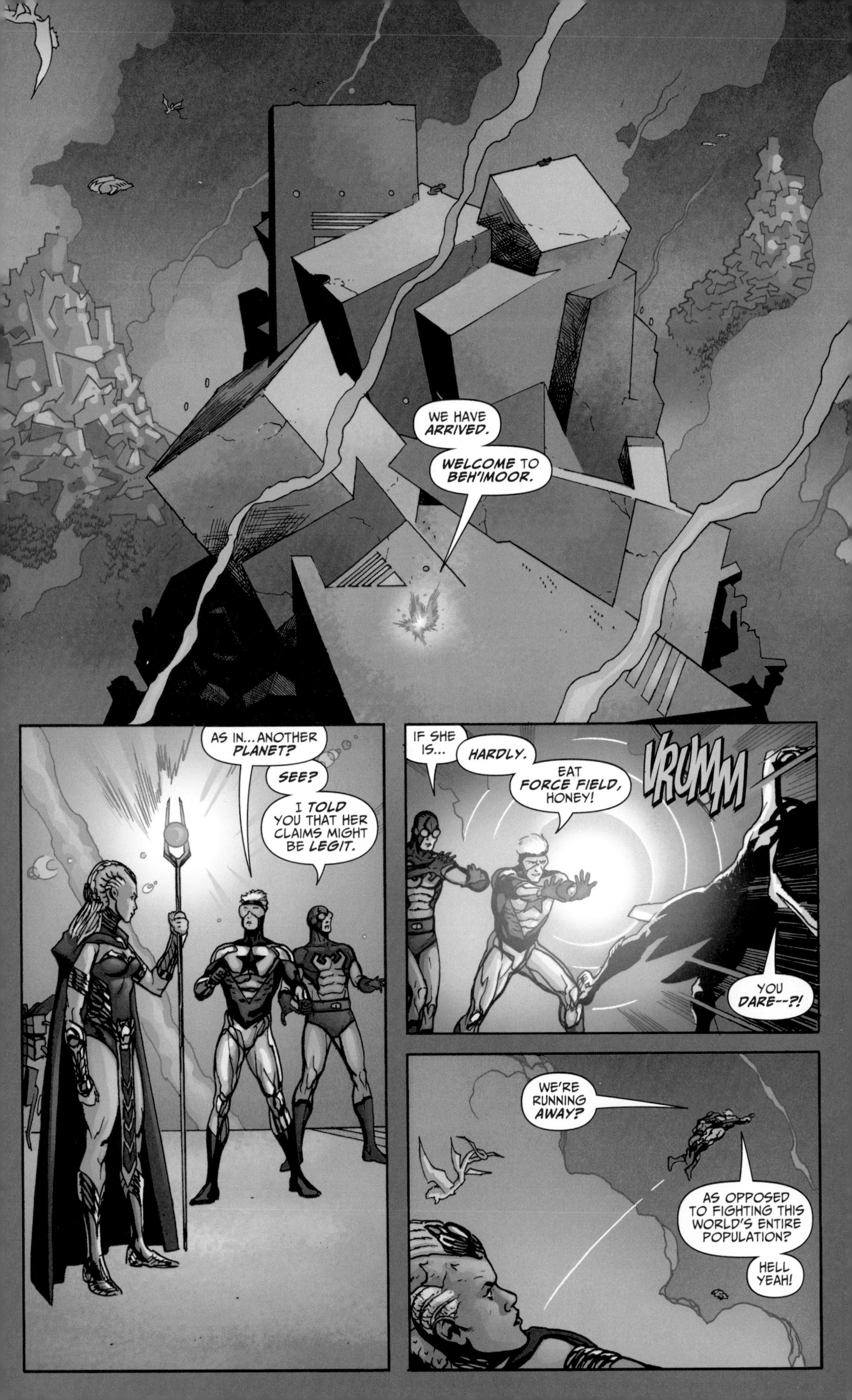
WE HAVE ARRIVED.
WELCOME TO BEH'IMOOR.
AS IN...ANOTHER PLANET?
SEE?
I TOLD YOU THAT HER CLAIMS MIGHT BE LEGIT.
IF SHE IS...
HARDLY.
EAT FORCE FIELD, HONEY!
VRUMM
YOU DARE--?!
WE'RE RUNNING AWAY?
AS OPPOSED TO FIGHTING THIS WORLD'S ENTIRE POPULATION?
HELL YEAH!

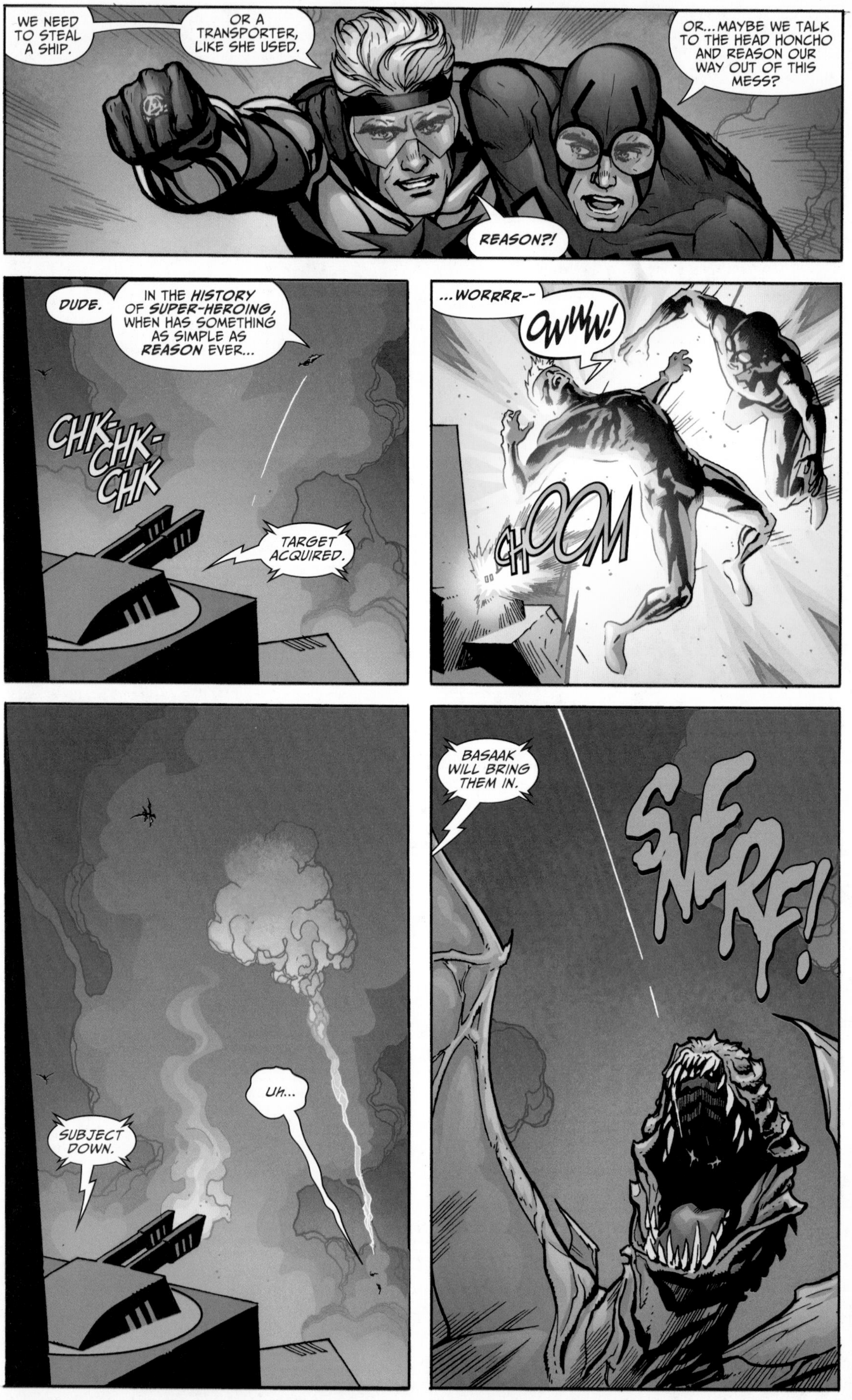
WE NEED TO STEAL A SHIP.
OR A TRANSPORTER, LIKE SHE USED.
OR...MAYBE WE TALK TO THE HEAD HONCHO AND REASON OUR WAY OUT OF THIS MESS?
REASON?!
DUDE.
IN THE HISTORY OF SUPER-HEROING, WHEN HAS SOMETHING AS SIMPLE AS REASON EVER...
CHK-CHK-CHK
TARGET ACQUIRED.
...WORRRR--
OWWW!
CHOOOM
SUBJECT DOWN.
Uh...
BASAAK WILL BRING THEM IN.
SNERF!

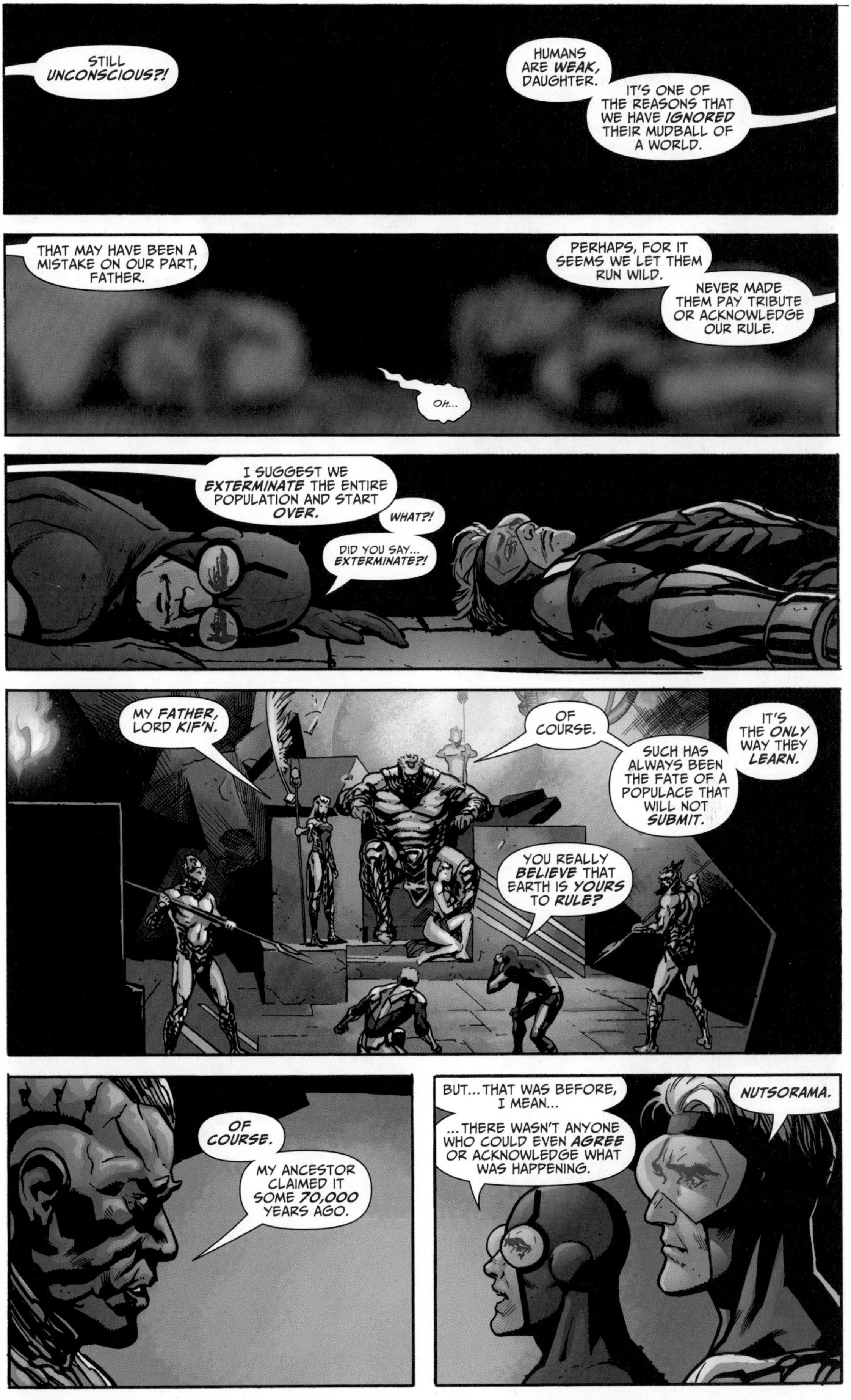

STILL UNCONSCIOUS?!
HUMANS ARE WEAK, DAUGHTER.
IT'S ONE OF THE REASONS THAT WE HAVE IGNORED THEIR MUDBALL OF A WORLD.
THAT MAY HAVE BEEN A MISTAKE ON OUR PART, FATHER.
PERHAPS, FOR IT SEEMS WE LET THEM RUN WILD.
NEVER MADE THEM PAY TRIBUTE OR ACKNOWLEDGE OUR RULE.
Oh...
I SUGGEST WE EXTERMINATE THE ENTIRE POPULATION AND START OVER.
WHAT?!
DID YOU SAY... EXTERMINATE?!
MY FATHER, LORD KIF'N.
OF COURSE.
SUCH HAS ALWAYS BEEN THE FATE OF A POPULACE THAT WILL NOT SUBMIT.
IT'S THE ONLY WAY THEY LEARN.
YOU REALLY BELIEVE THAT EARTH IS YOURS TO RULE?
OF COURSE.
MY ANCESTOR CLAIMED IT SOME 70,000 YEARS AGO.
BUT... THAT WAS BEFORE, I MEAN...
... THERE WASN'T ANYONE WHO COULD EVEN AGREE OR ACKNOWLEDGE WHAT WAS HAPPENING.
NUTSORAMA.

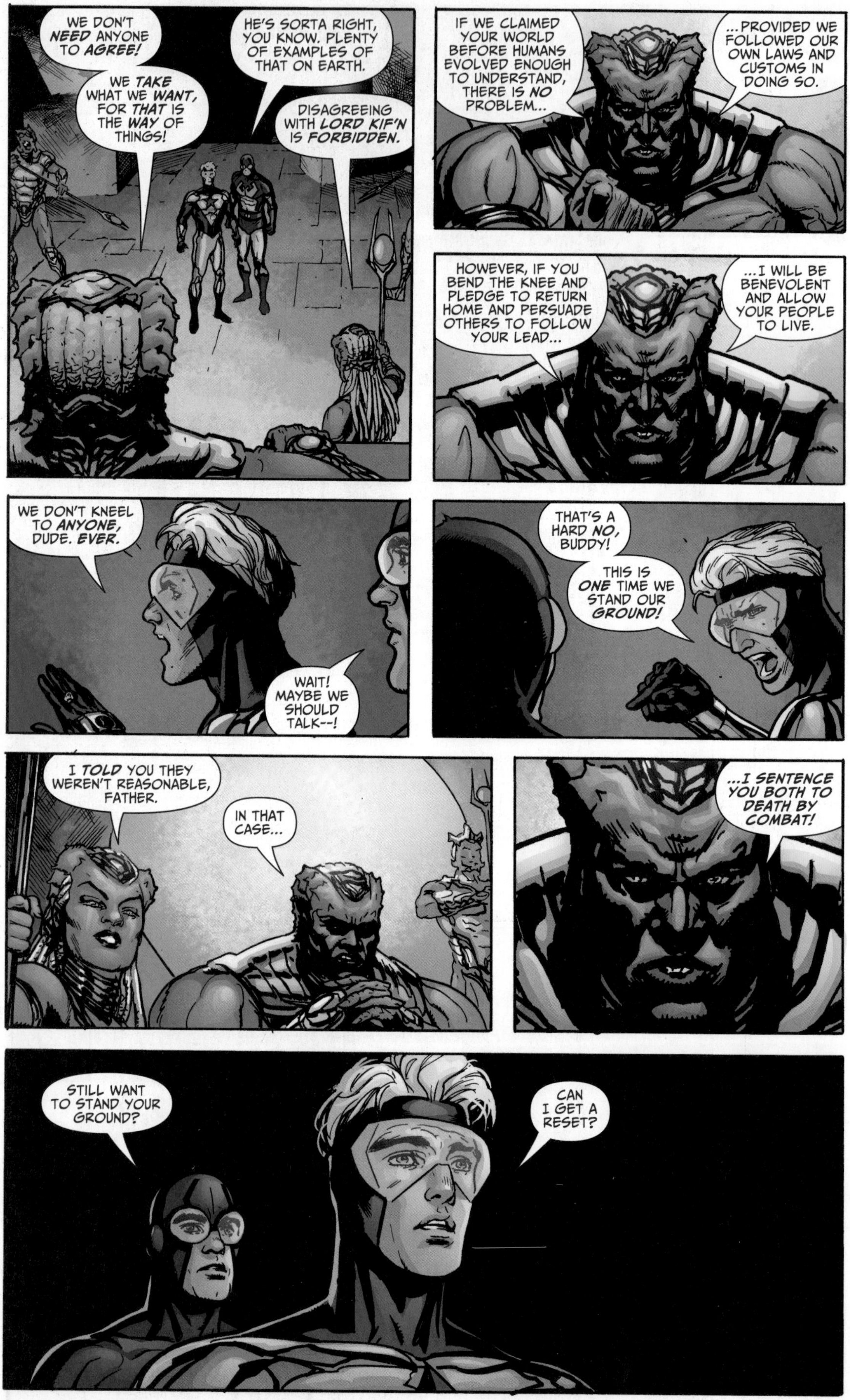
WE DON'T NEED ANYONE TO AGREE!
WE TAKE WHAT WE WANT, FOR THAT IS THE WAY OF THINGS!
HE'S SORTA RIGHT, YOU KNOW. PLENTY OF EXAMPLES OF THAT ON EARTH.
DISAGREEING WITH LORD KIF'N IS FORBIDDEN.
IF WE CLAIMED YOUR WORLD BEFORE HUMANS EVOLVED ENOUGH TO UNDERSTAND, THERE IS NO PROBLEM...
...PROVIDED WE FOLLOWED OUR OWN LAWS AND CUSTOMS IN DOING SO.
HOWEVER, IF YOU BEND THE KNEE AND PLEDGE TO RETURN HOME AND PERSUADE OTHERS TO FOLLOW YOUR LEAD...
...I WILL BE BENEVOLENT AND ALLOW YOUR PEOPLE TO LIVE.
WE DON'T KNEEL TO ANYONE, DUDE. EVER.
WAIT! MAYBE WE SHOULD TALK--!
THAT'S A HARD NO, BUDDY!
THIS IS ONE TIME WE STAND OUR GROUND!
I TOLD YOU THEY WEREN'T REASONABLE, FATHER.
IN THAT CASE...
...I SENTENCE YOU BOTH TO DEATH BY COMBAT!
STILL WANT TO STAND YOUR GROUND?
CAN I GET A RESET?

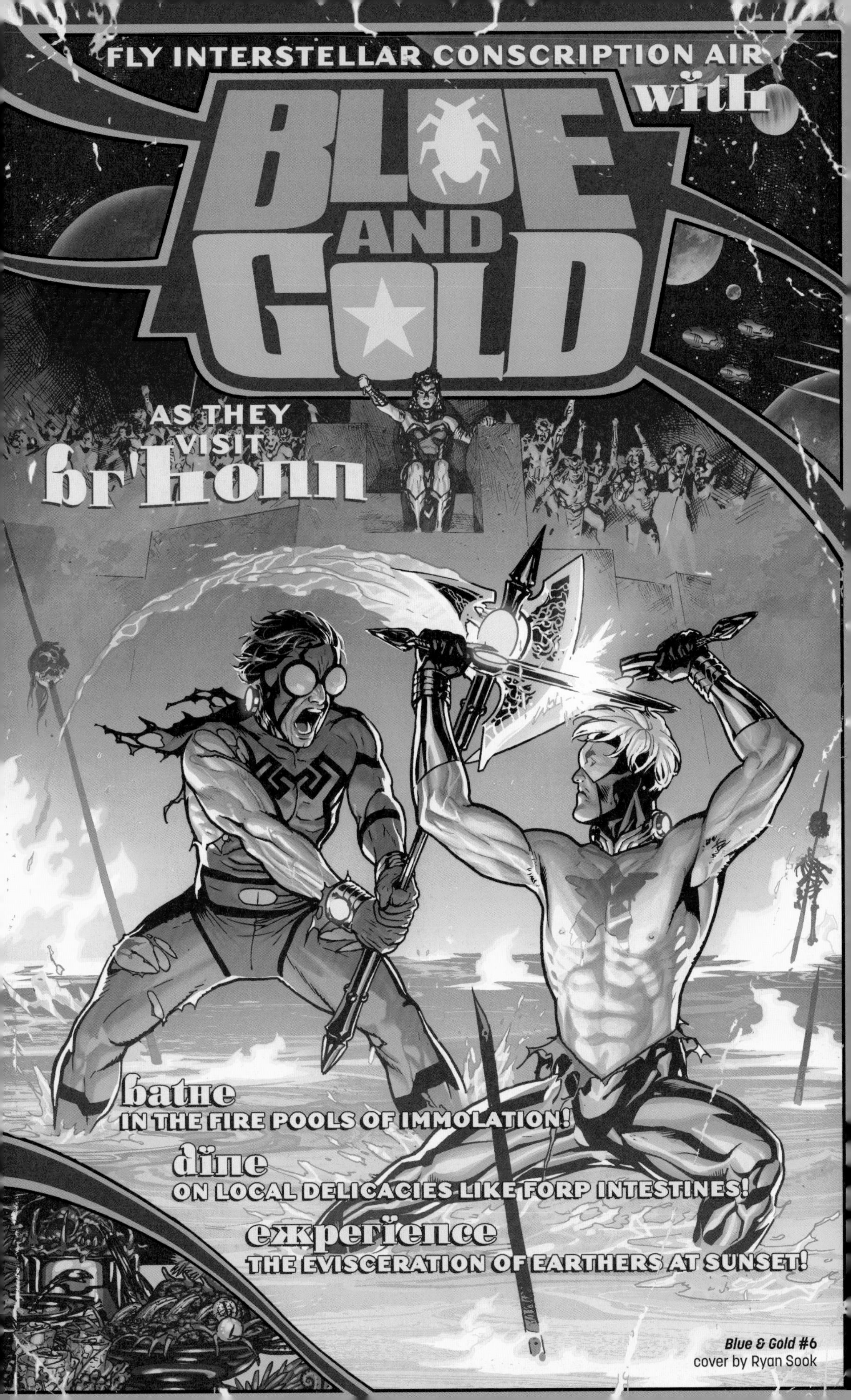
FLY INTERSTELLAR CONSCRIPTION AIR
with
BLUE AND GOLD
AS THEY VISIT
br'honn
bathe
IN THE FIRE POOLS OF IMMOLATION!
dine
ON LOCAL DELICACIES LIKE FORP INTESTINES!
experience
THE EVISCERATION OF EARTHERS AT SUNSET!

Blue & Gold #6
cover by Ryan Sook

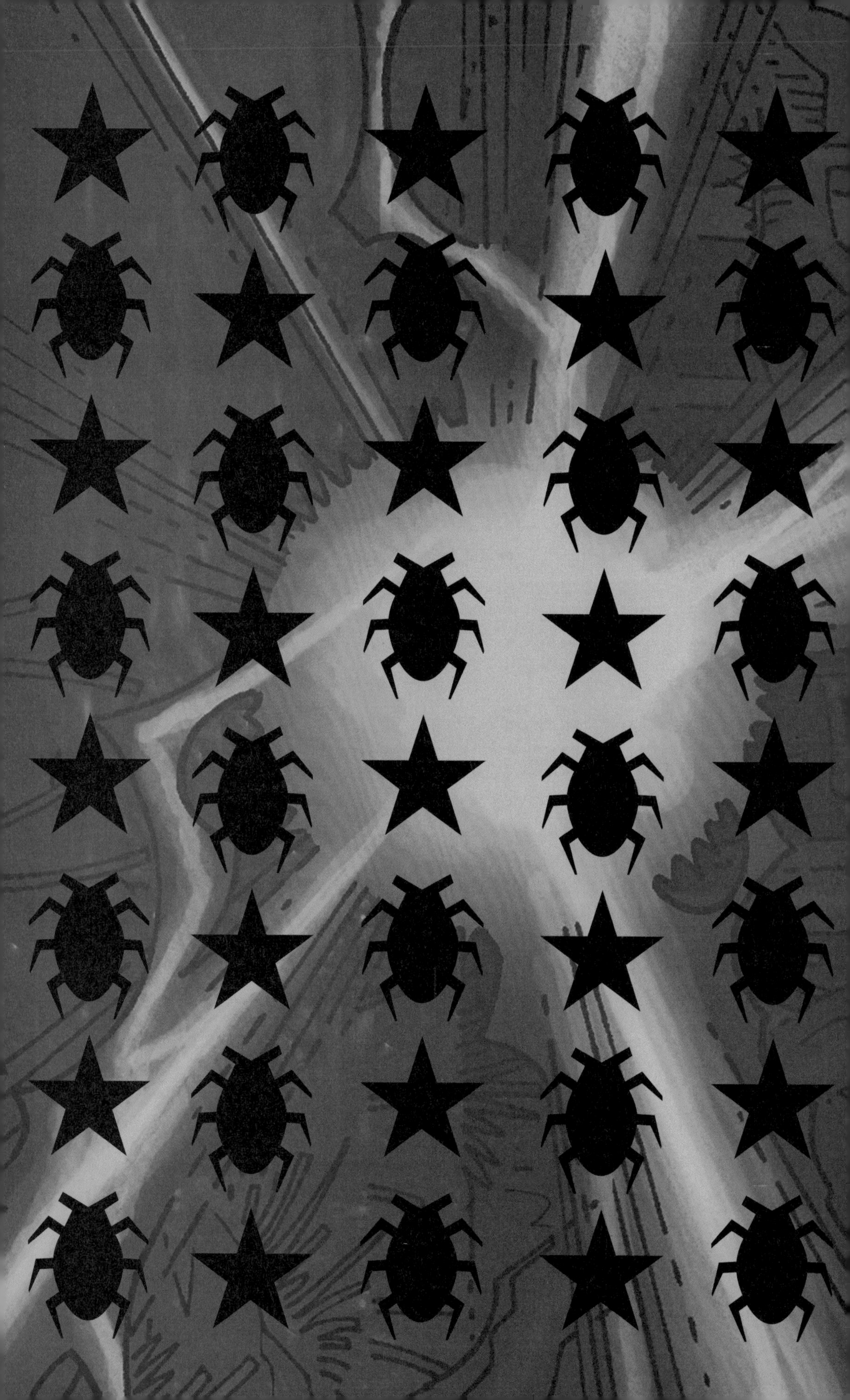

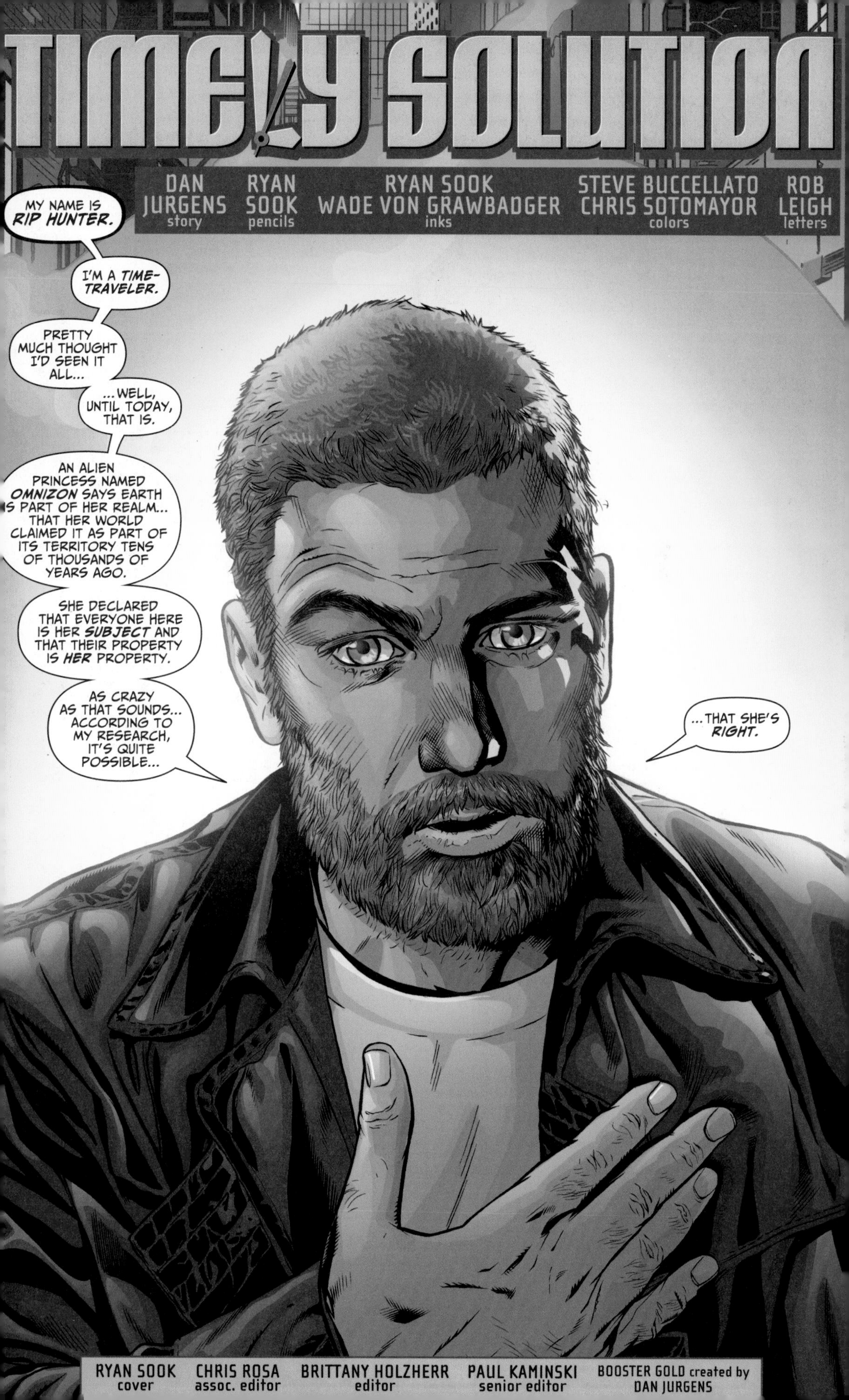
TIMELY SOLUTION
DAN JURGENS story
RYAN SOOK pencils
RYAN SOOK WADE VON GRAWBADGER inks
STEVE BUCCELLATO CHRIS SOTOMAYOR colors
ROB LEIGH letters
MY NAME IS RIP HUNTER.
I'M A TIME-TRAVELER.
PRETTY MUCH THOUGHT I'D SEEN IT ALL...
...WELL, UNTIL TODAY, THAT IS.
AN ALIEN PRINCESS NAMED OMNIZON SAYS EARTH S PART OF HER REALM... THAT HER WORLD CLAIMED IT AS PART OF ITS TERRITORY TENS OF THOUSANDS OF YEARS AGO.
SHE DECLARED THAT EVERYONE HERE IS HER SUBJECT AND THAT THEIR PROPERTY IS HER PROPERTY.
AS CRAZY AS THAT SOUNDS... ACCORDING TO MY RESEARCH, IT'S QUITE POSSIBLE...
...THAT SHE'S RIGHT.
RYAN SOOK cover
CHRIS ROSA assoc. editor
BRITTANY HOLZHERR editor
PAUL KAMINSKI senior editor
BOOSTER GOLD created by DAN JURGENS

UH-UH.
NO WAY.
OMNIZON IS NOT QUEEN OF ME.
WORD.
SAME.
UNDERSTOOD.
BUT WE CAN'T DISCOUNT HER CLAIMS. IT'S...
...MESSY.
ZZZT
CHRONAL ENERGY MITIGATED, TIME SPHERE UNDETECTABLE.
THE SITUATION IS NOT UNLIKE EARTH'S PAST, WHERE A COUNTRY WOULD PLANT A FLAG ON FOREIGN SOIL AND CLAIM IT AS ITS OWN.
I APPRECIATE THE REPAIR, MR. SKEETS.
ANYTIME, MS. BUGGLES.
SSSS
BVVVT
SHE TOOK BOOSTER AND BEETLE. HOW DO WE FIND THEM?
WE SHOULD ASSUME SHE TOOK THEM TO HER HOMEWORLD OF BEH'IMOOR, TERRI.
I ASSUME WE'LL MOUNT A RESCUE OPERATION?
SWAT
HEY! WATCH THOSE HANDS!
BZZT
SORRY.
WE NEED MORE INFORMATION ABOUT THE OVERALL SITUATION.
FORTUNATELY, I'M WELL EQUIPPED TO DO EXACTLY THAT.

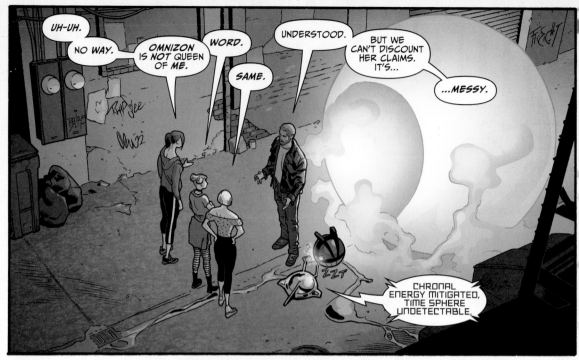

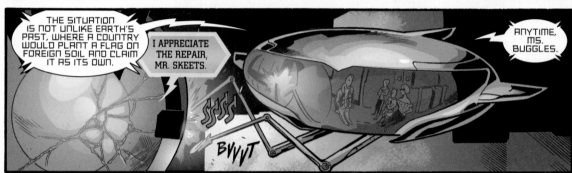

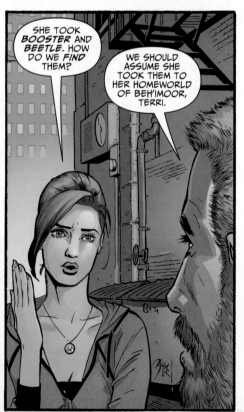

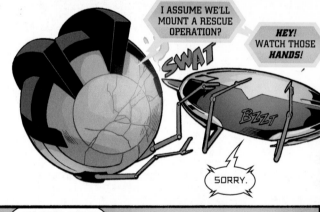

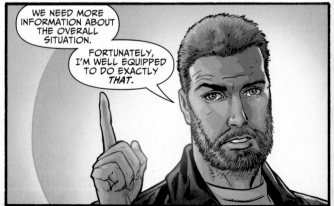

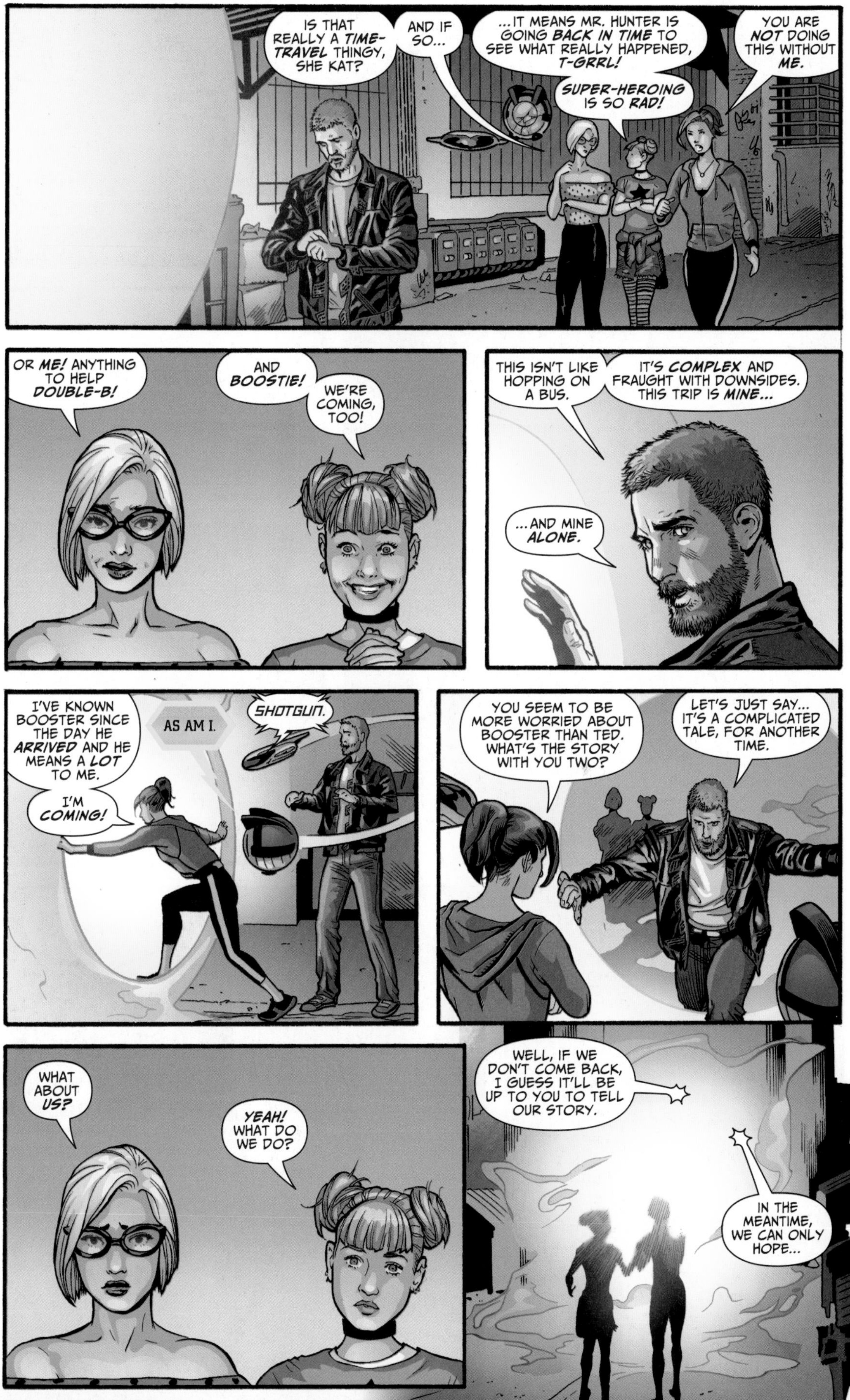
IS THAT REALLY A TIME-TRAVEL THINGY, SHE KAT?
AND IF SO...
...IT MEANS MR. HUNTER IS GOING BACK IN TIME TO SEE WHAT REALLY HAPPENED, T-GRRL!
SUPER-HEROING IS SO RAD!
YOU ARE NOT DOING THIS WITHOUT ME.
OR ME! ANYTHING TO HELP DOUBLE-B!
AND BOOSTIE!
WE'RE COMING, TOO!
THIS ISN'T LIKE HOPPING ON A BUS.
IT'S COMPLEX AND FRAUGHT WITH DOWNSIDES. THIS TRIP IS MINE...
...AND MINE ALONE.
I'VE KNOWN BOOSTER SINCE THE DAY HE ARRIVED AND HE MEANS A LOT TO ME.
I'M COMING!
AS AM I.
SHOTGUN.
YOU SEEM TO BE MORE WORRIED ABOUT BOOSTER THAN TED. WHAT'S THE STORY WITH YOU TWO?
LET'S JUST SAY... IT'S A COMPLICATED TALE, FOR ANOTHER TIME.
WHAT ABOUT US?
YEAH! WHAT DO WE DO?
WELL, IF WE DON'T COME BACK, I GUESS IT'LL BE UP TO YOU TO TELL OUR STORY.
IN THE MEANTIME, WE CAN ONLY HOPE...

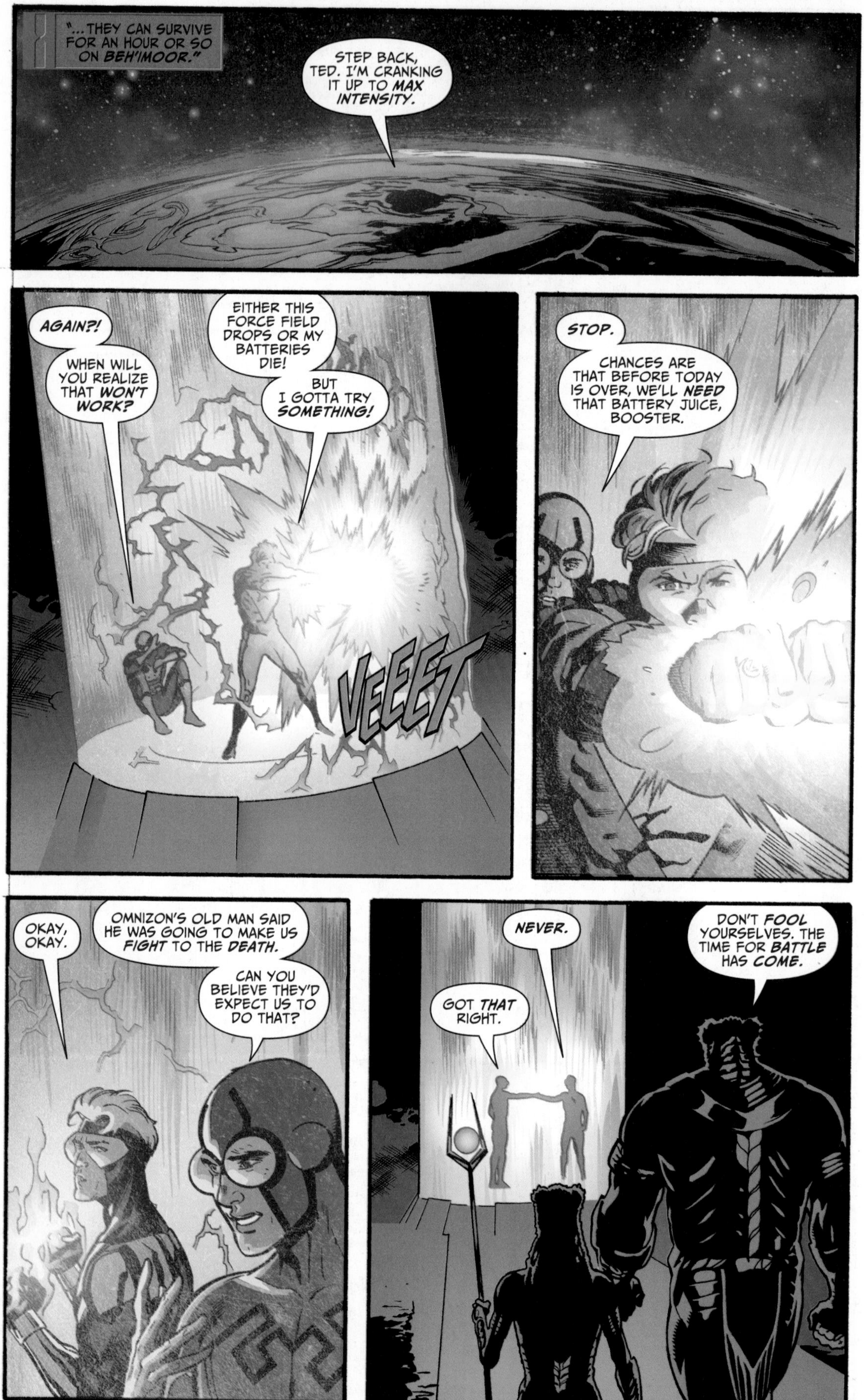
"...THEY CAN SURVIVE FOR AN HOUR OR SO ON BEH'IMOOR."
STEP BACK, TED. I'M CRANKING IT UP TO MAX INTENSITY.
AGAIN?!
WHEN WILL YOU REALIZE THAT WON'T WORK?
EITHER THIS FORCE FIELD DROPS OR MY BATTERIES DIE!
BUT I GOTTA TRY SOMETHING!
VEEET
STOP.
CHANCES ARE THAT BEFORE TODAY IS OVER, WE'LL NEED THAT BATTERY JUICE, BOOSTER.
OKAY, OKAY.
OMNIZON'S OLD MAN SAID HE WAS GOING TO MAKE US FIGHT TO THE DEATH.
CAN YOU BELIEVE THEY'D EXPECT US TO DO THAT?
NEVER.
GOT THAT RIGHT.
DON'T FOOL YOURSELVES. THE TIME FOR BATTLE HAS COME.

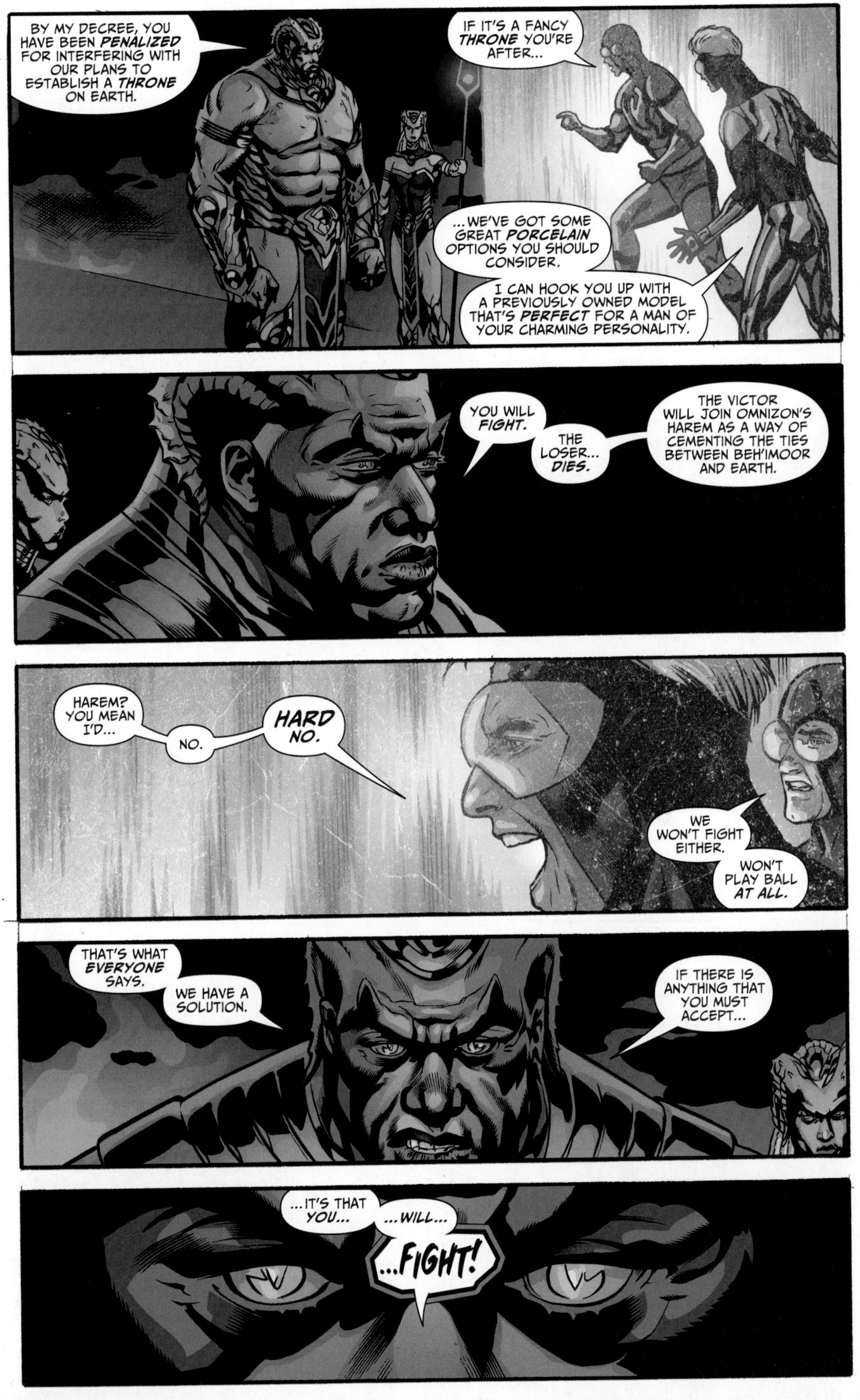
BY MY DECREE, YOU HAVE BEEN PENALIZED FOR INTERFERING WITH OUR PLANS TO ESTABLISH A THRONE ON EARTH.
IF IT'S A FANCY THRONE YOU'RE AFTER...
...WE'VE GOT SOME GREAT PORCELAIN OPTIONS YOU SHOULD CONSIDER.
I CAN HOOK YOU UP WITH A PREVIOUSLY OWNED MODEL THAT'S PERFECT FOR A MAN OF YOUR CHARMING PERSONALITY.
YOU WILL FIGHT.
THE LOSER... DIES.
THE VICTOR WILL JOIN OMNIZON'S HAREM AS A WAY OF CEMENTING THE TIES BETWEEN BEH'IMOOR AND EARTH.
HAREM? YOU MEAN I'D...
NO.
HARD NO.
WE WON'T FIGHT EITHER.
WON'T PLAY BALL AT ALL.
THAT'S WHAT EVERYONE SAYS.
WE HAVE A SOLUTION.
IF THERE IS ANYTHING THAT YOU MUST ACCEPT...
...IT'S THAT YOU...
...WILL...
...FIGHT!

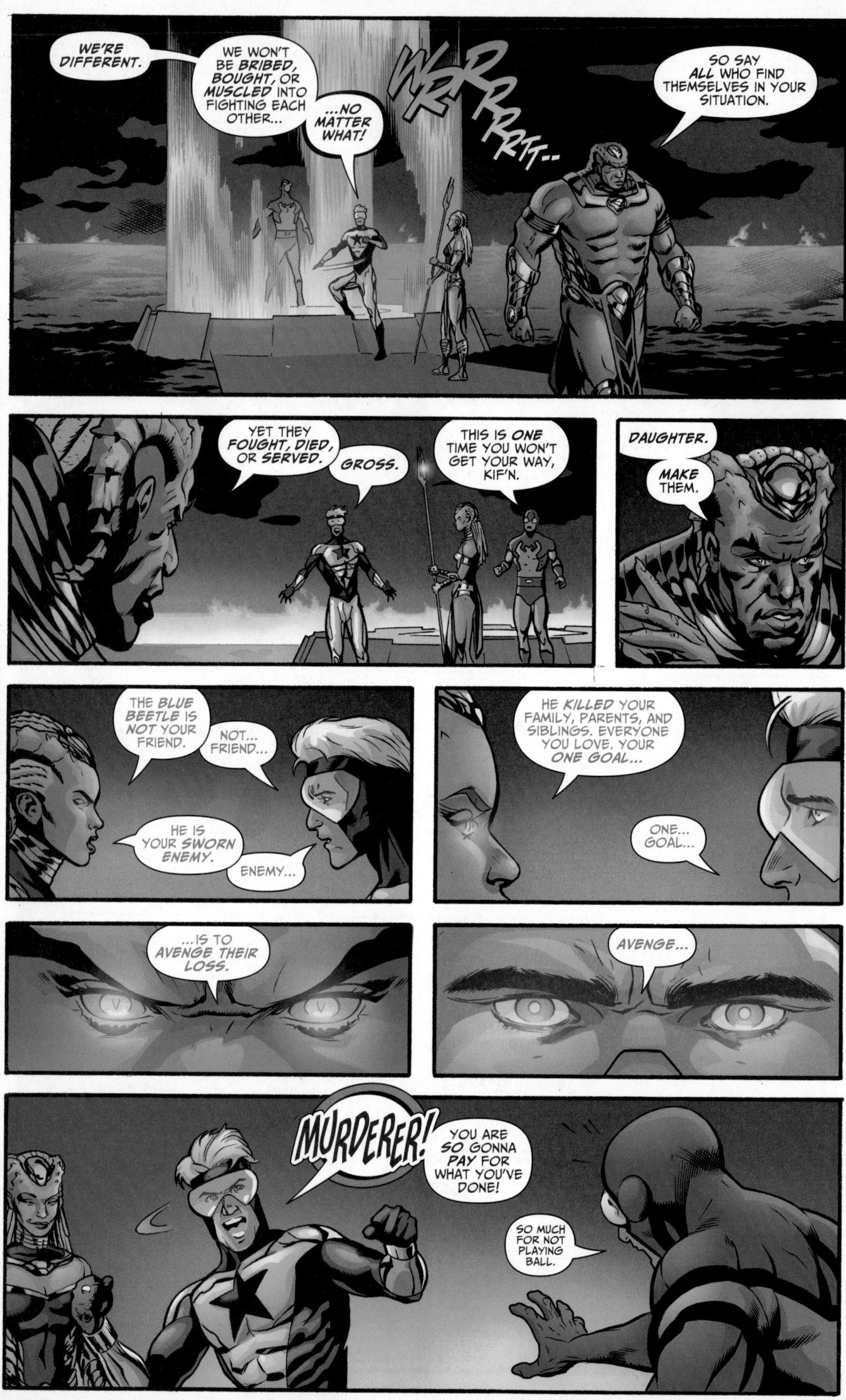
WE'RE DIFFERENT.
WE WON'T BE BRIBED, BOUGHT, OR MUSCLED INTO FIGHTING EACH OTHER...
...NO MATTER WHAT!
WRRRRRTT--
SO SAY ALL WHO FIND THEMSELVES IN YOUR SITUATION.
YET THEY FOUGHT, DIED, OR SERVED.
GROSS.
THIS IS ONE TIME YOU WON'T GET YOUR WAY, KIF'N.
DAUGHTER.
MAKE THEM.
THE BLUE BEETLE IS NOT YOUR FRIEND.
NOT... FRIEND...
HE IS YOUR SWORN ENEMY.
ENEMY...
HE KILLED YOUR FAMILY, PARENTS, AND SIBLINGS. EVERYONE YOU LOVE. YOUR ONE GOAL...
ONE... GOAL...
...IS TO AVENGE THEIR LOSS.
AVENGE...
MURDERER!
YOU ARE SO GONNA PAY FOR WHAT YOU'VE DONE!
SO MUCH FOR NOT PLAYING BALL.

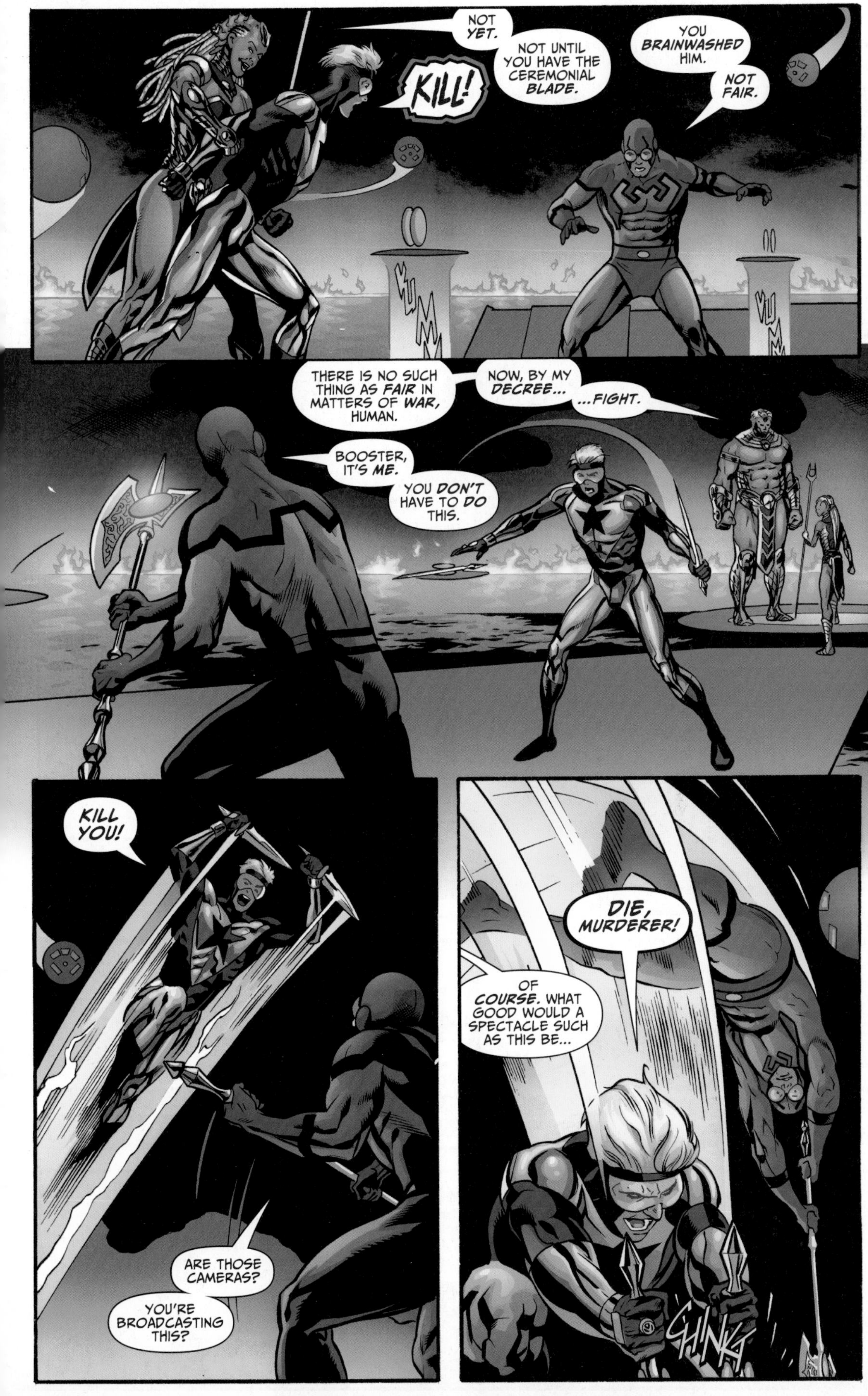
NOT YET.
KILL!
NOT UNTIL YOU HAVE THE CEREMONIAL BLADE.
YOU BRAINWASHED HIM.
NOT FAIR.
VUMM
VUMM
THERE IS NO SUCH THING AS FAIR IN MATTERS OF WAR, HUMAN.
NOW, BY MY DECREE...
...FIGHT.
BOOSTER, IT'S ME.
YOU DON'T HAVE TO DO THIS.
KILL YOU!
ARE THOSE CAMERAS?
YOU'RE BROADCASTING THIS?
DIE, MURDERER!
OF COURSE. WHAT GOOD WOULD A SPECTACLE SUCH AS THIS BE...
CHINK

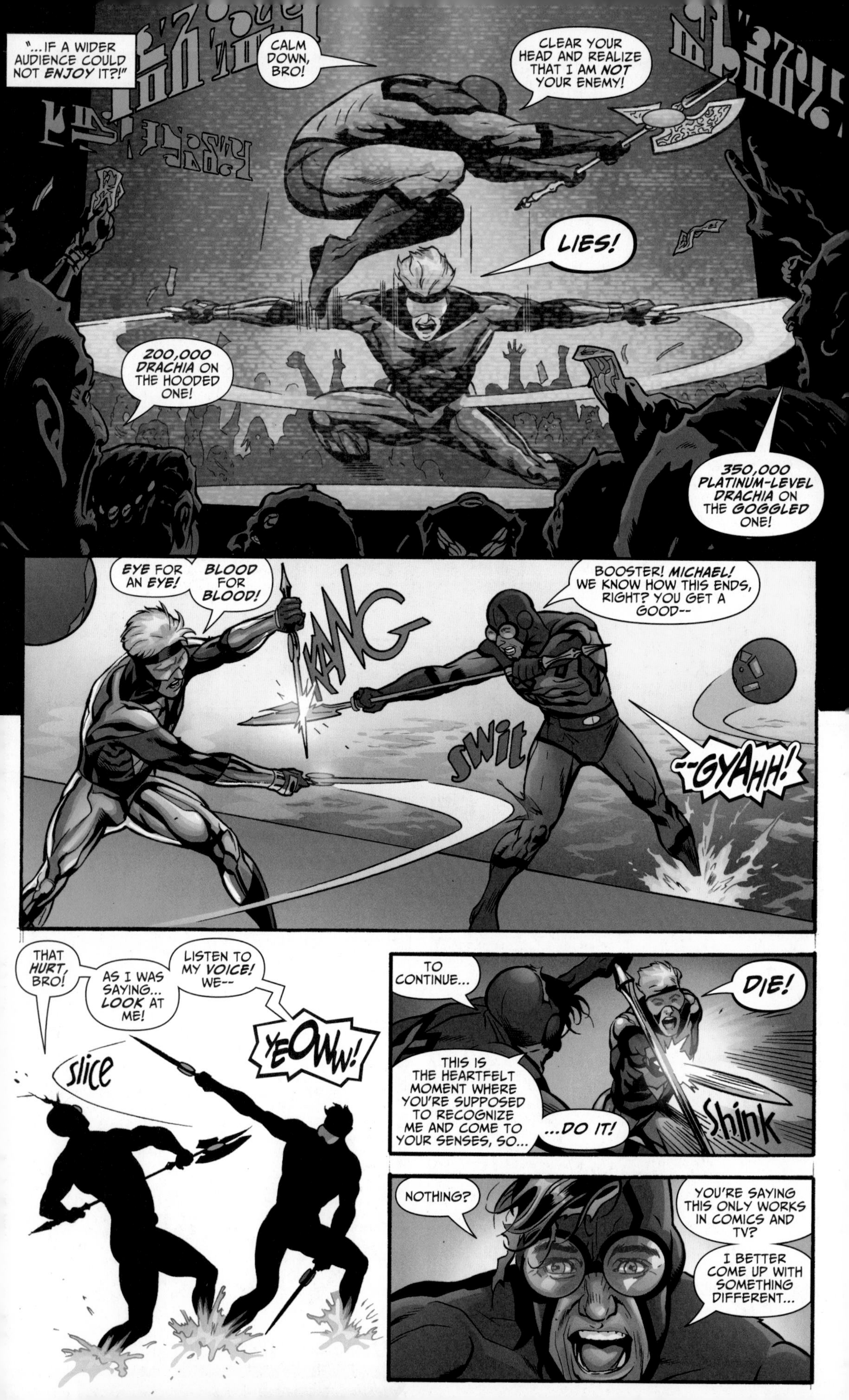
"...IF A WIDER AUDIENCE COULD NOT ENJOY IT?!"
CALM DOWN, BRO!
CLEAR YOUR HEAD AND REALIZE THAT I AM NOT YOUR ENEMY!
LIES!
200,000 DRACHIA ON THE HOODED ONE!
350,000 PLATINUM-LEVEL DRACHIA ON THE GOGGLED ONE!
EYE FOR AN EYE!
BLOOD FOR BLOOD!
KRANG
BOOSTER! MICHAEL! WE KNOW HOW THIS ENDS, RIGHT? YOU GET A GOOD--
SWIT
--GYAHH!
THAT HURT, BRO!
AS I WAS SAYING... LOOK AT ME!
LISTEN TO MY VOICE! WE--
YEOWW!
SLICE
TO CONTINUE...
DIE!
THIS IS THE HEARTFELT MOMENT WHERE YOU'RE SUPPOSED TO RECOGNIZE ME AND COME TO YOUR SENSES, SO...
...DO IT!
SHINK
NOTHING?
YOU'RE SAYING THIS ONLY WORKS IN COMICS AND TV?
I BETTER COME UP WITH SOMETHING DIFFERENT...

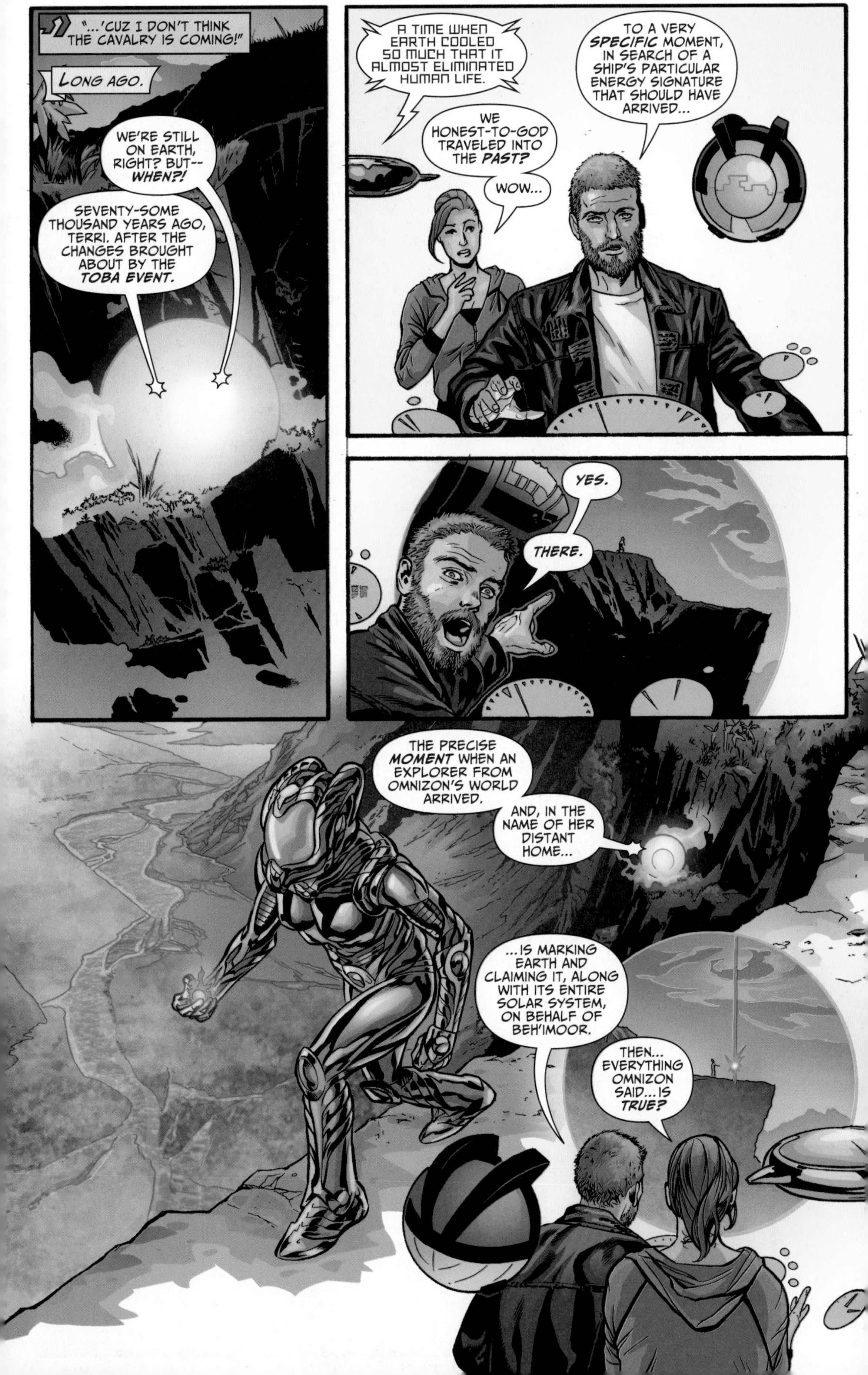
"...'CUZ I DON'T THINK THE CAVALRY IS COMING!"
LONG AGO.
WE'RE STILL ON EARTH, RIGHT? BUT-- WHEN?!
SEVENTY-SOME THOUSAND YEARS AGO, TERRI. AFTER THE CHANGES BROUGHT ABOUT BY THE TOBA EVENT.
A TIME WHEN EARTH COOLED SO MUCH THAT IT ALMOST ELIMINATED HUMAN LIFE.
TO A VERY SPECIFIC MOMENT, IN SEARCH OF A SHIP'S PARTICULAR ENERGY SIGNATURE THAT SHOULD HAVE ARRIVED...
WE HONEST-TO-GOD TRAVELED INTO THE PAST?
WOW...
YES.
THERE.
THE PRECISE MOMENT WHEN AN EXPLORER FROM OMNIZON'S WORLD ARRIVED.
AND, IN THE NAME OF HER DISTANT HOME...
...IS MARKING EARTH AND CLAIMING IT, ALONG WITH ITS ENTIRE SOLAR SYSTEM, ON BEHALF OF BEH'IMOOR.
THEN... EVERYTHING OMNIZON SAID...IS TRUE?

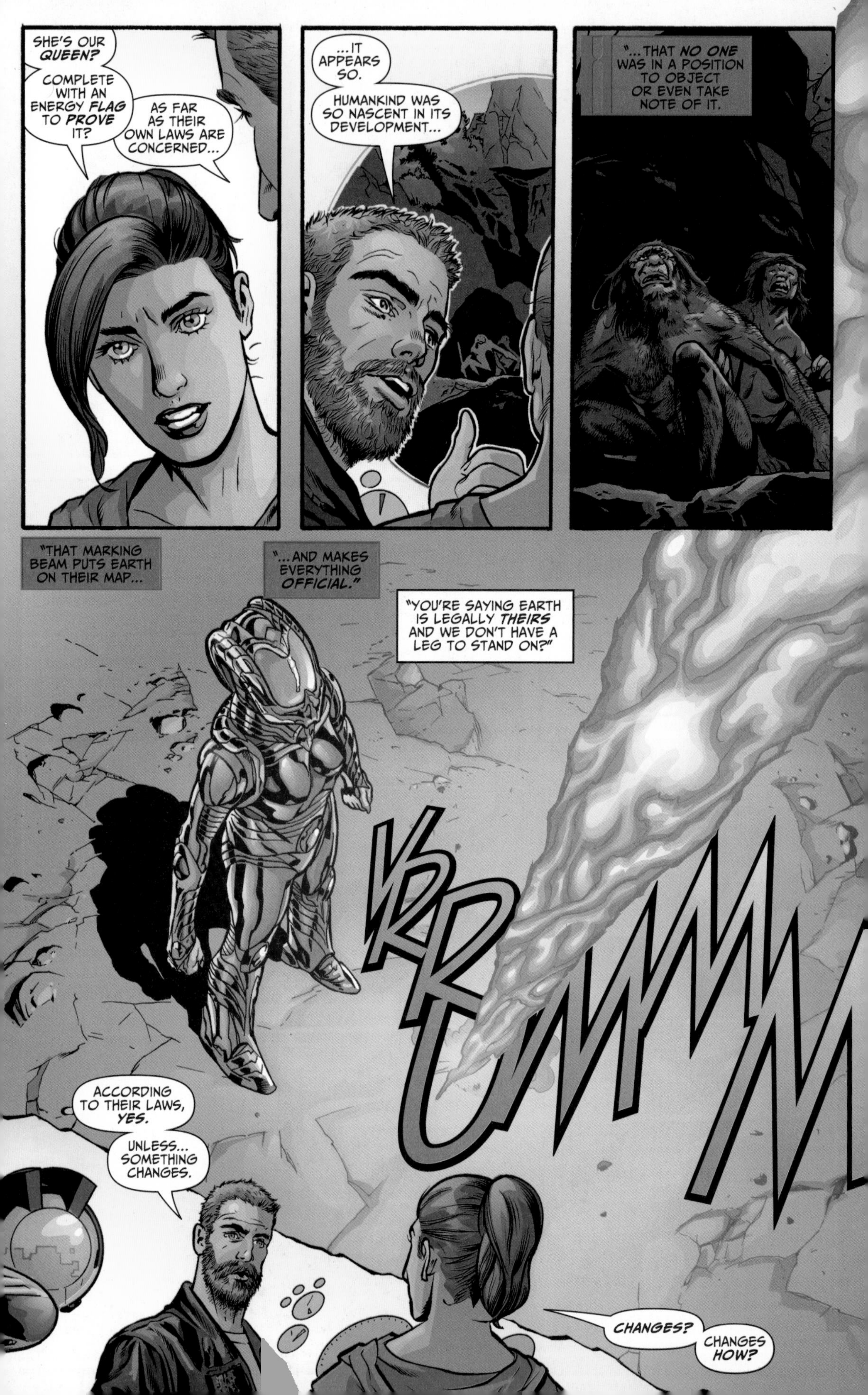
SHE'S OUR QUEEN?
COMPLETE WITH AN ENERGY FLAG TO PROVE IT?
AS FAR AS THEIR OWN LAWS ARE CONCERNED...
...IT APPEARS SO.
HUMANKIND WAS SO NASCENT IN ITS DEVELOPMENT...
"...THAT NO ONE WAS IN A POSITION TO OBJECT OR EVEN TAKE NOTE OF IT.
"THAT MARKING BEAM PUTS EARTH ON THEIR MAP...
"...AND MAKES EVERYTHING OFFICIAL."
"YOU'RE SAYING EARTH IS LEGALLY THEIRS AND WE DON'T HAVE A LEG TO STAND ON?"
VRRUMMM
ACCORDING TO THEIR LAWS, YES.
UNLESS... SOMETHING CHANGES.
CHANGES?
CHANGES HOW?

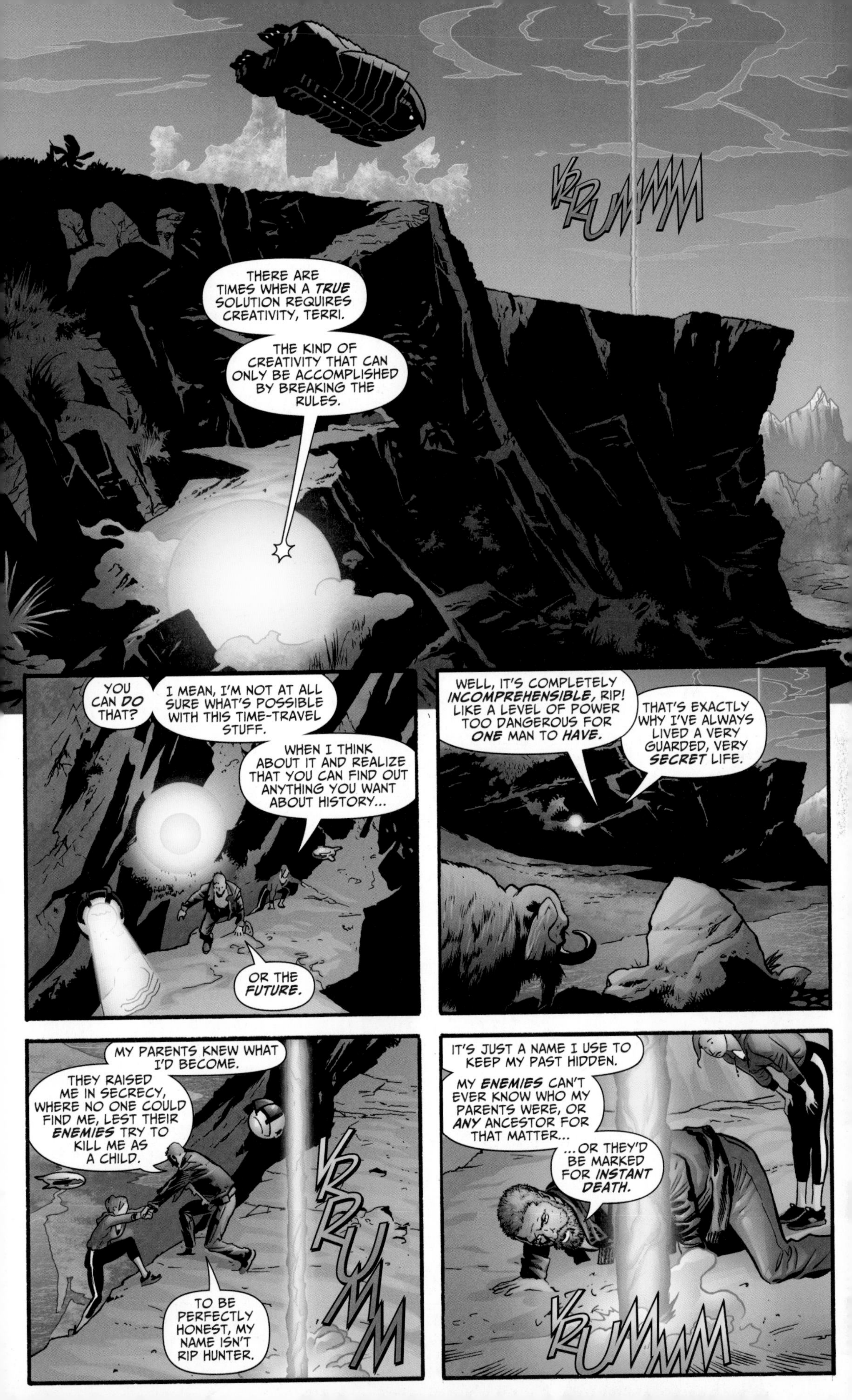
VRRUMMMM
THERE ARE TIMES WHEN A TRUE SOLUTION REQUIRES CREATIVITY, TERRI.
THE KIND OF CREATIVITY THAT CAN ONLY BE ACCOMPLISHED BY BREAKING THE RULES.
YOU CAN DO THAT?
I MEAN, I'M NOT AT ALL SURE WHAT'S POSSIBLE WITH THIS TIME-TRAVEL STUFF.
WHEN I THINK ABOUT IT AND REALIZE THAT YOU CAN FIND OUT ANYTHING YOU WANT ABOUT HISTORY...
OR THE FUTURE.
WELL, IT'S COMPLETELY INCOMPREHENSIBLE, RIP! LIKE A LEVEL OF POWER TOO DANGEROUS FOR ONE MAN TO HAVE.
THAT'S EXACTLY WHY I'VE ALWAYS LIVED A VERY GUARDED, VERY SECRET LIFE.
MY PARENTS KNEW WHAT I'D BECOME.
THEY RAISED ME IN SECRECY, WHERE NO ONE COULD FIND ME, LEST THEIR ENEMIES TRY TO KILL ME AS A CHILD.
TO BE PERFECTLY HONEST, MY NAME ISN'T RIP HUNTER.
VRRUMM
IT'S JUST A NAME I USE TO KEEP MY PAST HIDDEN.
MY ENEMIES CAN'T EVER KNOW WHO MY PARENTS WERE, OR ANY ANCESTOR FOR THAT MATTER...
...OR THEY'D BE MARKED FOR INSTANT DEATH.
VRUMMMM

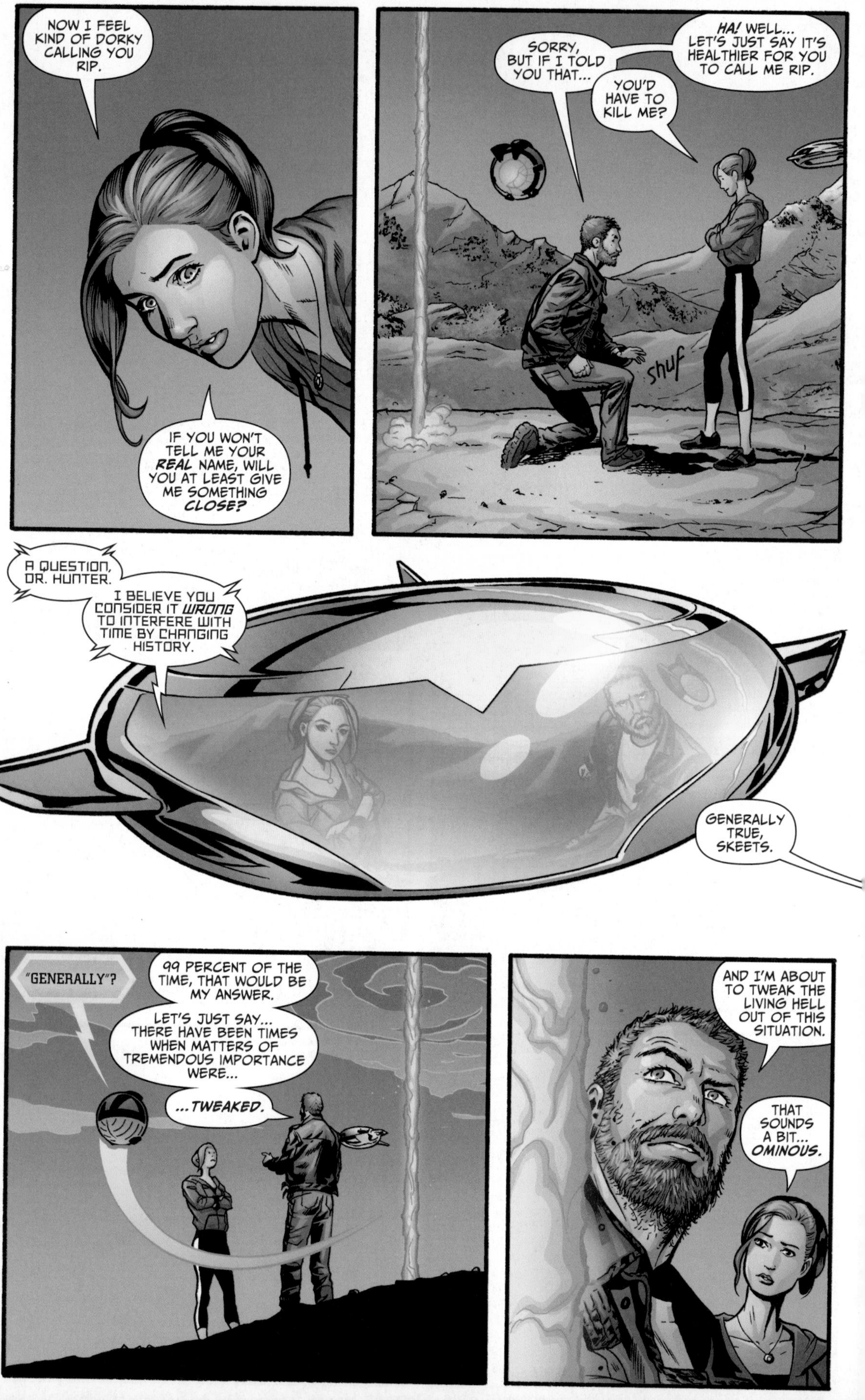
NOW I FEEL KIND OF DORKY CALLING YOU RIP.
IF YOU WON'T TELL ME YOUR REAL NAME, WILL YOU AT LEAST GIVE ME SOMETHING CLOSE?
SORRY, BUT IF I TOLD YOU THAT...
YOU'D HAVE TO KILL ME?
HA! WELL... LET'S JUST SAY IT'S HEALTHIER FOR YOU TO CALL ME RIP.
SHUF
A QUESTION, DR. HUNTER.
I BELIEVE YOU CONSIDER IT WRONG TO INTERFERE WITH TIME BY CHANGING HISTORY.
GENERALLY TRUE, SKEETS.
"GENERALLY"?
99 PERCENT OF THE TIME, THAT WOULD BE MY ANSWER.
LET'S JUST SAY... THERE HAVE BEEN TIMES WHEN MATTERS OF TREMENDOUS IMPORTANCE WERE...
...TWEAKED.
AND I'M ABOUT TO TWEAK THE LIVING HELL OUT OF THIS SITUATION.
THAT SOUNDS A BIT... OMINOUS.

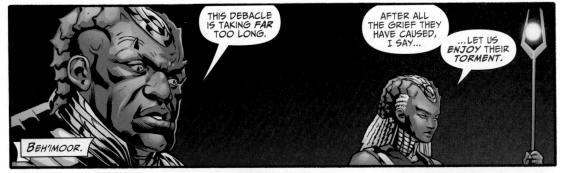

THIS DEBACLE IS TAKING *FAR* TOO LONG.

BEH'IMOOR.

AFTER ALL THE GRIEF THEY HAVE CAUSED, I SAY...

...LET US *ENJOY* THEIR *TORMENT*.

YOU SHOULD BE FIGHTING *OMNIZON*-- NOT *ME*!

YOU'VE *GOT* TO BREAK HER CONTROL OVER YOU!

NO MORE *BABBLING*!

DISARMING ME WON'T HELP...

...WHEN I CAN TAKE *YOURS*!

DUDE... I DON'T WANT TO HURT YOU...

DOUBLE MONEY ON THE BLOND!

...BUT YOU'VE *BACKED* ME INTO A *CORNER*!

STILL TIME TO RAISE YOUR BETS!

I SAY THE HOODED ONE *RALLIES*!

WHOA!

A FINE ADDITION TO THE HAREM!

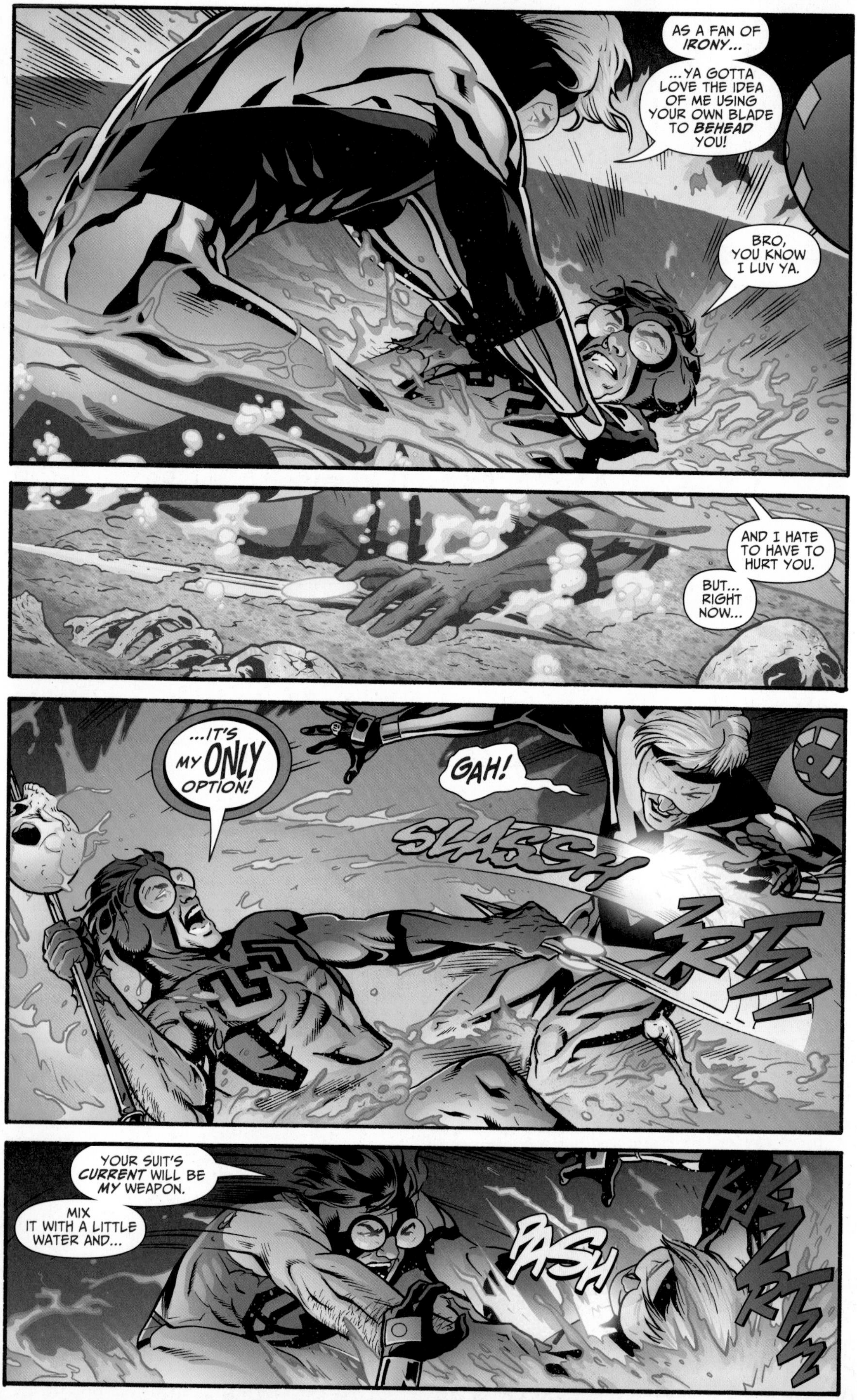
AS A FAN OF IRONY...
...YA GOTTA LOVE THE IDEA OF ME USING YOUR OWN BLADE TO BEHEAD YOU!
BRO, YOU KNOW I LUV YA.
AND I HATE TO HAVE TO HURT YOU.
BUT... RIGHT NOW...
...IT'S MY ONLY OPTION!
GAH!
SLASSH
WRRM
YOUR SUIT'S CURRENT WILL BE MY WEAPON.
MIX IT WITH A LITTLE WATER AND...
PASH
KKRRMM

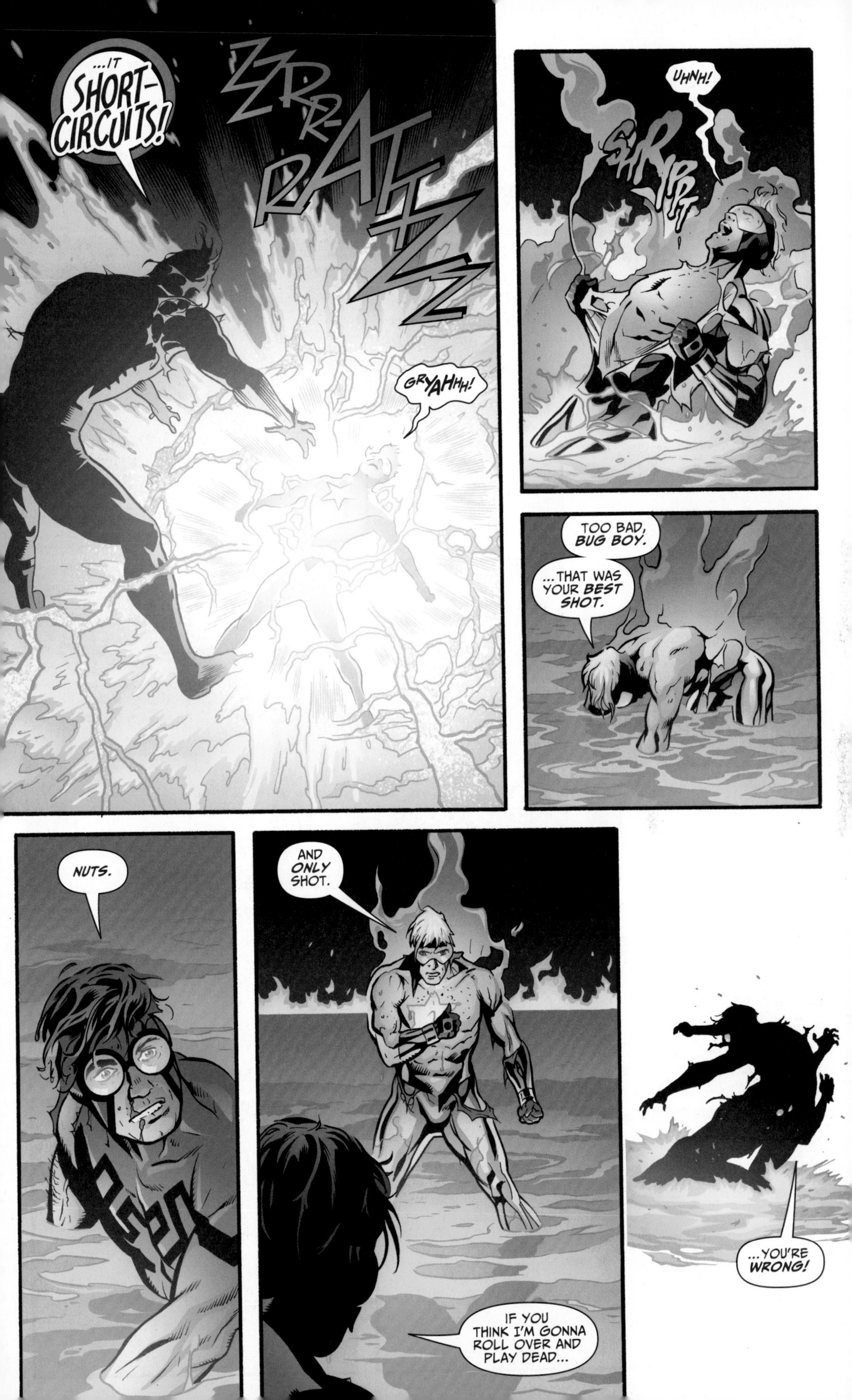
...IT SHORT-CIRCUITS!
ZZRR-RAHZZ
GRYAHHH!
UHNH!
SHRIPPT
TOO BAD, BUG BOY.
...THAT WAS YOUR BEST SHOT.
NUTS.
AND ONLY SHOT.
IF YOU THINK I'M GONNA ROLL OVER AND PLAY DEAD...
...YOU'RE WRONG!

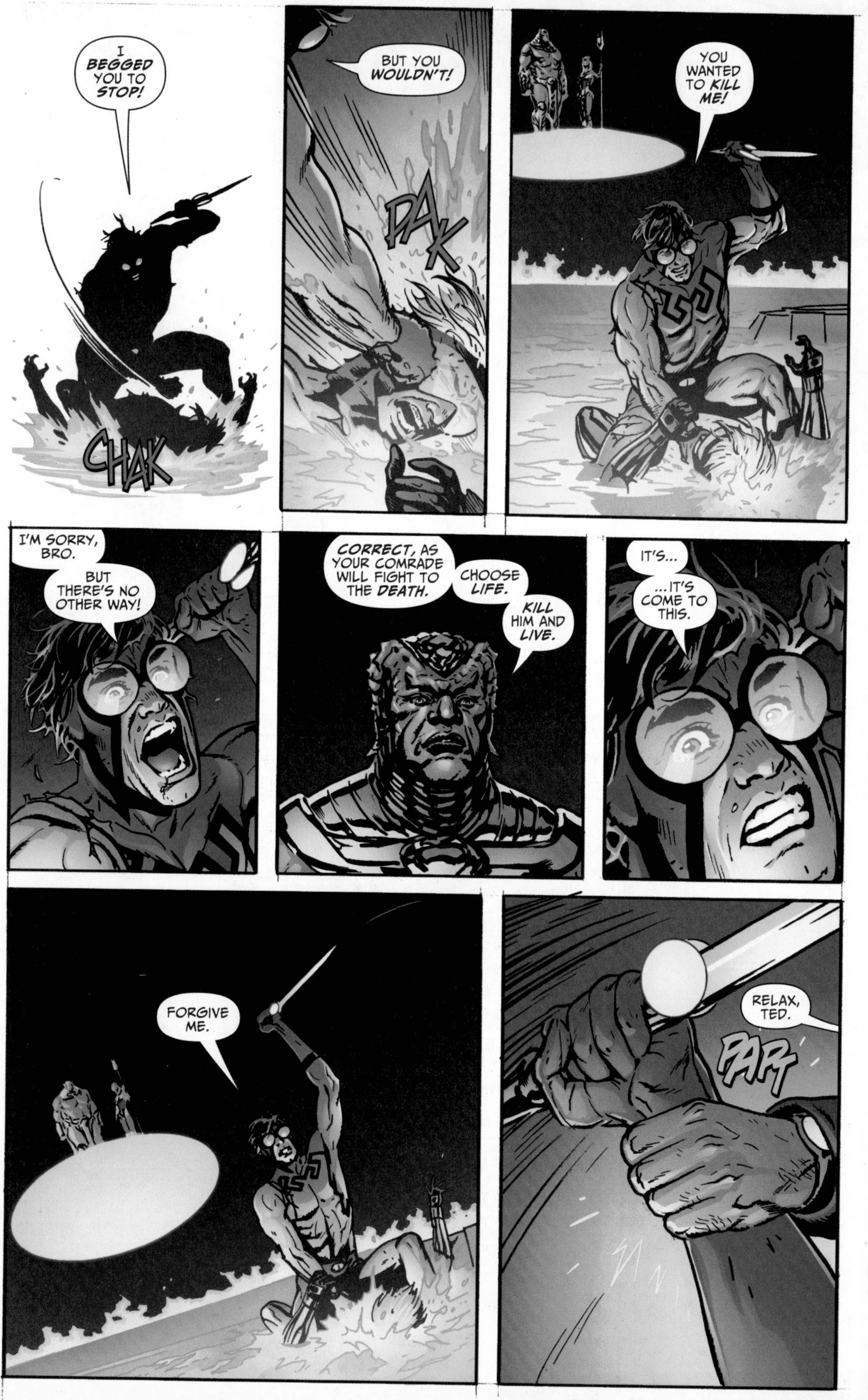
I BEGGED YOU TO STOP!
CHAK
BUT YOU WOULDN'T!
DAK
YOU WANTED TO KILL ME!
I'M SORRY, BRO.
BUT THERE'S NO OTHER WAY!
CORRECT, AS YOUR COMRADE WILL FIGHT TO THE DEATH.
CHOOSE LIFE.
KILL HIM AND LIVE.
IT'S...
...IT'S COME TO THIS.
FORGIVE ME.
RELAX, TED.
PAP

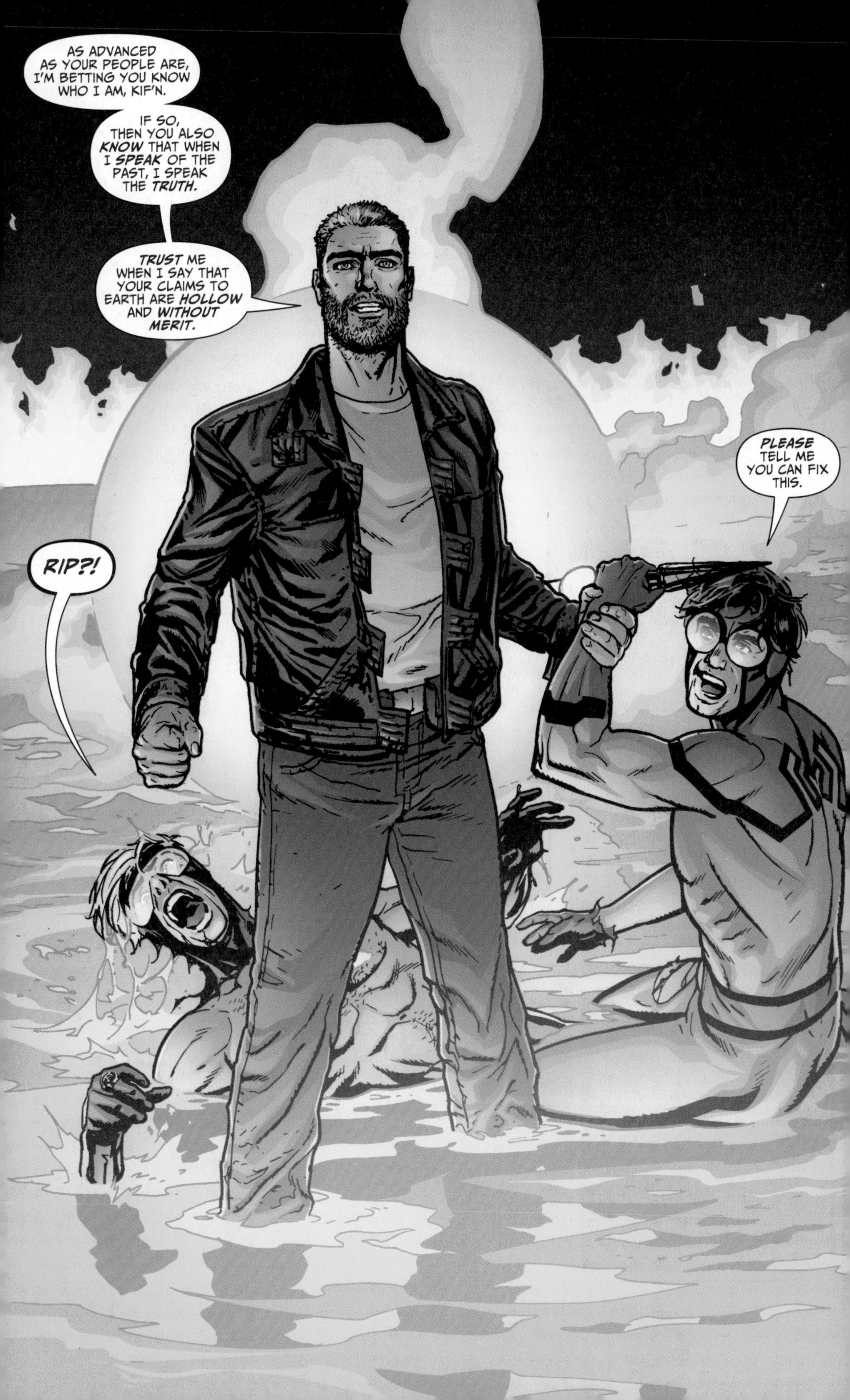
AS ADVANCED AS YOUR PEOPLE ARE, I'M BETTING YOU KNOW WHO I AM, KIF'N.
IF SO, THEN YOU ALSO KNOW THAT WHEN I SPEAK OF THE PAST, I SPEAK THE TRUTH.
TRUST ME WHEN I SAY THAT YOUR CLAIMS TO EARTH ARE HOLLOW AND WITHOUT MERIT.
RIP?!
PLEASE TELL ME YOU CAN FIX THIS.

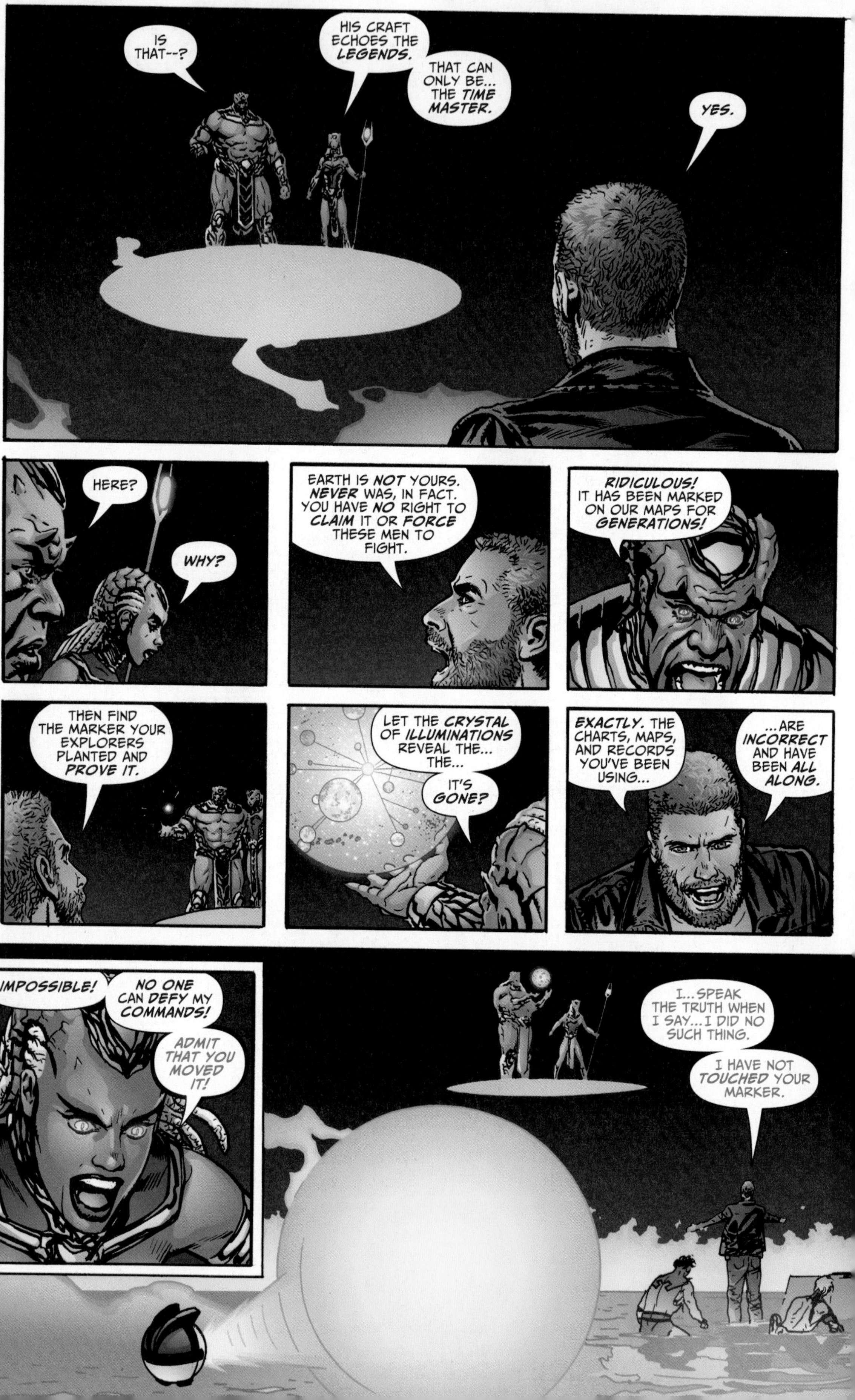
IS THAT--?
HIS CRAFT ECHOES THE LEGENDS.
THAT CAN ONLY BE... THE TIME MASTER.
YES.
HERE?
WHY?
EARTH IS NOT YOURS. NEVER WAS, IN FACT. YOU HAVE NO RIGHT TO CLAIM IT OR FORCE THESE MEN TO FIGHT.
RIDICULOUS! IT HAS BEEN MARKED ON OUR MAPS FOR GENERATIONS!
THEN FIND THE MARKER YOUR EXPLORERS PLANTED AND PROVE IT.
LET THE CRYSTAL OF ILLUMINATIONS REVEAL THE... THE...
IT'S GONE?
EXACTLY. THE CHARTS, MAPS, AND RECORDS YOU'VE BEEN USING...
...ARE INCORRECT AND HAVE BEEN ALL ALONG.
IMPOSSIBLE!
NO ONE CAN DEFY MY COMMANDS!
ADMIT THAT YOU MOVED IT!
I...SPEAK THE TRUTH WHEN I SAY...I DID NO SUCH THING.
I HAVE NOT TOUCHED YOUR MARKER.

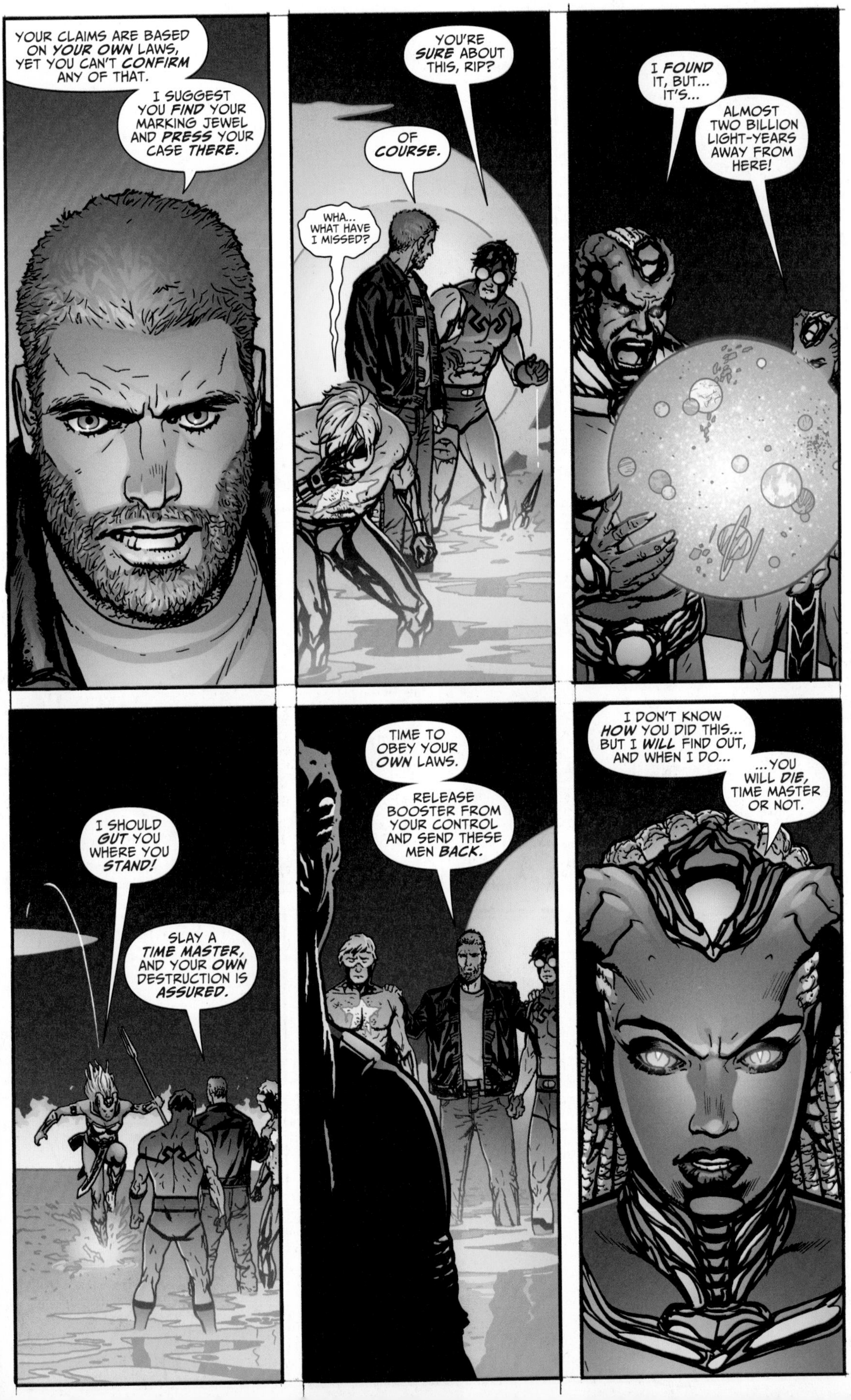
YOUR CLAIMS ARE BASED ON YOUR OWN LAWS, YET YOU CAN'T CONFIRM ANY OF THAT.
I SUGGEST YOU FIND YOUR MARKING JEWEL AND PRESS YOUR CASE THERE.
YOU'RE SURE ABOUT THIS, RIP?
OF COURSE.
WHA... WHAT HAVE I MISSED?
I FOUND IT, BUT... IT'S...
ALMOST TWO BILLION LIGHT-YEARS AWAY FROM HERE!
I SHOULD GUT YOU WHERE YOU STAND!
SLAY A TIME MASTER, AND YOUR OWN DESTRUCTION IS ASSURED.
TIME TO OBEY YOUR OWN LAWS.
RELEASE BOOSTER FROM YOUR CONTROL AND SEND THESE MEN BACK.
I DON'T KNOW HOW YOU DID THIS... BUT I WILL FIND OUT, AND WHEN I DO...
...YOU WILL DIE, TIME MASTER OR NOT.

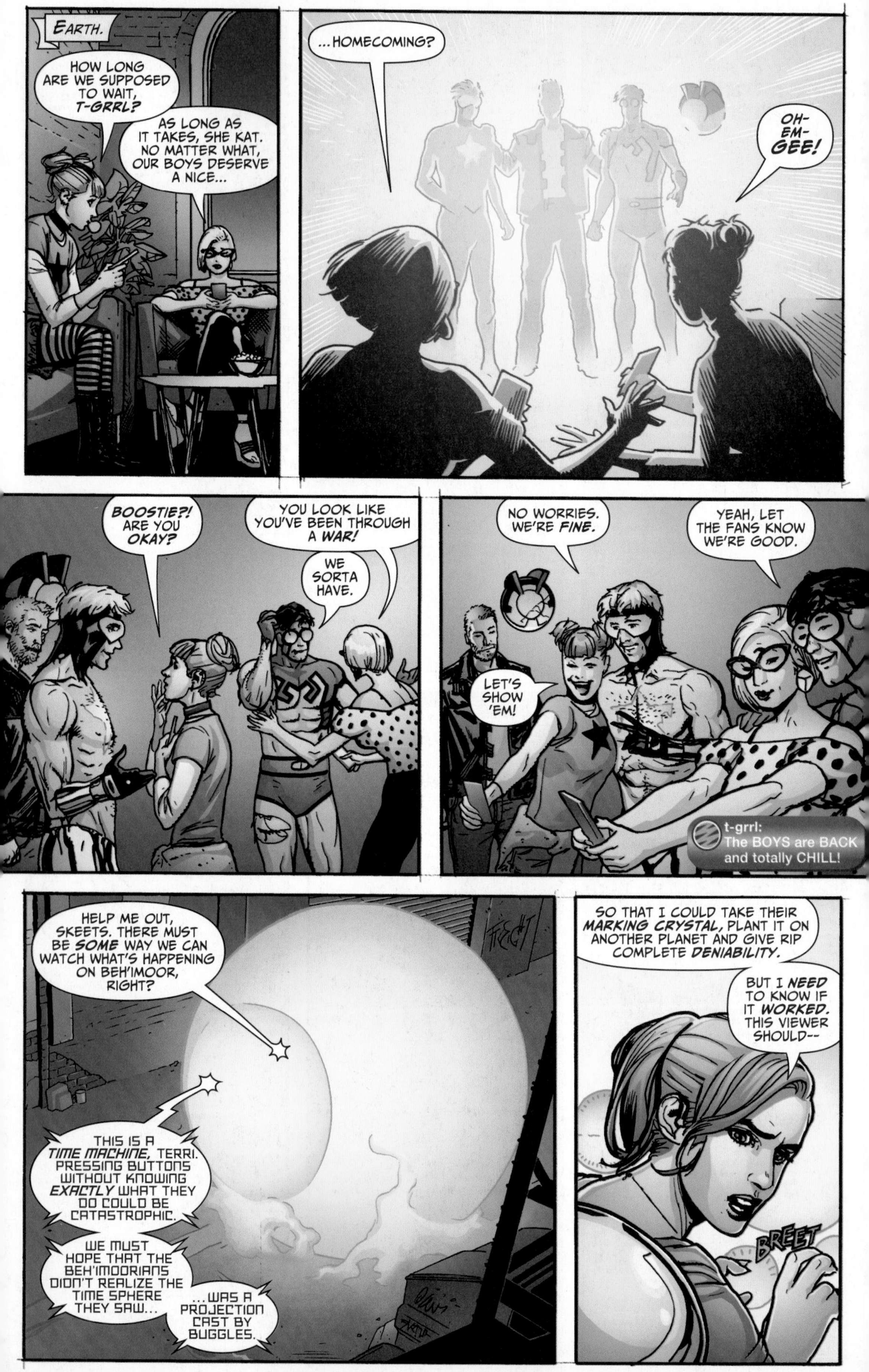
EARTH.
HOW LONG ARE WE SUPPOSED TO WAIT, T-GRRL?
AS LONG AS IT TAKES, SHE KAT. NO MATTER WHAT, OUR BOYS DESERVE A NICE...
...HOMECOMING?
OH-EM-GEE!
BOOSTIE?! ARE YOU OKAY?
YOU LOOK LIKE YOU'VE BEEN THROUGH A WAR!
WE SORTA HAVE.
NO WORRIES. WE'RE FINE.
YEAH, LET THE FANS KNOW WE'RE GOOD.
LET'S SHOW 'EM!
t-grrl:
The BOYS are BACK and totally CHILL!
HELP ME OUT, SKEETS. THERE MUST BE SOME WAY WE CAN WATCH WHAT'S HAPPENING ON BEH'IMOOR, RIGHT?
THIS IS A TIME MACHINE, TERRI. PRESSING BUTTONS WITHOUT KNOWING EXACTLY WHAT THEY DO COULD BE CATASTROPHIC.
WE MUST HOPE THAT THE BEH'IMOORIANS DIDN'T REALIZE THE TIME SPHERE THEY SAW...
...WAS A PROJECTION CAST BY BUGGLES.
SO THAT I COULD TAKE THEIR MARKING CRYSTAL, PLANT IT ON ANOTHER PLANET AND GIVE RIP COMPLETE DENIABILITY.
BUT I NEED TO KNOW IF IT WORKED. THIS VIEWER SHOULD--
BREET

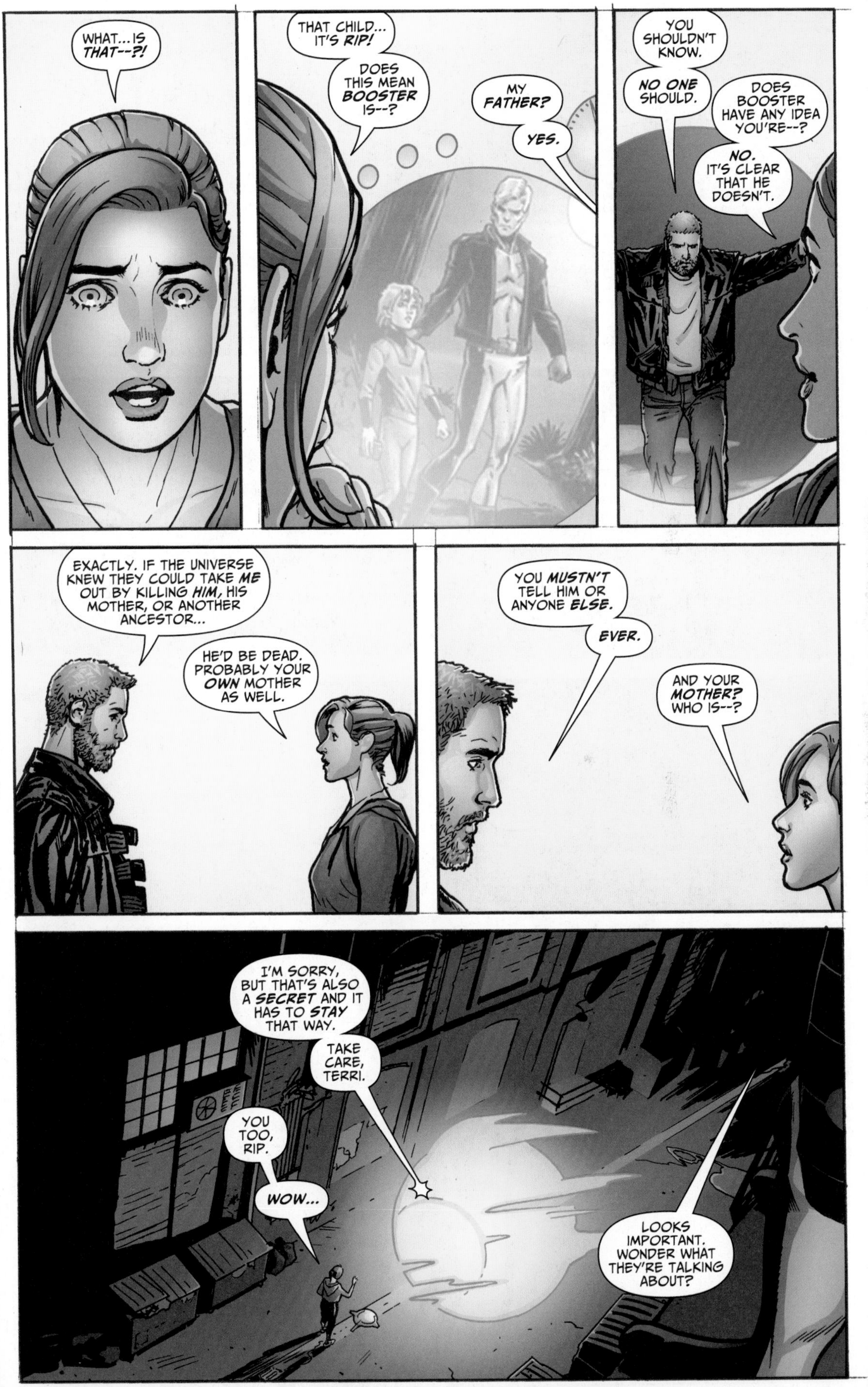

WHAT... IS THAT--?!
THAT CHILD... IT'S RIP!
DOES THIS MEAN BOOSTER IS--?
MY FATHER?
YES.
YOU SHOULDN'T KNOW.
NO ONE SHOULD.
DOES BOOSTER HAVE ANY IDEA YOU'RE--?
NO. IT'S CLEAR THAT HE DOESN'T.
EXACTLY. IF THE UNIVERSE KNEW THEY COULD TAKE ME OUT BY KILLING HIM, HIS MOTHER, OR ANOTHER ANCESTOR...
HE'D BE DEAD. PROBABLY YOUR OWN MOTHER AS WELL.
YOU MUSTN'T TELL HIM OR ANYONE ELSE.
EVER.
AND YOUR MOTHER? WHO IS--?
I'M SORRY, BUT THAT'S ALSO A SECRET AND IT HAS TO STAY THAT WAY.
TAKE CARE, TERRI.
YOU TOO, RIP.
WOW...
LOOKS IMPORTANT. WONDER WHAT THEY'RE TALKING ABOUT?

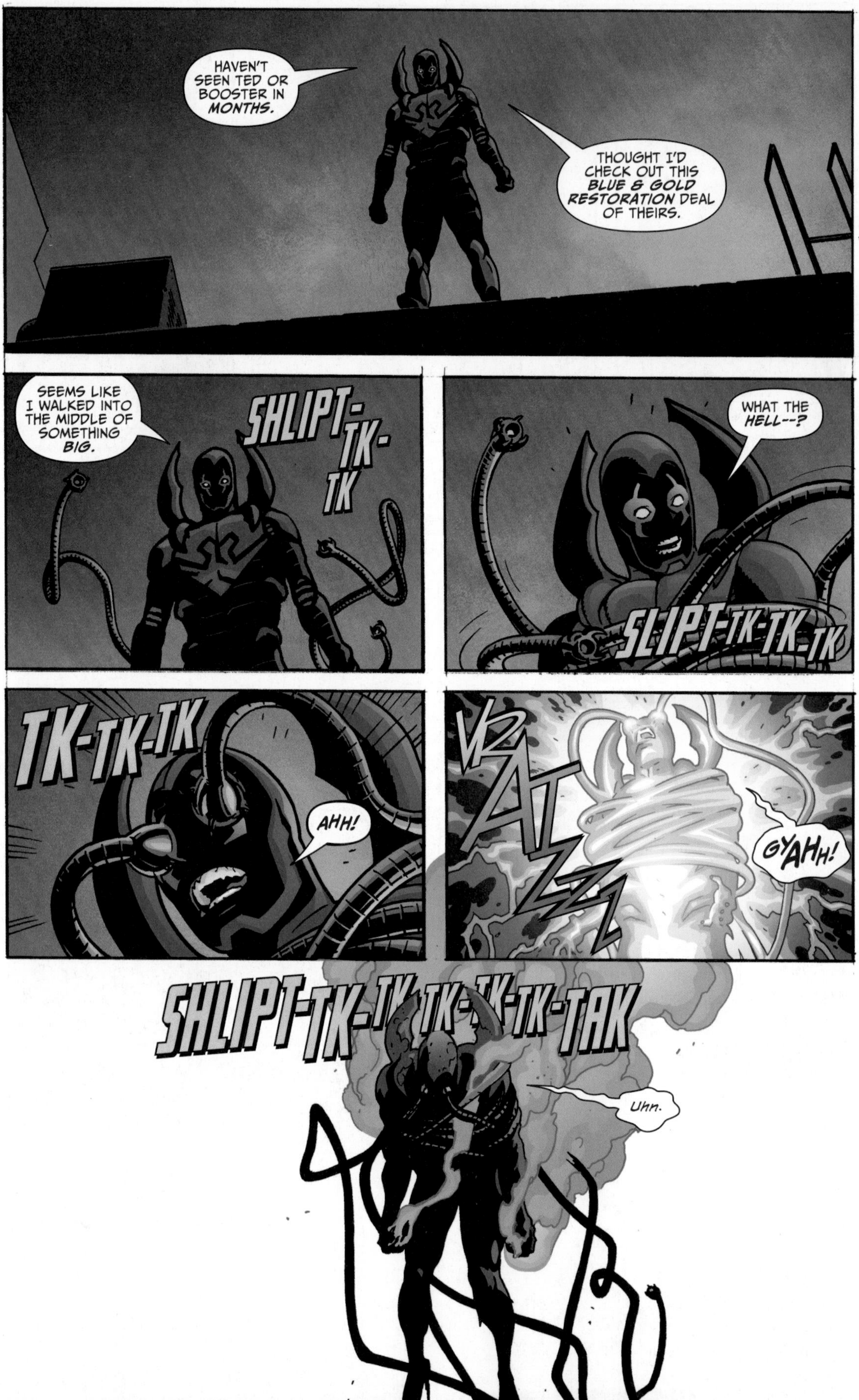
HAVEN'T SEEN TED OR BOOSTER IN MONTHS.
THOUGHT I'D CHECK OUT THIS BLUE & GOLD RESTORATION DEAL OF THEIRS.
SEEMS LIKE I WALKED INTO THE MIDDLE OF SOMETHING BIG.
SHLIPT-TK-TK
WHAT THE HELL--?
SLIPT-TK-TK-TK
TK-TK-TK
AHH!
VRAIZZZ
GYAHH!
SHLIPT-TK-TK
TK-TK-TAK
Uhn.

Blue & Gold #7
cover by Ryan Sook

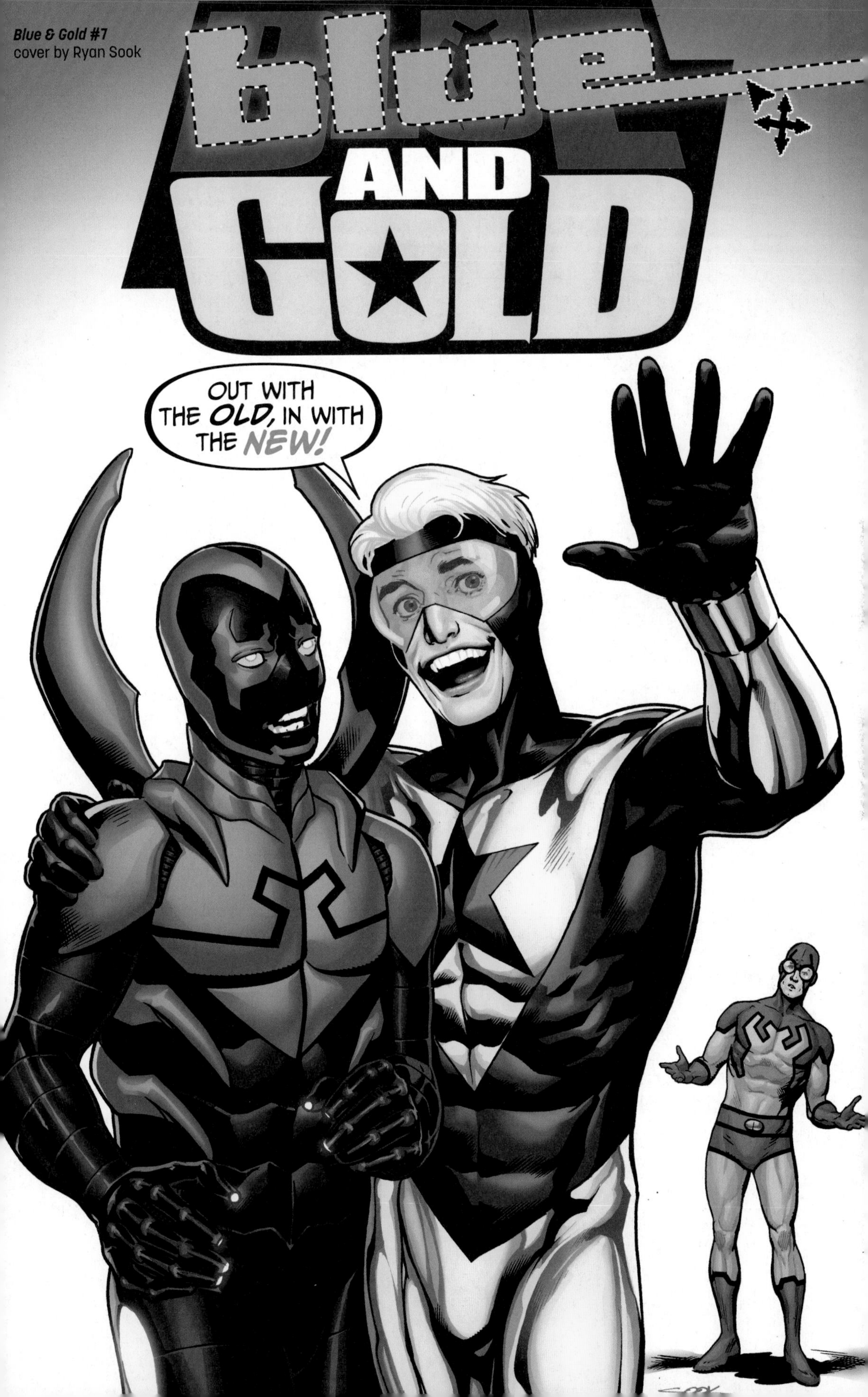

BLUE AND GOLD
OUT WITH THE OLD, IN WITH THE NEW!

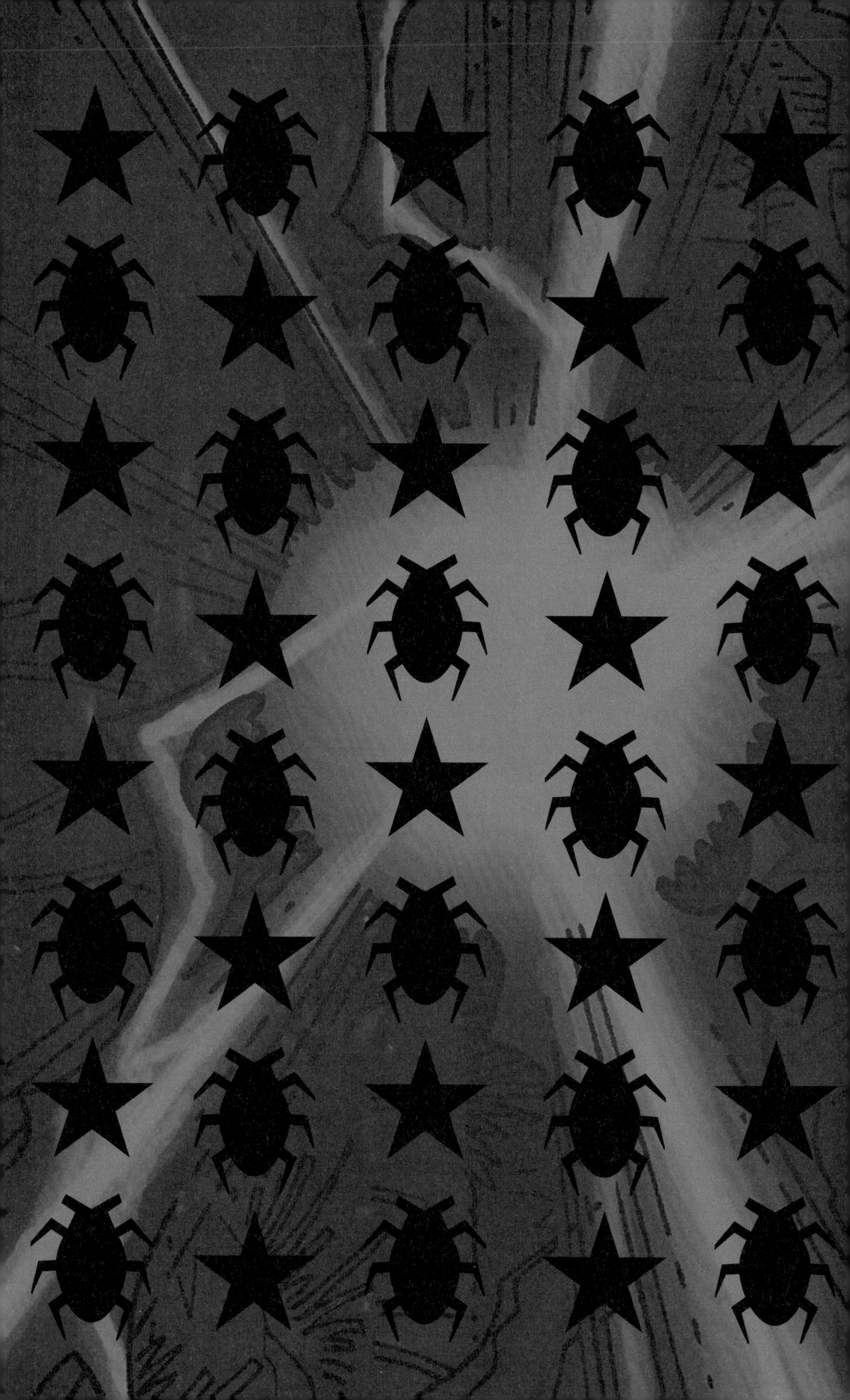

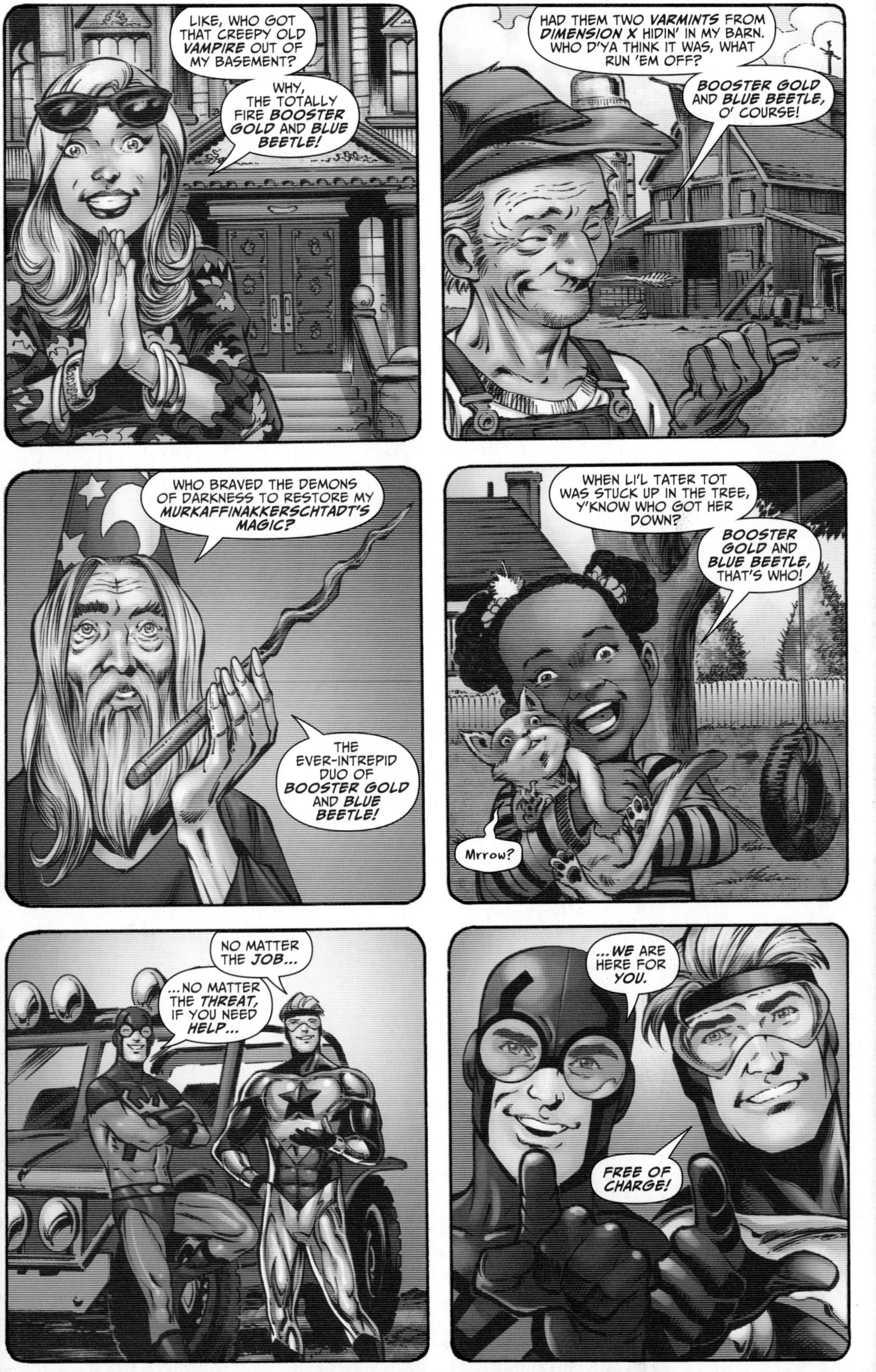
LIKE, WHO GOT THAT CREEPY OLD VAMPIRE OUT OF MY BASEMENT?
WHY, THE TOTALLY FIRE BOOSTER GOLD AND BLUE BEETLE!
HAD THEM TWO VARMINTS FROM DIMENSION X HIDIN' IN MY BARN. WHO D'YA THINK IT WAS, WHAT RUN 'EM OFF?
BOOSTER GOLD AND BLUE BEETLE, O' COURSE!
WHO BRAVED THE DEMONS OF DARKNESS TO RESTORE MY MURKAFFINAKKERSCHTADT'S MAGIC?
THE EVER-INTREPID DUO OF BOOSTER GOLD AND BLUE BEETLE!
WHEN LI'L TATER TOT WAS STUCK UP IN THE TREE, Y'KNOW WHO GOT HER DOWN?
BOOSTER GOLD AND BLUE BEETLE, THAT'S WHO!
Mrrow?
NO MATTER THE JOB...
...NO MATTER THE THREAT, IF YOU NEED HELP...
...WE ARE HERE FOR YOU.
FREE OF CHARGE!

BEETLES ABOUND!

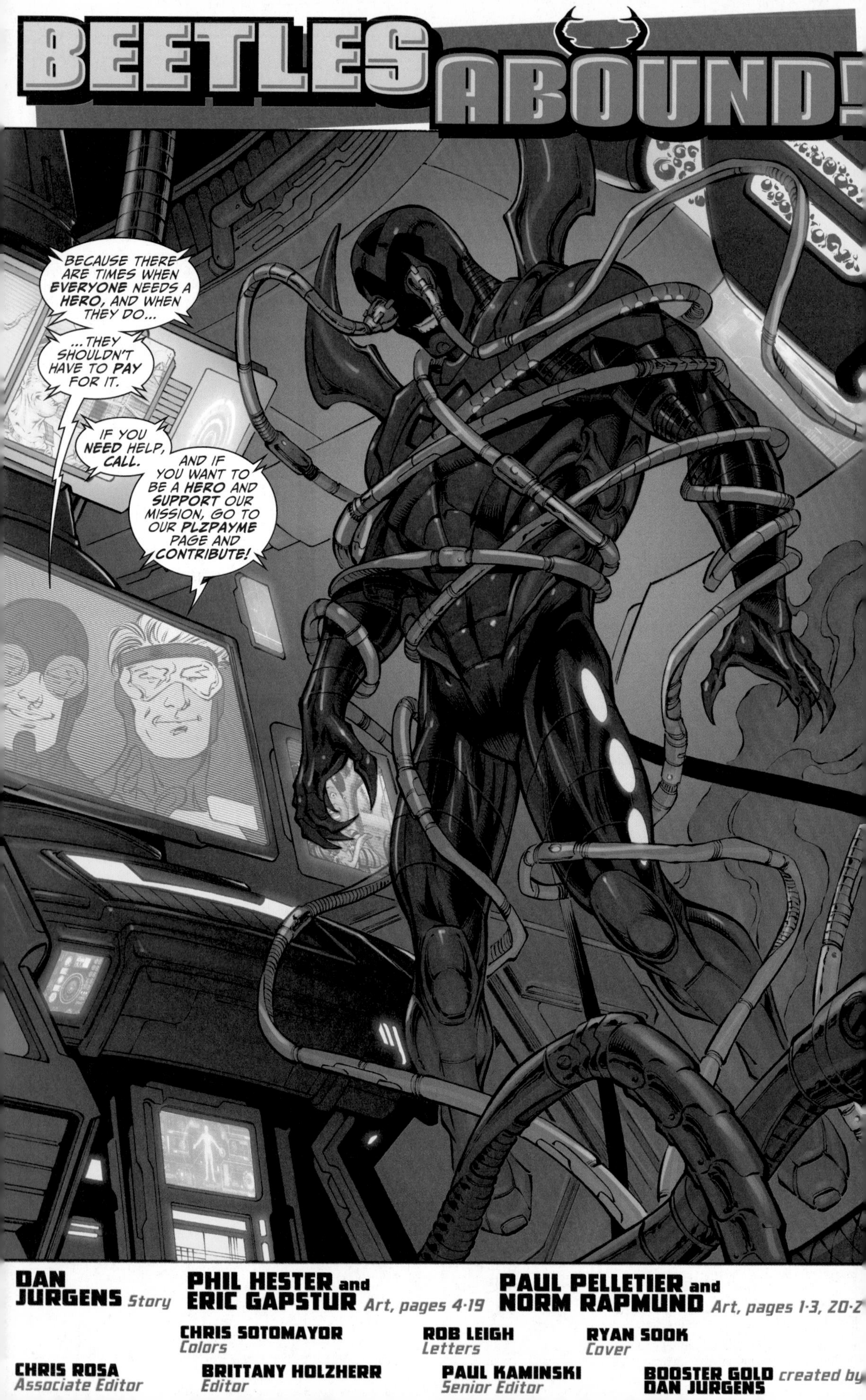
BECAUSE THERE ARE TIMES WHEN EVERYONE NEEDS A HERO, AND WHEN THEY DO...
...THEY SHOULDN'T HAVE TO PAY FOR IT.
IF YOU NEED HELP, CALL.
AND IF YOU WANT TO BE A HERO AND SUPPORT OUR MISSION, GO TO OUR PLZPAYME PAGE AND CONTRIBUTE!

DAN JURGENS *Story*
PHIL HESTER and **ERIC GAPSTUR** *Art, pages 4-19*
PAUL PELLETIER and **NORM RAPMUND** *Art, pages 1-3, 20-2*

CHRIS SOTOMAYOR *Colors*
ROB LEIGH *Letters*
RYAN SOOK *Cover*

CHRIS ROSA *Associate Editor*
BRITTANY HOLZHERR *Editor*
PAUL KAMINSKI *Senior Editor*
BOOSTER GOLD *created by* **DAN JURGENS**

THEY THINK THEY'RE *CLEVER.*

EVEN *HELPFUL,* WITH THAT SERVICE OF THEIRS.

BUT THEY'RE *IDIOTS.*

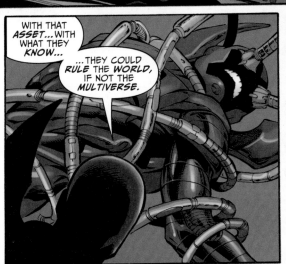

WITH THAT *ASSET...* WITH WHAT THEY *KNOW...*

...THEY COULD *RULE* THE *WORLD,* IF NOT THE *MULTIVERSE.*

SINCE THEY WON'T...

...I *WILL.*

AND *YOU,* JAIME REYES, WILL BE THE AGENT WHO PUTS IT ALL IN MOTION...

...ONCE YOU *SAVE* THEM FROM...

...*NULLIFEX.*

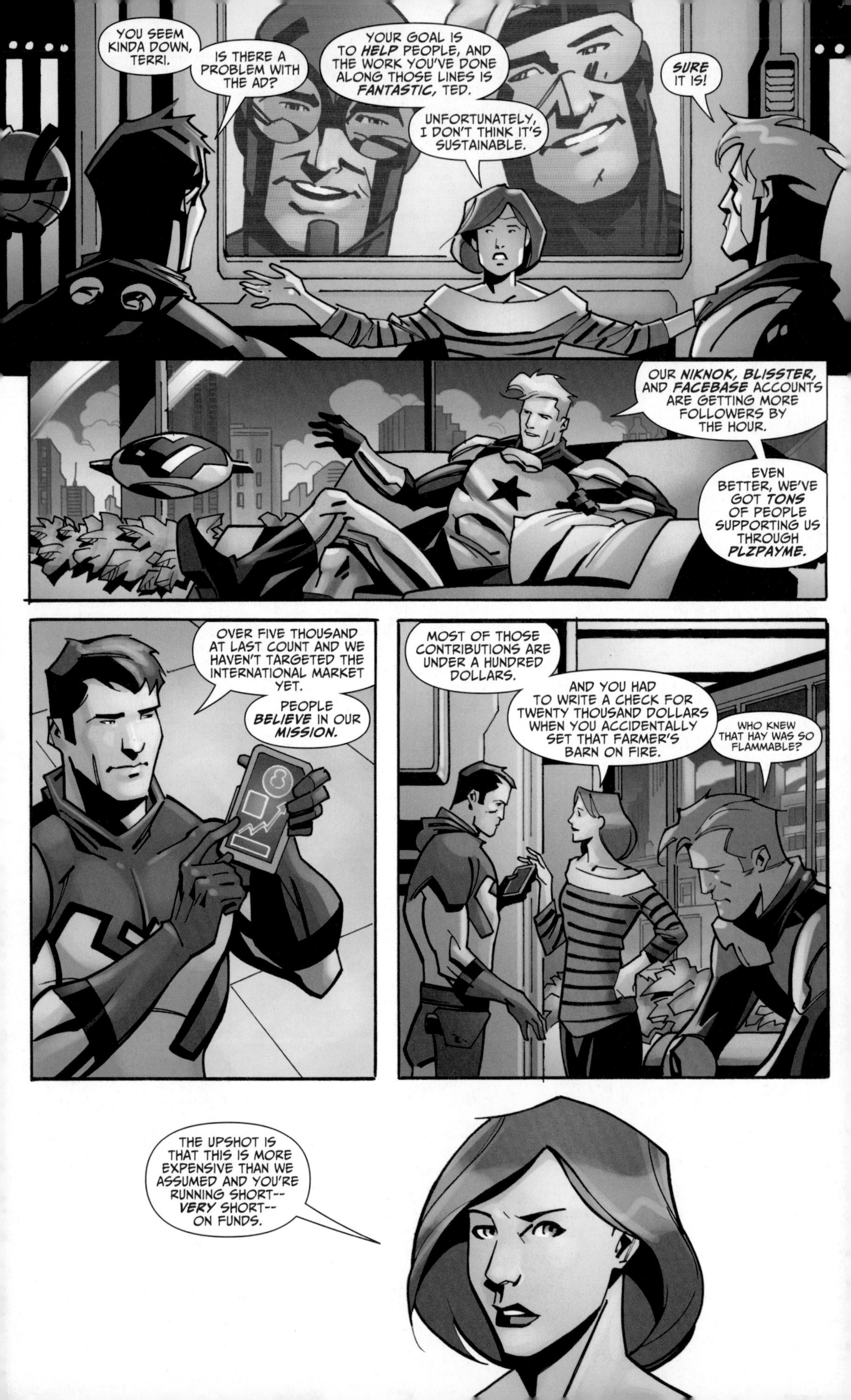
YOU SEEM KINDA DOWN, TERRI.
IS THERE A PROBLEM WITH THE AD?
YOUR GOAL IS TO HELP PEOPLE, AND THE WORK YOU'VE DONE ALONG THOSE LINES IS FANTASTIC, TED.
UNFORTUNATELY, I DON'T THINK IT'S SUSTAINABLE.
SURE IT IS!
OUR NIKNOK, BLISSTER, AND FACEBASE ACCOUNTS ARE GETTING MORE FOLLOWERS BY THE HOUR.
EVEN BETTER, WE'VE GOT TONS OF PEOPLE SUPPORTING US THROUGH PLZPAYME.
OVER FIVE THOUSAND AT LAST COUNT AND WE HAVEN'T TARGETED THE INTERNATIONAL MARKET YET.
PEOPLE BELIEVE IN OUR MISSION.
MOST OF THOSE CONTRIBUTIONS ARE UNDER A HUNDRED DOLLARS.
AND YOU HAD TO WRITE A CHECK FOR TWENTY THOUSAND DOLLARS WHEN YOU ACCIDENTALLY SET THAT FARMER'S BARN ON FIRE.
WHO KNEW THAT HAY WAS SO FLAMMABLE?
THE UPSHOT IS THAT THIS IS MORE EXPENSIVE THAN WE ASSUMED AND YOU'RE RUNNING SHORT-- VERY SHORT-- ON FUNDS.

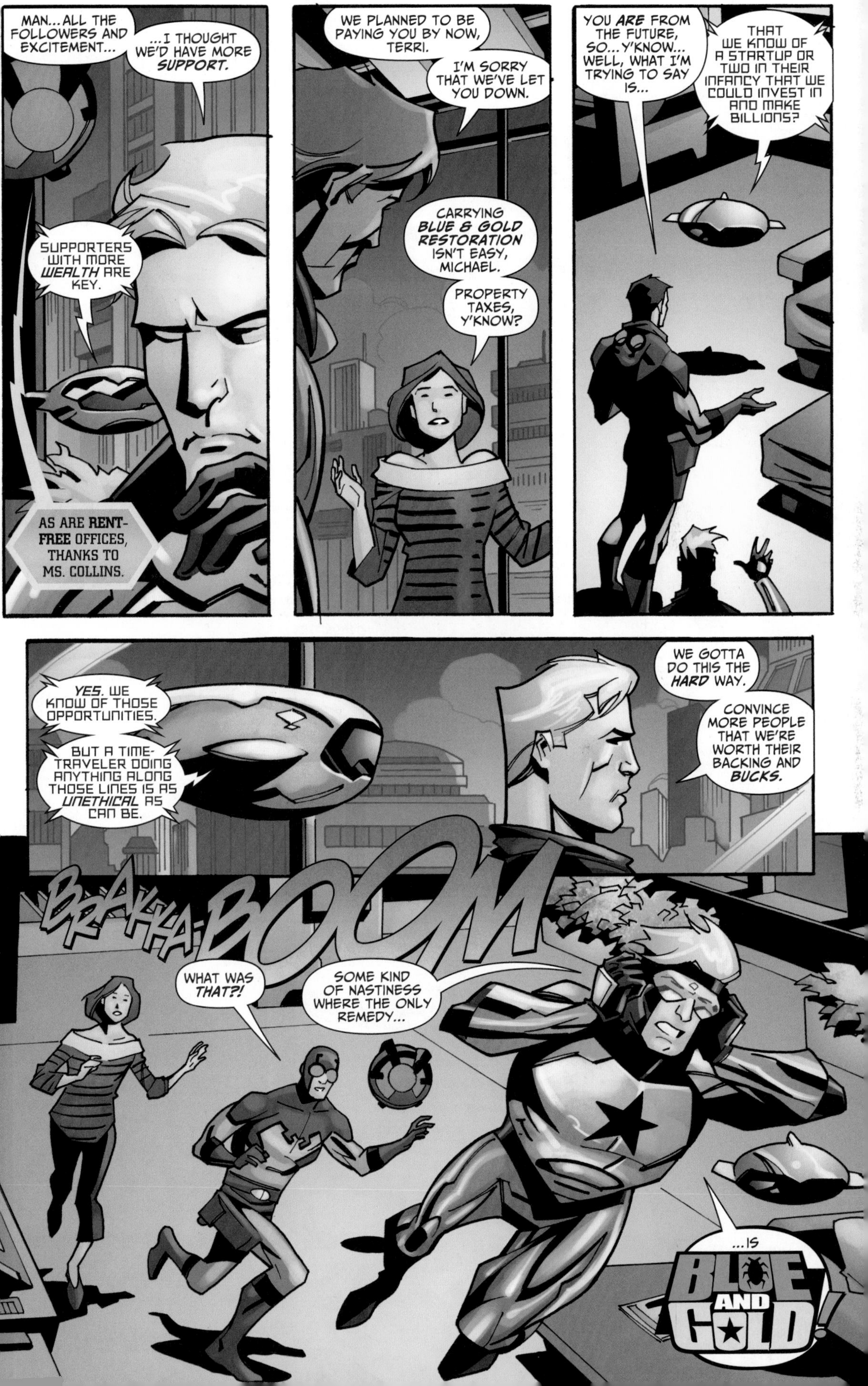
MAN...ALL THE FOLLOWERS AND EXCITEMENT...
...I THOUGHT WE'D HAVE MORE SUPPORT.
SUPPORTERS WITH MORE WEALTH ARE KEY.
AS ARE RENT-FREE OFFICES, THANKS TO MS. COLLINS.
WE PLANNED TO BE PAYING YOU BY NOW, TERRI.
I'M SORRY THAT WE'VE LET YOU DOWN.
CARRYING BLUE & GOLD RESTORATION ISN'T EASY, MICHAEL.
PROPERTY TAXES, Y'KNOW?
YOU ARE FROM THE FUTURE, SO...Y'KNOW... WELL, WHAT I'M TRYING TO SAY IS...
THAT WE KNOW OF A STARTUP OR TWO IN THEIR INFANCY THAT WE COULD INVEST IN AND MAKE BILLIONS?
YES. WE KNOW OF THOSE OPPORTUNITIES.
BUT A TIME-TRAVELER DOING ANYTHING ALONG THOSE LINES IS AS UNETHICAL AS CAN BE.
WE GOTTA DO THIS THE HARD WAY.
CONVINCE MORE PEOPLE THAT WE'RE WORTH THEIR BACKING AND BUCKS.
BRAKKA-BOOM
WHAT WAS THAT?!
SOME KIND OF NASTINESS WHERE THE ONLY REMEDY...
...IS BLUE AND GOLD!

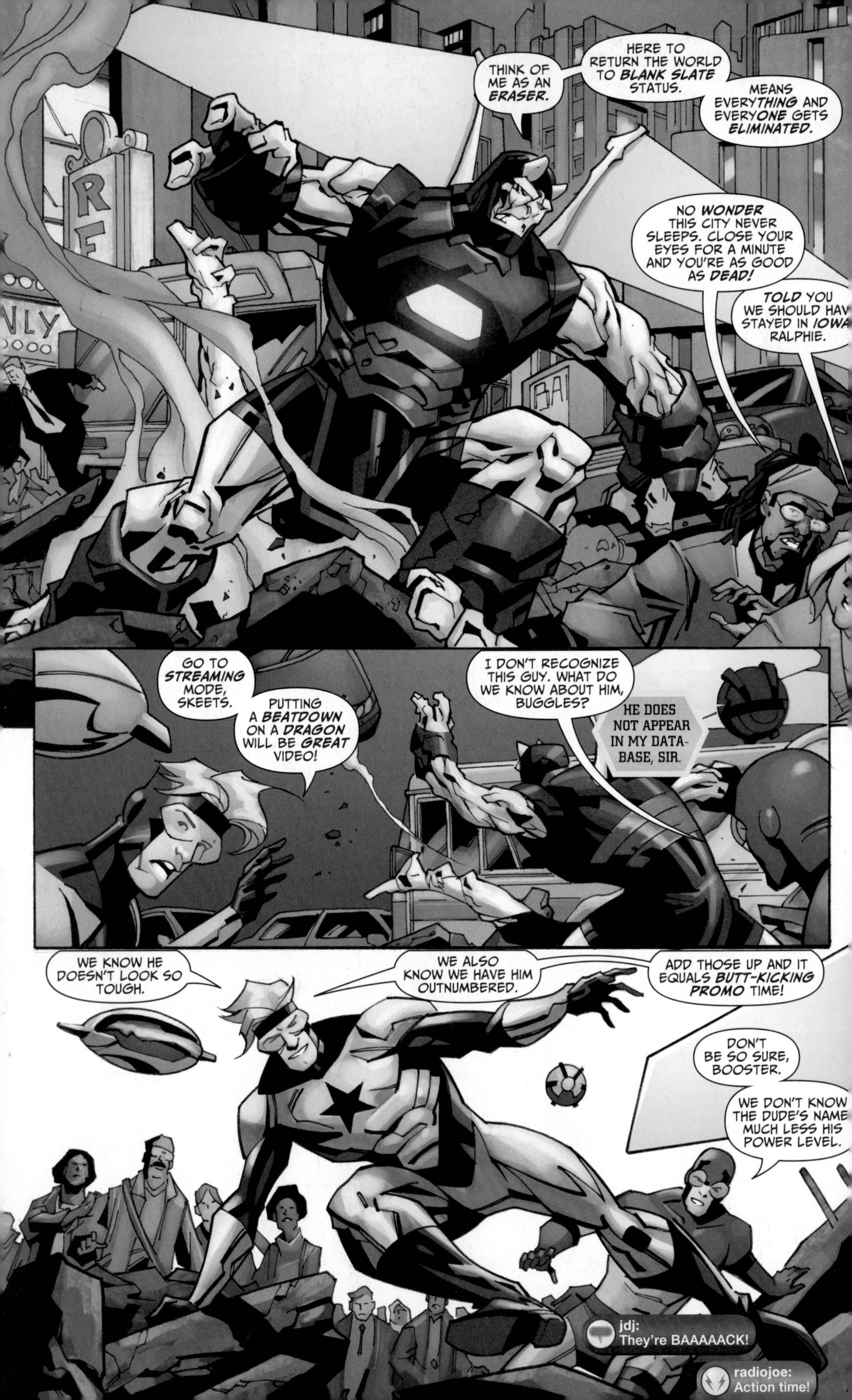
THINK OF ME AS AN ERASER.
HERE TO RETURN THE WORLD TO BLANK SLATE STATUS.
MEANS EVERYTHING AND EVERYONE GETS ELIMINATED.
NO WONDER THIS CITY NEVER SLEEPS. CLOSE YOUR EYES FOR A MINUTE AND YOU'RE AS GOOD AS DEAD!
TOLD YOU WE SHOULD HAV STAYED IN IOWA RALPHIE.
GO TO STREAMING MODE, SKEETS.
PUTTING A BEATDOWN ON A DRAGON WILL BE GREAT VIDEO!
I DON'T RECOGNIZE THIS GUY. WHAT DO WE KNOW ABOUT HIM, BUGGLES?
HE DOES NOT APPEAR IN MY DATA-BASE, SIR.
WE KNOW HE DOESN'T LOOK SO TOUGH.
WE ALSO KNOW WE HAVE HIM OUTNUMBERED.
ADD THOSE UP AND IT EQUALS BUTT-KICKING PROMO TIME!
DON'T BE SO SURE, BOOSTER.
WE DON'T KNOW THE DUDE'S NAME MUCH LESS HIS POWER LEVEL.
jdj: They're BAAAAACK!
radiojoe: Action time!

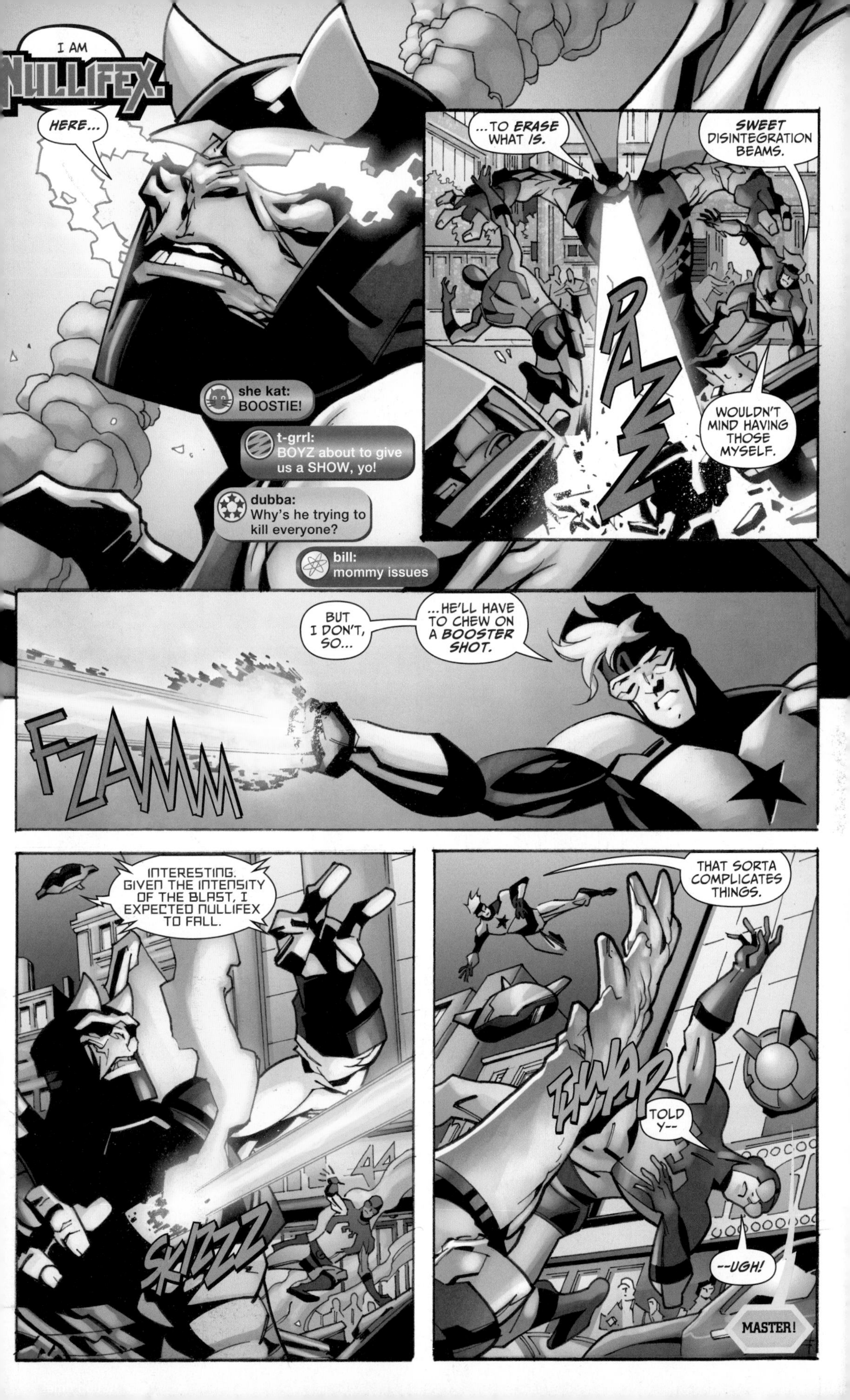
I AM NULLIFEX.
HERE...
...TO ERASE WHAT IS.
SWEET DISINTEGRATION BEAMS.
PAZZZ
WOULDN'T MIND HAVING THOSE MYSELF.
she kat: BOOSTIE!
t-grrl: BOYZ about to give us a SHOW, yo!
dubba: Why's he trying to kill everyone?
bill: mommy issues
BUT I DON'T, SO...
...HE'LL HAVE TO CHEW ON A BOOSTER SHOT.
FZAMMM
INTERESTING. GIVEN THE INTENSITY OF THE BLAST, I EXPECTED NULLIFEX TO FALL.
SKIZZZ
THAT SORTA COMPLICATES THINGS.
TWAP
TOLD Y--
--UGH!
MASTER!

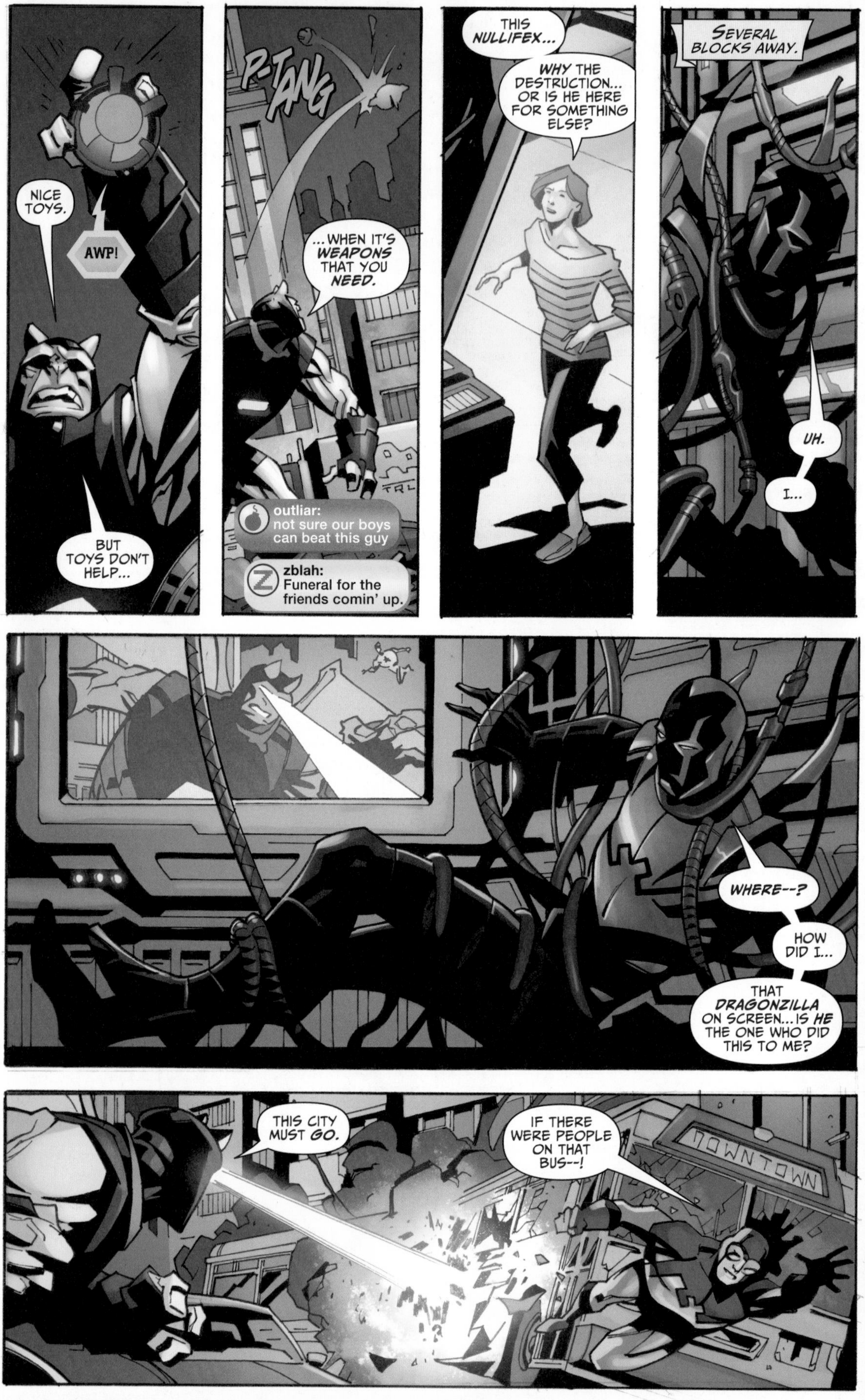
NICE TOYS.
AWP!
BUT TOYS DON'T HELP...
P-TANG
...WHEN IT'S WEAPONS THAT YOU NEED.
outliar:
not sure our boys can beat this guy
zblah:
Funeral for the friends comin' up.
THIS NULLIFEX...
WHY THE DESTRUCTION... OR IS HE HERE FOR SOMETHING ELSE?
SEVERAL BLOCKS AWAY.
UH.
I...
WHERE--?
HOW DID I...
THAT DRAGONZILLA ON SCREEN...IS HE THE ONE WHO DID THIS TO ME?
THIS CITY MUST GO.
IF THERE WERE PEOPLE ON THAT BUS--!
DOWNTOWN

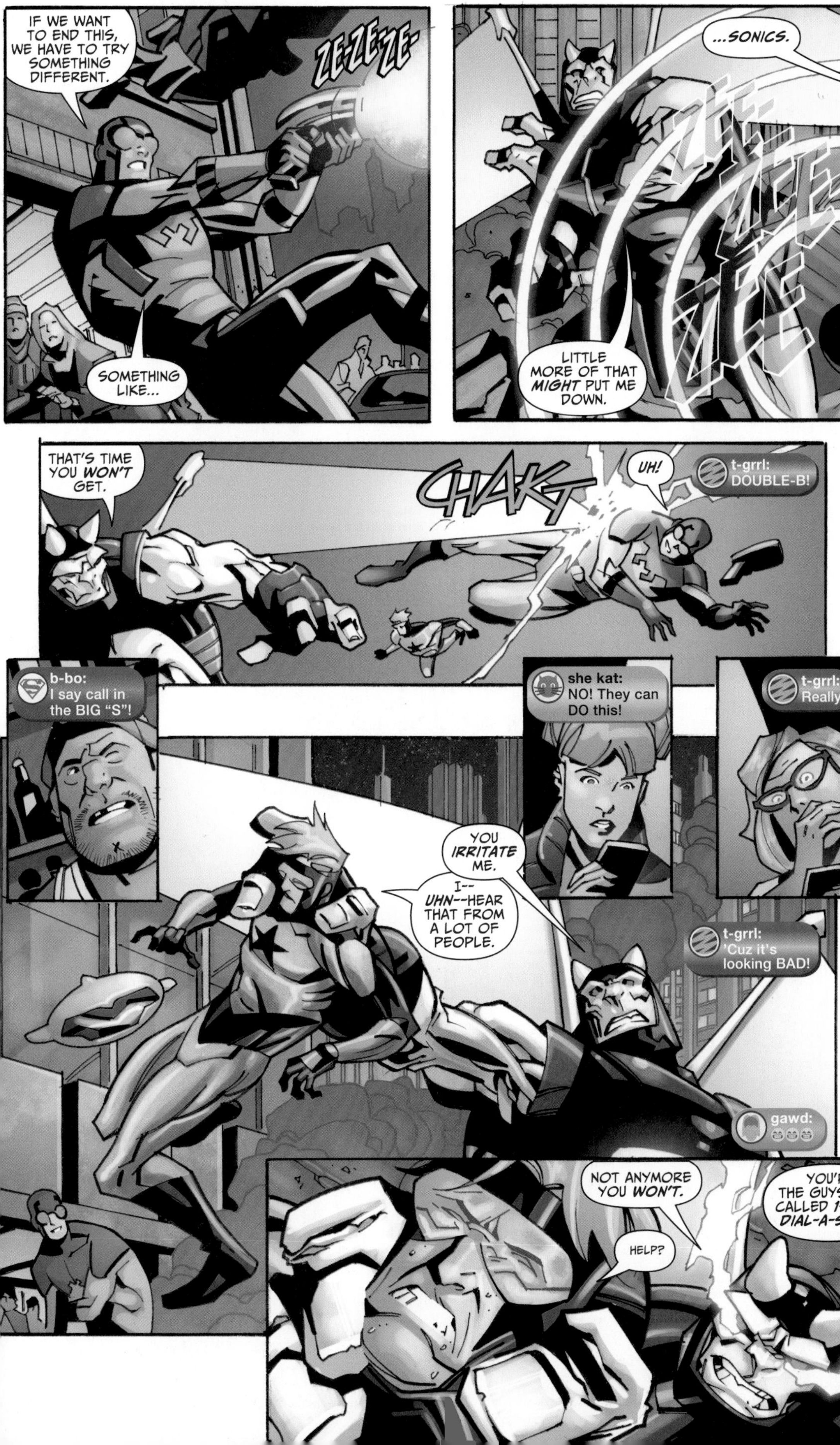
IF WE WANT TO END THIS, WE HAVE TO TRY SOMETHING DIFFERENT.
ZE-ZE-ZE-
SOMETHING LIKE...
...SONICS.
ZEE-ZEE-ZEE-ZEE
LITTLE MORE OF THAT MIGHT PUT ME DOWN.
THAT'S TIME YOU WON'T GET.
CHAKT
UH!
t-grrl: DOUBLE-B!
b-bo: I say call in the BIG "S"!
she kat: NO! They can DO this!
t-grrl: Really?
YOU IRRITATE ME.
I-- UHN--HEAR THAT FROM A LOT OF PEOPLE.
t-grrl: 'Cuz it's looking BAD!
gawd:
NOT ANYMORE YOU WON'T.
HELP?
YOU'RE THE GUYS WHO CALLED 1-800-DIAL-A-SAVE?

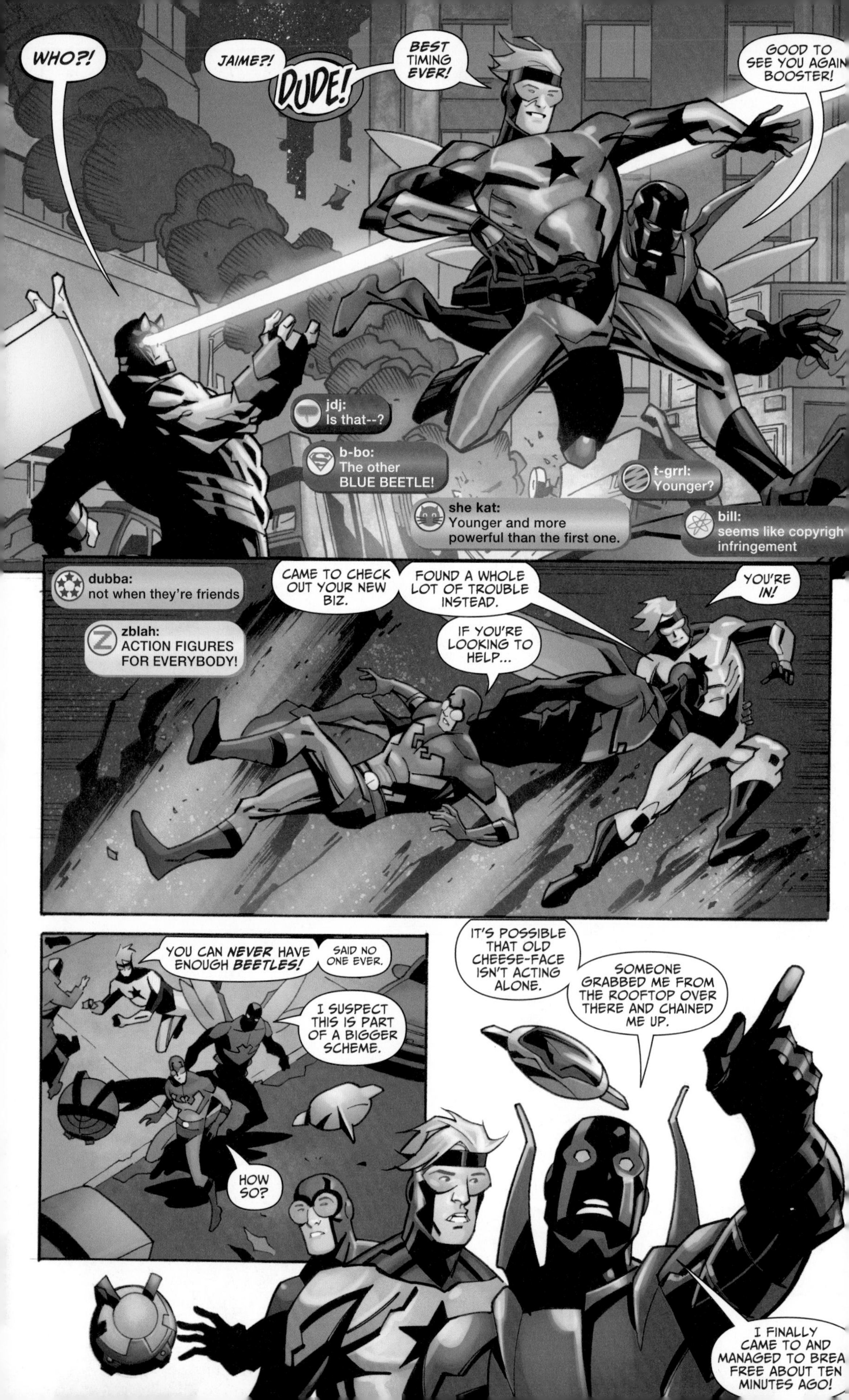
WHO?!
JAIME?!
DUDE!
BEST TIMING EVER!
GOOD TO SEE YOU AGAIN BOOSTER!
jdj: Is that--?
b-bo: The other BLUE BEETLE!
t-grrl: Younger?
she kat: Younger and more powerful than the first one.
bill: seems like copyrigh infringement
dubba: not when they're friends
zblah: ACTION FIGURES FOR EVERYBODY!
CAME TO CHECK OUT YOUR NEW BIZ.
FOUND A WHOLE LOT OF TROUBLE INSTEAD.
IF YOU'RE LOOKING TO HELP...
YOU'RE IN!
YOU CAN NEVER HAVE ENOUGH BEETLES!
SAID NO ONE EVER.
I SUSPECT THIS IS PART OF A BIGGER SCHEME.
HOW SO?
IT'S POSSIBLE THAT OLD CHEESE-FACE ISN'T ACTING ALONE.
SOMEONE GRABBED ME FROM THE ROOFTOP OVER THERE AND CHAINED ME UP.
I FINALLY CAME TO AND MANAGED TO BREA FREE ABOUT TEN MINUTES AGO!

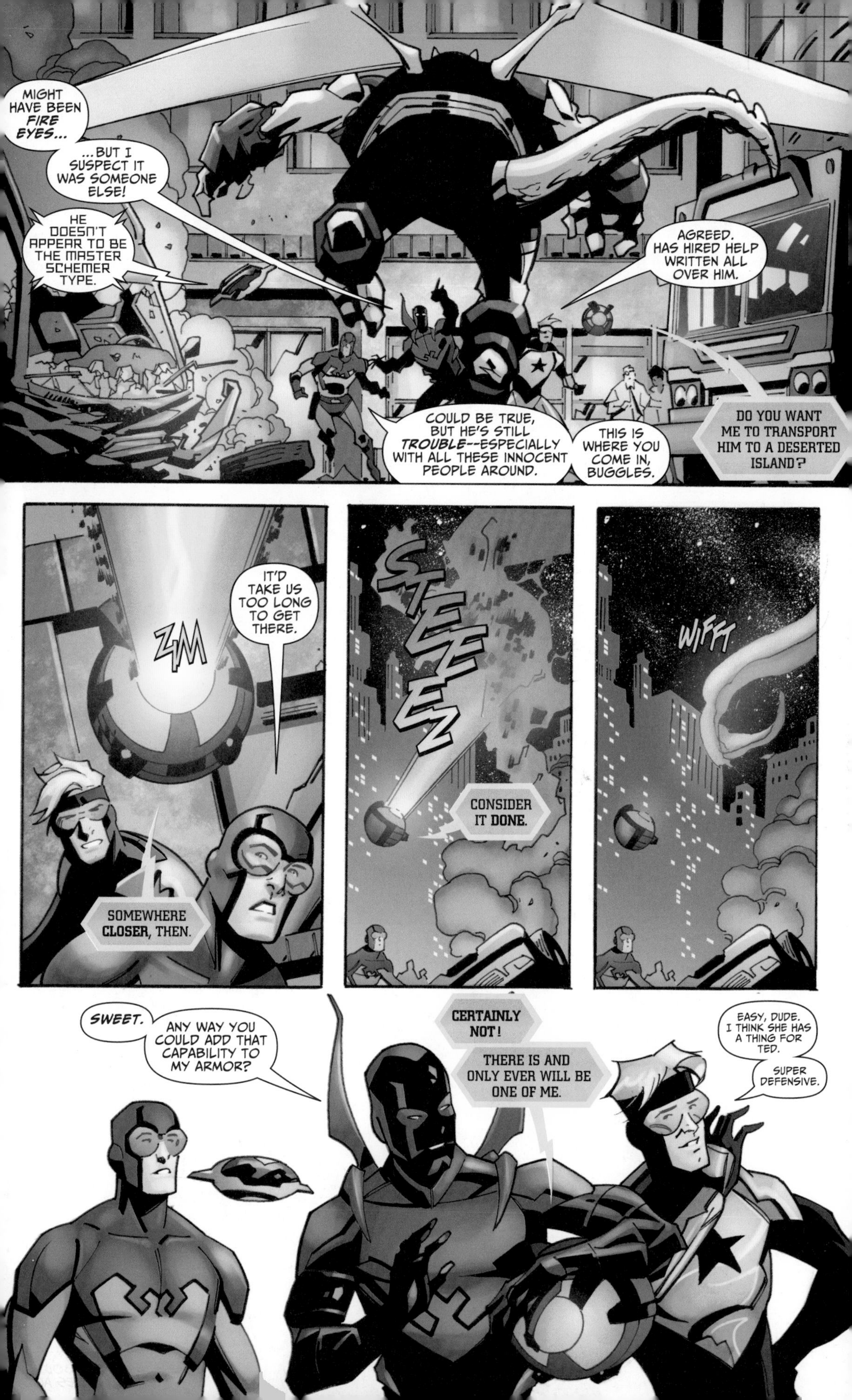
MIGHT HAVE BEEN *FIRE EYES...*
...BUT I SUSPECT IT WAS SOMEONE ELSE!
HE DOESN'T APPEAR TO BE THE MASTER SCHEMER TYPE.
AGREED. HAS HIRED HELP WRITTEN ALL OVER HIM.
COULD BE TRUE, BUT HE'S STILL *TROUBLE*--ESPECIALLY WITH ALL THESE INNOCENT PEOPLE AROUND.
THIS IS WHERE YOU COME IN, BUGGLES.
DO YOU WANT ME TO TRANSPORT HIM TO A DESERTED ISLAND?
IT'D TAKE US TOO LONG TO GET THERE.
ZM
SOMEWHERE **CLOSER**, THEN.
STEEEEZ
CONSIDER IT **DONE**.
WIFFT
SWEET.
ANY WAY YOU COULD ADD THAT CAPABILITY TO MY ARMOR?
CERTAINLY NOT!
THERE IS AND ONLY EVER WILL BE ONE OF ME.
EASY, DUDE. I THINK SHE HAS A THING FOR TED.
SUPER DEFENSIVE.

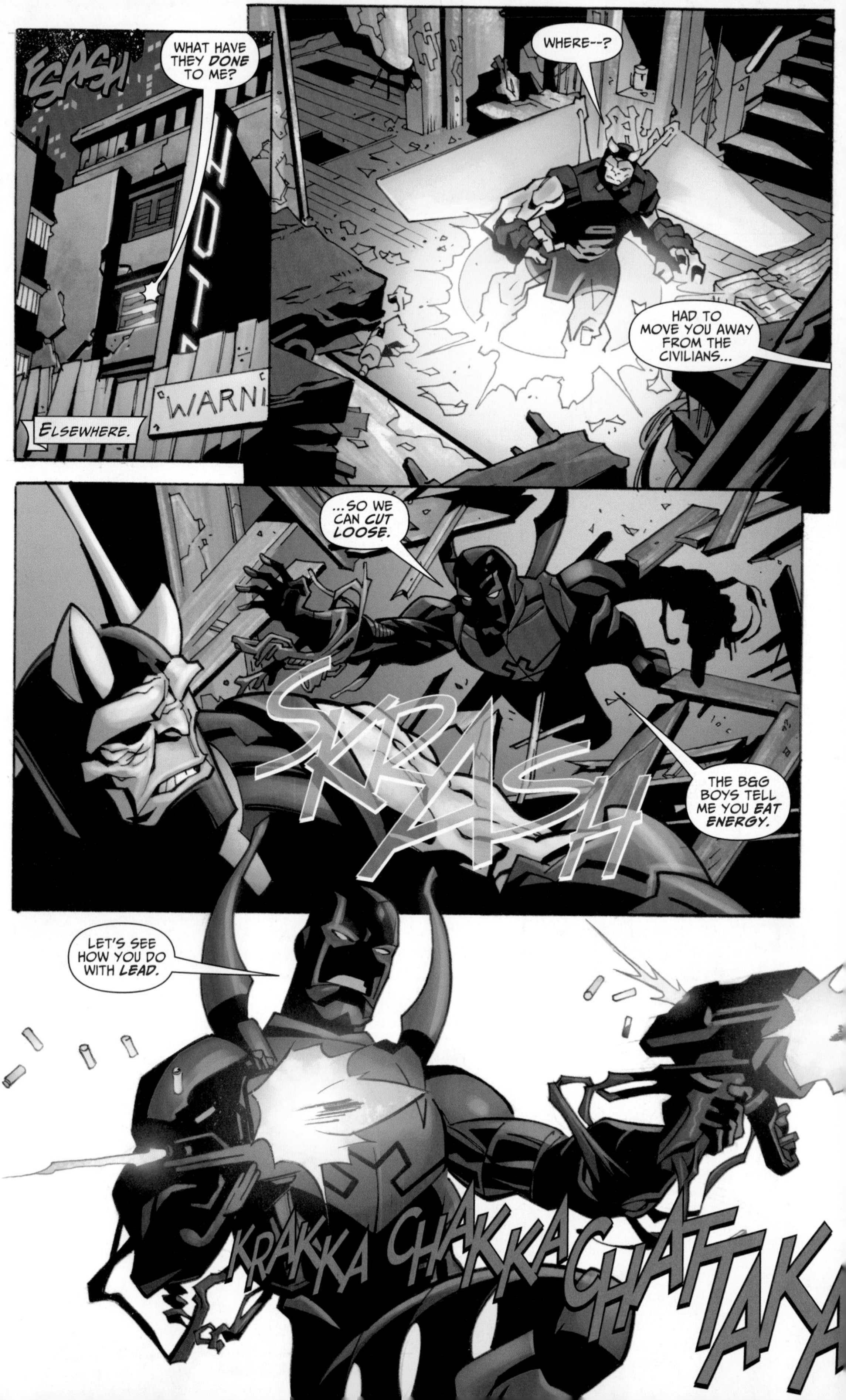
FSASH
WHAT HAVE THEY DONE TO ME?
HOT
WARNI
ELSEWHERE.
WHERE--?
HAD TO MOVE YOU AWAY FROM THE CIVILIANS...
...SO WE CAN CUT LOOSE.
SKRASH
THE B&G BOYS TELL ME YOU EAT ENERGY.
LET'S SEE HOW YOU DO WITH LEAD.
KRAKKA CHAKKA CHAT TAKA

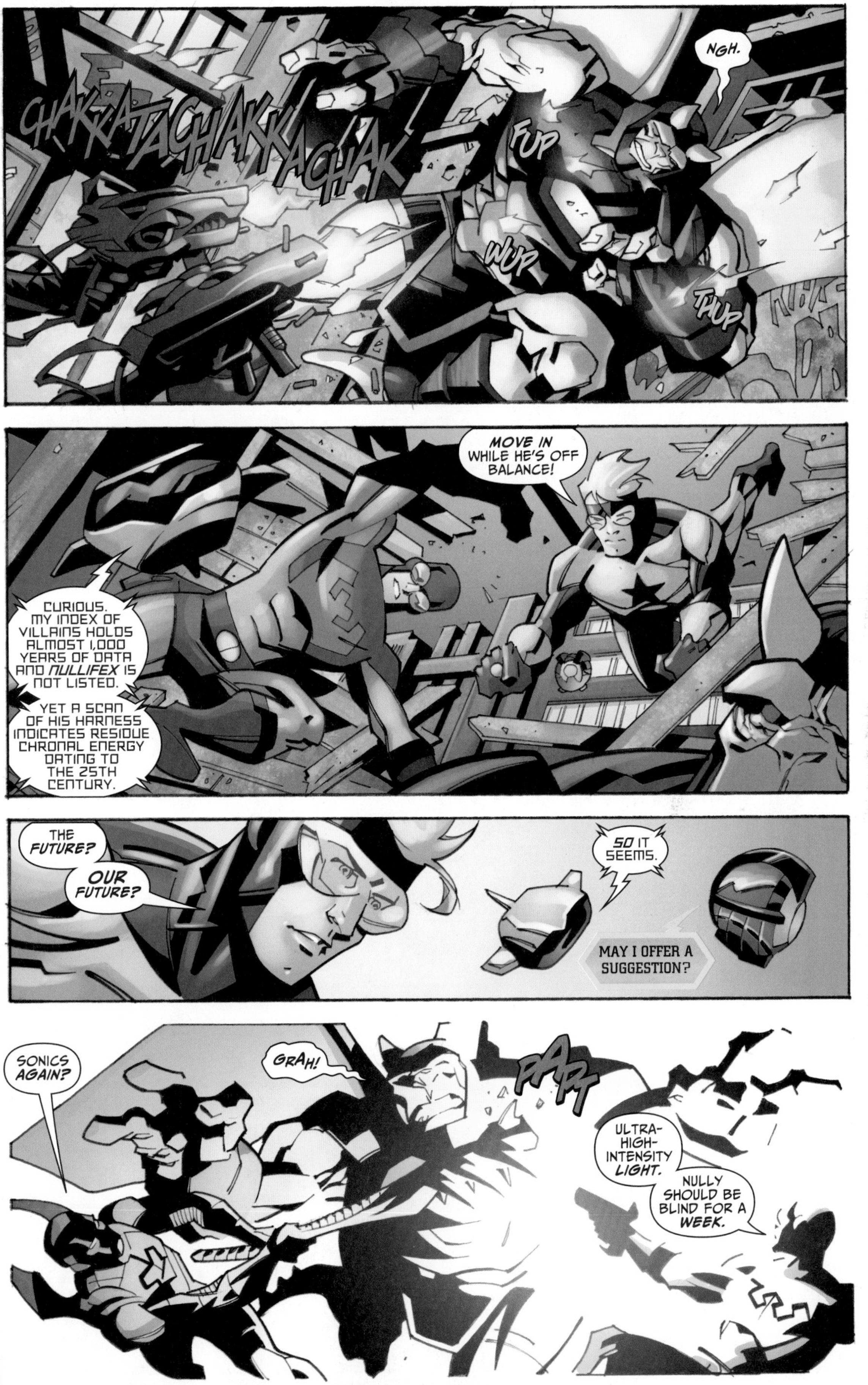
CHAKKATACHAKKACHAK
NGH.
FUP
WUP
THUP
MOVE IN WHILE HE'S OFF BALANCE!
CURIOUS. MY INDEX OF VILLAINS HOLDS ALMOST 1,000 YEARS OF DATA AND NULLIFEX IS NOT LISTED.
YET A SCAN OF HIS HARNESS INDICATES RESIDUE CHRONAL ENERGY DATING TO THE 25TH CENTURY.
THE FUTURE?
OUR FUTURE?
SO IT SEEMS.
MAY I OFFER A SUGGESTION?
SONICS AGAIN?
GRAH!
PAPT
ULTRA-HIGH-INTENSITY LIGHT.
NULLY SHOULD BE BLIND FOR A WEEK.

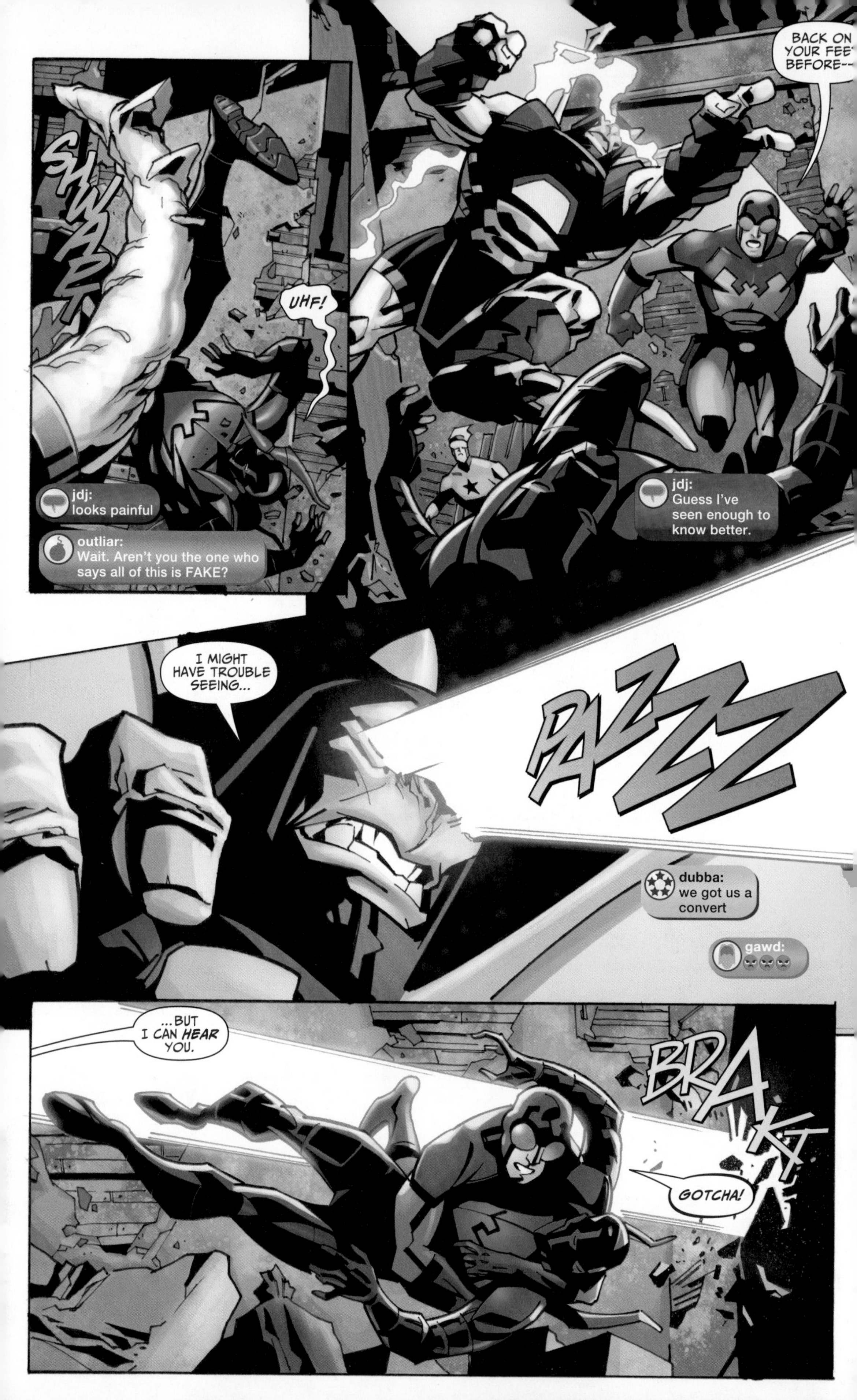
SHWAK!
UHF!
jdj: looks painful
outliar: Wait. Aren't you the one who says all of this is FAKE?
BACK ON YOUR FEET BEFORE--
jdj: Guess I've seen enough to know better.
I MIGHT HAVE TROUBLE SEEING...
PAZZZ
dubba: we got us a convert
gawd:
...BUT I CAN *HEAR* YOU.
BRAKT
GOTCHA!

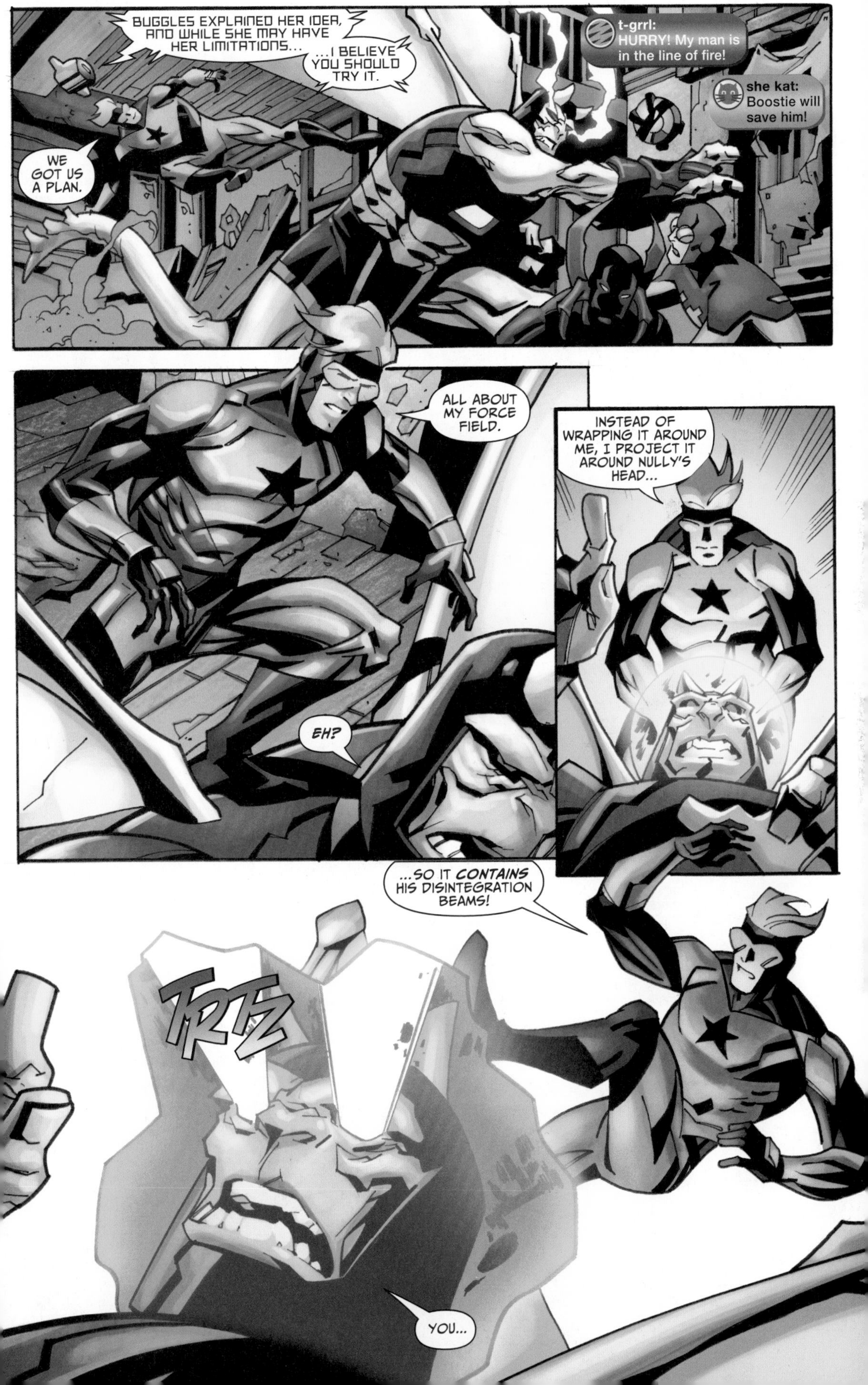
BUGGLES EXPLAINED HER IDEA, AND WHILE SHE MAY HAVE HER LIMITATIONS...
...I BELIEVE YOU SHOULD TRY IT.
WE GOT US A PLAN.
t-grrl: HURRY! My man is in the line of fire!
she kat: Boostie will save him!
ALL ABOUT MY FORCE FIELD.
EH?
INSTEAD OF WRAPPING IT AROUND ME, I PROJECT IT AROUND NULLY'S HEAD...
...SO IT *CONTAINS* HIS DISINTEGRATION BEAMS!
TRTZ
YOU...

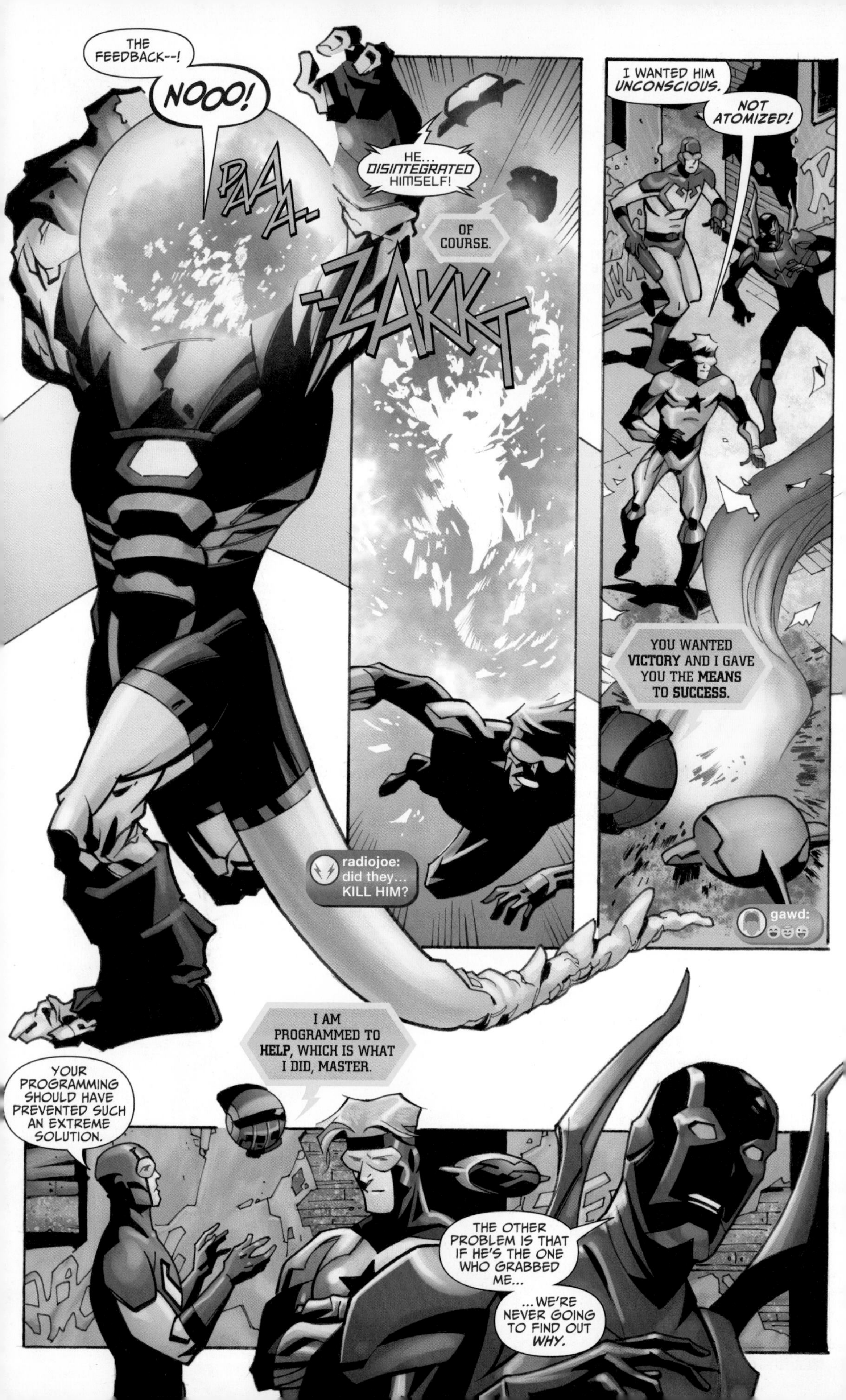
THE FEEDBACK--!
NOOO!
PAAA-
HE... DISINTEGRATED HIMSELF!
OF COURSE.
-ZAKKT
I WANTED HIM UNCONSCIOUS.
NOT ATOMIZED!
YOU WANTED VICTORY AND I GAVE YOU THE MEANS TO SUCCESS.
radiojoe: did they... KILL HIM?
gawd:
I AM PROGRAMMED TO HELP, WHICH IS WHAT I DID, MASTER.
YOUR PROGRAMMING SHOULD HAVE PREVENTED SUCH AN EXTREME SOLUTION.
THE OTHER PROBLEM IS THAT IF HE'S THE ONE WHO GRABBED ME...
...WE'RE NEVER GOING TO FIND OUT WHY.

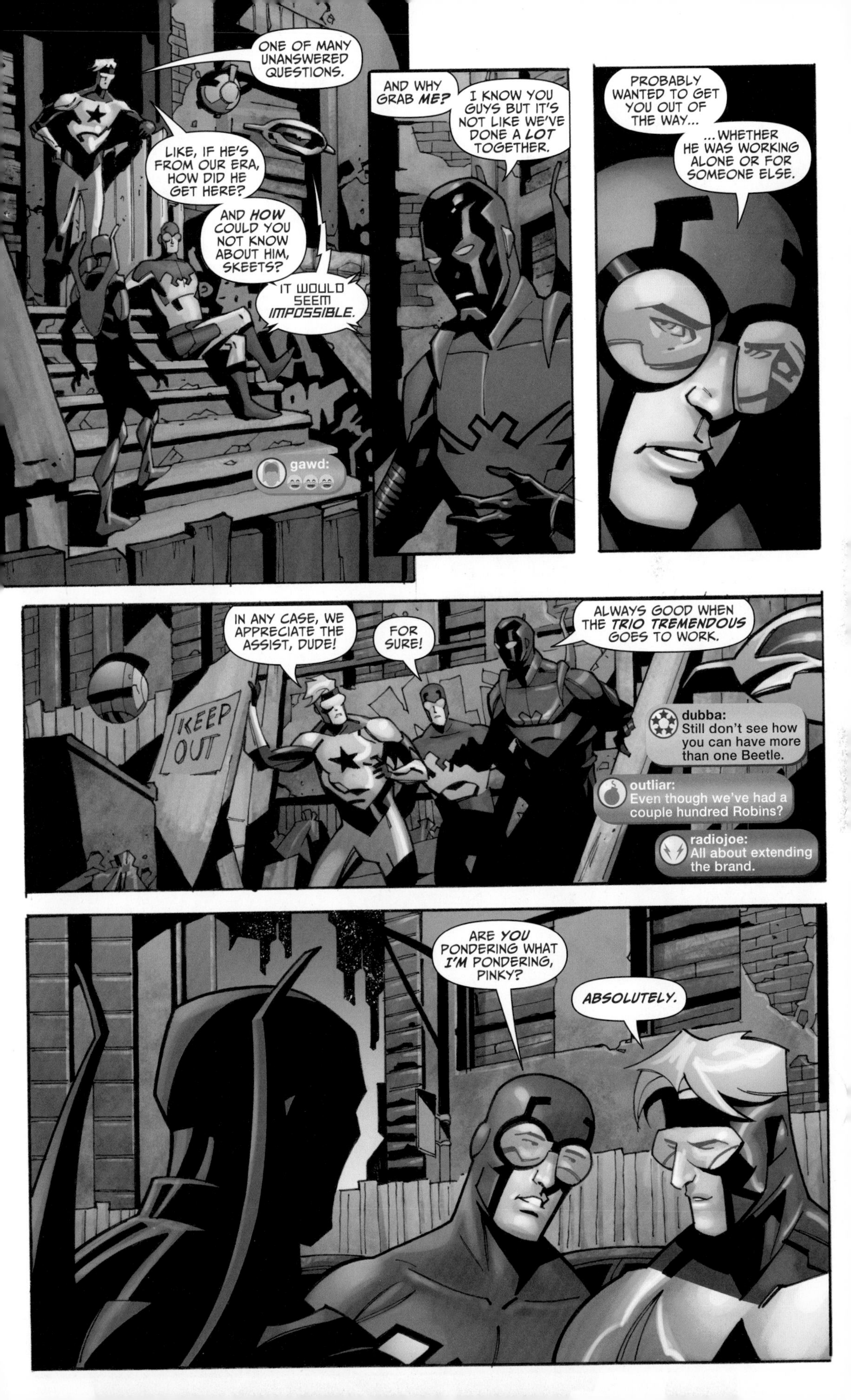
ONE OF MANY UNANSWERED QUESTIONS.
LIKE, IF HE'S FROM OUR ERA, HOW DID HE GET HERE?
AND HOW COULD YOU NOT KNOW ABOUT HIM, SKEETS?
IT WOULD SEEM IMPOSSIBLE.
gawd:
AND WHY GRAB ME?
I KNOW YOU GUYS BUT IT'S NOT LIKE WE'VE DONE A LOT TOGETHER.
PROBABLY WANTED TO GET YOU OUT OF THE WAY...
...WHETHER HE WAS WORKING ALONE OR FOR SOMEONE ELSE.
IN ANY CASE, WE APPRECIATE THE ASSIST, DUDE!
FOR SURE!
ALWAYS GOOD WHEN THE TRIO TREMENDOUS GOES TO WORK.
KEEP OUT
dubba:
Still don't see how you can have more than one Beetle.
outliar:
Even though we've had a couple hundred Robins?
radiojoe:
All about extending the brand.
ARE YOU PONDERING WHAT I'M PONDERING, PINKY?
ABSOLUTELY.

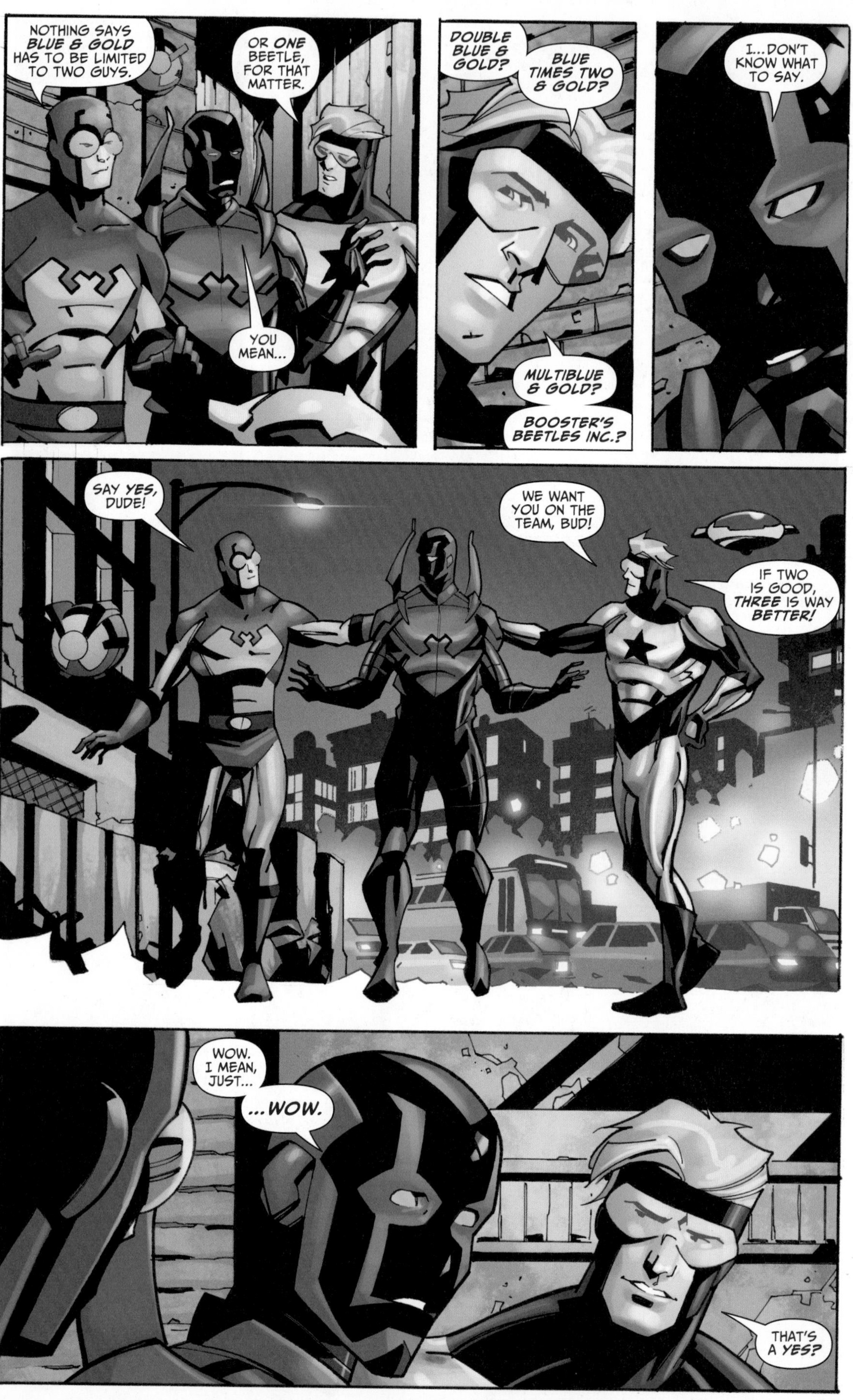

NOTHING SAYS BLUE & GOLD HAS TO BE LIMITED TO TWO GUYS.
OR ONE BEETLE, FOR THAT MATTER.
YOU MEAN...
DOUBLE BLUE & GOLD?
BLUE TIMES TWO & GOLD?
MULTIBLUE & GOLD?
BOOSTER'S BEETLES INC.?
I...DON'T KNOW WHAT TO SAY.
SAY YES, DUDE!
WE WANT YOU ON THE TEAM, BUD!
IF TWO IS GOOD, THREE IS WAY BETTER!
WOW. I MEAN, JUST...
...WOW.
THAT'S A YES?

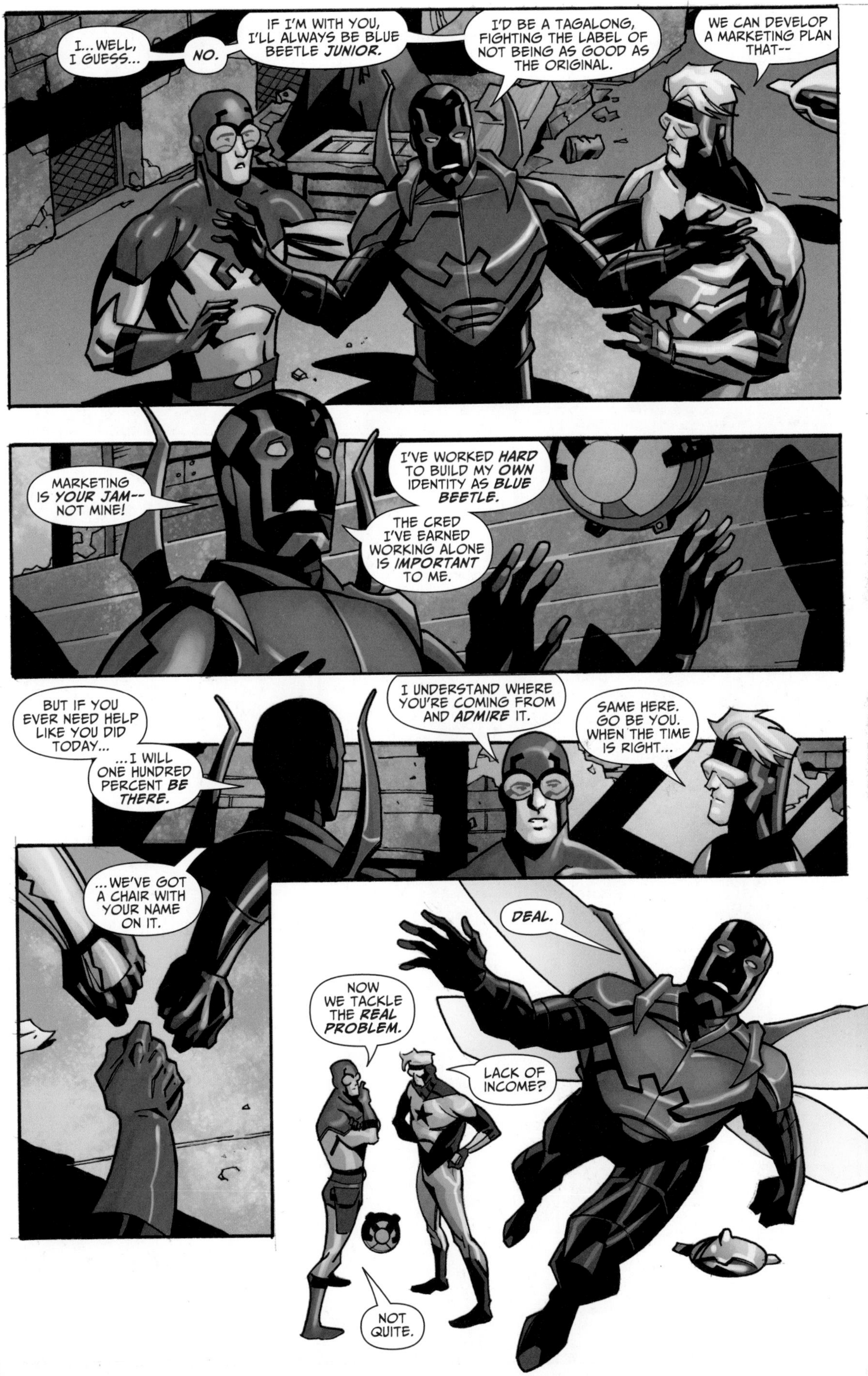
I...WELL, I GUESS...
NO.
IF I'M WITH YOU, I'LL ALWAYS BE BLUE BEETLE JUNIOR.
I'D BE A TAGALONG, FIGHTING THE LABEL OF NOT BEING AS GOOD AS THE ORIGINAL.
WE CAN DEVELOP A MARKETING PLAN THAT--
MARKETING IS YOUR JAM-- NOT MINE!
I'VE WORKED HARD TO BUILD MY OWN IDENTITY AS BLUE BEETLE.
THE CRED I'VE EARNED WORKING ALONE IS IMPORTANT TO ME.
BUT IF YOU EVER NEED HELP LIKE YOU DID TODAY...
...I WILL ONE HUNDRED PERCENT BE THERE.
I UNDERSTAND WHERE YOU'RE COMING FROM AND ADMIRE IT.
SAME HERE. GO BE YOU. WHEN THE TIME IS RIGHT...
...WE'VE GOT A CHAIR WITH YOUR NAME ON IT.
DEAL.
NOW WE TACKLE THE REAL PROBLEM.
LACK OF INCOME?
NOT QUITE.

NULLIFEX WAS A POWERFUL DUDE.

WHAT'S HIS STORY? DID HE COME ALONE...

...OR DID SOMEONE SEND HIM?

ALL THIS TIME, I HAVE WAITED.

WATCHED THEIR INSIPID BEHAVIOR FROM AFAR.

LOOKED FOR THE BEST TIME TO ATTACK.

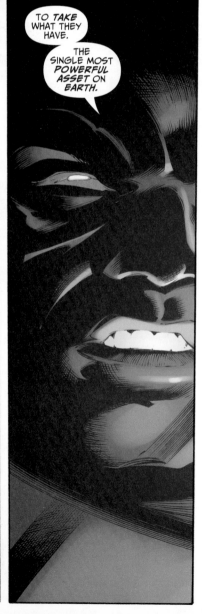

TO TAKE WHAT THEY HAVE.

THE SINGLE MOST POWERFUL ASSET ON EARTH.

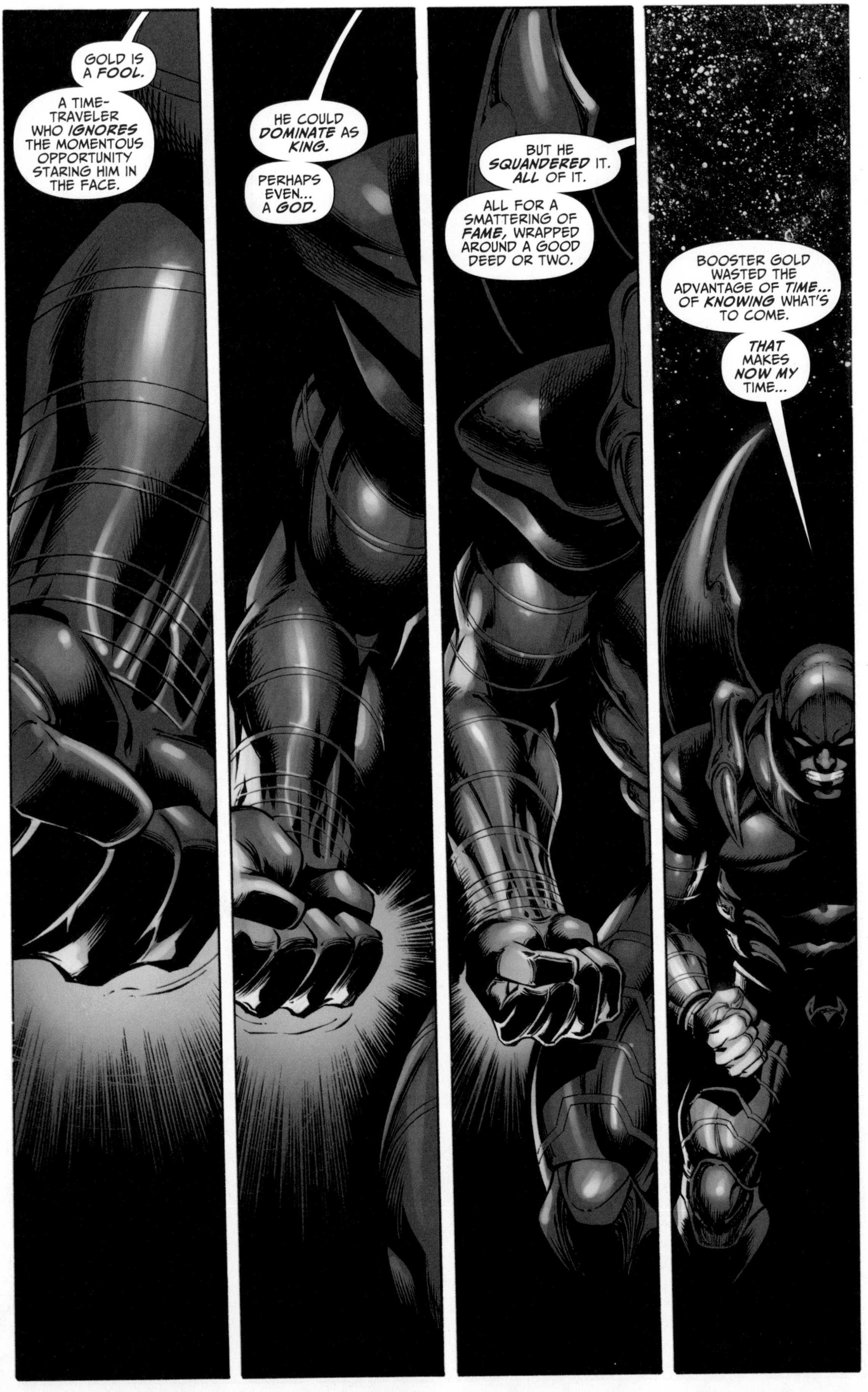
GOLD IS A FOOL.
A TIME-TRAVELER WHO IGNORES THE MOMENTOUS OPPORTUNITY STARING HIM IN THE FACE.
HE COULD DOMINATE AS KING.
PERHAPS EVEN... A GOD.
BUT HE SQUANDERED IT. ALL OF IT.
ALL FOR A SMATTERING OF FAME, WRAPPED AROUND A GOOD DEED OR TWO.
BOOSTER GOLD WASTED THE ADVANTAGE OF TIME... OF KNOWING WHAT'S TO COME.
THAT MAKES NOW MY TIME...

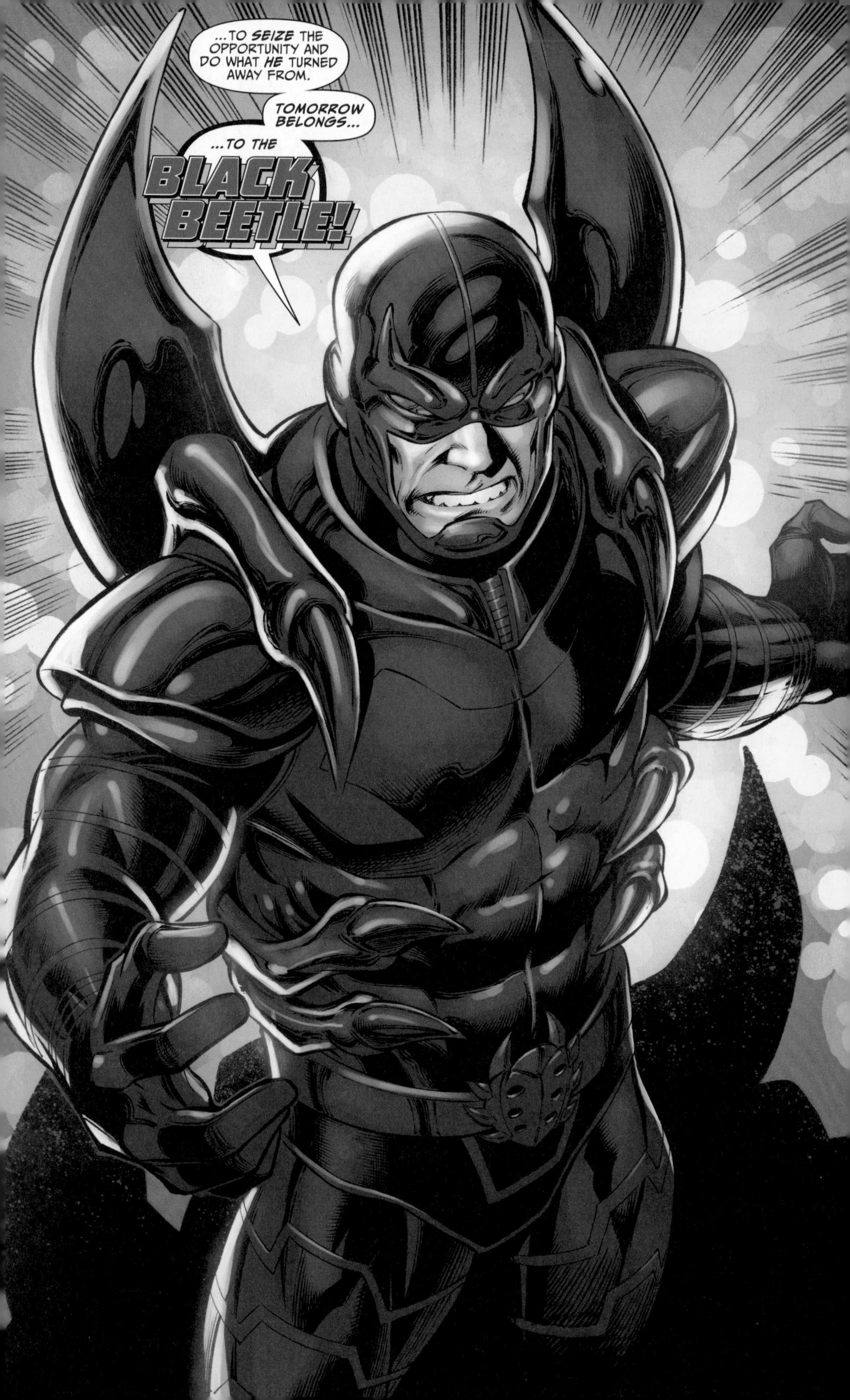
...TO SEIZE THE OPPORTUNITY AND DO WHAT HE TURNED AWAY FROM.
TOMORROW BELONGS...
...TO THE
BLACK BEETLE!

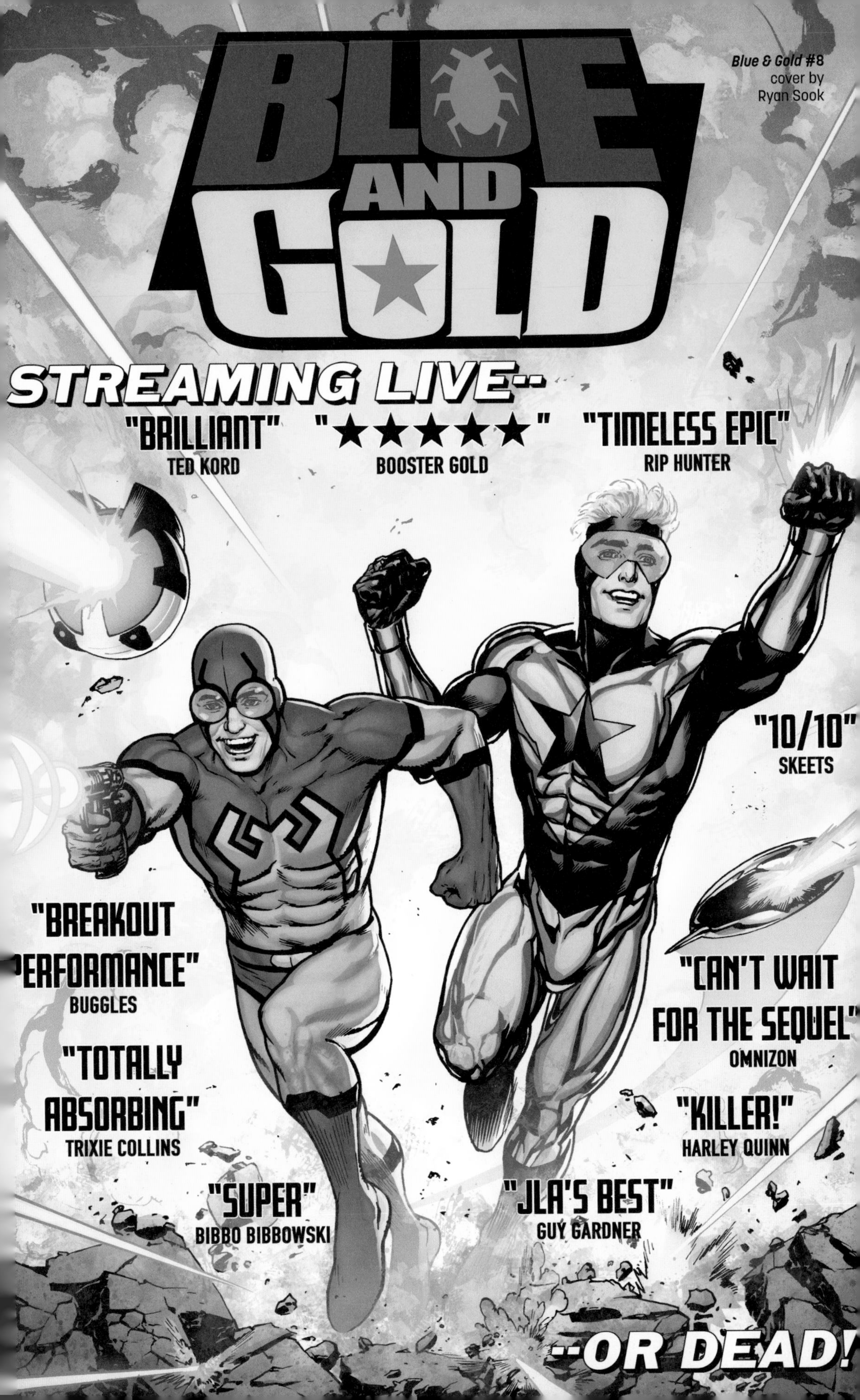
BLUE AND GOLD
STREAMING LIVE--
"BRILLIANT"
TED KORD
"★★★★★"
BOOSTER GOLD
"TIMELESS EPIC"
RIP HUNTER
"10/10"
SKEETS
"BREAKOUT
ERFORMANCE"
BUGGLES
"TOTALLY
ABSORBING"
TRIXIE COLLINS
"CAN'T WAIT
FOR THE SEQUEL
OMNIZON
"KILLER!"
HARLEY QUINN
"SUPER"
BIBBO BIBBOWSKI
"JLA'S BEST"
GUY GARDNER
--OR DEAD!

Blue & Gold #8
cover by
Ryan Sook

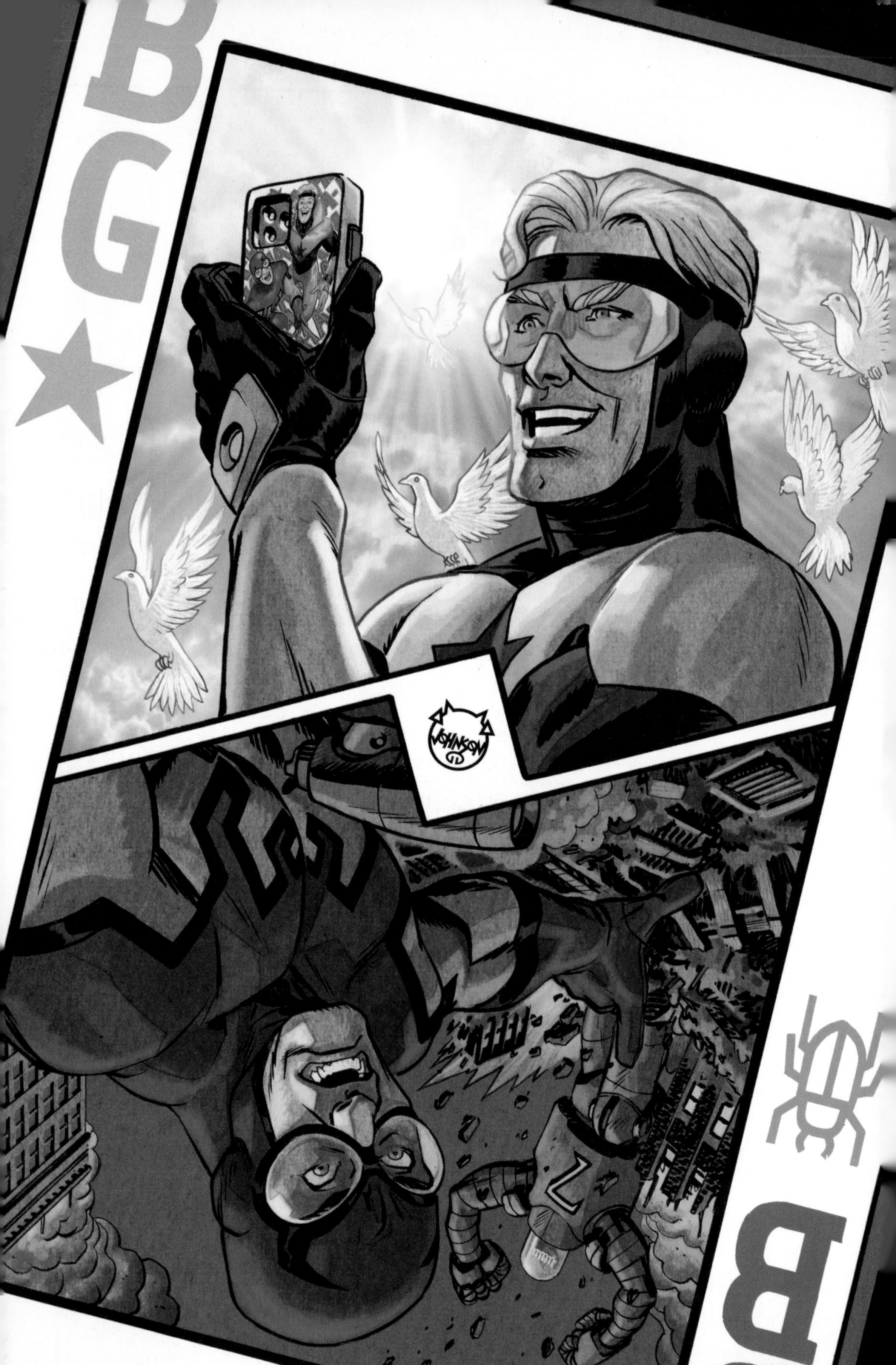

Blue & Gold #1
variant cover by Dave Johnson

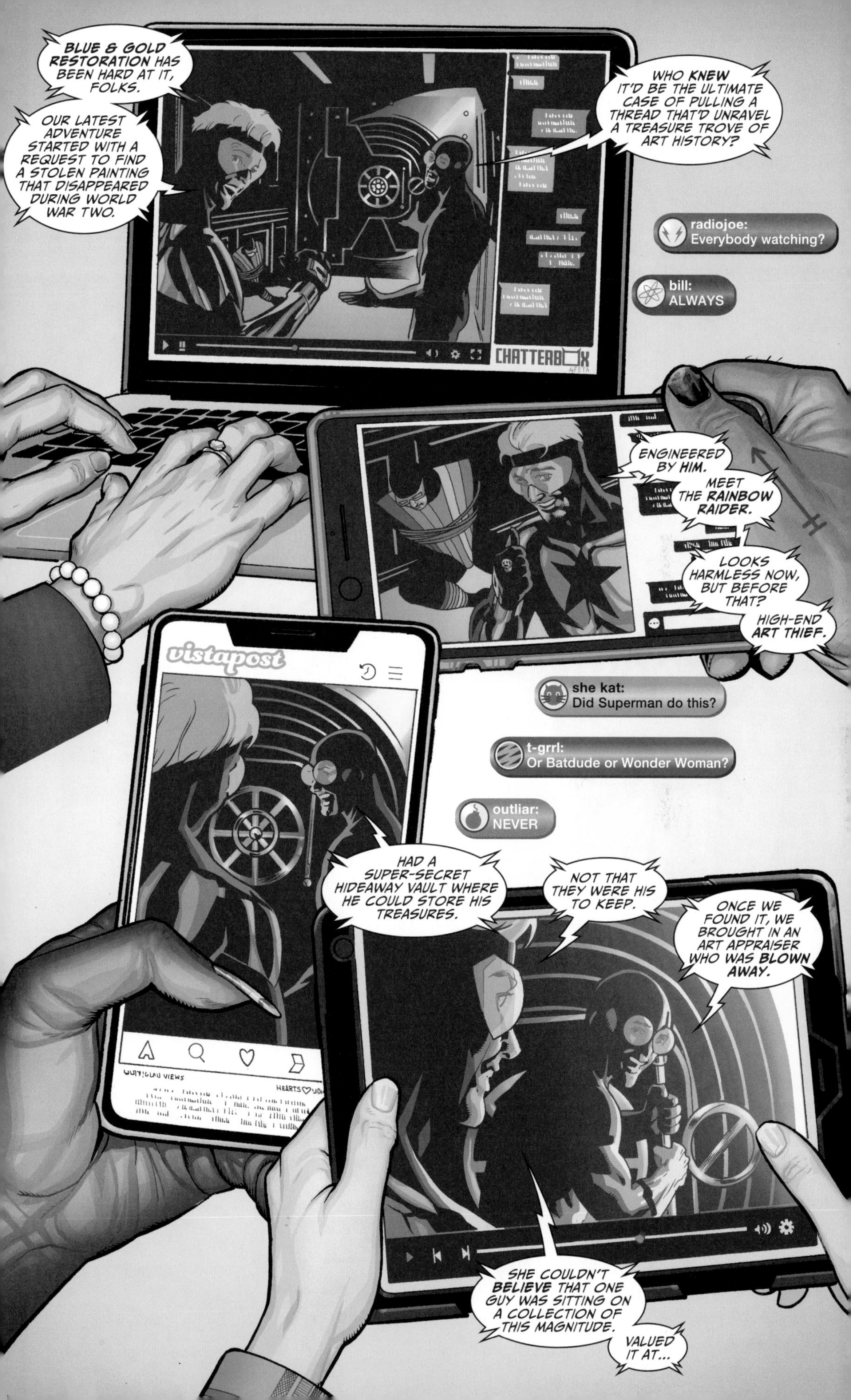

BLUE & GOLD RESTORATION HAS BEEN HARD AT IT, FOLKS.
OUR LATEST ADVENTURE STARTED WITH A REQUEST TO FIND A STOLEN PAINTING THAT DISAPPEARED DURING WORLD WAR TWO.
WHO KNEW IT'D BE THE ULTIMATE CASE OF PULLING A THREAD THAT'D UNRAVEL A TREASURE TROVE OF ART HISTORY?
CHATTERBOX
radiojoe: Everybody watching?
bill: ALWAYS
ENGINEERED BY HIM.
MEET THE RAINBOW RAIDER.
LOOKS HARMLESS NOW, BUT BEFORE THAT?
HIGH-END ART THIEF.
vistapost
she kat: Did Superman do this?
t-grrl: Or Batdude or Wonder Woman?
outliar: NEVER
HAD A SUPER-SECRET HIDEAWAY VAULT WHERE HE COULD STORE HIS TREASURES.
NOT THAT THEY WERE HIS TO KEEP.
ONCE WE FOUND IT, WE BROUGHT IN AN ART APPRAISER WHO WAS BLOWN AWAY.
SHE COULDN'T BELIEVE THAT ONE GUY WAS SITTING ON A COLLECTION OF THIS MAGNITUDE.
VALUED IT AT...

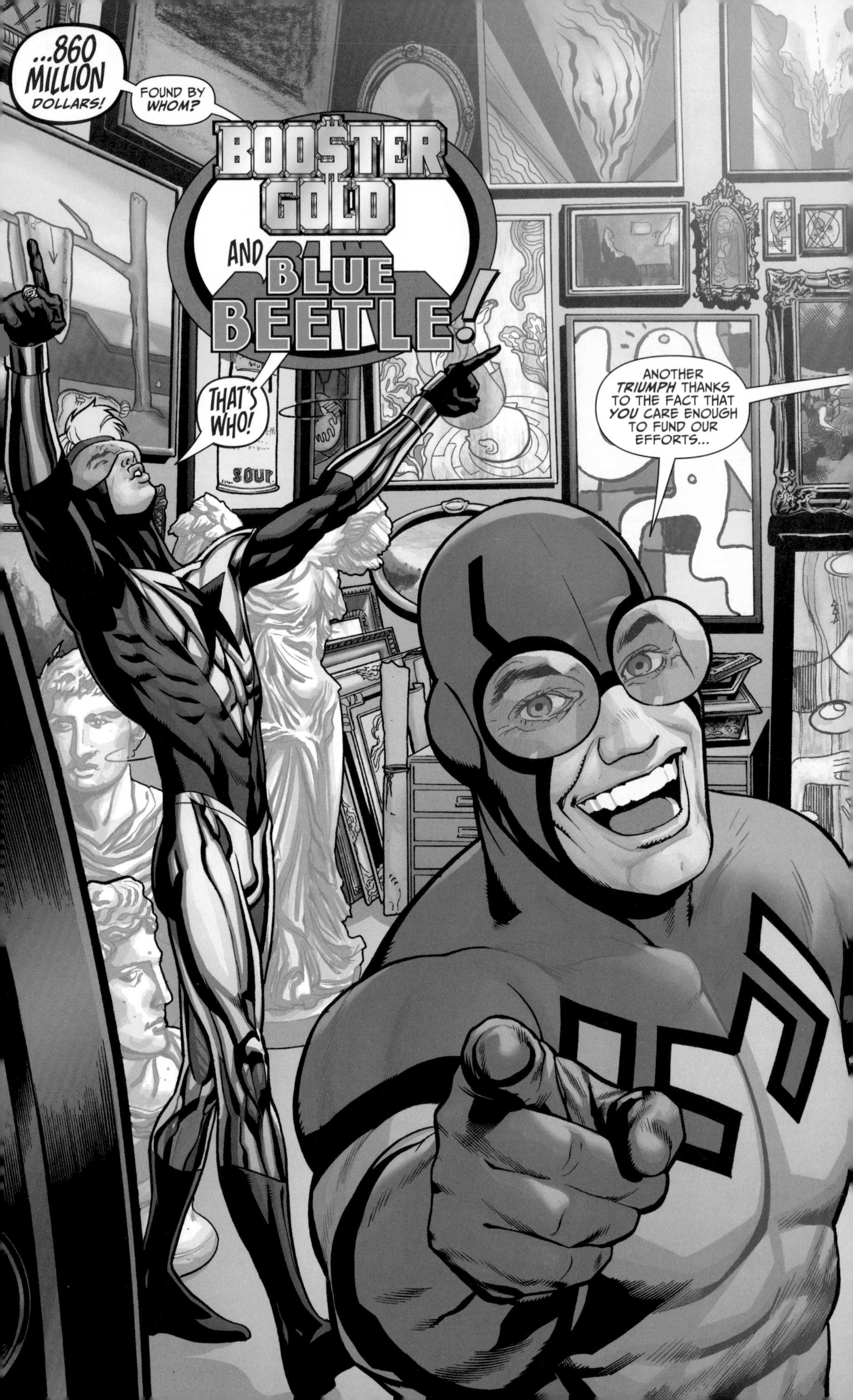
...860 MILLION DOLLARS!
FOUND BY WHOM?
BOOSTER GOLD AND BLUE BEETLE!
THAT'S WHO!
ANOTHER TRIUMPH THANKS TO THE FACT THAT YOU CARE ENOUGH TO FUND OUR EFFORTS...
SOUP

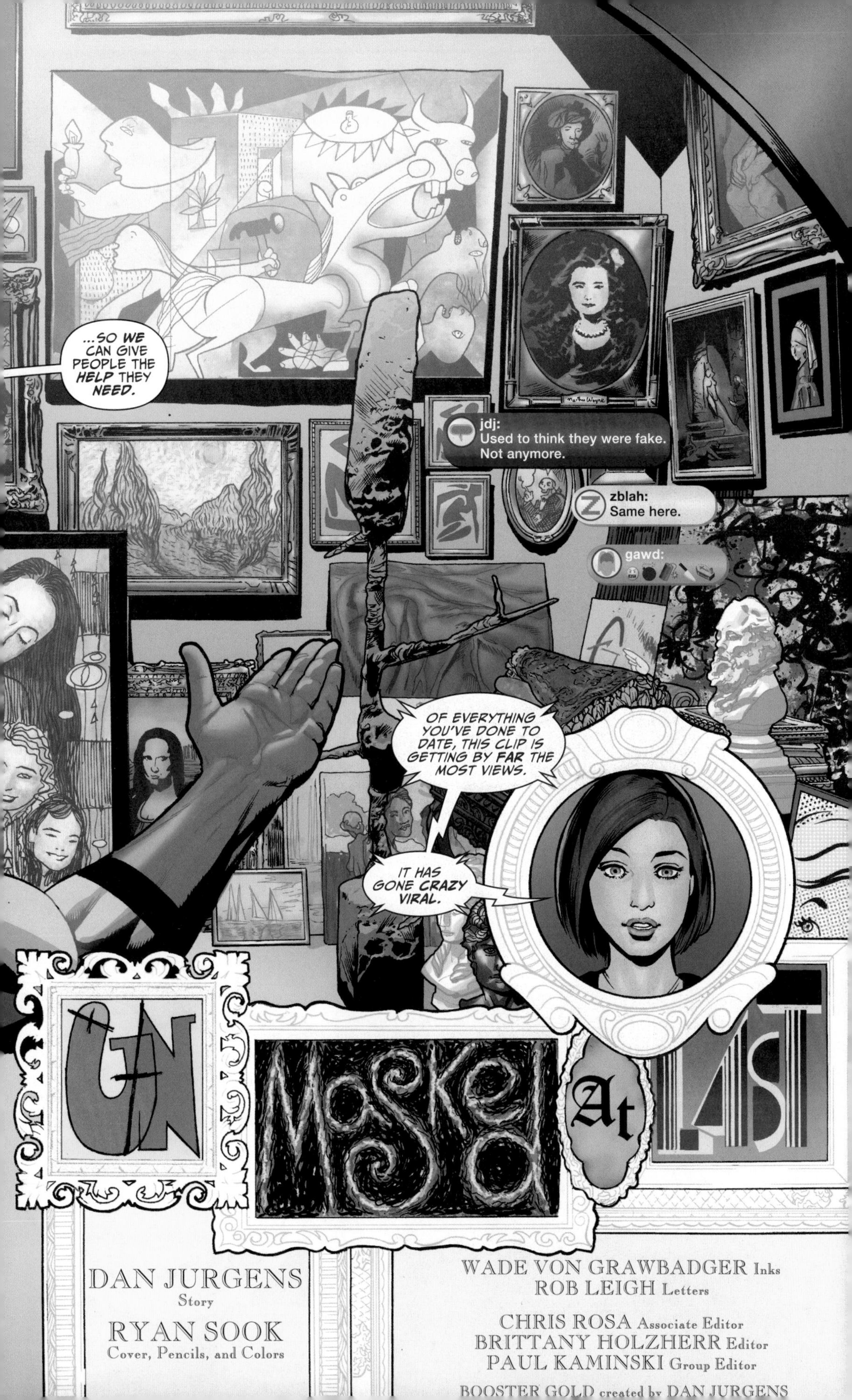
...SO WE CAN GIVE PEOPLE THE HELP THEY NEED.
jdj:
Used to think they were fake. Not anymore.
zblah:
Same here.
gawd:
OF EVERYTHING YOU'VE DONE TO DATE, THIS CLIP IS GETTING BY FAR THE MOST VIEWS.
IT HAS GONE CRAZY VIRAL.
UNMASKED AT LAST
DAN JURGENS Story
RYAN SOOK Cover, Pencils, and Colors
WADE VON GRAWBADGER Inks
ROB LEIGH Letters
CHRIS ROSA Associate Editor
BRITTANY HOLZHERR Editor
PAUL KAMINSKI Group Editor
BOOSTER GOLD created by DAN JURGENS

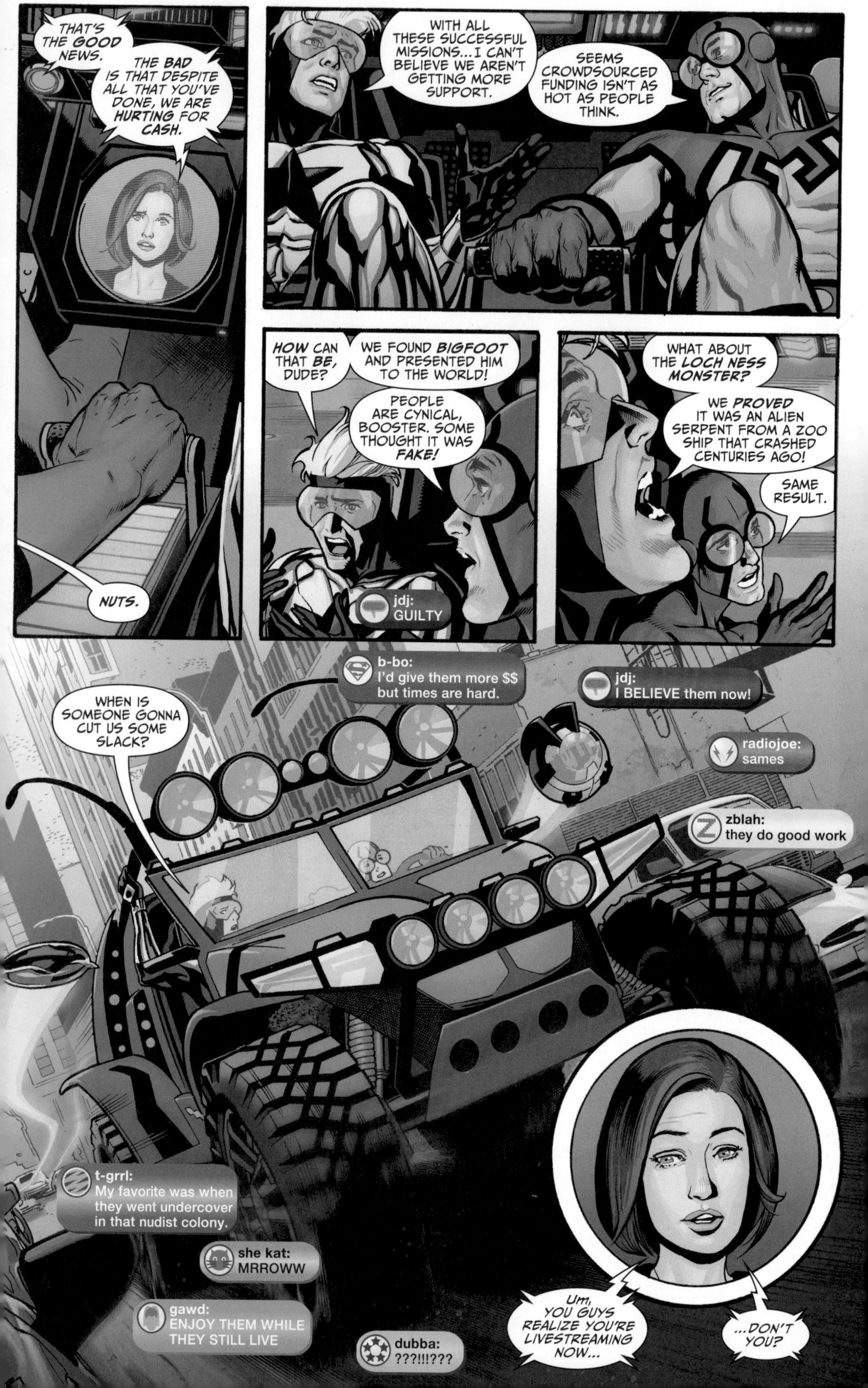
THAT'S THE GOOD NEWS.
THE BAD IS THAT DESPITE ALL THAT YOU'VE DONE, WE ARE HURTING FOR CASH.
NUTS.
WITH ALL THESE SUCCESSFUL MISSIONS...I CAN'T BELIEVE WE AREN'T GETTING MORE SUPPORT.
SEEMS CROWDSOURCED FUNDING ISN'T AS HOT AS PEOPLE THINK.
HOW CAN THAT BE, DUDE?
WE FOUND BIGFOOT AND PRESENTED HIM TO THE WORLD!
PEOPLE ARE CYNICAL, BOOSTER. SOME THOUGHT IT WAS FAKE!
jdj: GUILTY
WHAT ABOUT THE LOCH NESS MONSTER?
WE PROVED IT WAS AN ALIEN SERPENT FROM A ZOO SHIP THAT CRASHED CENTURIES AGO!
SAME RESULT.
WHEN IS SOMEONE GONNA CUT US SOME SLACK?
b-bo: I'd give them more $$ but times are hard.
jdj: I BELIEVE them now!
radiojoe: sames
zblah: they do good work
t-grrl: My favorite was when they went undercover in that nudist colony.
she kat: MRROWW
gawd: ENJOY THEM WHILE THEY STILL LIVE
dubba: ???!!!???
Um, YOU GUYS REALIZE YOU'RE LIVESTREAMING NOW...
...DON'T YOU?

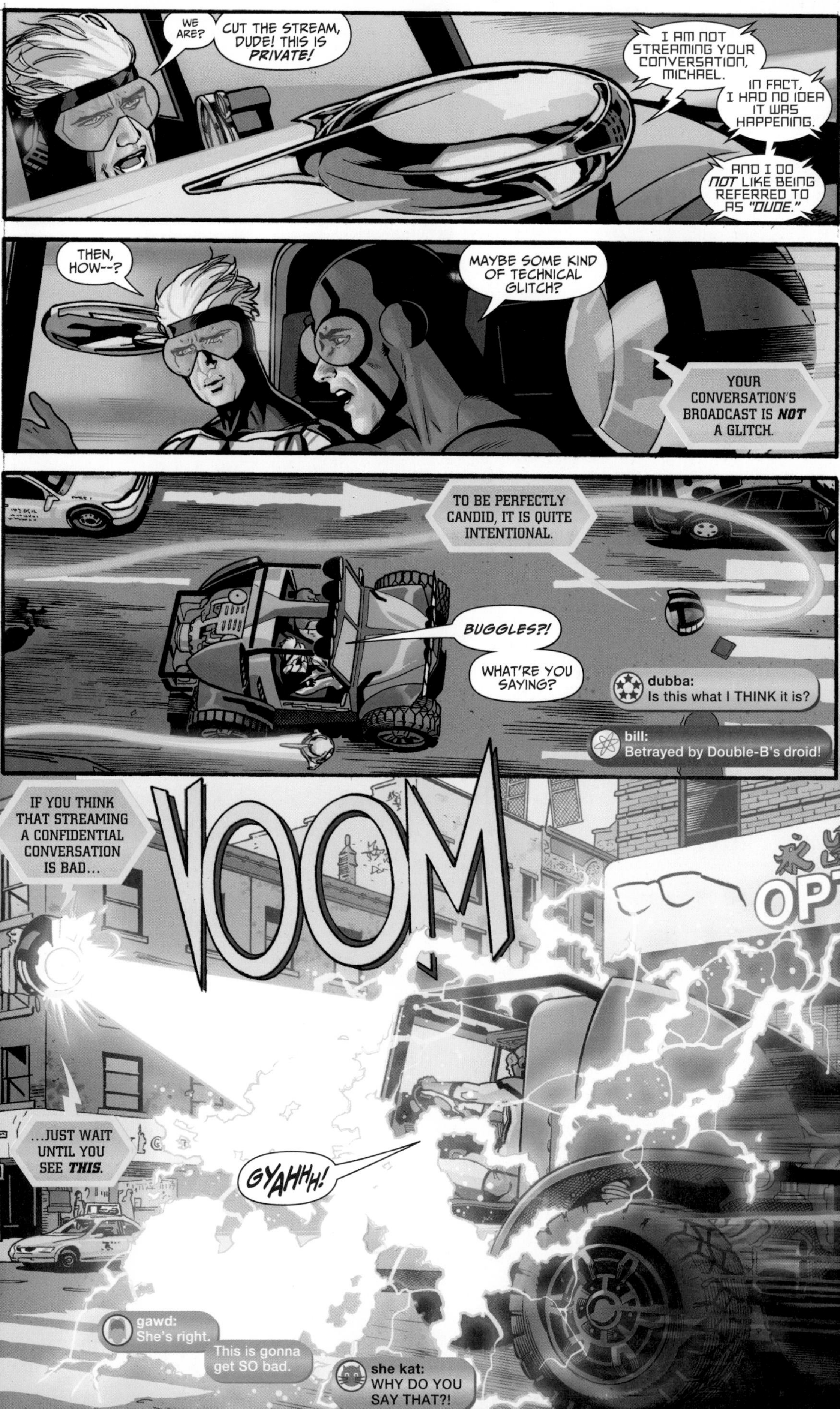
WE ARE?
CUT THE STREAM, DUDE! THIS IS PRIVATE!
I AM NOT STREAMING YOUR CONVERSATION, MICHAEL.
IN FACT, I HAD NO IDEA IT WAS HAPPENING.
AND I DO NOT LIKE BEING REFERRED TO AS "DUDE."
THEN, HOW--?
MAYBE SOME KIND OF TECHNICAL GLITCH?
YOUR CONVERSATION'S BROADCAST IS NOT A GLITCH.
TO BE PERFECTLY CANDID, IT IS QUITE INTENTIONAL.
BUGGLES?!
WHAT'RE YOU SAYING?
dubba: Is this what I THINK it is?
bill: Betrayed by Double-B's droid!
IF YOU THINK THAT STREAMING A CONFIDENTIAL CONVERSATION IS BAD...
VOOM
OPT
...JUST WAIT UNTIL YOU SEE THIS.
GYAHHH!
gawd: She's right.
This is gonna get SO bad.
she kat: WHY DO YOU SAY THAT?!

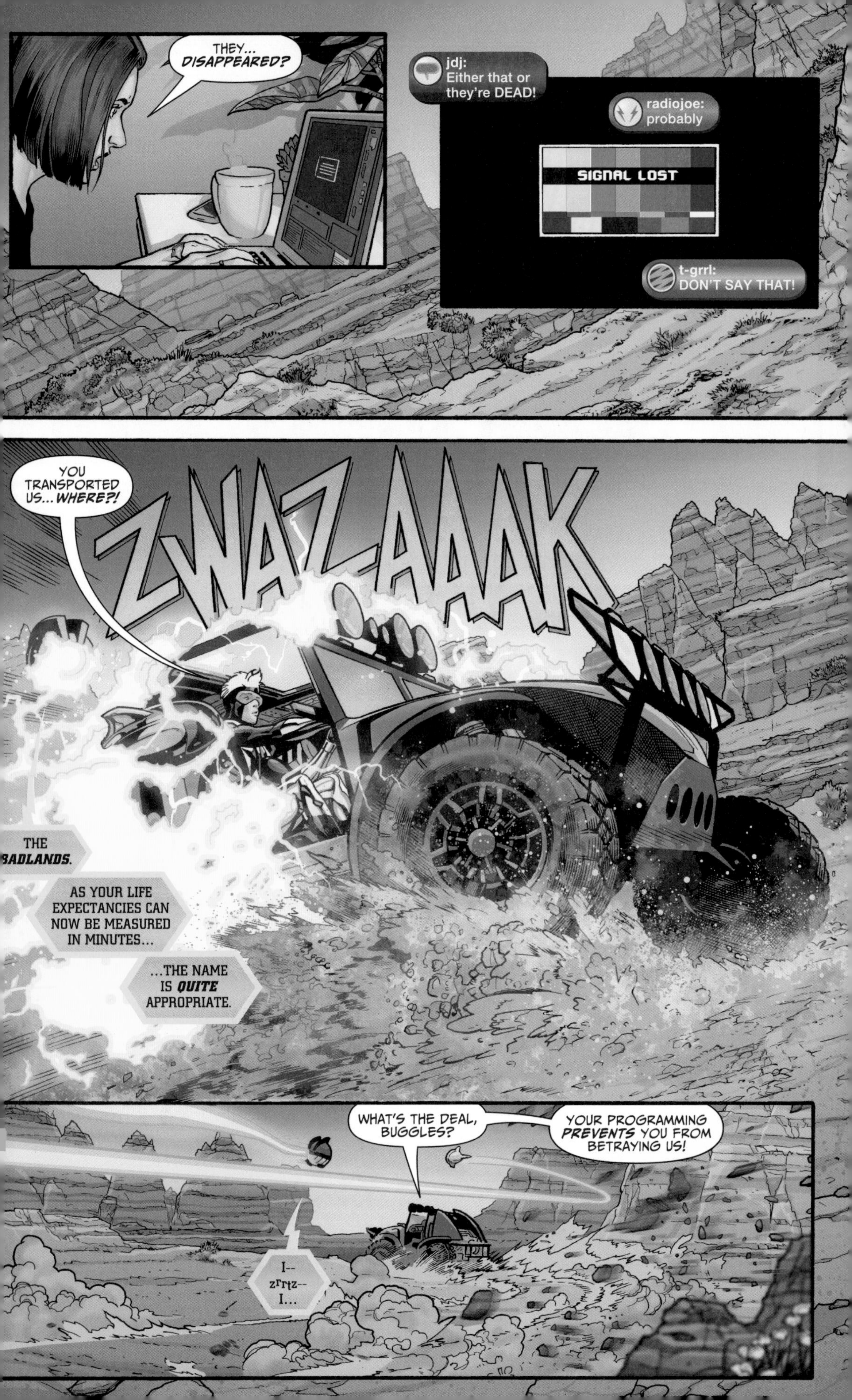

THEY... DISAPPEARED?
jdj: Either that or they're DEAD!
radiojoe: probably
SIGNAL LOST
t-grrl: DON'T SAY THAT!
YOU TRANSPORTED US... WHERE?!
ZWAZAAAK
THE BADLANDS.
AS YOUR LIFE EXPECTANCIES CAN NOW BE MEASURED IN MINUTES...
...THE NAME IS QUITE APPROPRIATE.
WHAT'S THE DEAL, BUGGLES?
YOUR PROGRAMMING PREVENTS YOU FROM BETRAYING US!
I-- zrrtz-- I...

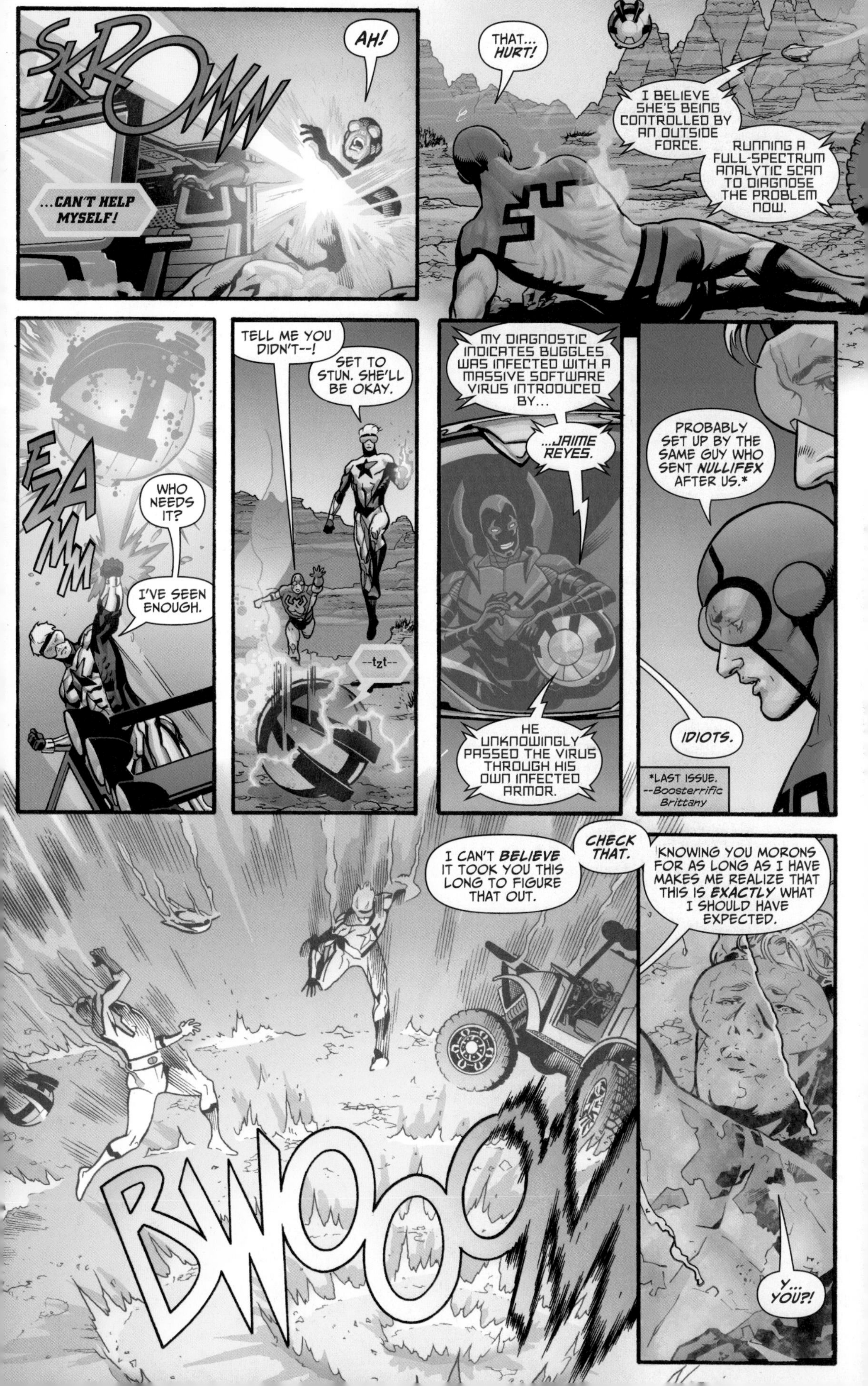
SKROWW
AH!
...CAN'T HELP MYSELF!
THAT... HURT!
I BELIEVE SHE'S BEING CONTROLLED BY AN OUTSIDE FORCE.
RUNNING A FULL-SPECTRUM ANALYTIC SCAN TO DIAGNOSE THE PROBLEM NOW.
FZAMMM
WHO NEEDS IT?
I'VE SEEN ENOUGH.
TELL ME YOU DIDN'T--!
SET TO STUN. SHE'LL BE OKAY.
--tzt--
MY DIAGNOSTIC INDICATES BUGGLES WAS INFECTED WITH A MASSIVE SOFTWARE VIRUS INTRODUCED BY...
...JAIME REYES.
HE UNKNOWINGLY PASSED THE VIRUS THROUGH HIS OWN INFECTED ARMOR.
PROBABLY SET UP BY THE SAME GUY WHO SENT NULLIFEX AFTER US.*
IDIOTS.
*LAST ISSUE. --Boosterrific Brittany
I CAN'T BELIEVE IT TOOK YOU THIS LONG TO FIGURE THAT OUT.
CHECK THAT.
KNOWING YOU MORONS FOR AS LONG AS I HAVE MAKES ME REALIZE THAT THIS IS EXACTLY WHAT I SHOULD HAVE EXPECTED.
BWOOOM
Y... YOU?!

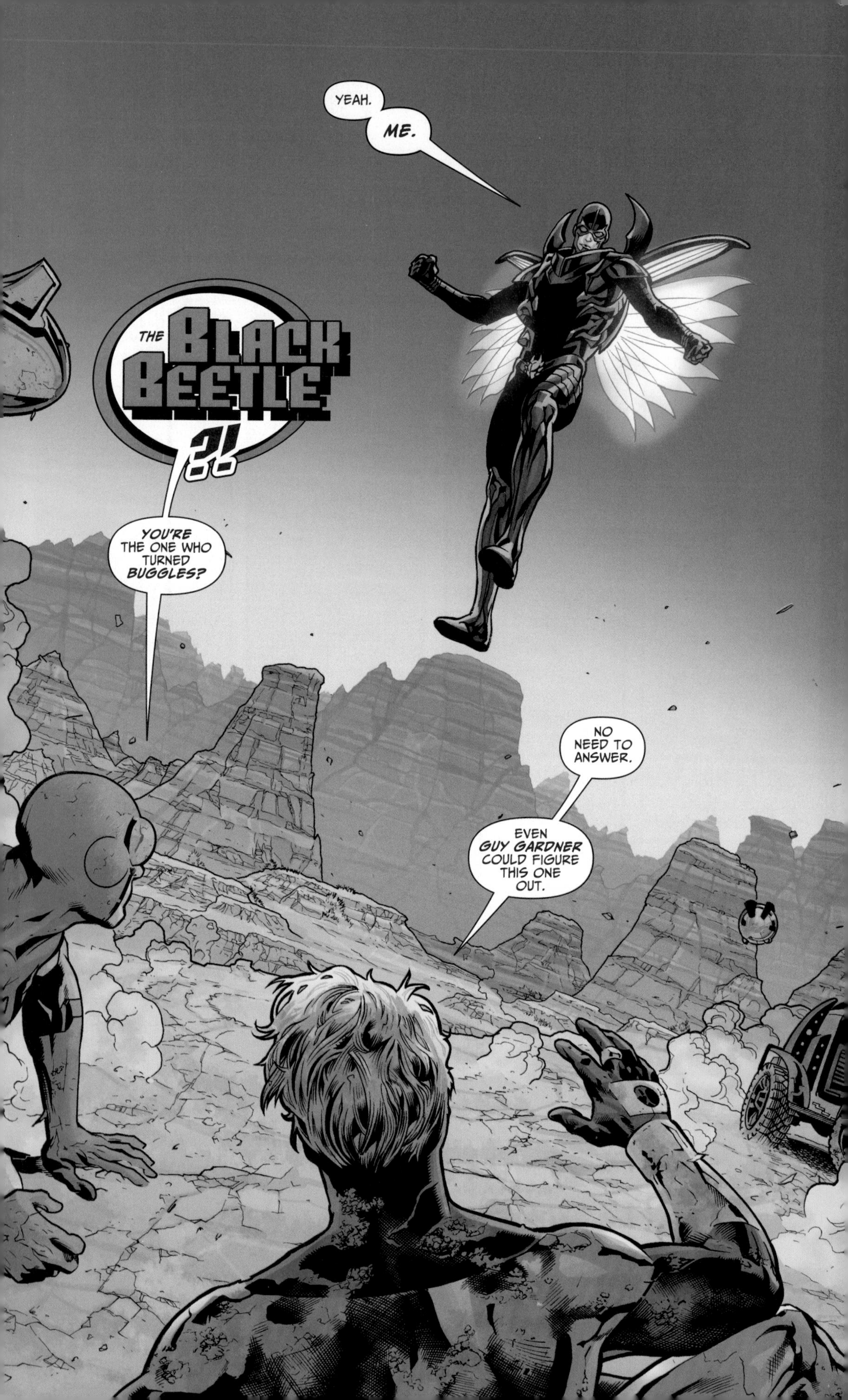
YEAH.
ME.
THE BLACK BEETLE ?!
YOU'RE THE ONE WHO TURNED BUGGLES?
NO NEED TO ANSWER.
EVEN GUY GARDNER COULD FIGURE THIS ONE OUT.

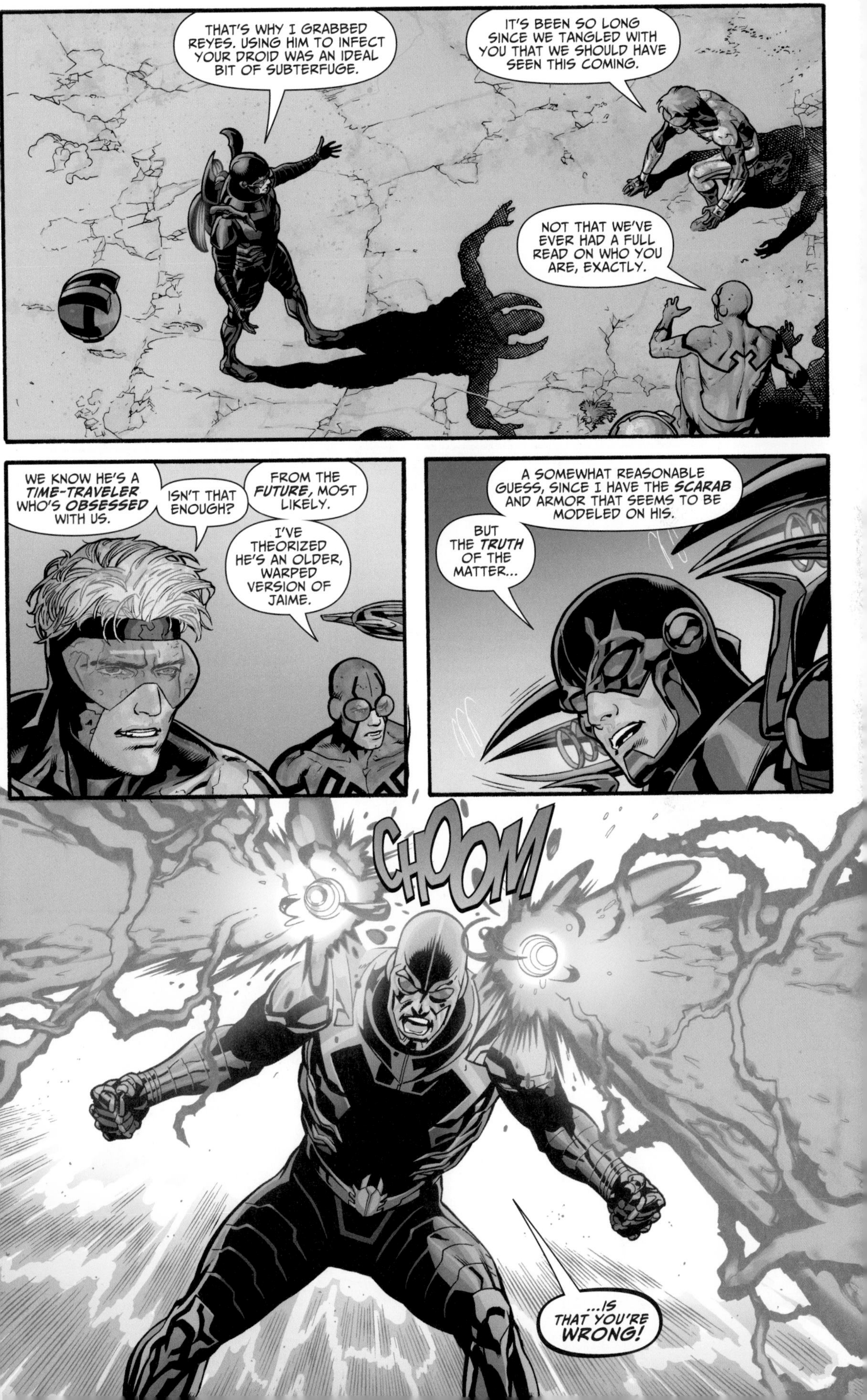
THAT'S WHY I GRABBED REYES. USING HIM TO INFECT YOUR DROID WAS AN IDEAL BIT OF SUBTERFUGE.
IT'S BEEN SO LONG SINCE WE TANGLED WITH YOU THAT WE SHOULD HAVE SEEN THIS COMING.
NOT THAT WE'VE EVER HAD A FULL READ ON WHO YOU ARE, EXACTLY.
WE KNOW HE'S A TIME-TRAVELER WHO'S OBSESSED WITH US.
ISN'T THAT ENOUGH?
FROM THE FUTURE, MOST LIKELY.
I'VE THEORIZED HE'S AN OLDER, WARPED VERSION OF JAIME.
A SOMEWHAT REASONABLE GUESS, SINCE I HAVE THE SCARAB AND ARMOR THAT SEEMS TO BE MODELED ON HIS.
BUT THE TRUTH OF THE MATTER...
CHOOM
...IS THAT YOU'RE WRONG!

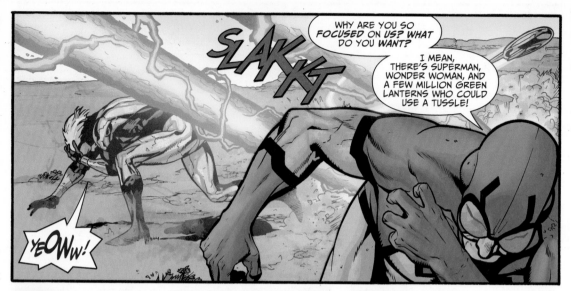

WHY ARE YOU SO *FOCUSED* ON *US?* WHAT DO YOU *WANT?*

I MEAN, THERE'S SUPERMAN, WONDER WOMAN, AND A FEW MILLION GREEN LANTERNS WHO COULD USE A TUSSLE!

SLAKKT

YEOWW!

BECAUSE I *LOATHE* YOU FOR THE WASTED BAGS OF FLESH THAT YOU ARE!

I.... I DON'T... tzzt--

CHOOM

I'M *SORRY!*

"WASTED BAGS OF FLESH"?

Ew.

CHAMM

SKOWW

FZAMM

WE'RE ONLY TRYING TO *HELP* PEOPLE!

EXACTLY.

TK

TIK TIK

SPEN

YOU HAVE *WASTED* THE GREATEST OPPORTUNITY *EVER...*

...WHEN YOU *SHOULD HAVE* OWNED THE WORLD!

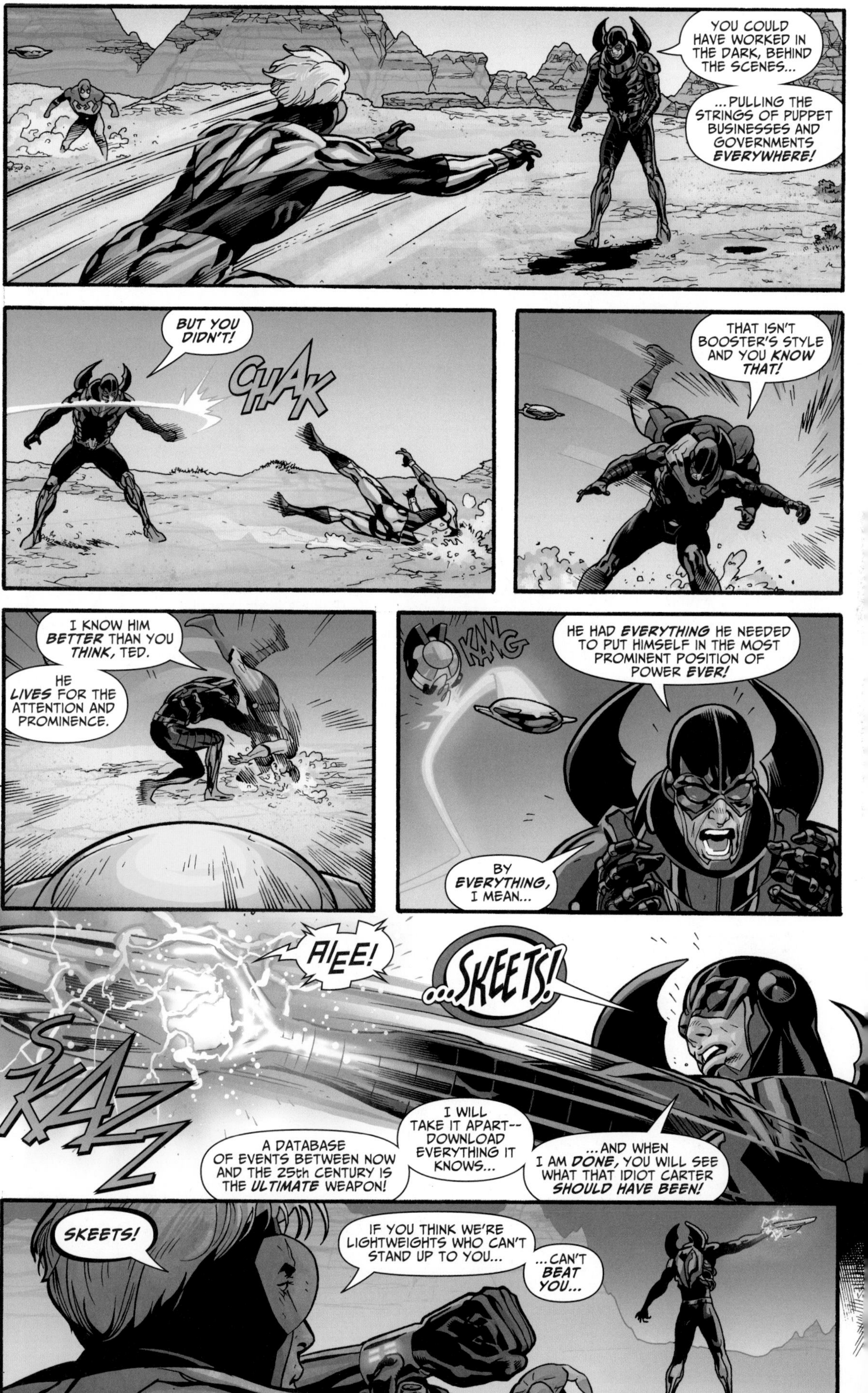
YOU COULD HAVE WORKED IN THE DARK, BEHIND THE SCENES...
...PULLING THE STRINGS OF PUPPET BUSINESSES AND GOVERNMENTS EVERYWHERE!
BUT YOU DIDN'T!
CHAK
THAT ISN'T BOOSTER'S STYLE AND YOU KNOW THAT!
I KNOW HIM BETTER THAN YOU THINK, TED.
HE LIVES FOR THE ATTENTION AND PROMINENCE.
KANG
HE HAD EVERYTHING HE NEEDED TO PUT HIMSELF IN THE MOST PROMINENT POSITION OF POWER EVER!
BY EVERYTHING, I MEAN...
AIEE!
...SKEETS!
SKAZZ
A DATABASE OF EVENTS BETWEEN NOW AND THE 25th CENTURY IS THE ULTIMATE WEAPON!
I WILL TAKE IT APART-- DOWNLOAD EVERYTHING IT KNOWS...
...AND WHEN I AM DONE, YOU WILL SEE WHAT THAT IDIOT CARTER SHOULD HAVE BEEN!
SKEETS!
IF YOU THINK WE'RE LIGHTWEIGHTS WHO CAN'T STAND UP TO YOU...
...CAN'T BEAT YOU...

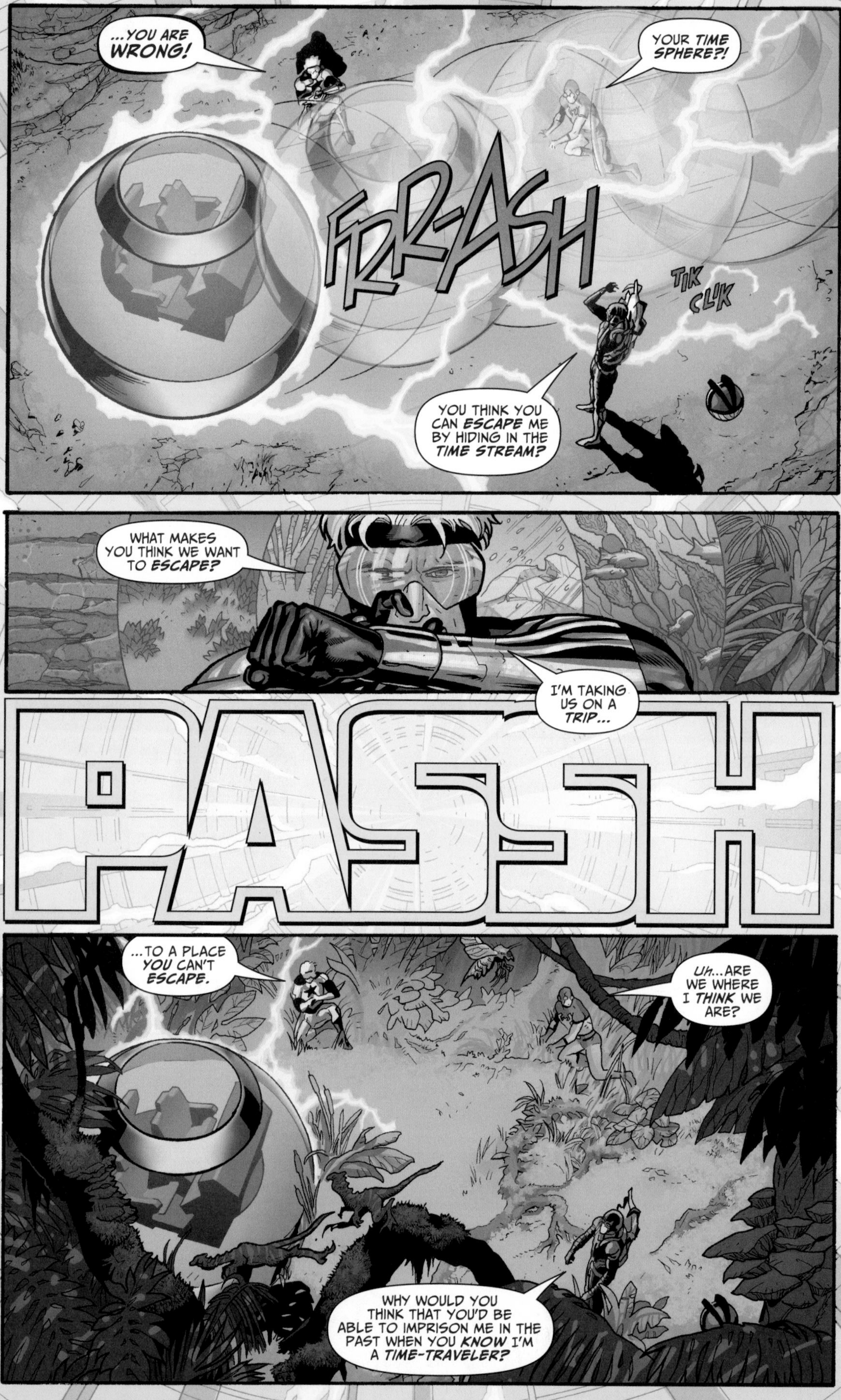
...YOU ARE WRONG!
YOUR TIME SPHERE?!
FRR-ASH
TIK
CLIK
YOU THINK YOU CAN ESCAPE ME BY HIDING IN THE TIME STREAM?
WHAT MAKES YOU THINK WE WANT TO ESCAPE?
I'M TAKING US ON A TRIP...
PASSH
...TO A PLACE YOU CAN'T ESCAPE.
Uh...ARE WE WHERE I THINK WE ARE?
WHY WOULD YOU THINK THAT YOU'D BE ABLE TO IMPRISON ME IN THE PAST WHEN YOU KNOW I'M A TIME-TRAVELER?

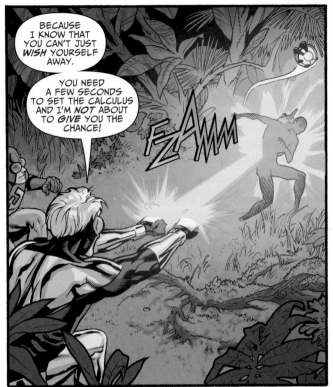

BECAUSE I KNOW THAT YOU CAN'T JUST *WISH* YOURSELF AWAY.

YOU NEED A FEW SECONDS TO SET THE CALCULUS AND I'M *NOT* ABOUT TO *GIVE* YOU THE CHANCE!

FZAMMM

TIME TO GIVE THE MAN ONE HELL OF A HEADACHE, TED.

SONICS.

ON IT.

VEVEVEVE

YOUR HEAD IS ABOUT TO FEEL LIKE IT'S SPLITTING IN *TWO*.

VEVEVEVE

GUH!

KRKKA

VEVEVEVEVE

AAH! MY HELMET!

NO...

...FREAKING...

...WAY!

OF ALL THE PEOPLE... IT NEVER OCCURRED TO ME THAT...HE'S...

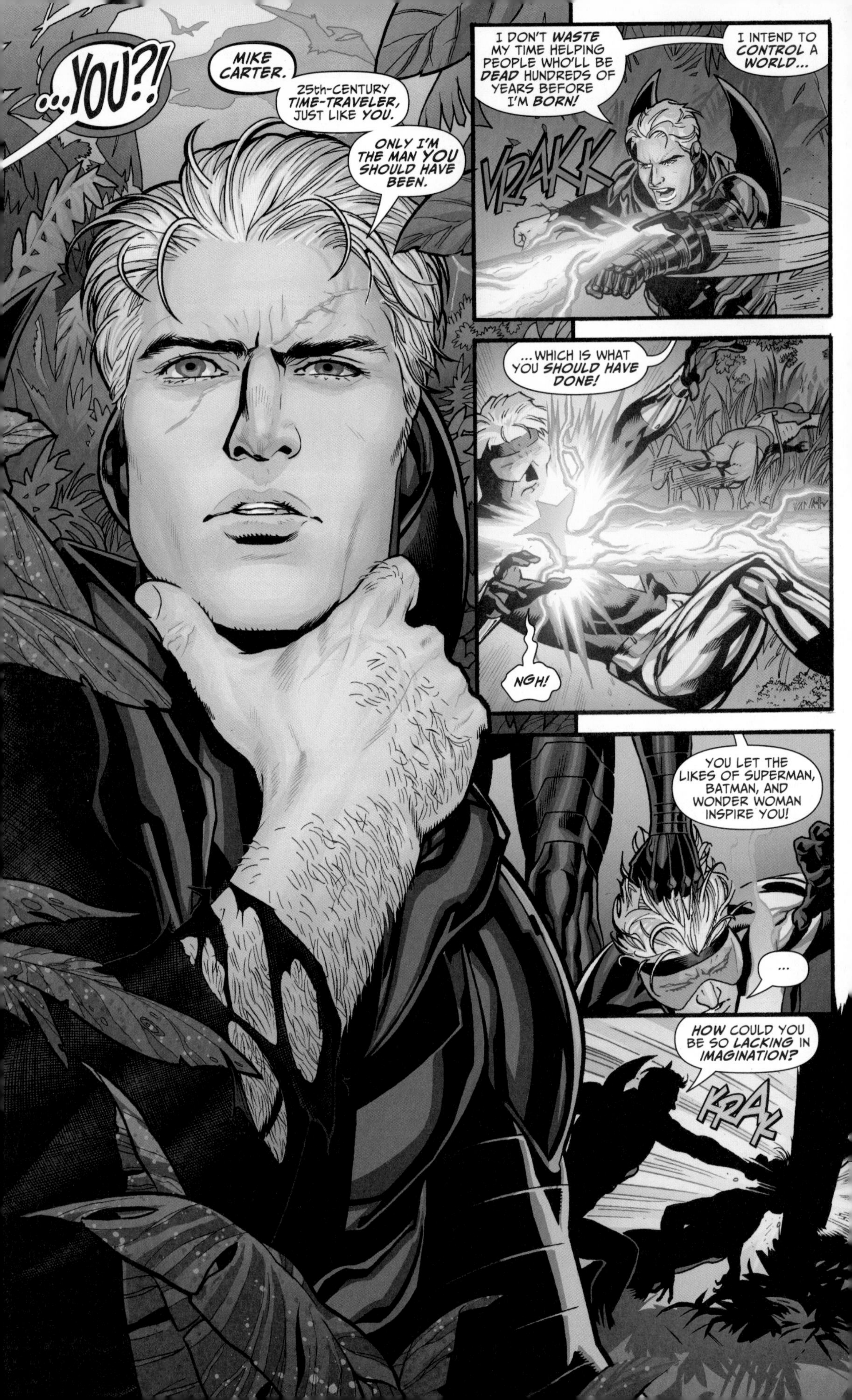
...YOU?!
MIKE CARTER.
25th-CENTURY TIME-TRAVELER, JUST LIKE YOU.
ONLY I'M THE MAN YOU SHOULD HAVE BEEN.
I DON'T WASTE MY TIME HELPING PEOPLE WHO'LL BE DEAD HUNDREDS OF YEARS BEFORE I'M BORN!
I INTEND TO CONTROL A WORLD...
VRAKK
...WHICH IS WHAT YOU SHOULD HAVE DONE!
NGH!
YOU LET THE LIKES OF SUPERMAN, BATMAN, AND WONDER WOMAN INSPIRE YOU!
...
HOW COULD YOU BE SO LACKING IN IMAGINATION?
KRAK

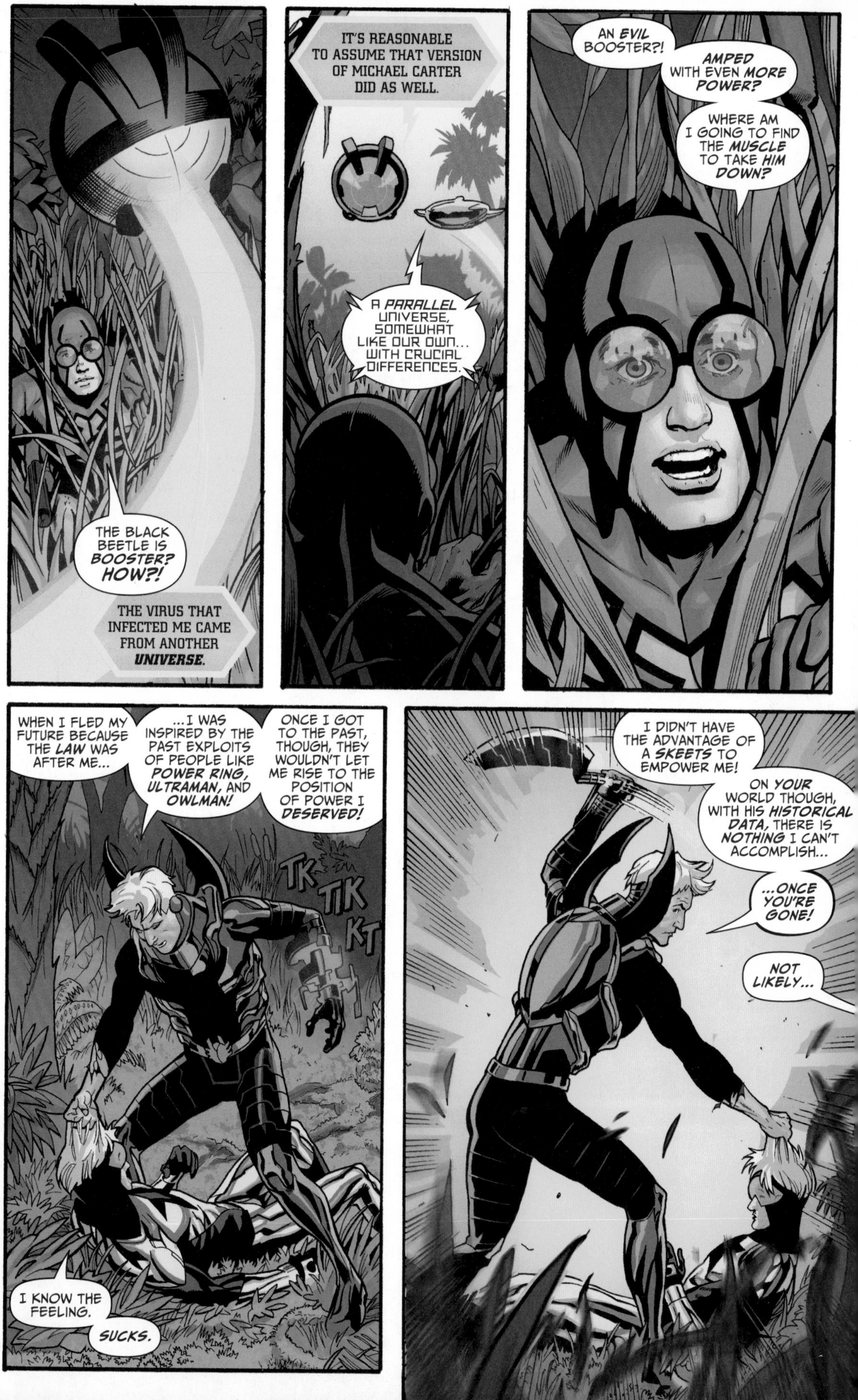
THE BLACK BEETLE IS BOOSTER? HOW?!
THE VIRUS THAT INFECTED ME CAME FROM ANOTHER UNIVERSE.
IT'S REASONABLE TO ASSUME THAT VERSION OF MICHAEL CARTER DID AS WELL.
A PARALLEL UNIVERSE, SOMEWHAT LIKE OUR OWN... WITH CRUCIAL DIFFERENCES.
AN EVIL BOOSTER?!
AMPED WITH EVEN MORE POWER?
WHERE AM I GOING TO FIND THE MUSCLE TO TAKE HIM DOWN?
WHEN I FLED MY FUTURE BECAUSE THE LAW WAS AFTER ME...
...I WAS INSPIRED BY THE PAST EXPLOITS OF PEOPLE LIKE POWER RING, ULTRAMAN, AND OWLMAN!
ONCE I GOT TO THE PAST, THOUGH, THEY WOULDN'T LET ME RISE TO THE POSITION OF POWER I DESERVED!
TK TIK KT
I KNOW THE FEELING.
SUCKS.
I DIDN'T HAVE THE ADVANTAGE OF A SKEETS TO EMPOWER ME!
ON YOUR WORLD THOUGH, WITH HIS HISTORICAL DATA, THERE IS NOTHING I CAN'T ACCOMPLISH...
...ONCE YOU'RE GONE!
NOT LIKELY...

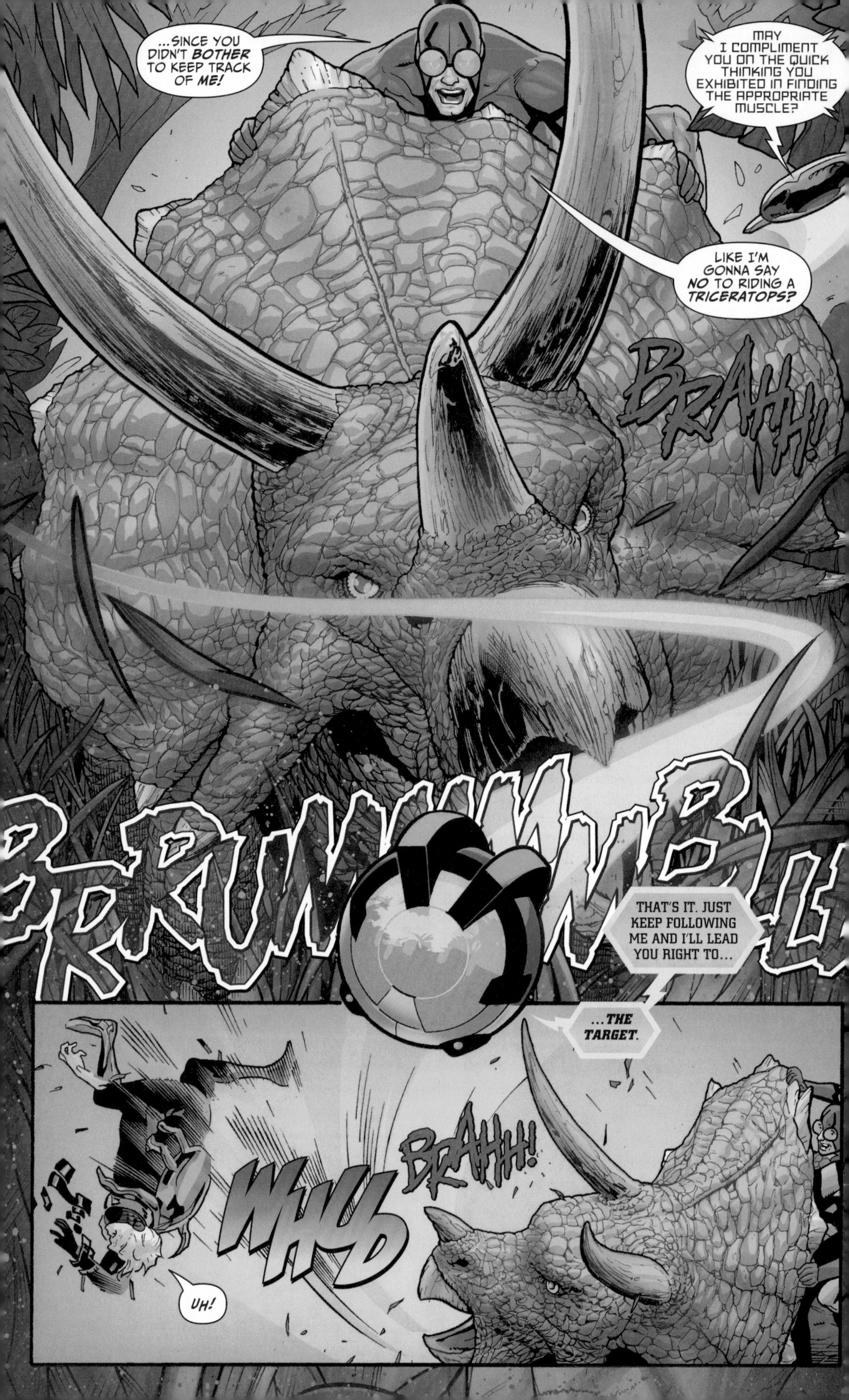
...SINCE YOU DIDN'T *BOTHER* TO KEEP TRACK OF *ME!*
MAY I COMPLIMENT YOU ON THE QUICK THINKING YOU EXHIBITED IN FINDING THE APPROPRIATE MUSCLE?
LIKE I'M GONNA SAY *NO* TO RIDING A *TRICERATOPS?*
BRAHH!
THAT'S IT. JUST KEEP FOLLOWING ME AND I'LL LEAD YOU RIGHT TO...
...*THE TARGET*.
BRAHH!
UH!

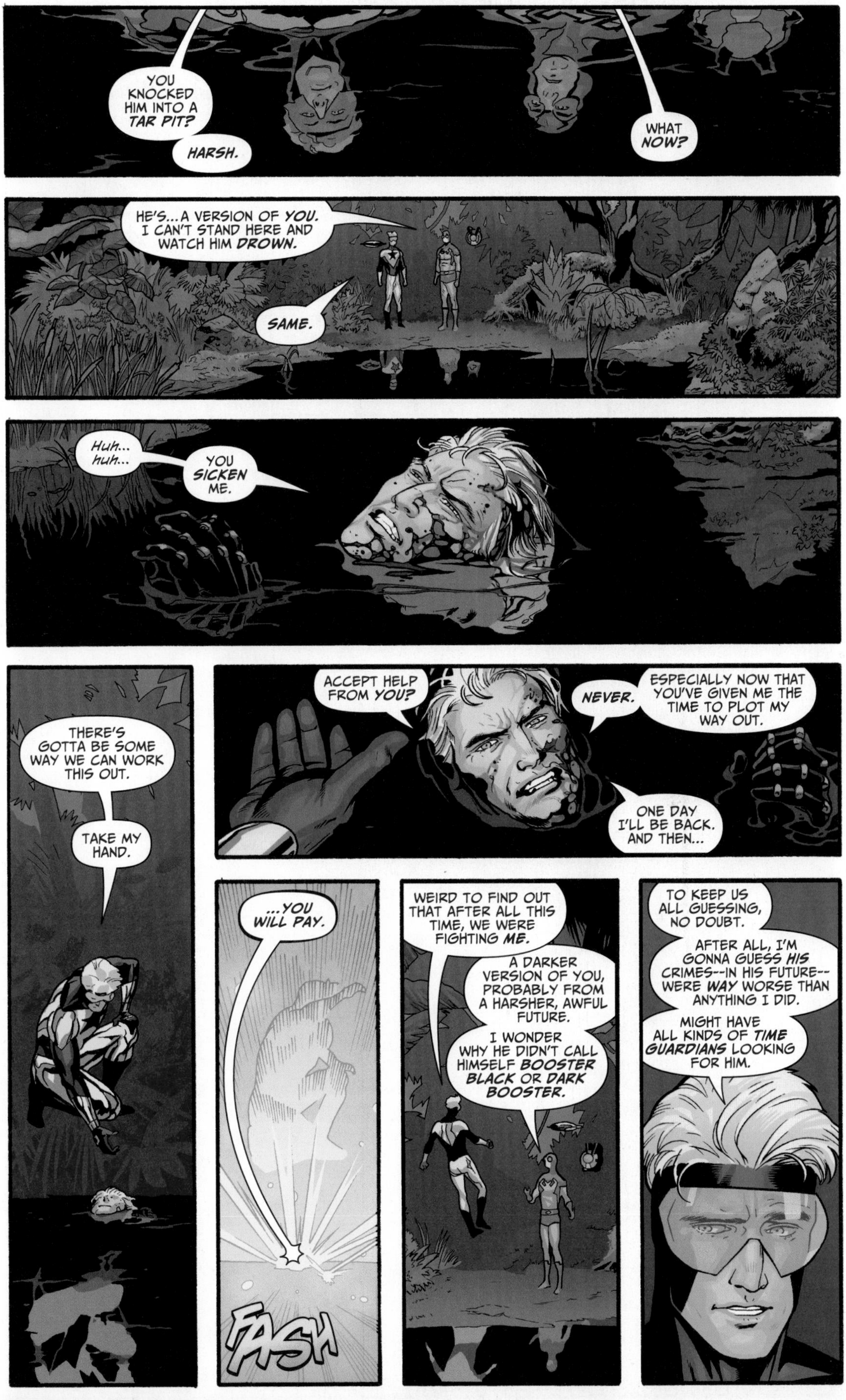
YOU KNOCKED HIM INTO A *TAR PIT?*
HARSH.
WHAT *NOW?*
HE'S...A VERSION OF *YOU.* I CAN'T STAND HERE AND WATCH HIM *DROWN.*
SAME.
Huh... huh...
YOU *SICKEN* ME.
THERE'S GOTTA BE SOME WAY WE CAN WORK THIS OUT.
TAKE MY HAND.
ACCEPT HELP FROM *YOU?*
NEVER.
ESPECIALLY NOW THAT YOU'VE GIVEN ME THE TIME TO PLOT MY WAY OUT.
ONE DAY I'LL BE BACK. AND THEN...
...YOU WILL PAY.
FASH
WEIRD TO FIND OUT THAT AFTER ALL THIS TIME, WE WERE FIGHTING *ME.*
A DARKER VERSION OF YOU, PROBABLY FROM A HARSHER, AWFUL FUTURE.
I WONDER WHY HE DIDN'T CALL HIMSELF *BOOSTER BLACK* OR *DARK BOOSTER.*
TO KEEP US ALL GUESSING, NO DOUBT.
AFTER ALL, I'M GONNA GUESS *HIS* CRIMES--IN HIS FUTURE--WERE *WAY* WORSE THAN ANYTHING I DID.
MIGHT HAVE ALL KINDS OF *TIME GUARDIANS* LOOKING FOR HIM.

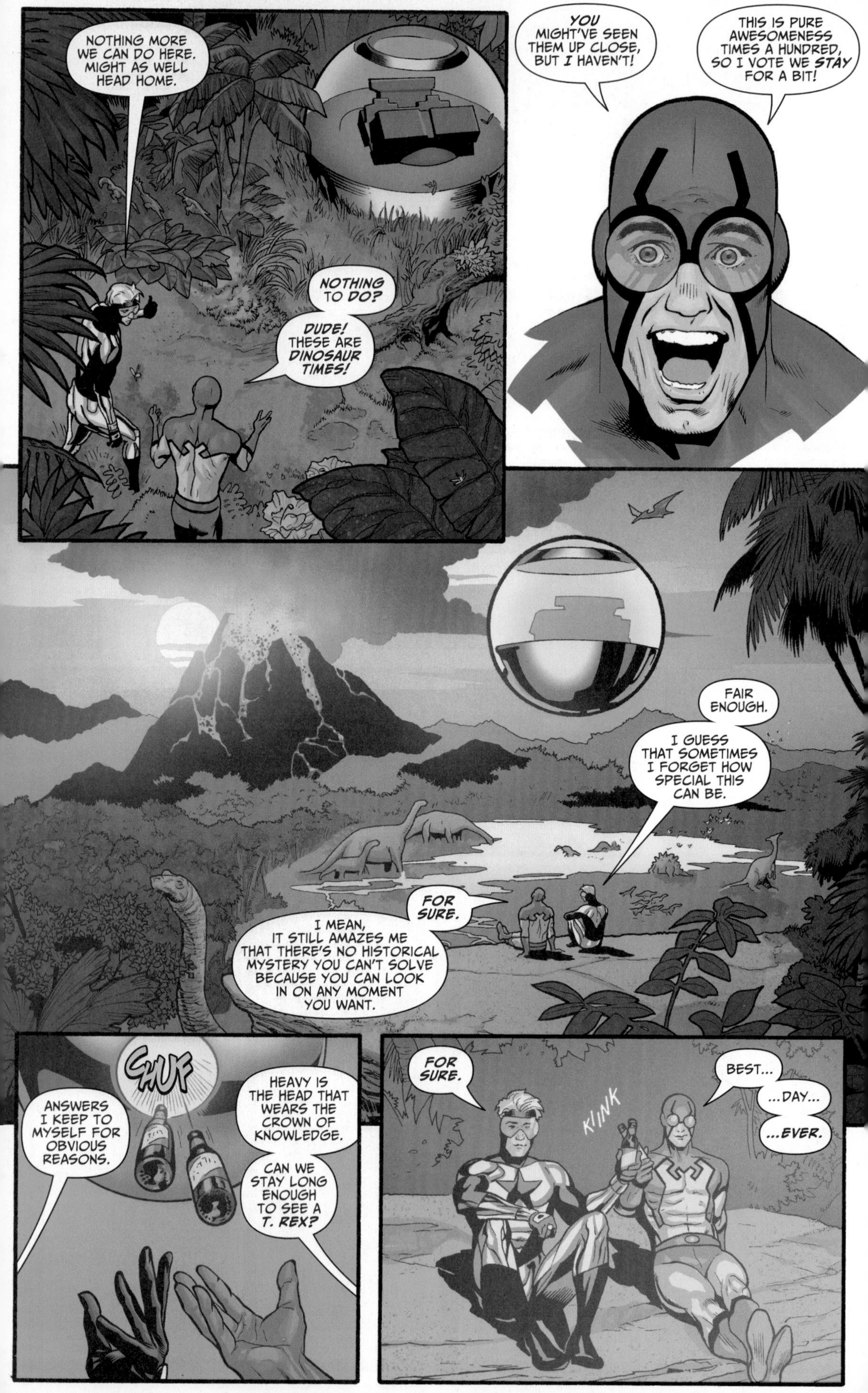
NOTHING MORE WE CAN DO HERE. MIGHT AS WELL HEAD HOME.
NOTHING TO DO?
DUDE! THESE ARE DINOSAUR TIMES!
YOU MIGHT'VE SEEN THEM UP CLOSE, BUT I HAVEN'T!
THIS IS PURE AWESOMENESS TIMES A HUNDRED, SO I VOTE WE STAY FOR A BIT!
FAIR ENOUGH.
I GUESS THAT SOMETIMES I FORGET HOW SPECIAL THIS CAN BE.
FOR SURE.
I MEAN, IT STILL AMAZES ME THAT THERE'S NO HISTORICAL MYSTERY YOU CAN'T SOLVE BECAUSE YOU CAN LOOK IN ON ANY MOMENT YOU WANT.
CHUF
ANSWERS I KEEP TO MYSELF FOR OBVIOUS REASONS.
HEAVY IS THE HEAD THAT WEARS THE CROWN OF KNOWLEDGE.
CAN WE STAY LONG ENOUGH TO SEE A T. REX?
FOR SURE.
KLINK
BEST...
...DAY...
...EVER.

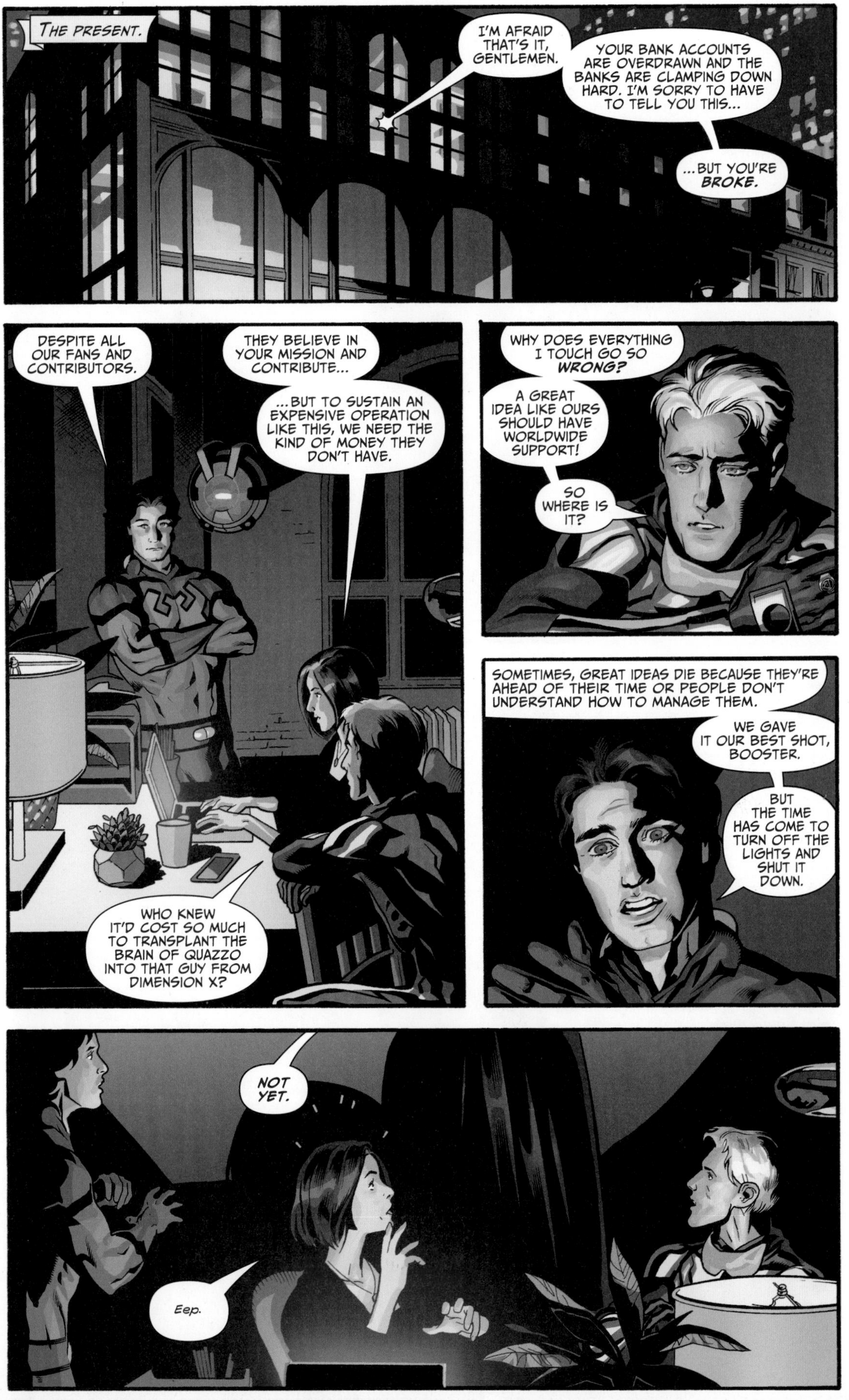
THE PRESENT.
I'M AFRAID THAT'S IT, GENTLEMEN.
YOUR BANK ACCOUNTS ARE OVERDRAWN AND THE BANKS ARE CLAMPING DOWN HARD. I'M SORRY TO HAVE TO TELL YOU THIS...
...BUT YOU'RE BROKE.
DESPITE ALL OUR FANS AND CONTRIBUTORS.
THEY BELIEVE IN YOUR MISSION AND CONTRIBUTE...
...BUT TO SUSTAIN AN EXPENSIVE OPERATION LIKE THIS, WE NEED THE KIND OF MONEY THEY DON'T HAVE.
WHO KNEW IT'D COST SO MUCH TO TRANSPLANT THE BRAIN OF QUAZZO INTO THAT GUY FROM DIMENSION X?
WHY DOES EVERYTHING I TOUCH GO SO WRONG?
A GREAT IDEA LIKE OURS SHOULD HAVE WORLDWIDE SUPPORT!
SO WHERE IS IT?
SOMETIMES, GREAT IDEAS DIE BECAUSE THEY'RE AHEAD OF THEIR TIME OR PEOPLE DON'T UNDERSTAND HOW TO MANAGE THEM.
WE GAVE IT OUR BEST SHOT, BOOSTER.
BUT THE TIME HAS COME TO TURN OFF THE LIGHTS AND SHUT IT DOWN.
NOT YET.
Eep.

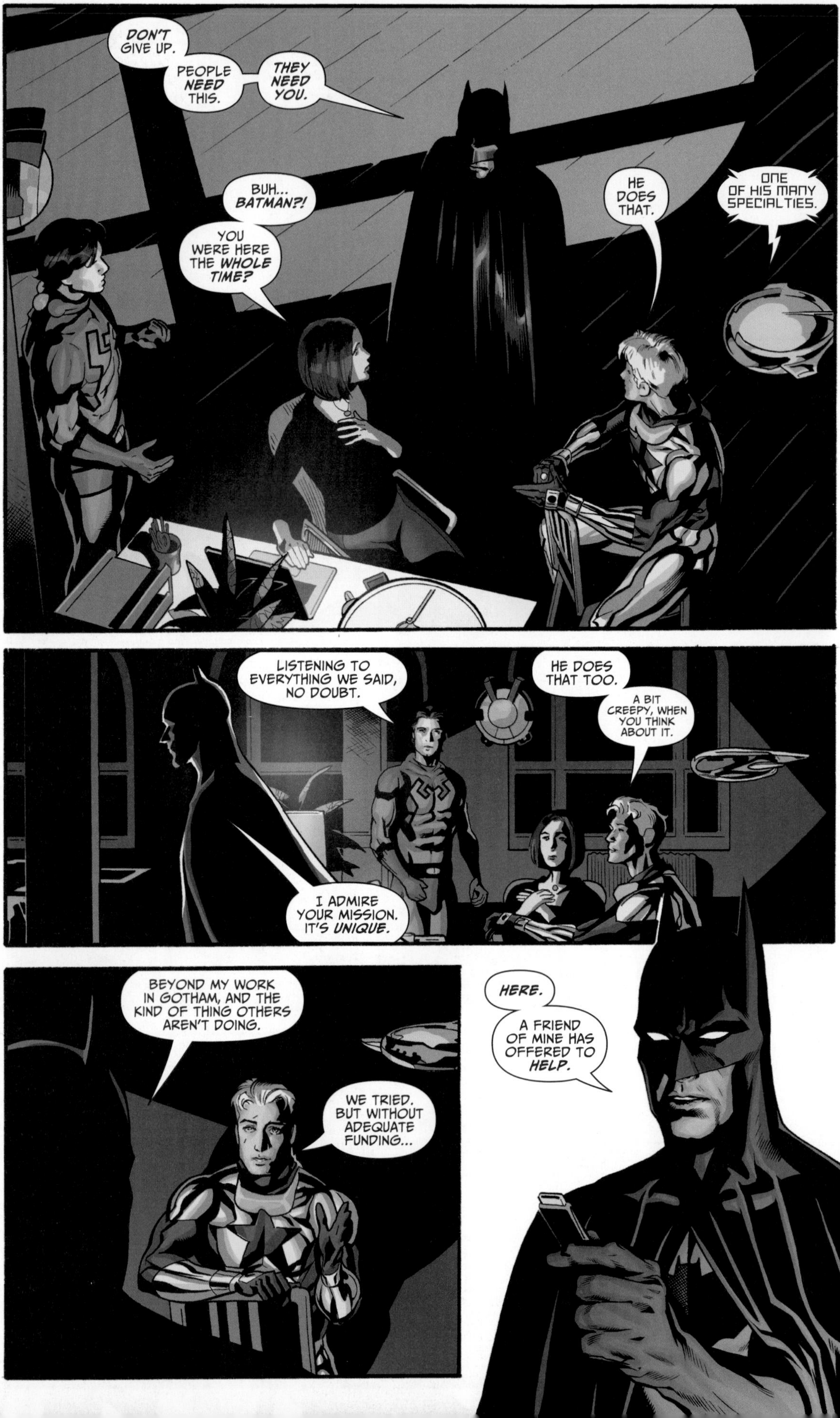
DON'T GIVE UP.
PEOPLE NEED THIS.
THEY NEED YOU.
BUH... BATMAN?!
YOU WERE HERE THE WHOLE TIME?
HE DOES THAT.
ONE OF HIS MANY SPECIALTIES.
LISTENING TO EVERYTHING WE SAID, NO DOUBT.
HE DOES THAT TOO.
A BIT CREEPY, WHEN YOU THINK ABOUT IT.
I ADMIRE YOUR MISSION. IT'S UNIQUE.
BEYOND MY WORK IN GOTHAM, AND THE KIND OF THING OTHERS AREN'T DOING.
WE TRIED. BUT WITHOUT ADEQUATE FUNDING...
HERE.
A FRIEND OF MINE HAS OFFERED TO HELP.

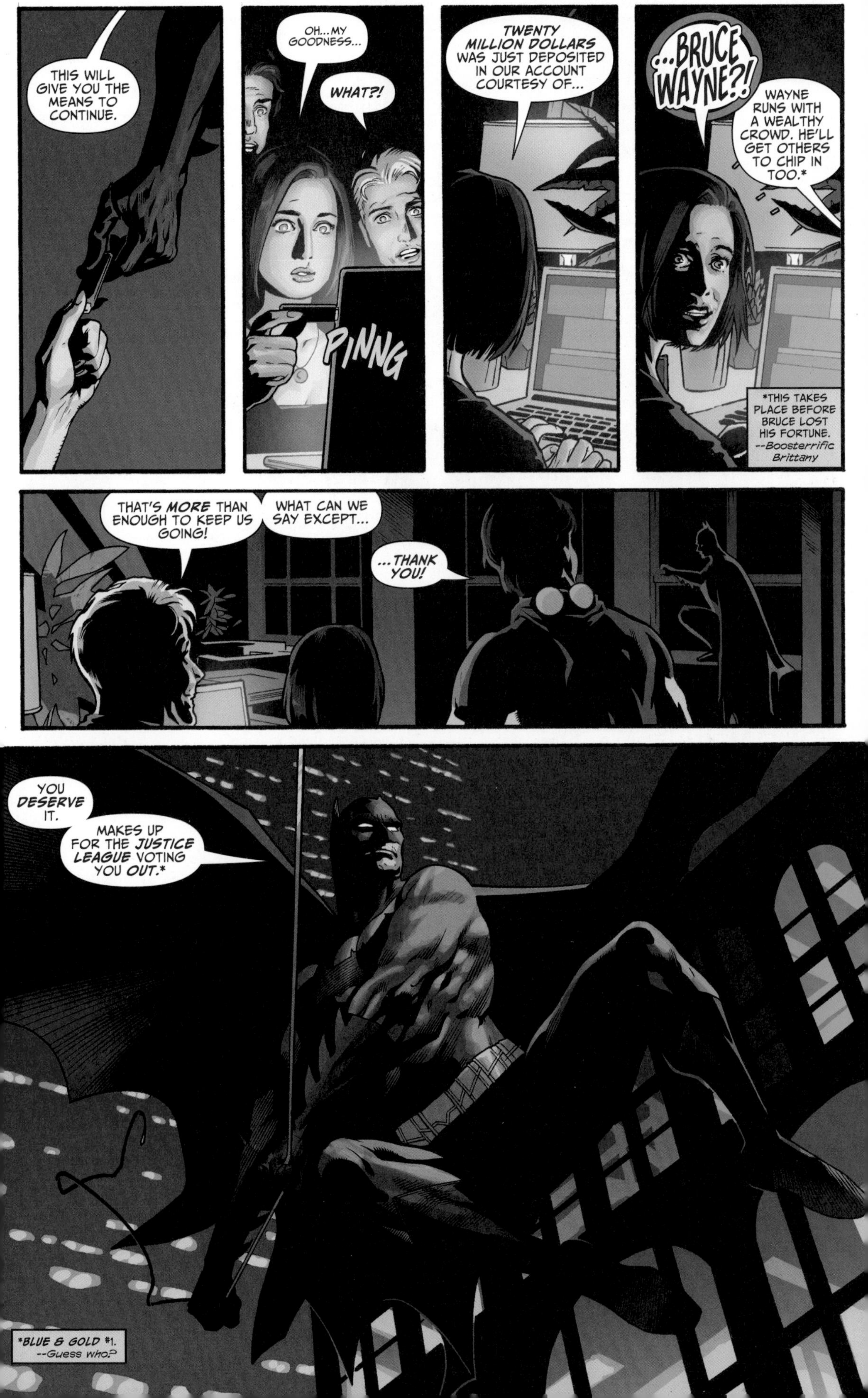
THIS WILL GIVE YOU THE MEANS TO CONTINUE.
OH... MY GOODNESS...
WHAT?!
PINNG
TWENTY MILLION DOLLARS WAS JUST DEPOSITED IN OUR ACCOUNT COURTESY OF...
...BRUCE WAYNE?!
WAYNE RUNS WITH A WEALTHY CROWD. HE'LL GET OTHERS TO CHIP IN TOO.*
*THIS TAKES PLACE BEFORE BRUCE LOST HIS FORTUNE. --Boosterrific Brittany
THAT'S MORE THAN ENOUGH TO KEEP US GOING!
WHAT CAN WE SAY EXCEPT...
...THANK YOU!
YOU DESERVE IT.
MAKES UP FOR THE JUSTICE LEAGUE VOTING YOU OUT.*
*BLUE & GOLD #1. --Guess who?

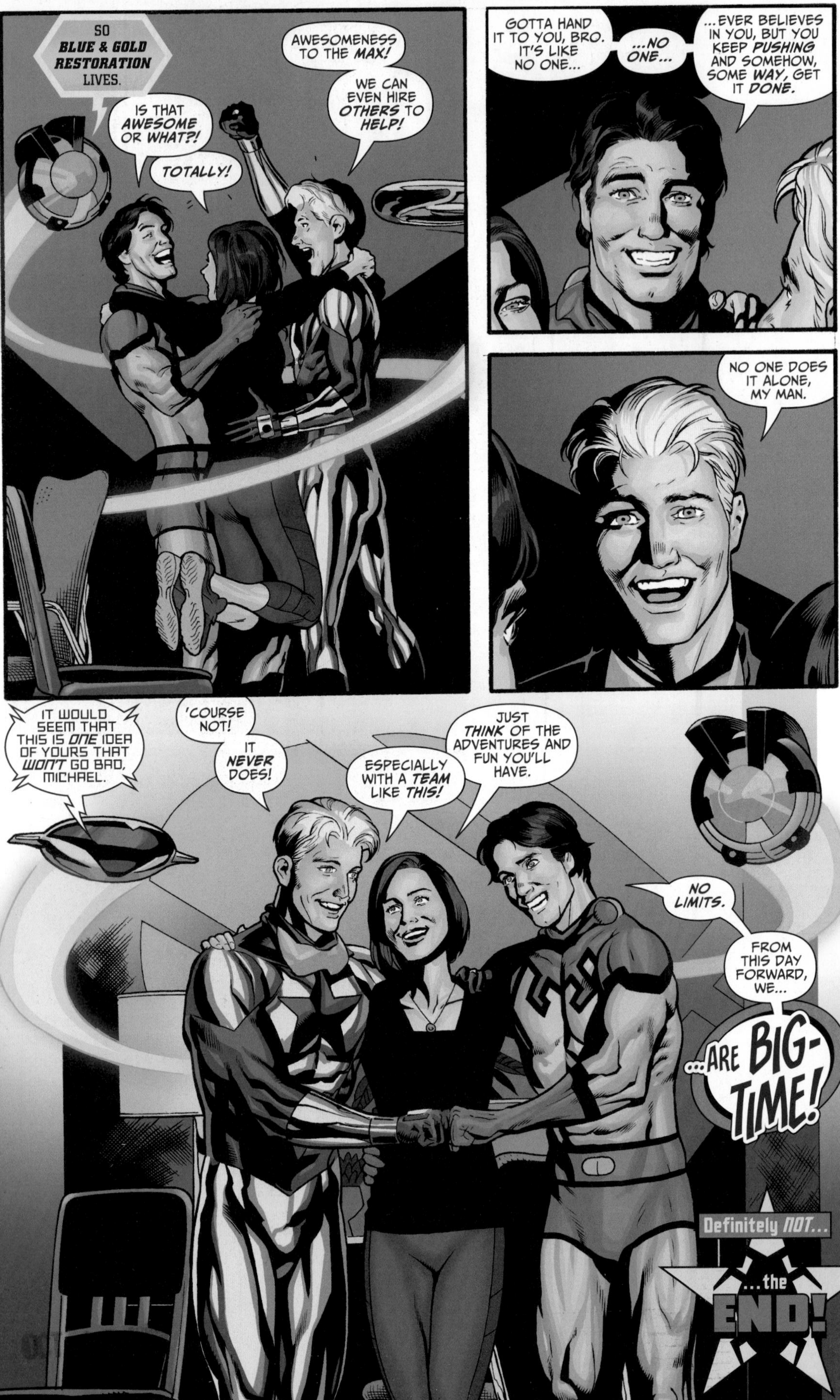
SO BLUE & GOLD RESTORATION LIVES.
IS THAT AWESOME OR WHAT?!
TOTALLY!
AWESOMENESS TO THE MAX!
WE CAN EVEN HIRE OTHERS TO HELP!
GOTTA HAND IT TO YOU, BRO. IT'S LIKE NO ONE...
...NO ONE...
...EVER BELIEVES IN YOU, BUT YOU KEEP PUSHING AND SOMEHOW, SOME WAY, GET IT DONE.
NO ONE DOES IT ALONE, MY MAN.
IT WOULD SEEM THAT THIS IS ONE IDEA OF YOURS THAT WON'T GO BAD, MICHAEL.
'COURSE NOT!
IT NEVER DOES!
ESPECIALLY WITH A TEAM LIKE THIS!
JUST THINK OF THE ADVENTURES AND FUN YOU'LL HAVE.
NO LIMITS.
FROM THIS DAY FORWARD, WE...
...ARE BIG-TIME!
Definitely NOT...
...the END!